Wiser Than Despair

The Evolution of Ideas in the Relationship
of Music and the Christian Church

Quentin Faulkner

www.religiousaffections.org

Wiser Than Despair/ The Evolution of Ideas in the Relationship of Music and the Christian Church, by Quentin Faulkner, was originally published in hard cover by Praeger, an imprint of ABC-CLIO, LLC, Santa Barbara, CA. Copyright © 1996 by Quentin Faulkner. Paperback edition by arrangement with ABC-CLIO, LLC, Santa Barbara, CA. All rights reserved.

No part of this book may be reproduced or transmitted in any form or by any means electronic or mechanical including photocopying, reprinting, or on any information storage or retrieval system, without permission in writing from ABC-CLIO, LLC.

Paperback edition printed by Religious Affections Ministries (*www.religiousaffections.org*) in 2012.

ISBN-13: 978-0-9824582-4-2
ISBN-10: 0-9824582-4-X

Printed in the United States.

In order to keep this title in print and available to the academic community, this edition was produced using digital reprint technology in a relatively short print run. This would not have been attainable using traditional methods. Although the cover has been changed from its original appearance, the text remains the same and all materials and methods used still conform to the highest book-making standards.

Copyright Acknowledgments

The author and publisher gratefully acknowledge permission for use of the following material:

Extracts from "The Organ in the Christian Church." Vol. 9, No. 1 of *Liturgy* (Fall 1990). Copyright The Liturgical Conference, 8750 Georgia Ave., Suite 123, Silver Spring, MD 20910-3621. All rights reserved. Used with permission.

Extracts from *The Organ from its Invention in the Hellenistic Period* . . . , by Jean Perrot. Translated by Norma Deane. Copyright 1971 Oxford University Press (London). Reprinted by permission of Oxford University Press.

Taken from *Bring Many Names* by Brian A. Wren. Copyright © 1989 by Hope Publishing Co., Carol Stream, IL 60188. All rights reserved. Used by permission.

Extracts from *Bring Many Names* by Brian A. Wren (1936-). World excluding USA and Canada: © Oxford University Press, 3 Park Road, London NW1 6XN; used by permission.

It was on a Friday Morning.Words: Sydney Carter. © 1960 by Stainer & Bell Ltd. All rights reserved. Used by permission of Hope Publishing Co., Carol Stream, IL 60188.

A brief quotation in a letter from Calvin Johansson to Quentin Faulkner, by Calvin Johansson. October 23, 1991. Used with permission.

Extracts from *The Best of G.A. Studdert-Kennedy*, by Geoffrey Anketel Studdert-Kennedy. Copyright 1929. Reproduced by permission of Hodder & Stoughton, Ltd.

"Give Thanks and Remember" by Jack Miffleton. Copyright 1975, WORLD LIBRARY PUBLICATIONS, a division of J.S. Paluch Company, Inc. 3825 N. Willow Rd., Schiller Park, IL 60176. All rights reserved. Reprinted with permission.

Extracts from *The Ethnomusicologist*, by Professor Mantle Hood. Copyright © 1982 McGraw-Hill Inc. (New York). Reprinted with permission.

Extracts from "Luther on Music," in *The Musical Quarterly*, by Walter E. Buszin. Vol. XXXII, No.1 (Jan. 1946), pp. 80–97. Reprinted by permission of Oxford University Press.

Extracts from *Papal Legislation on Sacred Music, 95 A.D. to 1977 A.D.*, by Robert F. Hayburn. Copyright 1979 The Liturgical Press, Collegeville, MN. Reprinted by permission of The Liturgical Press.

Extracts from $X\rho o\mu\alpha\ \theta\varepsilon o\upsilon$; *Musicae Sacrae Melethmata*, by Robert A. Skeris. Copyright 1976. Reprinted with permission.

Extracts from *Greek Musical Writings*, Vol. 1: The Musician and His Art, edited by Andrew Barker (1984). Reprinted with the permission of Cambridge University Press.

Extracts from *The Republic*, by Plato. Reprinted by permission of the publishers and the Loeb Classical Library from Plato: *The Republic*, Vol. II, pp. 491–93, 501–5, translated by Paul Shorey, Cambridge, Mass.: Harvard University Press, 1930.

Reprinted from *Music in Western Civilization* by Paul Henry Lang, with the permission of W.W. Norton & Company, Inc. Copyright 1941 by W. W. Norton & Company, Inc., renewed © 1969 by Paul Henry Lang.

Reprinted from *Source Readings in Music History* by Oliver Strunk, with the permission of W.W. Norton & Company, Inc. Copyright 1950 by W. W. Norton & Company, Inc.

Excerpt from *The Jerusalem Bible*, copyright © 1966 by Darton, Longman & Todd, Ltd. and Doubleday, a division of Bantam Doubleday Dell Publishing Group, Inc. Reprinted by permission.

Extracts from *Confessions* by Saint Augustine, translated by R. S. Pine-Coffin (Penguin Classics, 1961) copyright © R. S. Pine-Coffin, 1961.

Extracts from *Abbot Suger on the Abbey Church of St. Denis and its Art Treasures*, by Erwin Panofsky. Copyright 1946/79 Princeton University Press (Princeton, NJ). Reprinted by permission of Princeton University Press.

Richard F. French

--teacher

--mentor

--friend

Contents

Preface		xi
Acknowledgments		xv
Chronology		xvii
1.	Prologue	1
2.	Music in the Bible	17
3.	Music in Ancient Greece	29
4.	Music in the Early Church: The Patristic Era to Gregory the Great	49
5.	Integration and Transmission	73
6.	Interlude: Ecclesiastical Authority in Theory and Practice	87
7.	The Golden Age of Musical Speculation	93
8.	Speculation and Musical Practice	113
9.	The Reformation	135
10.	The Decline of Musical Speculation	143
11.	The Gifts of Christian Musical Speculation	149

Contents

12.	Humanism	153
13.	The Self-Conscious Revolution	161
14.	The Enlightenment and Music	171
15.	Romanticism and Music	183
16.	The Twentieth Century	191
17.	Questions	203
Appendix 1:	The Organ	215
Appendix 2:	Performance Practice	225
Bibliography		231
Index		243

Preface

The fact that human beings want to make music, as well as all other forms of art, is a given of human existence. Artistic expressions, however, are not isolated or autonomous. They are conditioned, among other things, by social and cultural factors, and these factors have a powerful influence in shaping any art form.

There is no more compelling example of a culture's power to condition art than the evolution of European art music during the Middle Ages under the influence of the Christian church and its theological stance with regard to the arts. The church's ideas about the purpose and function of music were the deciding factors in determining the directions that musical composition took during the Middle Ages. That direction has in turn helped determine not only modern compositional and performance practices, but indeed the very notion of what constitutes "quality" and "greatness" in Western art music.

This book traces the interaction of philosophical and theological ideas and attitudes with the conception and practice of music, beginning with the earliest ideas about music and the foundations laid by the ancient Greek philosophical systems, and continuing through the transformation of ideas and attitudes about music that happened from the sixteenth through the eighteenth centuries. The book's purpose is to explore--by means of many excerpts from primary sources, selected quotations from modern authors, and commentary on both--a highly complex and elusive matter: why the church was able to contribute so generously to music (and to the other arts, as well) from its earliest days up through the eighteenth century, and why it has suffered since that time from a creeping artistic paralysis. The opening chapters may be understood as a contribution to a more complete conception of the history and philosophy of music up through the eighteenth century. The final chapters are of greater interest to those who are specifically concerned with church music, especially as it has been conceived and practiced since the eighteenth century. I have presumed that the reader is familiar with the history of European art music and, within that, with the history of music in the service of the church.

It is presumptuous of me to attempt such a wide-ranging project, in particular because the nature of the evidence presently available is, on the whole, fragmentary, inconclusive, and not thoroughly understood. To the best of my knowledge, however, no one has previously attempted such a broad review of the effects that Christianity has had on the directions music has taken. It seemed that someone should initiate the discussion of those effects, if for no other reason than to promote interest and further research into the matter. It is in that spirit that I offer the following survey. It is a tentative survey, full of questions and matters that are only partially understood in our time; and it will have to be done over in the future, piece by piece and with more adequate documentation, as new information and fresh studies appear. Some of the facts it sets forth may prove to be incorrect, but not, I believe, its general direction and its way of looking at the matter.

The view of music's development offered in this book is only part of the whole picture. It does not deal with the inevitable interaction and cross-fertilization between varying musical practices that keep the art vital. Nor does it take into account musical sensitivity and intuition, or the unique creativity of purely musical genius. These elements cannot be omitted from any complete view of music's historical development; but this book does not aspire to completeness. Its appointed task limits it to the realm of ideas about music, and how those ideas shaped and energized musical developments. Ideas (since they are capable of being recorded), are more amenable to documentation. At the same time, they are also more liable to be ignored by succeeding generations, for their effect on music is not always acknowledged or understood.

If much of what is set forth here seems strange and foreign, then, it is for the very reason just stated above: we are dealing here not with the practice of music, but with musical *ideas* and *ideals*. Thus our investigation must extend beyond musical scores, and even further than writings about musical practice. Musical compositions and practices do indeed reflect ideas and attitudes, but succeeding generations and eras are likely to comprehend and interpret them in light of their own attitudes, presuppositions, and ideals. Only a broad survey of earlier modes of thought can reintegrate composition and performance into their original matrix. I therefore ask the reader to suspend judgment for the present (especially in the earlier chapters of the book). Do not ask, "Does this idea or attitude seem reasonable to me? Is what this source says accurate and true?" Ask instead, "Do I understand thoroughly what is being said here?" In other words, try to understand earlier ideas and attitudes solely on their own terms, and not on yours.

I have adopted the policy of paying greater attention to ideas that influenced the development of musical style and substance than to the evolving relationship of music and text. Words that are set to music do, of course, condition musical style in subtle ways, but twentieth-century church music's emphasis on social injustices and the agony of war or medieval music's preoccupation with the cult of the Virgin have essentially nothing to do with the style or substance of the music to which they are set, and I have chosen to pass over them in the interests of brevity and coherence. I have also chosen to emphasize the church's art music at the expense of its more popular hymnody, believing the ideas that impel the people's song are relatively simple and straightforward, while the ideas that have given rise to art music are far more complex and elusive.

It is no secret that the path church music has taken since the eighteenth century has not been an especially smooth one. This book has been written to help those who are involved with church music, either in deed or in spirit, to make sense of the conflicting claims and allegiances that tug at them in this age of contradictions and uncertainties. Readers will find here no answers to the problems and perplexities of the present situation; they may only hope for aid in formulating the right questions to ask, and thus gain a new perspective that may become part of a foundation on which to build a more secure future.

Acknowledgments

This book has had a gestation period of over 10 years. Anyone undertaking a project so protracted cannot help but be beholden to a multitude for assistance, great and small, along the way. With the awareness that I have inevitably slighted some whose gracious help has greatly aided and improved this undertaking, I offer my thanks to a host of kind people, among whom are:

Prof. Kerry Grant, formerly Director of the School of Music, University of Nebraska-Lincoln; the University of Nebraska-Lincoln Research Council; Ludwig-Maximilians-Universität of Munich (and especially Frau Musselmann, of the University Administration)

Prof. Jean-Claude Zehnder, Schola Cantorum Basiliensis; Mr. Oskar Birchmeyer, Gebenstorf, Switzerland

Prof. Robert Audi, University of Nebraska-Lincoln; Dr. Eugenia Earle, Columbia Teachers College; Mr. William Parsons, Library of Congress; Msgr. Francis Schmitt; Mrs. Louise Small; Prof. William Small, University of Maine; Dr. Robert H. Winthrop

Prof. Calvin Johansson, Evangel College, and the Rev. Mr. O.J. Scott, who read the manuscript and made numerous helpful suggestions

My faculty colleagues at the University of Nebraska-Lincoln School of Music, especially Profs. George Ritchie, Pamela Starr, and Raymond Haggh, all of whom read the manuscript and patiently offered advice and help on countless occasions.

My students, who have questioned and prodded, and who have corrected the text and forced me to rewrite it until my ideas could be understood and defended.

Ms. Alicia Merritt and Mr. David Palmer, of the Greenwood Publishing Group, for shepherding this undertaking to its final publication.

and especially Prof. Richard French of Yale University and the Juilliard School of Music, to whom this volume is dedicated; and my wife, Mary Murrell Faulkner, who listened, advised, corrected, encouraged and put up with.

Chronology

1500 B.C.   Moses

1200   Joshua invades Palestine
                  Period of the Judges

                  Samuel (c.1040)
                  Saul (c.1030-c.1010)
1000   David (c.1010-c.970)
                  Solomon (c.970-931) - building of the temple at Jerusalem

          Israel   Judah
          (northern kingdom)   (southern kingdom)

                       PERIOD OF THE LATER
                            PROPHETS

          Fall of the
          northern kingdom
                (721)
700

                            Fall of Jerusalem and southern kingdom (587)
                            BABYLONIAN CAPTIVITY
                            Return from exile (538)
                            Rebuilding of the temple (537-515)
500

200   Period of foreign domination
                                     (Macabees)

xviii Chronology

100 B.C.
                        Pompey (Roman general) takes Jerusalem (63)
                        Roman rule

A.D. Jesus's life, ministry, death and resurrection
       Saul/Paul's letters to the churches (c.45-63)
          Fall of Jerusalem and destruction of the temple (70)
             Writing of the gospels (c.60-100)
100
      Periodic persecution of Christians (c.60-c.300)
        Conflicts over heresies (arising from Christianity's encounter with
             gnosticism (c.100-c.450)
        Rise of Christian asceticism (forerunner of monasticism)
200
      Tertullian, Christian writer (c.160-220)

300
      Edict of Milan, 313 (Emperor Constantine legalizes Christianity)
        Augustine, Bishop of Hippo (354-430) - *De musica*
        Canon of New Testament established
400 Disintegration of Roman Empire underway; separation into Eastern and
           Western empires

500 Boethius (c.480-524) -*De institutione musica*
       Benedict of Nursia (c.480-549), founder of western
          (Benedictine) monasticism
       Cassiodorus (c.485-c.580)

600 Gregory I, Bishop of Rome (reigned 590-604) - regulates Roman Schola
          cantorum
       Rise of Islam
         Missionary activity of Irish monks (until c.800)
700
      Rise to prominence of schools run by monasteries

800 Charlemagne (reigned 768-814)
       Johannes Scotus Erigena (810-886)

900 *Scholia enchiriadis* (earliest treatise on polyphony)

1000 Rise to prominence of polyphony

1100 Schools run by cathedrals (*maîtrises*) begin to assume former role of monastic
         schools
        School of Notre Dame, Paris (Leonin, Perotin)
1200

1300 Rise of universities, assuming former role of *maîtrises*.
        Papal bull *Docta sanctorum* (Pope John XXII)

Chronology

1400
- Fall of Byzantium (Constantinople), 1453, provides impetus for rise of humanism (Renaissance)
- Musical speculation and number symbolism appear in polyphonic composition

1500
- Reformation: Luther, Zwingli, Calvin
- Counter Reformation: Council of Trent

1600
- Enlightenment (c.1600-c.1800)
  - Pietism (from now on)

1700
- J.S. Bach (1685-1750)
- Evangelical revivals (Wesleys; England and North America)
  - Declaration of Independence (1776); birth of United States (institutionalization of egalitarian democracy)

1800 Romanticism (in music, c.1800-c.1900)
- Retrospective ecclesiastical revivals: Oxford and Ecclesiological Movements, Solesmes, *Kirchenagenden*
- Simultaneous rise of literary biblical criticism and Christian Fundamentalism

1900
- Jazz
  - Liturgical Mvt.
    - Rock-&-Roll
      - Second Vatican Council (institutionalization of principles of Liturgical Movement)
- Rise of the Church Growth Movement and entertainment evangelism

2000

1

Prologue

> The history of music is the history of the human species.
> François-Joseph Fétis, *Histoire Générale de la Musique*, 1869

"WORLD-CONSCIOUS" VERSUS "SELF-CONSCIOUS"

Human beings are born into a universe that presents them with endless unanswered questions. Of those questions, none are more elemental than these: "Why? Why do I exist? What do I mean? Is my life worthwhile, and how is it worthwhile?" Compare if you will these two hypothetical answers to such basic questions:

An inherently mysterious, awesome power has created me to be part of the world, a world I can never hope to understand or control. Following the teachings or laws revealed to my people will enable me to remain pleasing to that creating force and at one with my family and tribe, and thus will provide my life with meaning because it is integrated with theirs. Following the teachings or laws requires me to fulfill certain duties and obligations, and I am fulfilled in doing these the best I can. Indeed I am compelled to do them: since living is an everlasting struggle between life and death, good and evil, blessing and curse, growth and decay, unfaithfulness to my duties and obligations will lead to my destruction.

I am significant because it is a matter of common knowledge and observation that our species is superior and in control on this planet. The democratic ideal guarantees me freedom and the right to pursue my happiness. Therefore I am free to follow my own personal goals and to pursue comfort, satisfaction and personal pleasure. That which I do not now understand about the universe will eventually be explained by science, so that things which now seem mysterious will ultimately be provided with rational explanations. I am not compelled to be faithful to any higher order of existence, since there is none.

The first of these statements stresses integration into an orderly world or universe (governed and ordered by some higher or transcendent power or powers);

2   Wiser than Despair

it is *world*[1]*-conscious*. It excels at symbolism, myth, ceremony, and ritual--at providing the general, the "big" picture. The primary satisfaction it offers its adherents is security in belonging. (It is typically unconcerned with organization and efficiency.) The second statement, on the other hand, stresses the supreme worth of individuals, their comfort, their physical security and well-being; it is *self-conscious*. It excels in detail, in providing reasonable answers to various specific elements of the complex mysteries of the universe. To do this, it insists on organization and efficiency. The primary satisfactions it offers its adherents are a sense of freedom, initiative, and adventure.

The first statement represents a stance that, as far as we can tell, has been characteristic of human thought since the dawn-time of human existence. It may be regarded as a classical formulation of the "primitive worldview"--providing one clearly understands what the word "primitive" means. In the modern popular mind, that word immediately evokes images of half-naked people who paint their skin, shrink heads and engage in other barbaric practices. From its derivation, however, the word "primitive" (as well as the related word "aboriginal") merely conveys the sense of existing "from the first" or "from the beginning." Long and unbiased studies of aboriginal cultures have revealed that, far from being inferior to more developed cultures, they are potentially as capable or more capable than developed cultures of creating and sustaining stable and humane societies.

From a historical perspective, allegiance to various elements of the first statement were in the course of time gradually conditioned by more rational modes of thought. As examples we may take some of the Old Testament prophets, or the Greek philosopher Socrates, all of whom rejected and defied elements of their society as a result of principles they held to be nobler and more valid than adherence to prevailing norms. For another example, the concept of obedience to tribal deities and laws was gradually supplanted in some societies by obedience to a single sovereign god and to laws and standards derived from that god's revelation. For yet another example, a rising standard of living (brought on in part by a division of labor) suppressed in some measure the immediate perception of the continual, grim struggle between life and death. Yet in spite of these subtle alterations, some recognizable form of the first statement seems to have enjoyed almost total allegiance in the Western world until the coming of the complex of views we label the Enlightenment. Most of its tenets had well-nigh universal support until the eighteenth century (previously they had been questioned only in very limited intellectual circles), and they lost ground substantially only in the nineteenth and especially in the twentieth centuries.

The second statement will be recognized as an extreme form of the modern secular worldview. Its tenets are relatively familiar, since they have been berated in recent years from pulpit and political platform. This worldview began to be propounded in the seventeenth and eighteenth centuries, and is the driving force behind the phenomenon we know as the Enlightenment. At first it belonged exclusively to the domain of intellectuals, but during the nineteenth and especially the twentieth centuries it has come to enjoy more widespread popular

---

[1]"World" here is used in an older sense, synonymous with "universe" or "cosmos" (see *Dictionary: O.E.D.*, "World," II.9); but it also implies integration into an infinitely greater whole, and thus belief in transcendent creative power(s).

support. It would probably be possible to find some people in the developed countries of the world who would subscribe in large measure to it, though their number would be relatively few. Many more would still subscribe to the first statement, especially those people in the developing countries of the world. The vast majority of the world's people, however, would adopt an ambivalent stance toward the two statements.

If you are by upbringing or inclination religious, and if you live and have been educated in one of the developed countries, you would probably count yourself among that majority. A comparison of the two statements tells us that they are fundamentally opposed to each other and at heart probably irreconcilable. The more extreme proponents of each often roundly detest each other. But if you are honest with yourself about your stance toward life, you will probably realize, curiously enough, that you instinctively react positively to aspects of both. Thus neither of them ought to be regarded as absolutes, but rather as opposing poles, within whose strong magnetic fields people have been living and acting for a very long time. The contradictions they embody still form a very real part of the human predicament today: in the relations between developed and undeveloped countries of the world; in the interaction between various elements within a country or society; in the individual human being's striving for wholeness, integration and well-being.

It is only fair to assert, then, that, although neither of the statements provides a completely satisfactory answer to the questions posed at the outset, both are more or less viable options for developing and maintaining a stance toward living, and for allowing people to fulfill some degree of their human potential. Since the words "primitive" (or "aboriginal") and "modern" are often misused and misunderstood, I have chosen to avoid them and to substitute in their place the terms "world-conscious" versus "self-conscious."

The stances toward life inherent in the two statements inevitably dictate in some measure judgments about what is important and what is not. Those judgments in turn help to determine what people will strive to excel in and what they will cultivate less intensively. Indeed, they help to form an entire approach to living. Each of the statements shapes any number of more specific ideas and attitudes about what is authentic, what is moral, what is appropriate.

WORLD-CONSCIOUS RELIGION: THE CULT

World-conscious humans are typically religious. The word "religious" should be understood here apart from the connotations of "pious" or "church-going" that attend the word in present-day Western societies. In this context, it connotes a stance toward life that is occasioned by an awareness of the supernatural, by a sense of living in the constant presence of a mysterious "spirit-world" that impinges on daily life, resulting at least in a sense of reverence for the forces of the spirit-world, and at most in the experience of awe-ful fascination with a numinous[2] force that is overwhelmingly powerful and active in the world of the

---

[2]Simply defined, the word means "divine" or "full of holy awe"; for a full explanation and definition of the term, together with an extensive inquiry into this primal aspect of religious experience, see Rudolf Otto, *The Idea of the Holy*.

senses. This awareness is expressed in many different ways: as magic, spirits resident in animate and inanimate natural objects, good and evil spirits, spirits of ancestors, unseen (or only occasionally seen) beings of a higher order (gods or spirits), the Holy Spirit, the one God. The awareness of a spirit-world is not exclusively a feature of early societies; it was prevalent everywhere in the Western world until the Enlightenment, and is in fact still very powerful in the world today. The spirit-world may be menacing: demons, witches, sorcerers.

People [in this case, in the later Middle Ages] lived close to the inexplicable. The flickering lights of marsh gas could only be fairies or goblins; fireflies were the souls of unbaptized dead infants. In the terrible trembling and fissures of an earthquake or the setting afire of a tree by lightning, the supernatural was close at hand. Storms were omens, death by heart attack or other seizures could be the work of demons. Magic was present in the world: demons, fairies, sorcerers, ghosts, and ghouls touched and manipulated human lives. (Tuchman, pp. 54-55)

Or it may be benign and even sanctifying, such as the coming of the Holy Spirit upon Jesus's disciples at Pentecost, as recorded in the second chapter of the Acts of the Apostles. Whether menacing or benign, however, visions and epiphanies are for world-conscious humans an inevitable part of the fabric of life, and the awareness of an ever-present spirit-world ensures a more or less continuous attitude of awe or reverence in the presence of the holy. Therefore, the sacred-secular dichotomy that pervades a great deal of Western religious thought finds no place in fully world-conscious thinking, since everything--time, nature, human existence--is understood as being subject to the forces of the spirit-world. In this sense, everything is sacred.[3]

Among world-conscious peoples, religion manifests itself in three primary aspects: in myth (content and teachings), in ethos (behavior or morals), and in cult. We will consider each of these aspects in turn; but it is to the cult that we must first direct our attention, since music is related to religion chiefly through this aspect. Today, "cult" is a word that that has fallen into ill repute; it has assumed a slightly repulsive odor, having become tinged with connotations such as "barbarism," "fanaticism," and "brain-washing." Thus we have been robbed of a word that is crucial to the understanding of religion (and music in the service of religion), and we need to try to reclaim its original meaning.[4] Sigmund Mowinckel offers the following definition of the word:

Cult...may be defined as the socially established and regulated holy acts and words in which the encounter and communion of the Deity with the congregation is established, developed, and brought to its ultimate goal...a relation in which a

---

[3]Cf. Eliade, *Myths, Rites, Symbols*, pp. 137-8 & 140.

[4]The original meaning still remains current to some degree in continental European cultures, for example, in the French *culte* and German *Kultus* (e.g., *Kultusministerium* means "ministry of public worship and education"), but it has been entirely lost in the United States, where "cult" is synonymous in the popular mind either with "fad" or with unquestioning allegiance and devotion to occult, deviant religious fanaticism. The original French title of Father Joseph Gelineau's book *Voices and Instruments in Christian Worship* is *Chant et Musique dans le Culte Chrétien*. Although the French title is straightforward and easily translatable, it is obvious why the book's American publishers chose not to translate it directly.

religion becomes a vitalizing function as a communion of God and congregation, and of the members of the congregation among themselves...the visible and audible expression of the relation between the congregation and the deity. (Mowinckel, pp. 15 & 16)

After reading and digesting the definition, you may be tempted to ask whether "cult" is not simply another word for "worship." Indeed it is--provided you understand the degree of intensity the word "cult" connotes. "Worship" is conceived today as being a good and fitting thing for God-fearing people to do, but it is by no means normally understood as being the life-and-death matter implicit in the concept of cult. The meaning of the word "cult" is immediately compromised the moment any suggestion of convenience or indifference is connected with it. To cite an example: in present U.S. society, church members who are moderately ill (e.g., a bad cold or a case of the flu) would normally be inclined not to attend a service of worship, not only because they do not feel well, but because they would want to inhibit the spread of disease (a gesture of thoughtfulness). When fully world-conscious people are ill, on the other hand, attendance at cultic observances is a vital necessity; if their own strength fails them, then they are carried to the cultic assembly by their relatives, or the assembly comes to them. Cult is the means by which life is secured and the forces that threaten life (demons, disease, curses) are vanquished or held at bay. To be cut off from the cult is to die--both spiritually and ultimately physically as well. Therefore participation in the cult is hardly a take-it-or-leave-it affair; it is an essential prerequisite for living, indeed for survival. No matter what other aspects of religious observance might have to be curtailed (e.g., alms-giving or religious instruction), it is imperative that cultic celebrations be conducted in all their fullness, since the strengthening of the cult is the central concern in people's lives. The idea of cult inevitably involves the notions of covenant, solidarity, ritual, sacrament, and ornament, and we must now examine each of these in turn.

At the heart of the cult is the believers' realization that there is a relationship between them and their god or gods. In this relationship, the god or gods are more powerful than the people; they initiate the relationship with the people, their will takes precedence, and the people must follow it. The god or gods agree to protect and increase their people, and the people agree to praise and adore, to worship and to obey their god or gods. In ancient Israel, for example, this relationship was understood as a covenant, initiated by Yahweh through Moses at Mount Sinai and ratified by all the people of Israel. Yahweh promised to be the God of Israel, to bless his people. In return, Israel agreed to obey a number of Yahweh's precepts (the foremost being the Ten Commandments). This mutual up-building or blessing is the primary reason for the existence of the cult. The First and Second Commandments ("You shall have no other gods before me; you shall not make for yourself a graven image," Exodus 20:3-4[5]) do not occupy their position by chance; the primary concern of the Israelite cult was the praise and worship[6] of Yahweh.

---

[5] Today the cultic significance of these statements is largely ignored or forgotten.

[6] The word "worship" originated as a compound of "worth" and "ship"--"worth-ship"; thus it fundamentally means "ascribing worth to."

It is self-evident from what has just been said that cult and public government cannot be separated; there cannot be, in modern terms, any separation of church and state. In Israel (as in many highly world-conscious societies), the king (or chief) was a primary figure in the cult. The cult is likewise financed not primarily by voluntary donations, but by some form of universal taxation[7] imposed by the cult and enforced (if necessary) by the government. Furthermore, the cult perpetuates the fundamentally hierarchical nature of the world-conscious worldview: first the god or gods, then the king, and finally the people (and often many other hierarchical substrata, such as classes of priests or nobles, as well). The worship of a transcendent god or gods and reverence for the king (or chief) and priests as their earthly representatives create a society that lives comfortably and naturally with bowing, kneeling and other forms of self-abasement. Indeed, that society has an innate affinity for the notion of "quality," both with regard to people (a concept that has had fateful ramifications, both good and evil) and to that which people do and create.

World-conscious humans normally regard themselves first and foremost as part of a people, a tribe or a family, instead of understanding themselves primarily as individuals. That is the reason why cultic observances are inevitably communal. Each of the cult's adherents is conscious of owing a debt of gratitude to the god or gods and to the human social institutions that create and sustain; each possesses a sense of obligation to fulfill a responsibility, to be accountable. This sense of responsibility underlies sentiments that are as superficially diverse as tribal loyalty and national patriotism,[8] as animal sacrifice and Sunday morning church attendance.[9] Fully world-conscious humans do not have the option of rejecting this responsibility, for to do so would be to incur divine wrath and cut themselves off from the blessings (life, health, well-being, increase) that can only be secured through full participation in the community and its religious, cultic life.

World-conscious humans are driven by the impulse to discover, confirm, and express their existence in the greater whole of things seen and unseen, by symbolically acting out in ritual and ceremony the realities of life as they perceive them.[10] In this (inherently religious) context, ritual and ceremony evolve so slowly and subtly as to seem immutable. Thus they create and perpetuate a tradition, both in themselves and in what they signify. The emphasis on wholeness and integration that is characteristic of world-conscious peoples seems to allow ceremonial formality and personal feeling to coexist and cooperate naturally, without uneasiness. It is not yet entirely clear today why this is so, but to confirm the truth of it, we need only compare the graceful 'appropriateness' of world-conscious ceremonies such as African tribal dances or British royal coronations with the rather uneasy, stilted formalities of a modern secular wedding or a U.S. state university commencement exercise.

---

[7]In ancient Israel, this was the imposition of the tithe; see Leviticus 27: 30-33.

[8]Especially of the "my country, right or wrong, but my country" variety.

[9]Self-conscious humans may also possess a sense of responsibility to their fellow creatures, but it is motivated by fundamentally different ideals: altruistic love of nature or humanity, or perhaps enlightened self-interest ("What benefits the community benefits me as well").

[10]Cf. Eliade, *Myths, Rites, Symbols*, pp. 136, 138, & 164.

Ritual and ceremony--symbolic actions--are also carried out to some degree in the conviction that by means of words and actions humans can influence their relations with the spirit-world. Indeed, the belief in the efficacy of prayer-- certainly of communal prayer--is based entirely on this conviction. The influence may either be for protection (such as exorcism; cf. Mark 1:21ff., where Jesus drives out demons) or for blessing (such as the Sacraments of the Christian church). Whatever the intent, it is ordinarily clear that a causal relationship exists between words and actions and what they are meant to accomplish. There are many examples of this in the Judaeo-Christian religious heritage. It is evident in the book of Numbers 6:22-27 that the unconditional force of blessing is contained in the benediction that God commands Aaron and his sons to pronounce upon the people of Israel: "The Lord bless you and keep you...." In the Eastern Orthodox Christian churches and in the entire Western church (up to the Reformation), the words and actions of the priest in the Eucharist combine to render the body and blood of Christ truly present under the species of bread and wine.[11] Furthermore, the actions and words of the bishop or priest at confirmation are intended not merely to invite the presence of the Holy Spirit, but to convey it. An *ex opere operato* force is inherent in all of these examples: human words and actions are understood as being able to combine to trigger the creation of an unseen reality.

When believers engage in cultic activities such as prayer or ritual and ceremony, they are trying to establish, renew, or strengthen their relationship with the deity. Cultic activities normally result in a confirmation of that relationship through some sort of divine epiphany, some sign that the deity exists, and is powerful, and places a claim on its creatures. The possibility that what exists in the perceptible world can serve as a sign of the unseen lies at the heart of most world-conscious cultic awareness. Anything in the world of the senses may potentially serve as a channel through which the divine manifests itself, anything may act as a bridge from the other world to this: elements of nature (storms, animals, the beauty of nature), artifacts (idols, the Ark of the Covenant, music, bread and wine), human words and actions (an embrace, a sign or word of blessing), or human beings themselves (god-kings, the messiah).[12] The potential of the divine for using the created order to reveal itself, for making creation transparent to divine being and will, may be referred to as the "sacramental principle," or more simply as sacrament.[13]

World-conscious humans unquestioningly accept the value, indeed the inevitability of ornament and adornment in the service of religious ritual and ceremony, as an integral part of praising the deity and of symbolizing who they are. Not only records of ancient religious ceremonies, but also archaeological

---

[11] Disregarding for the moment the more specific issue of Transubstantiation, which explains *how* they come to be present.

[12] To the degree that they enter on the process of becoming holy, believers realize their capacity to develop an ever more acute awareness of all creation as a sign of divine being, power, and will; in the Christian tradition, people who are more advanced in this process are recognized as "saints."

[13] In the narrower, more specifically Christian sense of the term, then, the "Sacraments" are those human acts that the church throughout its history has recognized as the unmistakable and paradigmatic channels, ordained by God, through which God communicates with humans (i.e., as channels of grace).

discoveries at excavations of ancient religious sites confirm that there is an irresistible human urge to ornament the worship of the deity, to devote the best of human artistry and skill in the service of loving, ceaseless elaboration. That artistry may take the form of physical adornment (e.g., skin painting or tattooing), of religious figures, signs or paintings, of religious costume, of religious poetry and music, or of religious architecture. In any of these cases, however, a people's best efforts are normally expended in the creation of such art because only the best is appropriate to the cult.

MUSIC IN THE CULT

In a context such as the one described above, poetry and music, ritual movement (sacred dance)--indeed, all art forms[14] that are cultural manifestations of cultic societies--are typically understood as gifts of the deity, as infinitely precious mysterious signs of the presence of the spirit-world and of human response to that presence, as signs of solidarity with a family, tribe or people, as basic elements of ritual and ceremony, as a means of contacting and influencing the spirit-world, and as a means of adorning the worship of the deity. All words, music, ritual movement--all art forms--have a spiritual significance, because there is understood to be a fundamental continuity between the spiritual and the physical world, and all of life is lived in the consciousness of that larger reality. The sacred/secular distinction so fundamental to more self-conscious people is therefore meaningless in such a context, and the concept of "art for art's sake" is unknown.[15] For world-conscious people there is urgent reason to sing and to make all kinds of music, and there is pressing cause to value music, because it is both a primary sign of blessing and well-being (of human wholeness, integration, mental health--of human joy) and a primary instrument in the creation of blessing and well-being. This holds equally true for tribal ceremonies and for the medieval Roman Catholic Mass. The obvious and inevitable evolution of religious ideas that has taken place between these two stages of world-consciousness has naturally brought about changes in people's perceptions of music and their attitude toward it. We will explore these changes in due time. For the present, we ought to review a number of basic characteristics of music that can be perceived in those world-conscious societies that have evolved the least from their human beginnings.

The experience of the numinous is fundamentally emotional and nonrational. The primary significance of music as a response to the numinous is also in its most primal manifestation emotional and nonrational. Human beings cry out in fear, they shout for help, they groan in pain; it is inevitable that they come to sing as they entreat the deity, as they plead for divine mercy. Human beings cry out in joy and delight; that cry becomes the sung prayer of thanksgiving. Human beings devise repeated chants to remember and interiorize words of wisdom; these chants naturally become transformed into songs of meditation on the divine wisdom. The solidarity engendered by humans singing together is

---

[14]All forms of art tend to be integrated and interdependent in world-conscious cultures.

[15]See Sachs, *Wellsprings of Music*, p. 16.

Prologue   9

transferred to song's creation of oneness with the divine.[16] World-conscious music in general, but in particular world-conscious music in the service of the cult, is in its origin spontaneous and improvisational rather than conscious and deliberative, and its style and substance are originally perpetuated by oral tradition instead of being written down. Therefore aboriginal music, the earliest manifestation of world-conscious music-making, usually encompasses only short, simple units, with much repetition and an absence of formal complication.[17]

Because world-conscious living is primarily communal, being rooted in the family, tribe, or people, music normally has a superpersonal, communal significance. It does not express primarily the thoughts or feelings of a single individual, but of an individual (or individuals) within the life of the larger community. Music seems to have begun with singing instead of with performance on musical instruments,[18] and almost until the advent of the modern era music and poetry were linked.[19] Singing did not exist without words, and poetry was never delivered apart from singing. This holds true for music in general, and in particular for music in the service of the cult. Furthermore, cultic words are inevitably sung:

> The word which is merely spoken is a somewhat incomplete form of human language. It suffices for ordinary utilitarian communications. But as soon as the word becomes charged with emotion, as soon as it is filled with power, as soon as it tends to identify itself with the content of its message--when...it has to signify the sacredness of actions being performed--then it calls imperatively...for a musical form... The complete word, the fully developed word, the sacred word, has the nature of song. (Gelineau, p. 44)

The specific ways in which the relationship between the cult and music unfolds in the many world-conscious cultures are manifold and fascinating. There is now a considerable body of scholarly information about these ways, constantly increasing in its scope. As examples we might mention the role of music among the Suya people, an aboriginal tribe in Brazil,[20] or among the Balinese people,[21] or (to approach more nearly the Western cultural heritage) among the ancient Israelites (as seen in the Old Testament). Some cultures are preoccupied (some might say "obsessed") with religion, whereas others seem to take it more as a matter of course and to wear its mantle more lightly. Therefore the energy and attention assigned to the practice of music in the service of the cult vary considerably. But no matter how different these specific ways are, the ideas and principles discussed above seem in every case to underlie them.

Even though music had an omnipresent spiritual significance, there is every good reason to suppose that in the dawn-time of humanity it had a number of

---

[16]For a more complete development of these ideas, see Joseph Gelineau, S.J., *Voices and Instruments in Christian Worship*, pp. 15-22.
[17]See Sachs, *Wellsprings of Music*, p. 123; see also Alan P. Merriam, *African Music in Perspective*, pp. 87-88.
[18]See Sachs, *Rise of Music...*, p. 21f.
[19]Ibid., p. 30.
[20]See Anthony Seeger, *Why Suyá Sing*.
[21]See Mantle Hood, *The Ethnomusicologist*, pp. 9-16.

utilitarian functions, just as it does in all cultures today. Music lightened toil, it served as a mnemonic or teaching tool, it amused and entertained. We are concerned, however, with none of these. Our task is to trace and explain the evolution of ideas that underlies the development of music in the service of religion, specifically of Christianity. Until the dawn of the modern age such ideas were clear and forceful, and they decisively determined the nature of music and music-making in the Christian church.

NEW IDEAS AS THE CULT EVOLVES

In the previous section we made passing reference to the obvious and inevitable development in religious ideas that took place as Judaeo-Christian religious consciousness evolved, and the effect this evolution had on people's perception of music and their attitude toward it. To the degree that religion came to be subject to rational thought processes, a tension arose between the primal, irrational world-conscious religious conception and newer, more rational ideas. The net effect of these new ideas was to condition (but never entirely to negate) the primal force of cultic characteristics and requirements.

The image of a covenant between Yahweh and Israel dominates the Old Testament: an agreement in which both parties have obligations. The covenant image is intensified in the New Testament, however, because Christ is understood as having made the ultimate sacrifice, thus fulfilling the old covenant. God has already met, indeed, far exceeded the covenant obligation, proving the boundlessness of divine love. Accordingly, there is no imaginable circumstance or human condition in which the believer is not compelled to offer the praise and worship that are due to God, without condition, question, or hesitation:

> My God, I love thee; not because I hope for heaven thereby,
> Nor yet for fear that loving not I might forever die;
> But for that thou didst all mankind upon the cross embrace;
> For us didst bear the nails and spear and manifold disgrace,
> And griefs and torments numberless, and sweat of agony;
> E'en death itself; and all for man, Who was thine enemy.
>
> Then why, most loving Jesus Christ, should I not love thee well,
> Not for the sake of winning heav'n, nor any fear of hell;
> Not with the hope of gaining aught, not seeking a reward;
> But as thyself hast lovèd me, O ever-loving Lord!
> E'en so I love thee, and will love, and in thy praise will sing,
> Solely because thou art my God and my eternal King
> (Spanish, seventeenth century; trans. Edward Caswall (1849).
> *The Hymnal of the Protestant Episcopal Church, 1940*, no. 456)

The obligation to praise is therefore more intense and uncompromising than ever before.

Although the communal aspect of the cult was never rejected, the idea that each individual is important in the sight of God gained ground steadily. Already detectable in the writings of some Old Testament prophets,[22] it was given powerful impetus through the teachings of Jesus and his followers, in particular through the concept of substitutionary atonement ("Christ died for our sins") and the call for individual repentance and conversion: "For God so loved the world that he gave his only Son, that whoever believes in him should not perish but have eternal life" (John 3: 16). Indeed, the notion that God could become incarnate in a single human being, or that he could be given birth by an individual human mother, powerfully fosters the idea of the worth of the individual. In our time that idea has come to be taken for granted; it is the very foundation of modern democratic society. It need not negate the importance of the individual's role in a people, tribe, or family; the two ideas can exist in fruitful tension with each other. In point of fact, however, the appreciation of human individuality grew steadily stronger in the wake of Renaissance humanism. Among its many effects were a rise in the estimation of private, individual worship as over against cultic worship (which is always communal in spirit) and a corresponding slackening of the indispensable requirement for full participation in cultic events that is a constitutive feature of cult. An increasing emphasis on the unique worth of each human individual inevitably resulted in some shift of activity from the cultivation of music for communal cultic events (formal music that expressed communal consensus and obligation more than personal feeling) to the advancement of music intended to promote private, individual religious sentiment.

The intimate cooperation of elaborate, artistic ritual and ceremony in cultic celebrations was first conditioned (in the Judaeo-Christian heritage) by the messages of some Old Testament prophets: "I hate, I despise your feasts, and I take no delight in your solemn assemblies.... Take away from me the noise of your songs; to the melody of your harps I will not listen. But let justice roll down like waters, and righteousness like an ever-flowing stream" (Amos 5: 21; 23-24). Of course, the prophet Amos is not calling here for an end to ritual and ceremony in public worship, nor is he condemning artistry in worship per se. Rather, he is insisting on righteousness and fidelity to the will of God, so that the heart and mind may truly mean what the body and lips do and say. Were this not true, the elaborate ritual of worship at the Jerusalem temple would surely have been curbed. In point of fact, that ritual was still thriving when the Romans destroyed the Jerusalem temple in A.D. 70, and early rabbis subsequently recorded its details carefully, with an eye toward the day when it might be resumed. Early Christian writings do not reject the importance of solemn ritual; on the contrary, the book of Acts records that early Christians were faithful in their attendance at temple worship.[23] Nor do Christian writings condemn ornament and adornment in the service of worship; on the contrary, they seem to approve of it. It is difficult to interpret the story of the woman anointing Jesus's feet with precious ointment[24] in any other way. The Jews, Jesus, the early Christians--all of them seem never to have questioned, indeed they seem to have taken for granted that the elaborate, artistically splendid worship of the temple

---

[22]Cf. Ezekiel 18:19ff. See also Gerhard von Rad, *Old Testament Theology*, p. 396.
[23]Acts 2:46; 3:1.
[24]Luke 7:37-50; John 12:1-8.

was an appropriate way to worship God. Any disparagement of such a mode of worship occurs only in the context of condemning hypocrisy,[25] of requiring sincerity of devotion. The story of the woman anointing Jesus's feet, mentioned above, also suggests that the adornment of worship can coexist with a more rational approach to righteousness and faithfulness to God's will (in that case, with the moral requirement to care for the poor, a requirement that Jesus certainly never abolished). But in fact the history of the church reveals a constant tension between the spontaneous and the deliberative on this point. The first clear breach with earlier attitudes comes with the rise of early Christian asceticism, with its strong emphasis on individual contrition of heart, its suspicion of art, and its iconoclastic tendencies (but more on this later).

The *ex opere operato* relationship of ritual words and actions with the unseen reality they are meant to convey was perhaps one of the earliest casualties of the advent of more rational modes of thought. At the earlier stages of ancient Israel's history (even as late as the period of the prophets), such a relationship was clearly taken for granted. For example, at the word of the prophet Elijah the fire of the Lord descended from heaven and devoured the burnt offering.[26] But later in the Old Testament (after the Babylonian Captivity), Job called in distress time after time for God's help, and finally received the reply that the ways of God are inscrutable, beyond human knowing; human words and acts cannot control the Almighty: "Where were you when I laid the foundations of the earth? Tell me, if you have understanding" (Job 38: 4). By the time of the New Testament, there is a consensus that neither human voices nor acts, neither song nor any human art in itself, can please or placate God; the faithfulness and righteousness of the speaker or the doer is all that God regards.[27]

Although these new ideas have tended to condition and perhaps to dilute the primal force of cultic worship and the music that accompanies it, all of them could be and have been accommodated within the framework of world-consciousness as it gradually evolved toward modern times. That is because they only modify the world-conscious worldview and do not negate it. The negation of world-consciousness (together with the elimination of cult and its accompanying music) may be accomplished only when the primary frame of reference for humans comes to be the human self, and not the "other" (i.e., the spirit-world, the divine).

MUSIC IN CREATION MYTHS

Myths are stories about the doings of divine beings and their interaction with human beings. They offer reasons why life is meaningful; they tell how and why things came into being, and how they are nourished and sustained. Myths flourish and are accorded the profound respect due to them primarily in

---

[25]The very notion of hypocrisy is inconceivable in connection with cult in its purest, most uncompromising form.

[26]I Kings 18:38.

[27]This is in stark contrast to pagan views, which regarded music as a means of placating the gods. See Quasten, *Music and Worship in Pagan and Christian Antiquity*, p. 1.

prescientific cultures, cultures whose people are united in a world-conscious worldview. Myths are the basis for and the energizing force behind the cult, and cult and myth cooperate in the creation of reality.[28]

Myths mean many things to many people.[29] Self-conscious humans ordinarily understand myths to be quaint fairy tales. Some anthropologists and sociologists understand them as ways for a people to define who they are, to express their self-image. Although there is an element of truth in both of these views, there is relatively little to be gained from speaking of myths in this manner, and much to be gained from trying to understand them from the vantage point of those to whom they belong. Most educated musicians recognize that the only way to approach a true understanding of the music of a past era is to attempt to do so not through the eyes and ears of the present time, but through the eyes and ears of the age to which that music belonged. For example, the music of J. S. Bach is best realized in terms of how Bach himself intended to realize it (insofar as that is possible today). That is how it is with myths; they belong to world-conscious people, people of faith, and in order to understand their true significance, we must try to understand them as do those people to whom they belong.

For world-conscious people, myths are products of divine revelation. They are a means by which people come to understand who they are in relation to the divine. People of faith believe wholeheartedly and without reservation in the myths that underlie and inform their faith. On the other hand, people who are in some measure affected by the self-conscious, scientific worldview often have a difficult time understanding how myths can be considered true. The key lies in distinguishing between fact and truth. The analogy of an adopted child's relationship with adoptive parents[30] may help clarify that distinction. On the level of fact, for the adoptive child to say of adoptive parents, "This is my mother" or "This is my father," would be patently untrue; a legal document, a birth certificate, exists to attest to the *fact* that child and parents are biologically unrelated. But "mother-ness" and "father-ness" belong to an entirely different category of reality from biological fact. For the adoptive child, the adoptive mother is undeniably truly mother, and the adoptive father is truly father; the biological "fact" is, on this level of reality, inconsequential. It is in this way that myths must be considered true: they embody and express truths that are far deeper (and infinitely truer) than factual truth. This is not to say, however, that myths are always completely divorced from facts. They may indeed be based in part or wholly on historical facts, but that is not why they are myths, nor why they are powerful and valid. They are powerful and true only because they reveal to human beings the nature of the divine and how the divine relates to the human sphere.

To repeat, then: for world-conscious people, myths are a means of understanding who they are in relation to the divine. For people of faith, myths are of

---

[28]"...a *living myth* is always connected with a cult, inspiring and justifying a religious behavior" (Eliade, *Myths, Rites, Symbols*, p. 19).

[29]For a more detailed discussion of the nature and significance of myths, see Eliade, *Myths, Rites, Symbols*, p. 2ff. In addition, Joseph Campbell's *The Power of Myth* is an engaging popular introduction to this topic.

[30]The apostle Paul indeed uses this metaphor in a similar way in Galatians 4:5.

surpassing importance, of ultimate significance. They have no option but to believe in them, to stake their existence on them, because if they were not true, life would not be worth living, would not be bearable. The analogy with adoptive motherhood and fatherhood is *only* an analogy; belief in myths is much more intense and decisive for the world-conscious person. That person can face (albeit with difficulty) surviving without parents, but cannot conceive of surviving without the myths that give life meaning and certitude.

Because myths are of surpassing importance and ultimate significance, they cannot help but establish and perpetuate (in cooperation with the cult) a view of what reality is: a worldview. They define what is important to a people, what a people understands as central to existence, what a people particularly respects and reverences. As long as certain myths are perpetuated among a people, they continue to reinforce that worldview, defining the important features of reality as that people perceives it. The ideas propagated by myths generate presuppositions and attitudes, and in the final analysis these are as important as the ideas behind them. By their very nature, then, such myths establish the *ideals* to which a people subscribes. How do these ideals relate to the world of events, actions, situations: the "real world"? Certainly they are not the same, but just as certainly the former conditions the latter. For example, if a myth depicts a people as having been created out of the blood of a wounded god, then that people may well be fierce and cultivate the making of war as an ideal; this is indeed the case with the Yanomamö, an aboriginal people that inhabits the jungles of Venezuela and Brazil.[31] The interrelatedness of ideal and real world is in fact basic to any history of ideas (such as this book). Myths cooperate in the creation of a vision of how things *ought to be*. Those ideals correlate only imperfectly with the reality of the situation, but their influence on it is unmistakable.

Myths appear to have their birth in prerecorded history, one might even dare to say, from the earliest moments of humanity. Perhaps the most fundamental distinguishing characteristic of being human is an awareness of oneself within a greater whole. In the dawn-time of human existence one of the primary ways this burgeoning 'cosmic' awareness was expressed was in terms of myths. Myths were at first perpetuated as part of tribal oral traditions, but they came to be recorded in writing at the earliest stages of a people's literacy. Here is a myth that tells about the creation of the world:

There was Eru, the One, who in Arda is called Ilúvatar; and he made first the Ainur, the Holy Ones, that were the offspring of his thought, and they were with him before aught else was made. And he spoke to them, propounding to them themes of music; and they sang before him, and he was glad...

And it came to pass that Ilúvatar called together all the Ainur and declared to them a mighty theme... Then Ilúvatar said to them: 'Of the theme that I have declared to you, I will now that ye make in harmony together a Great Music...ye shall show forth your powers in adorning this theme, each with his own thoughts and devices, if he will. But I will sit and hearken, and be glad that through you great beauty has been wakened into song.'

Then the voices of the Ainur...began to fashion the theme of Ilúvatar to a great music; and a sound arose of endless interchanging melodies woven in harmony that

---

[31] See: Napolean A. Chagnon, *Yanomamö: The Fierce People*, pp. 47-48.

passed beyond hearing into the depths and into the heights, and the places of the dwelling of Ilúvatar were filled to overflowing, and the music and the echo of the music went out into the Void, and it was not void...

...Ilúvatar arose in splendour, and he went forth from the fair regions that he had made for the Ainur; and the Ainur followed him.

But when they were come into the Void, Ilúvatar said to them: 'Behold your Music!' And he showed to them a vision,...and they saw a new World made visible before them... And when the Ainur had gazed for a while and were silent, Ilúvatar said again: 'Behold your Music! This is your minstrelsy. (J.R.R. Tolkien, *The Silmarillion*, pp. 3-4, 6)

In some ways this is a most unusual myth: it is modern, having been written in the first half of the twentieth century, and its author, J.R.R. Tolkien, unlike the first tellers of ancient myths, is known. But in its substance it might just as easily have been written 3,500 years ago. It is similar to myths encountered among ancient Egyptians, Indians, and Chinese in this very important way: it reveals music as a transcendent power used by the gods to create the universe and the world.[32] It is hardly surprising that music is very highly regarded indeed in cultures that perpetuate such myths. Those cultures often consider music to be a means by which cosmic order is maintained, as well as a way of allowing human lives to participate in that order. The Hebrew Book of Genesis does not accord to music such an exalted role in the creation of order from chaos. But the *Timaeus*, the Greek philosopher Plato's story of the creation of the cosmos, does indeed grant music such a role.[33] And, as we will see, Plato's *Timaeus* was highly influential in the development of the Christian church's understanding of the role of music.

---

[32]See: Reinhold Hammerstein, "Music as Divine Art," in Philip P. Wiener, ed.-in-chief, *Dictionary of the History of Ideas*, Vol. III, p. 268.

[33]Plato's creation account may well be indebted to earlier Egyptian and Mesopotamian sources.

2

Music in the Bible

MUSIC IN THE OLD TESTAMENT

Judaeo-Christian religious tradition can trace a direct line of descent from the earliest religious expression of ancient Israel. There is nothing particularly distinctive about ancient Israel as a tribal people except its religious expression: the religion of Yahweh, the one all-powerful God. That religion was remarkably intense and demanding, and its uncompromising monotheism represented an extraordinarily mature, sophisticated level of religious awareness for a tribal people. Ancient Israel's evolving religious awareness unfolds in the Old Testament, whose earliest writings offer a record of what was surely first an oral tradition of great antiquity.

The Old Testament offers only a fragmentary image of musical thought and practice in ancient Israel. The chief reason for this incompleteness is that it was not the intention of the authors of the Old Testament to offer an explanation of ideas about music. Therefore, although there are many references to music, most of them are in the form of incidental comments, and it is hardly surprising that these comments present only a partial record of musical ideas and practices.

Ancient Israel's ideas about music do exert some influence on the evolution of Christian musical thought, though proportionately far less influence than Greek philosophy. It is important to examine those ideas, however, for a number of reasons. First, as sacred scripture, incontestably accepted as divine revelation by Jews and Christians alike, the Old Testament cannot ever be dismissed without carefully considering what it has to say. Second, the chronicle of ancient Israel's evolution as a society provides a specific example of the force of cult as a determining factor in sacred music. Finally, the comparison of undiluted world-conscious modes of thought with more modern ones is endlessly fascinating and instructive.

The Old Testament records the religious development of the Jewish people and its covenant relationship with Yahweh. It begins with tribal Judaism (the books

18   Wiser than Despair

of Genesis through Judges, as well as many of the Psalms), and then proceeds to chronicle the rise and fall of the monarchy, beginning shortly before 1000 B.C. (the books of Samuel through Chronicles, and most of the prophetic writings) and Israel's return to the Holy Land after the Babylonian Captivity, at which point Jewish culture exhibited a marked self-identity. Even though the Old Testament offers only a fragmentary view of musical thought, it has manifold references to music at all stages of this development. Consequently the ideas it expresses about music continue to evolve throughout the course of the narrative. At the earliest tribal stages, all that has been said in the prologue about music in primitive societies undoubted held true for Israel as well: music was a prominent feature of the cult of Yahweh; it was the result of the outpouring of emotion[1] (in the Yahweh cult it was often a concomitant of ecstatic states); it was the property, not of the specialist but of the entire people.

The first mention of music in the Old Testament is in Genesis 4:19-22[2]:

Lamech married two women: the name of the first was Adah and the name of the second was Zillah. Adah gave birth to Jabal: he was the ancestor of the tent-dwellers and owners of livestock. His brother's name was Jubal: he was the ancestor of all who play the lyre and the flute. As for Zillah, she gave birth to Tubal-cain: he was the ancestor of all metalworkers, in bronze or iron.

In this passage three primal professions are singled out for mention, and curiously, music is one of them. Perhaps it is an indication of the importance that ancient Israel attached to music.

At the earliest stage of the Yahweh cult, the Old Testament shows music functioning in two ways: it accompanied ecstatic states and prophecy, and it was closely linked with magic.

Ecstasy is the state of trance that is concomitant with prophetic inspiration.[3] It is a phenomenon frequently encountered in connection with cult in its more primitive manifestations. In the Yahweh cult it was the mark of a prophet, and until the later years of Israel's monarchy it was inevitably accompanied by music. Such a view of music presumes that Israel considered it to be of divine origin, a gift from Yahweh. Although there is only one Hebrew word for prophet, *nabi*, nevertheless two types of prophets are recorded in the Old Testament, roughly corresponding to the period before and the period after the institution of the monarchy (c. 1000 B.C.).

Of the many instances of prophecy recorded in the Old Testament, several are of special note with regard to music. The first is recorded in I Samuel 10:1-12 (the anointing of Saul). According to that account, after Samuel had anointed Saul king over Israel, he instructed Saul to seek a sign of his new status. One of his assignments was to go to Gibeah where he would meet a group of prophets "headed by harp, tambourine, flute and lyre; they will be in an ecstasy."

---

[1] See Sachs, *Rise of Music*, p. 59.
[2] All biblical quotations are taken from *The Jerusalem Bible* (see *Holy Bible*), since that translation often clarifies and intensifies the cultic matrix of scripture.
[3] See *Dictionary: O.E.D.*, "Ecstasy," 3.b.

Saul obeyed Samuel and was caught up in the prophets' ecstatic fervor. Here the connection between music and ecstasy is quite clear. It is less clear in I Chronicles 25: 1-7, in which David is organizing the music of the Jerusalem temple. In that passage David sets apart a number of men to serve as musicians in the temple liturgies; all of them were singers who accompanied themselves with various instruments ("lyre and harp and cymbal"). Only by consulting the original Hebrew text does it become evident that the word used here for the singing of the levitical musicians, *nibba*, is the same word used elsewhere for the ecstatic states of prophets. The prophetic office thus became institutionalized in the priestly practice of the temple, although it was clearly still linked with music (and probably with ecstatic states as well).

In addition to music, two other elements seem to be common to prophetic utterances: the use of instruments and dancing. The use of instruments we have already encountered in I Samuel 10, but both are evident in the familiar passage that relates David's dancing before the Ark of the Lord: II Samuel 6:1-2, 5-6, & 14-15.

David again mustered all the picked troops of Israel, thirty thousand men. Setting off with the whole force then with him, David went to Baalah of Judah, to bring up from there the ark of God which bears the name of Yahweh Sabaoth who is seated on the cherubs... David and all the House of Israel danced before Yahweh with all their might, singing to the accompaniment of lyres, harps, tambourines, castanets, and cymbals... And David danced whirling round before Yahweh with all his might, wearing a linen loincloth round him. Thus David and all the House of Israel brought up the ark of Yahweh with acclaim and the sound of the horn.

The account of Israel's early history also testifies that women as well as men could be counted as prophets: for example, in Exodus 15: 19-21, Aaron's sister Miriam is called a "prophetess" and leads the people of Israel in their song of rejoicing for deliverance from Egypt: Exodus 15:19-21 (Israel's deliverance from Egypt).

Pharaoh's cavalry, both his chariots and horsemen, had indeed entered the sea, but Yahweh had made the waters of the sea flow back on them, yet the sons of Israel had marched on dry ground right through the sea.
Miriam, the prophetess, Aaron's sister, took up a timbrel, and all the women followed her with timbrels, dancing. And Miriam led them in the refrain:
'Sing of Yahweh: he has covered himself in glory,
horse and rider he has thrown into the sea'.

In Judges 4:1-10, Deborah prophesies Israel's victory over Sisera, the commander of Jabin's army. Although Deborah is also called a judge in this passage, it was not from that office that she gained her status as a prophetess; rather it was from her ability to sing the message of Yahweh, as the account in Judges 5:1-7 makes clear.

The period between the institution of the monarchy and the Babylonian Captivity that began in 587/6 B.C. witnessed a transformation in the role of the prophet. Prophets of this era, such as Isaiah, Jeremiah, Ezekiel, Hosea, Joel, and Amos, were not merely local figures, nor were they connected with the liturgy of the Jerusalem temple. They were men of national significance, tellers

20   Wiser than Despair

of the future and witnesses to Yahweh's wrath at Israel's unfaithfulness. The case for music's connection with the delivery of their prophecies is not as strong as for earlier prophets, since singing and the use of instruments are not specifically mentioned. Yet the poetic form in which the majority of the later prophetic writings is cast certainly suggests the possibility that they might have been sung. There is at least one instance of a specific link, in 2 Kings 3:9-20, in which it appears that the playing of an instrument actually helped to induce Elisha's prophetic ecstasy.

An intriguing idea that seems to be related to human prophetic song is the attribution of song to the realm of nature. The book of Job records that the natural world praises Yahweh for its creation and preservation (e.g., Job 38:7), and Psalm 65:13 speaks of the desert, the hillsides, the meadows and the valleys acclaiming and singing to Him out of their fruitfulness.

In the New Testament it is the book of Revelation that most clearly resembles the Old Testament prophetic books. It is not mere chance, then, that Revelation has more references to music than any other book in the New Testament. It testifies that the idea of prophetic ecstasy connected with music was still alive in the early Christian church, though it is not clear to what degree the ecstatic music described in its pages was translated into actual song by early Christians.

Music in the Old Testament is also closely linked with magic (i.e., supernatural occurrences); it has the power not only to speak, but also to act. Music may invoke Yahweh; it may drive away evil spirits; and it may have the power to frighten and to cooperate in destroying the enemy. In this connection of music with magic, just as in the union of music and prophecy, ancient Israel resembles other primitive, tribal societies.

Ancient Israel invoked Yahweh with a loud voice or with noisy instruments, in order to gain his attention and invite his presence. They did not "speak" to God; rather, they "invoked" him (*kar'a*), they "shouted" to him (*za'ak*), or they "exulted" in him (*teru'ah*). Indeed, I Samuel 1:1-17 reveals that silent prayer was unheard of. In that passage Hannah is praying silently to Yahweh for a son; overcome with emotion, she moves her lips without uttering a sound. Eli the priest, watching her, cannot imagine that she is praying, even though she is standing in the temple; he can only presume that she is drunk. In II Chronicles 5:11-4, Yahweh's advent is associated with a loud invocation, marked by forceful singing and powerful instrumental music. In that passage the "cloud of Yahweh's glory" may be interpreted as a metaphor for the ecstatic state that possessed the assembly, thus preventing the continuation of the normal temple ritual. If this is true, it is yet another piece of evidence that music was a concomitant of ecstatic states. In I Kings 18:25-29 Elijah challenges the prophets of Baal to summon their god. The main point of the passage is, of course, to express Elijah's mocking sarcasm at the impotence of the priests of Baal. His command, "Call louder," however, reflects the usual primitive practice of invoking the deity with a loud noise, a practice that Elijah then rejects in the subsequent narrative.[4] The instrument most frequently mentioned to invoke Yahweh is the shofar or ramshorn, an instrument that makes a sound not unlike

---

[4]Elijah's prophetic ministry occurred at a later time in Israel's history, c. 742-687 B.C.; his rejection of the primitive practice of invocation with a loud noise is evidence of a more evolved and refined religious consciousness.

an amplified human shriek. The instrument may have been viewed as a means of augmenting the volume of the human voice. In the later prophets, God himself is depicted as blowing the shofar to announce his own coming: Zechariah 9:14.

> Yahweh will appear above them
> and his arrow will flash out like lightning.
> Yahweh will sound the trumpet [i.e., shofar]
> and advance in the storms of the south.

The power of music to drive away evil spirits is evident in the report (I Samuel 16:14-23) of David's ability to alleviate Saul's fits of madness by playing the lyre or harp (Hebrew *kinnor*). As in other primitive societies, ancient Israel understood human madness as being possessed by a spirit[5] that music was capable of exorcising.

Music also had the power to frighten and to cooperate in destroying the enemy. This is confirmed by the famous story of the fall of Jericho (Joshua 6), as well as the account of Gideon and his troops routing the Midianite army (Judges 7:16-22).

It may strike the reader as strange that in the foregoing analysis of ancient Israel's musical thought little mention is made of music in communal cultic celebrations. The earliest stages of the Old Testament in fact record nothing substantive about such music. That is indeed odd, especially since the early books of the Bible are full of instructions regulating cultic observances. Only one portion of the Bible reveals something of the important place music occupied in those primitive cultic observances, and that is the psalms. In his pioneering study of the psalms, Sigmund Mowinckel[6] made a convincing case that their origin and purpose were intimately connected with the Yahweh cult. Since the psalms are cultic poetry (hymns), they were invariably sung (among primitive peoples poetry is always sung, never simply spoken). It is impossible to isolate any of the most primitive psalms in their original form, however, since they were later combined with more recent psalm poetry in the organizational structure known as the Psalter (the 150 canonical Psalms), apparently a product of post-exilic worship at the Jerusalem temple. Only a comparative study of ancient Israel's worship with practices of other primitive peoples can reveal to us the original cultic matrix of the psalms and music's original role in Israel's earliest cultic practices. The vivid language and arresting imagery of many of the psalms (e.g., Psalm 44, or Psalm 149), however, provide eloquent testimony to the apparent intensity of music in the Yahweh cult.

The Old Testament does not reveal anything substantive about music in communal cultic celebrations until the time of the monarchy, when David and Solomon centralized the Yahweh cult in the national capital by building the

---

[5] Ancient Israel was decisively different from other primitive cultures, however, in its monotheism. The spirit that possessed Saul is therefore "from God," and not an evil spirit, as in other cultures; there are no powerful spirits other than Yahweh.

[6] Mowinckel, *The Psalms in Israel's Worship*.

Jerusalem temple. The building of the temple and the regulation of Israel's religious life and practice gave impetus to a gradual but fundamental transformation of music in Israel's worship. The earlier spontaneity apparent in music's link with prophecy (and characteristic of primitive cultic expression) began to yield to musical organization and specialization. The account of David's organization of music in the temple is recorded in I Chronicles 25 as well as in I Chronicles 15:16-22 and 16:4-7, in which he assigned to the Levites the task of being temple priests, one contingent of whom were to serve as musicians. Thereafter music is recorded as holding a permanent place in the temple liturgy: "There before the ark of the covenant of Yahweh David left Asaph and his kinsmen to maintain a permanent ministry before the ark as each day's ritual required" (I Chronicles 16:37). I Chronicles 16:8-36 records what the musicians sang in the temple liturgy; these verses consist of portions of psalms, principally Psalms 105 and 96. It seems probable that already during this early period of the monarchy the psalms were gradually being collected and organized into a hymnbook for the temple, although it is only much later, after the Babylonian exile, that unequivocal evidence for this exists.

Ezra 3:10-11 records that following the return from Babylon and the reconstruction of the temple, the liturgy was reinstituted together with its full complement of music. Although by that time the earlier spontaneous, ecstatic worship seems to have been curtailed in favor of a more organized ritual, the Davidic temple liturgy in all likelihood continued essentially intact until the destruction of Jerusalem and the temple by Roman forces in A.D. 70. Passages in the rabbinic writings, the *Talmud*, apparently written in an attempt to preserve the temple ritual for the restoration of the temple by some future generation, are quite detailed in their description of it,[7] and what they say is in basic accord with the accounts in I Chronicles, written perhaps 600 years earlier. This was the temple liturgy in which Jesus himself took part (cf. Luke 2:41), as well as his disciples and followers after his death and resurrection (cf. Acts 2:46). It was far from austere; in fact, it seems to have been exotic, splendid, artistic, sensuous, overwhelming--and quite emotional.

In contrast to temple worship, however, is the worship of the synagogue, an institution that seems to have arisen or at least been given its definitive form during the Babylonian exile. Early Christian worship drew much more heavily on the synagogue service (as the subsequent shape of the Christian eucharistic and office liturgies shows), which consisted primarily of readings, the singing of Psalms, prayers and an address or sermon. Synagogue worship, in contrast to the temple, was more sober, thoughtful and reflective: "The original aim of Sabbath meetings was not divine service, but rather study of the law. This explains why, even in later times, a mere subordinate role has been assigned to the worship and praise of Yahveh in the Synagogue as compared with religious instruction" (Sendrey, *Music in Ancient Israel*, p. 179). Sobriety, rather than splendor, came to be the chief characteristic of early Christian worship;[8] as the

---

[7]*Talmud, Tamid* tractate, 7:3-4; see Sachs, *Rise of Music*, p. 61.

[8]In this statement, "sobriety" should be understood as "modest, simple in outward form and appearance." It is clear that the element of ecstasy played an important role in early Christian worship, as we learn from the account of the day of Pentecost (Acts 2) and from the practice of speaking in tongues.

original Jewish sect gradually became transformed into a new religion, Jewish temple worship was rejected and forgotten. When elaborate ceremony later appeared in Christian worship, it was more the product of Christianity's favored status in the later days of imperial Rome (together with the natural impetus to ornament the worship of God) than any direct continuity with cultic celebrations at the Jerusalem temple.

MUSIC IN THE NEW TESTAMENT

The Old Testament tells the story of the development of the Jewish people, a story encompassing more than two thousand years. It traces the gradual growth and maturation of that people's religious consciousness to a point where religion and culture are highly unified. The New Testament, on the other hand, covers a period of less than one century; it tells the story of a small, struggling new religion, embracing people of very different cultural backgrounds that celebrated their newfound unity only in their intense religious beliefs and practice, not in a broad cultural unity. The New Testament, then, since it covers only the earliest stages of Christianity, presents a neutral picture of most manifestations of culture (if indeed it presents any picture at all), while the Old Testament offers us a rather detailed picture of culture as it relates to religion. Furthermore, the Old Testament represents a religion that had, over a very long period of time, created its accompanying, sympathetic culture, while the New Testament represents a religion at odds with the alien culture in which it found itself (indeed, awaiting the imminent destruction of that culture in the second coming of Christ). Finally, while many passages in the Old Testament are concerned with some aspect of the cult, the New Testament is notably shy of specifically Christian cultic references. (In the early years of Christianity's existence, Jewish cultic observances continued to fulfill most of Christianity's cultic requirements, the single exception being the reenactment of the Lord's Supper.)

In light of these observations, it is only to be expected that the picture of music is even more fragmentary in the New Testament than in the Old. The Old Testament presents a sympathetic view of making music in the service of religion, whereas the New Testament is largely neutral to music. The Old Testament shows no suspicion of music's power, while the early Christian church (living in a hostile cultural environment) quickly came to be suspicious of it. And while religious music-making as reflected in the New Testament is largely simple, modest, and undeveloped, religious music-making in the Old Testament is unabashedly (yea, enthusiastically) lavish, elaborate, splendid, and highly developed.

It is a significant (though seldom adequately recognized) fact that the earliest Christians took worship at the Jerusalem temple for granted as part of their life. Temple worship in tandem with the simpler, more sober synagogue-based worship of the early Christian assembly offered a balanced cultic life as long as Christianity was still a Jewish sect. When Christianity extended itself to gentile peoples, however, the rejection of Jewish temple worship left a void that eventually was filled by the adoption of imperial Roman or Byzantine court ceremonial practices, coupled with the natural urge to adorn and beautify the worship of God. There was no New Testament scriptural basis for such embel-

24   Wiser than Despair

lishment, however. This explains why, when later generations of Christians sought to explain and to justify the practice of elaborate, highly organized and sophisticated religious music, they turned primarily to the Old Testament and the accounts of worship in the Jerusalem temple, and only secondarily to the New Testament.[9]

The references to music in the New Testament can be sorted into a number of categories, as follows:

1. There are direct reports of music-making, pertaining either to the contemporary culture at large, or specifically to the fledgling Christian community: Matthew 9:23 (Jesus raises the official's daughter to life);

> When Jesus reached the official's house and saw the flute-players, with the crowd making a commotion he said, "Get out of here; the little girl is not dead, she is asleep."

Mark 14:26 (the close of the Last Supper).

> After Psalms had been sung they left for the Mount of Olives.

2. In his letters the apostle Paul occasionally admonishes Christians to sing not superficially, but sincerely from the heart: Colossians 3:16 (Paul exhorts the community to Christian behavior; cf. also Ephesians 5:18-20).

> Let the message of Christ, in all its richness, find a home with you. Teach each other, and advise each other, in all wisdom. With gratitude in your hearts sing psalms and hymns and inspired songs to God.

---

[9]For example:

...everybody knows that not only the prophets and kings of Israel (who praised God with vocal and instrumental music, with songs and stringed instruments), but also the early Christians, who sang especially psalms, used music already in the early stages of the Church's history. (Martin Luther, Preface to *Geistliches Gesangbüchlein*, 1524; trans. in Buszin, "Luther on Music," pp. 87-88)

...both Kings David and Solomon, when they wished to arrange the worship of God in the temple and tabernacle at Jerusalem as magnificently and elegantly as possible, appointed to the task any number of musicians, both singers and instrumentalists, sparing neither effort nor expense, to create all the more ardor and zeal among the people. For this purpose David himself even used his own harp, and doubtless had several magnificent organs built and set up, because of the size of the temple. (Michael Prætorius, *Syntagma musicum* II, p. 82.

NB. This chapter is the true foundation of all God-pleasing church music. (J. S. Bach's marginal comment on I Chronicles, Chap. 25, in his copy of Luther's German Bible with commentary by Abraham Calov. See Leaver, *J. S. Bach and Scripture*, p. 93.)

Music in the Bible 25

3. Musical instruments are occasionally used as metaphors: Matthew 6:2 (Jesus expounds the Law);

So when you give alms, do not have it trumpeted before you; this is what the hypocrites do in the synagogues and in the streets to win men's admiration.

I Corinthians 13:1 (Paul speaks of the primacy of love);

If I have all the eloquence of men or of angels, but speak without love, I am simply a gong booming or a cymbal clashing.

Hebrews 12:18-19 (Paul compares the new vision of the Kingdom of God to the old).

What you have come to is nothing known to the senses: not a blazing fire, or a gloom turning to total darkness, or a storm; or trumpeting thunder or the great voice speaking which made everyone that heard it beg that no more should be said to them.

4. By far the most frequent references to music in the New Testament mention it in an eschatological connection: I Corinthians 15:51-52 (Paul describes the end-time).

I will tell you something that has been secret: that we are not all going to die, but we shall all be changed. This will be instantaneous, in the twinkling of an eye, when the last trumpet sounds. It will sound, and the dead will be raised, imperishable, and we shall be changed as well.

All the references to music in the Book of Revelation fall into this category.

5. Some passages seem to record early Christian hymns or canticles; the Gospel of Luke is particularly rich in this regard, containing Mary's song (the Magnificat, 1:46-55), Zechariah's song (The Benedictus, 1:68-79), and Simeon's song (The Nunc Dimittis: 2:29-32). Elsewhere in the New Testament (particularly in Paul's letters), there are passages that possibly enshrine fragments of early Christian hymns no longer extant, for example, Ephesians 5:13-14 (Paul speaks of the new life in Christ).

The things which are done in secret are things that people are ashamed even to speak of; but anything exposed by the light will be illuminated and anything illuminated turns into light. That is why it is said:

> Wake up from your sleep,
> rise from the dead,
> and Christ will shine on you.

Here Paul seems to have inserted a few lines of hymnic poetry into his text, much in the same way Christian preachers in later ages might quote a few phrases of a familiar hymn appropriately to emphasize a point in a sermon.

6. Related to hymn-singing (and of course to prophecy as well) is the practice of *glossolalia* or speaking in tongues, an ecstatic, unintelligible outpouring of praise that was apparently well established among some early Christians. Paul looked upon the practice with something less than enthusiasm: I Corinthians 14: 2-12 (Paul speaks of spiritual gifts, especially prophecy).

> Anybody with the gift of tongues speaks to God, but not to other people; because nobody understands him when he talks in the spirit about mysterious things. On the other hand, the man who prophesies does talk to other people, to their improvement, their encouragement and their consolation. The one with the gift of tongues talks for his own benefit, but the man who prophesies does so for the benefit of the community. While I should like you all to have the gift of tongues, I would much rather you could prophesy, since the man who prophesies is of greater importance than the man with the gift of tongues, unless of course the latter offers an interpretation so that the church may get some benefit.
>
> Now suppose, my dear brothers, I am someone with the gift of tongues, and I come to visit you, what use shall I be if all my talking reveals nothing new, tells you nothing, and neither inspires you nor instructs you? Think of a musical instrument, a flute or a harp: if one note on it cannot be distinguished from another, how can you tell what tune is being played? Or if no one can be sure which call the trumpet has sounded, who will be ready for the attack? It is the same with you: if your tongue does not produce intelligible speech, how can anyone know what you are saying? You will be talking to the air. There are any number of different languages in the world, and not one of them is meaningless, but if I am ignorant of what the sounds mean, I am a savage to the man who is speaking, and he is a savage to me. It is the same in your own case: since you aspire to spiritual gifts, concentrate on those which will grow to benefit the community.

Speaking in tongues seems to have been well established among certain Christians, however, and it persisted as a phenomenon in Christian worship at least through the patristic era (see p. 56 below for a statement by St. Augustine defending ecstatic utterance).

7. Finally, in the context of his remarks on speaking in tongues Paul voices the single New Testament statement that can qualify as a unique and potentially fruitful idea about music: I Corinthians 14:13-15.

> That is why anybody who has the gift of tongues must pray for the power of interpreting them. For if I use this gift in my prayers, my spirit may be praying but my mind is left barren. What is the answer to that? Surely I should pray not only with the spirit but with the mind as well? And sing praises not only with the spirit but with the mind as well?

Such an idea, balancing the two poles--mind and spirit--and setting them in creative tension, has enormous potential for exegesis. It was indeed quoted by later Christian writers,[10] yet it was never probed deeper than the most obvious level. When Christian theologians and authors finally came to consider music's place in the church, they did not return to the New Testament as the basis for their work. Rather, they reverted to their early (pagan) education and thought about music in categories devised centuries before by early Greek philosophers.

---

[10]For example: St. John Chrysostom, fourth century, *Exposition of Psalm XLI*:

Hear what Paul says: "Be not drunk with wine, wherein is excess, but be filled with the Spirit." He adds, moreover, what the cause of this filling is: "Singing and making melody in your heart to the Lord." What is the meaning of "in your heart"? With understanding, he says; not so that the mouth utters words while the mind is inattentive, wandering in all directions, but so that the mind may hear the tongue. (trans. in Strunk, *Source Readings*, p. 68)

See also McKinnon, *Music in Early Christian Literature*, 134 & 303.

3

Music in Ancient Greece

> The mental process necessary to pass from imitative reproduction to conscious creation was beyond the capacity of primitive men. It eventually developed when the conflux of tribes, somewhere in Asia, had produced the phenomenon that we call 'high civilization.' Due to science, which was the essential achievement of high civilization, music progressed to an art. It needed mathematicians to express in numbers and ratios what seemed to exist in an imaginary, unmeasurable space of its own. And since analysis and synthesis were functions of logic, it needed philosophy to disintegrate melody into single notes and intervals and to rearrange the elements in ever new configurations. (Sachs, *Rise of Music*, pp. 52-53)

What Curt Sachs says about music in ancient high civilizations[1] holds true for the far East (China), for the Near Eastern Mesopotamian cultures, for Egypt, and for Greece. It is necessary to understand, however, that when Sachs speaks of science, he does not mean empirical science based on the modern scientific method. To be sure, the results of experiments and the recognition of natural laws of physics did play a role in ancient musical learning. But they were inextricably intermingled with intuition, rationalization, and revelation. What distinguished all of this from primitive music (and what made it *science*) was the engagement of the human intellect, of rational thought. Music for these cultures came to be more and more a matter of logical thinking and knowing rather than of feeling.

The common threads that run through the musical thought of all the more advanced cultures of the ancient world make it interesting to draw parallels and comparisons between them.[2] But for our purposes that exercise is beside the point, since only one of them was of consequence for church music: the musical thought of ancient Greece. Particularly as it was formulated and expressed by the philosopher Plato, this thought was decisive in determining the way Christian church music developed.

---

[1] See also Sachs: *Rise of Music*, pp. 57-58.
[2] See Bukofzer, "Speculative Thinking," p. 165.

30   Wiser than Despair

Underlying ancient Greek ideas on music, and indeed ancient Greek thinking in general, is the concept of *harmonia*, later referred to (in the Christian era) as world harmony or cosmic harmony. The root of this word, "ar," means "to fit together," to "adapt" or "adjust" one thing to another. Today the word *harmony* has a meaning that is essentially musical, and its subsidiary connotations are conceived with reference to the musical meaning of the term. In ancient Greek thought, however, the musical meaning of *harmonia* was subsidiary to the cosmic meaning of the term as described above.[3]

Greek philosophy presupposed *harmonia* as a basic quality of all that exists. Like all other ancient philosophical systems, it did not allow the possibility that anything could be absurd or even capricious. (Plato is notably without a sense of humor!) Since Greek philosophers were predisposed to *harmonic* thinking, to perceiving connections and interrelations between ostensible disparates, they eventually hit upon the notion that music was related to two other disciplines: (1) mathematics and (2) ethics or human morality. The philosophers could hardly have been unmindful that music can have a powerful effect on the senses and emotions (they surely were aware of the Orpheus legend), but they largely ignored the emotional, sensual aspect of music and left it undeveloped. Rather, music was understood primarily as a matter of intellectual understanding and contemplation, of *knowing* (i.e., a "science," in the ancient sense of the term) rather than of *feeling* (i.e., an "art," in the modern sense of the term). It was a scientific rather than an artistic endeavor.

Most Greek philosophers believed that music was related to mathematics or, as they themselves expressed it, to "number":

Number, fitting all things into the soul through sense-perception, makes them recognisable and comparable with one another... You may see the nature of Number and its power at work not only in supernatural and divine existences but also in all human activities and words everywhere, both throughout all technical production and also in music. (Philolaus of Tarentum, (fl. c. 475 B.C.), trans. in Anderson, *Ethos and Education*, p. 37)

Among the earliest protagonists of this relationship were the Pythagoreans, followers of the half-legendary yet enormously influential figure Pythagoras. Perhaps the most succinct statement of their doctrines was written by the Greek philosopher Aristotle, whose deprecatory tone is to be explained by the fact that he did not agree with them:

---

[3]In *Ethos and Education in Greek Music* (p. 38), Warren Anderson writes:

[The Greek philosopher] Philolaus maintained...that the basic principles of the cosmos, which underlie reality and enable us to apprehend it, have no meaningful interrelation through their own powers... This want, he says, is supplied by the cosmic force of *harmonia*, for "unlike and unrelated and unevenly ranked elements" must necessarily be brought into combination by the kind of *harmonia* that will enable them to be included in a cosmic order.

See also Routley, *The Church and Music*, p. 19.

Music in Ancient Greece   31

Illustration 1:
This thirteenth-century manuscript illustration portrays the legend of Pythagoras. In the upper panel Pythagoras is overhearing iron hammers striking an anvil, while in the lower there is depicted a *Chordotonos* (or monochord), the instrument Pythagoras devised to illustrate his discovery.

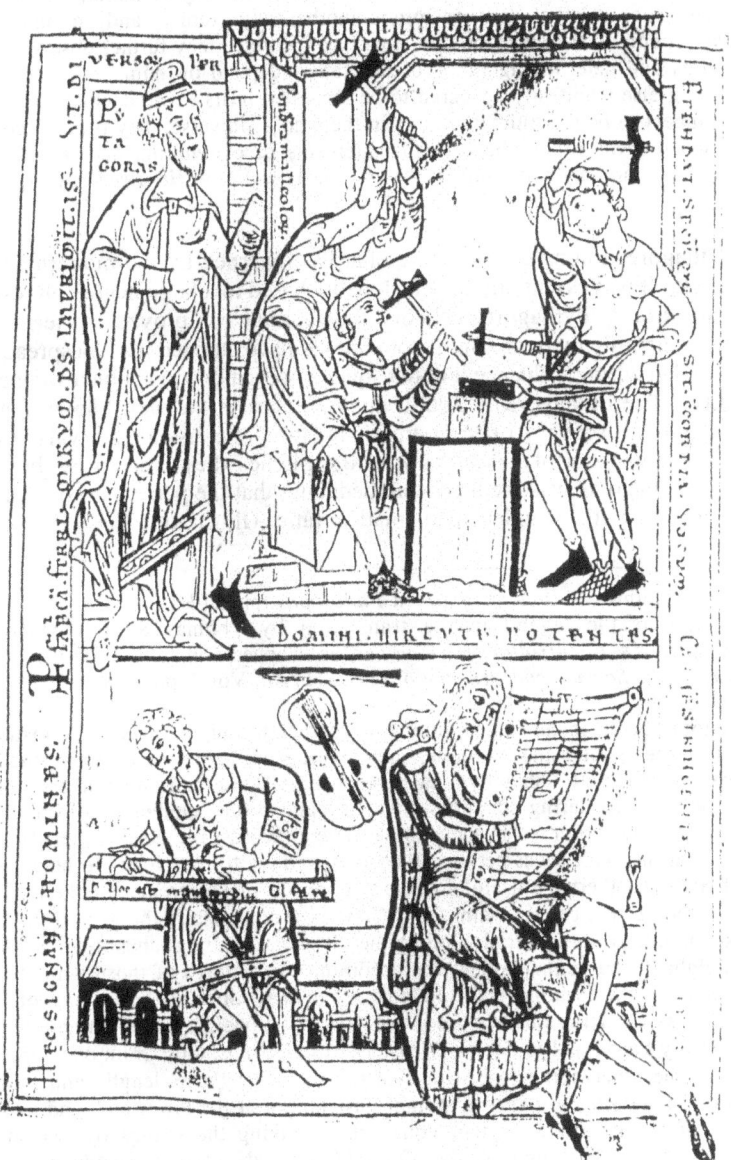

Source: a manuscript containing John of Cotton's *De Musica*, Clm 2599, fol. 96v.; courtesy of the Bavarian State Library, Munich, Germany.

32   Wiser than Despair

...the so-called Pythagoreans attached themselves to the mathematics and were the first to advance that science by their education, in which they were led to suppose that the principles of mathematics are the principles of all things. So as numbers are logically first among these principles, and as they fancied they could perceive in numbers many analogues of what is and what comes into being, much more readily than in fire and earth and water (such and such a property of number being justice, such and such another soul or mind, another opportunity, and so on, speaking generally, with all the other individual cases), and since they further observed that the properties and determining ratios of harmonies depend on numbers--since, in fact, everything else manifestly appeared to be modelled in its entire character on number, and numbers to be the ultimate things in the whole Universe, they became convinced that the elements of numbers are the elements of everything, and that the whole "Heaven" is harmony and number. (Aristotle, *Aristotle on His Predecessors*, pp. 91-92)

Pythagorean number theory was hardly governed by the modern scientific approach. It was essentially mystical, being based to a large degree on revelation and intuition.[4] Pythagorean theory thus cannot be "proved" in terms of the modern scientific method. But it could never have attained its widespread acceptance and enduring influence without some empirically perceptible evidence of its validity. The Pythagoreans found this evidence in the well-known legend of Pythagoras's discovery of the numerical ratios of musical intervals: by comparing the weights of hammers with the pitches they created as they struck anvils, Pythagoras was credited with deducing that the perfect musical intervals were created by the simplest mathematical ratios (Illustration 1):[5]

---

[4] See Guthrie, *A History of Greek Philosophy*, pp. 212-3.

[5] Here is the legend in the translation by Thomas Stanley (1701) from Nichomachus's *Enchiridion harmonices*, as it appears in John Hawkins's *General History of the Science and Practice of Music* (1776), Vol. I, pp. 9-10:

Pythagoras being in an intense thought whether he might invent any instrumental help to the ear, solid and infallible, such as the sight hath by a compass and rule, as he passed by a smith's shop by a happy chance he heard the iron hammers striking on the anvil, and rendering sounds most consonant to one another in all combinations except one. He observed in them these three concords: the octave, the fifth and the fourth; but that which was between the fourth and the fifth he found to be a discord in itself, though otherwise useful for the making up of the greater of them, the fifth. Apprehending this came to him from God, as a most happy thing, he hastened into the shop, and by various trials finding the difference of the sounds to be according to the weight of the hammers, and not according to the force of those who struck, nor according to the fashion of the hammers, nor according to the turning of the iron which was in beating out: having taken exactly the weight of the hammers, he went straightway home, and to one beam fastened to the walls, cross from one corner of the room to the other, tying four strings of the same substance, length, and twist, upon each of them he hung a several weight, fastening it at the lower end, and making the length of the strings altogether equal; then striking the strings by two at a time interchangeably, he found out the aforesaid concords, each in its own combination; for that which was stretched by the greatest weight, in respect of that which was stretched by the least weight, he found to sound an octave. The greatest weight was of twelve pounds, the least of six; thence he determined that the octave did consist in double proportion, which the weights themselves did show. Next he found that the

Music in Ancient Greece   33

Pythagoras probably did not discover those ratios; he is known to have traveled in the ancient Near East, where they were already known and venerated as possessing cosmological significance. They must have had a special appeal to him, however, since they employ only the first four numbers (1:2, 2:3, 3:4) and are therefore a sensually perceptible manifestation of the sacred Pythagorean tetraktys: $1 + 2 + 3 + 4 = 10$, the formula that the Pythagoreans regarded as the source of all things. The legend thus assumed a far greater significance than simply musical, since it was decisive "proof" for Pythagorean claims that the quality of *harmonia* is fundamentally mathematical, residing in the essential "numerosity"[6] of all things. The musical interval ratios came to be accepted as the mathematical formulas underlying all creation; as Oskar Söhngen writes, "Whoever occupied himself with music also stood in the workshop of the secrets of the structure of the world."[7] It is not difficult to understand, then, why music came to play such a crucial role in Pythagorean philosophical systems, such as Plato's.

The Greek philosopher Plato (427?-347 B.C.) was one of the chief exponents of Pythagorean thought, and his writings on the subject of the creation and operation of the universe in particular bear the stamp of Pythagorean doctrine. Plato's creation story is set forth in his epic *Timaeus*, a Greek counterpart to the biblical book of Genesis. As the first component of the act of creating, God composed the world-soul, the invisible animating force that underlies the visible creation, beginning that process by fusing the qualities of changeless eternity with those of transient temporality. God then began to make appropriate subdivisions of this whole:

---

greatest to the least but one, which was of eight pounds, sounded a fifth; whence he inferred this to consist in the proportion 3:2, in which proportion the weights were to one another; but unto that which was less than itself in weight, yet greater than the rest, being of nine pounds, he found it to sound a fourth; and discovered that, proportionably to the weights, this concord was 4:3; which string of nine pounds is naturally 3:2 to the least; for nine to six is so, viz., 3:2, as the least but one, which is eight, was to that which had the weight six, in proportion 4:3; and twelve to eight is 3:2; and that which is in the middle, between a fifth and a fourth, whereby a fifth exceeds a fourth, is confirmed to be in 9:8 proportion. The system of both was called *Diapason*, or octave, that is both the fifth and the fourth joined together, as duple proportion is compounded of 3:2 and 4:3, or on the contrary, of 4:3 by 3:2.

Applying both his hand and ear to the weights which he had hung on, and by them confirming the proportion of the relations, he ingeniously transferred the common result of the strings upon the crossbeam to the bridge of an instrument, which he called *Chordotonos*; and for stretching them proportionably to the weights, he invented pegs, by the turning whereof he distended or relaxed them at pleasure. Making use of this foundation as an infallible rule, he extended the experiment to many kinds of instruments, as well pipes and flutes as those which have strings; and he found that this conclusion made by numbers was consonant without variation in all.

[6] For St. Augustine's use of this word in a related context, see Chap. 5, p. 75 below.
[7] Oskar Söhngen, "Music and Theology: A Systematic Approach," p. 2.

34 Wiser than Despair

He first marked off a section of the whole, and then another twice the size of the first; next a third, half as much again as the second and three times the first, a fourth twice the size of the second, a fifth three times the third, a sixth eight times the first, a seventh twenty-seven times the first. Next he filled in the double and treble intervals by cutting off further sections and inserting them in the gaps, so that there were two mean terms in each interval, one exceeding one extreme and being exceeded by the other by the same fraction of the extremes, the other exceeding and being exceeded by the same numerical amount. These links produced intervals of 3/2 and 4/3 and 9/8 within the previous intervals, and he went on to fill all intervals of 4/3 with the interval 9/8 ; this left, as a remainder in each, an interval whose terms bore the numerical ratio of 256 to 243. And at that stage the mixture from which these sections were being cut was all used up.

Building on this proportional foundation, God then constructed the world-soul as a framework on which to anchor the physical world.

And when the whole structure of the soul had been finished to the liking of its framer, he proceeded to fashion the whole corporeal world within it, fitting the two together centre to centre: and the soul was woven right through from the centre to the outermost heaven, which it enveloped from the outside and, revolving on itself, provided a divine source of unending and rational life for all time. (Plato, *Timaeus*, pp. 47-50)

For our purposes, we need note only three conclusions that are easily drawn from this esoteric speculation.[8] First, creation for Plato is "rational," that is, it is constructed according to numerical ratios or proportions, it is inherently mathematical; in the act of creation, God worked with numbers and proportions, and these are immanent in all that is created. Second, the ratios of creation, 1:2, 2:3 and 3:4, are also those of musical intervals: the octave, the fifth, and the fourth. Thus for Plato, the universe is not only "rational," it is musical--musical harmony lies at the very heart of the cosmos.

The attentive reader will perhaps already have sensed the third conclusion to be drawn: Plato's creation epic is a *myth* (albeit a relatively sophisticated one). It is a product of divine revelation, establishing how the creation is related to and ordered by the creator. Plato's description of the workings of the cosmos, found in Book X of the *Republic*, is cast even more clearly in the form of a myth, and furnishes the same conclusions about music (though from a different perspective):

...the tale of a warrior bold, Er, the son of Armenius, by race a Pamphylian. He once upon a time was slain in battle, and when the corpses were taken up on the tenth day already decayed, was found intact, and after coming to life, related what he said he had seen in the world beyond...[Here Plato commences to tell Er's story of the afterlife, eternal reward and punishment, followed by an explanation of the construction and operation of the cosmos according to Er's eye-witness account, derived from Pythagorean teachings, as follows.] They came in four days to a spot whence they discerned, extended from above throughout the heaven and the earth, a straight light like a pillar, most nearly resembling the rainbow, but brighter and purer. To this

---

[8]For a modern author's explanation of these concepts, see Spitzer, *Classical and Christian Ideas of World harmony*, pp. 10-14.

they came after going forward a day's journey, and they saw there at the middle of the light the extremities of its fastenings stretched from heaven; for this light was the girdle of the heavens like the undergirders of triremes, holding together in like manner the entire revolving vault. And from the extremities was stretched the spindle of Necessity, through which all the orbits turned. Its staff and its hook were made of adamant, and the whorl of these and other kinds was commingled. And the nature of the whorl was this: Its shape was that of those in our world, but from his description we must conceive it to be as if in one great whorl, hollow and scooped out, there lay enclosed, right through, another like it but smaller, fitting into it as boxes that fit into one another, and in like manner another, a third, and a fourth, and four others, for there were eight of the whorls in all, lying within one another, showing their rims as circles from above and forming the continuous back of a single whorl about the shaft, which was driven home through the middle of the eighth... And the spindle turned on the knees of Necessity, and up above on each of the rims of the circles a Siren stood, borne around in its revolution and uttering one sound, one note, and from all the eight there was the concord of a single harmony. And there were other three who sat round about at equal intervals, each one on her throne, the Fates, daughters of Necessity, clad in white vestments with filleted heads, Lachesis, and Clotho, and Atropos, who sang in unison with the music of the Sirens, Lachesis singing the things that were, Clotho the things that are, and Atropos the things that are to be. (Plato, *Republic*, Vol. II, pp. 491-3; 501-5)

Again music is depicted as central to the process of creating and ordering the universe (much as it was in Tolkien's modern "myth" recounted above, pp. 14-15). The modern reader is likely to read this myth with a mounting sense of confusion and skepticism. It is, however, essential to keep in mind the ultimate significance myths hold for world-conscious people. Many of Plato's followers, and many Greeks in the centuries after Plato, held his narration of Pythagorean doctrine to be divine revelation. And later still, many Christian scholars and theologians (decisively influenced by neo-Platonism) accorded to Plato's accounts a significance nearly equal to that of the biblical account of creation in the Book of Genesis--but now we are getting ahead of our tale.

The tale of Er also elucidates Plato's conception of reality: the real world is invisible, lying behind the world of appearances. The human body lives entirely in the world of appearances; it is only the human soul, the intellect, that is capable of comprehending the real world that lies hidden behind it. The impact of that vision of reality continued to reverberate well into the Christian era; for example, its assumption fueled the Thomist conception of substance and accidents upon which the doctrine of Transubstantiation is based. Again, music is at the heart of this vision; it is at the very heart of universal processes, and these processes are inconceivable without it.

The myth of Er constitutes one of the primary sources for the persistent (and persistently contested) assertion that there is a "harmony of the spheres" or "music of the spheres", that the heavenly bodies actually make a sound (albeit imperceptible to human ears) as they revolve in their orbits. The argument as to whether the heavenly bodies actually make a sound as they revolve, or whether their music is to be understood only in a symbolic sense, was one that persisted through the Renaissance. Aristotle argued against it, but in the long run the Platonic view prevailed. Macrobius (fifth century A.D.), for example, wrote a commentary on Cicero's "Dream of Scipio" (*De Re Publica*, VI:xviii: 18-9), in which he expounded the "great and pleasing sound" of the heavenly spheres, to which humans were deaf due to their limited range of hearing. Macrobius's commentary retained its influence throughout the Middle Ages and into the Renaissance. As a poetic symbol of universal harmony, the concept actually persisted well into the seventeenth and even the eighteenth century, especially in English metaphysical poetry (see Chap. 7, pp. 98-9 below), and the great astronomer Johannes Kepler propounded a variant of it in his *Harmonices Mundi* (1619: see Chap. 7, p. 97 below). The "harmony of the spheres", then, was more than simply a mathematical or astronomical theory. It formed the basis for a unified world-view, a vision of all existence as interrelated and interdependent. For the arts in particular it assumed a unifying role, giving impulse, direction, and form, not just to music, but to other arts such as architecture as well.[9]

If the characteristic quality of all being is *harmonia*, then the highest good to which human beings can aspire is to integrate themselves into it, to align their lives with it. The Greeks understood music (sounding, "earthly" music, that is) as the means by which cosmic harmony could be transferred to the human soul;[10] for them it was a phenomenon of divine origin given to humans for the betterment, the ennobling of their souls. Implicit in this idea was the Greek assumption of the duality of soul and body, an idea not encountered in the Old Testament (where body and soul are viewed as one and indivisible) and alien to Jewish thought until the era of hellenic influence following the conquests of Alexander the Great, but already met with in the New Testament (e.g., I Corinthians 15:44-57; Galatians 5:17; I Peter 3:18-19) and axiomatic in the post-apostolic Christian church (though later rejected in its extreme form--Gnosticism--as heretical).

Plato asserted that music forms good people, creating good character and gracefulness; later scholars have referred to that teaching as the Doctrine of Ethos.[11] It is an idea that Plato seems to have inherited from his predecessor, the philosopher Damon (fifth century B.C.): "Song and dance necessarily rise when the soul is in some way moved; liberal and beautiful songs and dances create a similar soul, and the reverse kind create a reverse kind of soul" (quoted in Anderson, *Ethos and Education*, p. 39; see also Barker, *Greek Musical Writings*, Vol. I, pp. 168-9). Plato himself (speaking through Socrates) expressed it as the ability to recognize and to rejoice in that which is fine and good, an ability that is the result of the development of good character; that development is in turn the result of proper training in *mousike* (music and poetry), training that allows it to penetrate and 'harmonize' the soul.[12] Thus

---

[9]See Nabers and Wiltshire, "The Athena Temple at Paestum and Pythagorean Theory."

[10]See Hollander, *The Untuning of the Sky*, p. 28; Spitzer, *Classical and Christian Ideas of World Harmony*, pp. 15-16.

[11]See Hollander, *The Untuning of the Sky*, pp. 32-34.

[12]Plato, *Republic* 401-2:

...'good diction [said Socrates] and good *harmonia* and gracefulness and good rhythm follow good character, not the foolishness to which we give that name by way of a euphemism, but the mind that is genuinely well and beautifully constituted in its character.'

'I entirely agree,' he [i.e., Glaucon] said.

there is both good music and bad music: Plato held that certain modes (namely, the Dorian and Phrygian) infuse the soul with life and health, while others (such as the Mixolydian, Syntonolydian, and Iastian) enervate it.[13] It does not matter that we no longer know the musical substance of these modes; the important thing is that Plato considers the modes to have specific characters and these characters to have particular effects on the soul of the listener. Plato is vague as to exactly how music accomplishes its effects on the soul, though it has something to do with music's ability to represent or imitate either noble or base states of mind which by continuous exposure are supposed to "rub off" on the listener.

Now don't we say that all music is representational and imitative?
Yes...
Then those who are looking for the best kind of singing and music must look not for the kind that is pleasant but that which is correct: and as we have said, an imitation is correct if it is made like the object imitated, both in quantity and in quality. (Plato, *Laws* 668, in Barker, *Greek Musical Writings*, Vol. I, p. 152)

Since music was considered to have such a powerful effect on the soul, its proper use was a primary constituent of the education process, or more correctly, of *paideia*, a Greek word connoting not only education, but also the formation of good character. Plato expressed this in the passage quoted above (p. 36, n. 12), as well as in the following:

So in order that the child's soul should not become habituated to enjoying and disliking things in defiance of the law and those who obey the law, but should follow it, enjoying and disliking the same things as an old man does, for these purposes there exist what we call 'songs'... I say that all the choruses, of which there are three,

---

'Then mustn't these things be universally pursued by our young men, if they are to do the work proper to them?'
'They must.'
'Now painting and all crafts of that kind are certainly full of them, as are weaving and embroidery and house-building and the making of all other artefacts, and so is the structure of our bodies and that of other living things: for in all of them there is gracefulness and its opposite. And gracelessness and bad rhythm and bad *harmonia* are sisters of bad speech and bad character, whereas their opposites are sisters and imitations of the opposite, of a self-restrained and good character.'
'Undoubtedly,' he said...
'For these reasons, then, Glaucon,' I said, 'isn't training in *mousike* [music/poetry] of overriding importance, because rhythm and *harmonia* penetrate most deeply into the recesses of the soul and take a powerful hold on it, bringing gracefulness and making a man graceful if he is correctly trained, but the opposite if he is not? Another reason is that the man who has been properly trained in these matters would perceive most sharply things that were defective, and badly crafted or badly grown, and his displeasure would be justified. He would praise and rejoice in fine things, and would receive them into his soul and be nourished by them, becoming fine and good: but he would rightly condemn ugly things, and hate them even when he was young, before he was able to lay hold on reason. And when reason grew, the person trained in this way would embrace it with enthusiasm, recognising it as a familiar friend. (Barker, *Greek Musical Writings*, Vol. I, pp. 135-6)

[13]See Barker, *Greek Musical Writings*, Vol. I, pp. 130-1.

must sing incantations over the souls of the children, while they are still young and tender, enunciating all the good things that we have gone through previously or may go through later; and let their overall gist be this: by saying that it is the gods' assertion that the most pleasant life is identical with that which is best, we shall simultaneously be saying what is most true and persuading those who have to be persuaded more readily than we could by speaking in any other way. (Plato, *Laws* 659; 664, in Barker, *Greek Musical Writings*, Vol. I, pp. 147 & 148)

This process of education was not, however, merely for the young; it was to be applied to all ages and conditions.[14]

Logically, then, music ought to be either exciting or calming, as the situation and personalities of the listeners require. (This is in fact what Aristotle taught.) But Plato spoke almost exclusively of music as a means of ridding the body of excess passion, not of infusing passion into it; he did not commend music's ability to raise emotions. There is a passage in the *Laws* (790d-791e) in which he compares the treatment of Corybants (those in a frenzied religious state) with the method by which mothers calm their infants. The latter rock their children and sing to them; the former are made to dance accompanied by music. In both instances, violent internal motion is quieted by the application of a calm, ordered external motion, producing rational composure in place of frenzy. Indeed, music's ability to calm unruly passions is a persistent theme in Greek antiquity.[15] In the *Republic* (411) Plato even holds that too much music can actually be enervating, contributing to the enfeeblement of the spirit.[16] From that passage as well as from others, we may infer that Plato conceived music's basic purpose as making people *noble*; it was to express and to create nobility of soul.[17]

---

[14]See Plato, *Laws*, 664 & 665, in: Barker, *Greek Musical Writings*, Vol. I, pp. 148 & 149.

[15]Cf. Athenaus, *Deipnosophistae* 623-4, in Barker, *Greek Musical Writings*, Vol. I, p. 281.

[16]Plato, *Republic* 411:

...whenever anyone lets music entrance his soul with its piping, and lets pour into his soul through his ears, as though through a funnel, the sweet and soft and mournful *harmoniai* [Greek musical 'modes'], and when he uses up the whole of his life humming, enraptured by song, then to begin with, if he has anything of the spirited element in him, this man will temper it like iron, and make useful what was useless and hard. But if he persists in entrancing it without ceasing, he will eventually dissolve it and melt it away, till he pours away his spirit, and cuts, as it were, the sinews from his soul, and makes of it a "feeble warrior" [quoting *Iliad* XVII.588]... And if to begin with...his natural character lacks spirit, this process will be quickly completed. But if it is spirited, then by weakening his spirit he will make it easily swayed, quickly inflamed and extinguished by trifling matters. Such people become quick-tempered and quarrelsome instead of spirited, full of peevishness. (Barker, *Greek Musical Writings*, Vol. I, pp. 137-8)

[17]See Chapter 4, n. 68; this notion has become so firmly entrenched in ensuing western European culture that it has continued to exert a strong influence even up to the present.

Plato's understanding of the word *mousike* (the activity of the muses) presumed the inseparable association of music and words. He considered the use of instruments for music-making permissible, but they were to be used only to accompany a sung text, and the text was always the dominant partner in the union.

> ...song is put together out of three things, words, *harmonia*, and rhythm... So far as its words are concerned, they surely don't differ from words that are not sung, in that they must be uttered in the same mould and in the same manner as we said just now [i.e., imitating what is good]... And *harmonia* and rhythm must follow the words. (Plato, *Republic* 398, in Barker, *Greek Musical Writings*, Vol. I, p. 130)

Musicians who played only on instruments, without at the same time singing words, were to be considered both foolish and inartistic.[18]

For Plato, sound *paideia* consisted of a mixture of physical education/gymnastics and *mousike*, and the true "musician" was not a performer, but one who in his character could hold the two elements in balance.[19] Thus gymnastics and *mousike* were to be considered the two basic elements in education. From the *Republic* 411-2 we may infer two conclusions: (1) the true musician is by nature reflective, well-formed, well-educated, balanced, and emotionally restrained, and (2) the one who simply composes or performs music is inferior to the true musician as just characterized. Elsewhere Plato is quite specific about this second point: the mere musical composer or performer is not competent to

---

[18]Plato, *Laws* 669-70:

> ...human composers, weaving and jumbling all such things [i.e., musical incongruities] nonsensically together, would be laughed at by everyone who, as Orpheus puts it, 'has attained the full bloom of joyfulness'. For they can see all these things jumbled together: and further, the composers tear rhythm and posture away from melody, putting bare words into metres, setting melody and rhythm without words, and using the *kithara* and the *aulos* without a voice, a practice in which it is extremely difficult--since rhythm and *harmonia* occur with no words--to understand what is intended, and what worthwhile representation it is like. It is essential that we accept the principle that all such practices are utterly inartistic... (Barker, *Greek Musical Writings*, Vol. I, p. 154)

[19]Plato, *Republic* 411-2:

> I should say then that God seems to have given us two skills for the sake of these two elements in us, *mousike* and gymnastics, that is, for the spirited and the philosophic parts, and not for the soul and the body, except as an unimportant by-product. Their task is to tune those two elements to one another by tightening and relaxing them until the proper relation is reached... Then the man who can best blend gymnastics with *mousike* and administer them, perfectly measured, to the soul, is the one whom we should most correctly call the complete musician and the true expert in harmony, much more than the man who can tune strings to one another. (Barker, *Greek Musical Writings*, Vol. I, pp. 138-9)

distinguish between what is good and what is bad, and should not be entrusted with this responsibility.[20]

Plato's attitude toward music was, like his philosophical outlook in general, conservative; that is, he viewed continuity with long-established tradition as an unquestioned good. In this he showed himself to be akin to the Pythagoreans; W.C.K. Guthrie (*A History of Greek Philosophy*, p. 216) speaks of "the conservatism and respect for tradition which were a natural consequence of the religious character of Pythagoreanism." Thus Plato condemned any sort of innovation in music, and it is a measure of the power he ascribed to music that he insisted musical change and decay are at the root of deterioration and disintegration in the state.[21] It is self-evident, then, that Plato proscribed any sort of variety or novelty in music.[22]

---

[20]Plato, *Laws* 801:

...Isn't it the fact that poets as a class are not entirely competent to understand properly what is good and what is not? Surely then, when a poet incorporates this error in his composition of words or song--composing prayers that are not correct-- he will be making our citizens pray for the opposite of what is good, in matters of the greatest importance. (Barker, *Greek Musical Writings*, Vol. I, p. 160)

Plato, *Laws* 660:

...the lawgiver who acts correctly will persuade the poet by fine words and flattery, and will compel him if he fails to persuade, to compose correctly in his rhythms the postures of men who are moderate and brave and in all respects good, and to compose their melodies in his *harmoniai*. (Barker, *Greek Musical Writings*, Vol. I, p. 148)

In the *Laws* 670, Plato seems to relent in his harsh judgment of performers by entrusting to singers the selection of music appropriate to *paideia*; yet he insists that singers must be thoroughly educated in the elements that comprise good music before they are allowed to influence the young. See Barker, Vol. I, pp. 155-6.

[21]Plato, *Republic* 424-5:

'To put it briefly, then, those in charge of the city must devote themselves to ensuring that this principle is not destroyed without their noticing it, and to guarding it above all else, the principle, I mean, that no innovations shall be made in gymnastics and music beyond what is laid down, but that what is laid down shall be preserved as closely as possible [cf. e.g. *Laws* 799a-b]. When someone says that
> People praise more highly the song
> That is most newly come to minstrels' lips

they should fear that people might easily suppose the poet to mean not just new songs, but a new style of song, and that they would applaud the latter. Such a thing should not be applauded, nor should the poet be so understood. People should beware of change to new forms of music, for they are risking change in the whole. Styles of music are nowhere altered without change in the greatest laws of the city: so Damon says, and I concur.'

'You can count me in as another of those who concur,' said Adeimantus. 'It seems then,' I said, 'that it is here, in music, that the guardians must build their guard-house.'

'It is easy for this law-breaking to creep in undetected,' he said.

'Yes,' I replied. 'It is treated as a matter of mere amusement and as doing no harm.

Music in Ancient Greece 41

That Plato recognized music gives pleasure is evident in his writings, but he consistently disparaged this factor in music:[23] "...most people certainly say that musical correctness consists in the power to provide pleasure for the soul. But that assertion is intolerable and cannot even be uttered without blasphemy" (Plato, *Laws* 655, in Barker, *Greek Musical Writings*, Vol. I, p. 143). He also condemns any musical practices that smack of virtuosity or clownishness, labeling "speed and precision [i.e., technical facility] and animal noises" as "utterly inartistic."[24]

'That's because it does nothing,' he said, 'except to establish itself little by little, and quietly insinuates itself into characters and practices. From there it emerges enlarged, and enters men's dealings with one another, and from these dealings it moves to attack laws and constitutions with the most wanton extravagance, Socrates, until in the end it overturns everything in both public and private life.'
'I see,' I said. 'Is all that really so?'
'I think so,' he said.
'Then as we were saying at the very beginning, mustn't our children be set, from the start, to more law-abiding amusements, since when amusements are lawless, children are so too, and it is impossible for law-abiding and honest men to grow up out of these?'
'Inevitably,' he said.
'Then surely when children make a good start with their amusements, and are equipped through *mousike* with a law-abiding spirit, this spirit, the opposite of what you have described, will follow along with everything and augment it, and will set right anything in the city that was previously laid low.' (Barker, *Greek Musical Writings*, Vol. I, pp. 139-40)

[22]Plato, *Republic* 399:

...we shall have no need of a multiplicity of strings or an assemblage of all the *harmoniai* in our songs and melodies...we shall not bring up craftsmen to make *trigonoi* or *pektides* or any of the instruments that have many strings and all *harmoniai*... Following on from *harmoniai* we should next deal with rhythms, to ensure that we do not pursue intricately varied ones with every kind of movement, but discover the rhythms that are those of an orderly and courageous life. (Barker, *Greek Musical Writings*, Vol. I, p. 132-3)

Plato, *Republic* 404:

...if we likened that kind of food and regimen [i.e., one characterized by much variety] to music and song expressed in the 'pan-harmonic' [i.e., using all the *harmoniai*] and in every variety of rhythm it would be a fair comparison... And there [i.e., in music and song] variety engendered licentiousness, did it not, but here [i.e., in the body] disease? While simplicity in music begets sobriety in the souls, and in gymnastic training it begets health in bodies. (trans. Paul Shorey; p. 269)

[23]Plato, *Protagoras* 347c-d:

Second-rate and commonplace people, being too uneducated to entertain themselves as they drink by using their own voices and conversational resources, put up the price of female musicians, paying well for the hire of an extraneous voice--that of the pipe--and find their entertainment in its warblings. But where the drinkers are men of

To ensure that his prescriptions for music's use were properly carried out for the well-being of the state, Plato advocated strict music censorship.[25] He

---

worth and culture, you will find no girls piping or dancing or harping. They are quite capable of enjoying their own company without such frivolous nonsense, using their own voices in sober discussion and each taking his turn to speak or listen--even if the drinking is really heavy. (trans. Hamilton & Cairns, *The Collected Dialogues of Plato*, p. 340.)

[24]Plato, *Laws* 670:

...if they are so enamoured of speed and precision and animal noises that they use the music of the *aulos* and *kithara* for purposes other than the accompaniment of dance and song: the use of either by itself is characteristic of uncultured and vulgar showmanship. (Barker, *Greek Musical Writings*, Vol. I, p. 154)

[25]Plato, *Laws* 656-7:

'What sort of laws do you say they have concerning such matters in Egypt?'
'Even to hear them described is astonishing. Once, long ago, so it seems, they came to understand the argument that we have just been setting out, according to which the young men in each city must become practised in good postures and good melodies. These they prescribed, and they advertised which they are and what they are like in the temples: it was forbidden, as it still is, for painters or any other portrayers of postures and representations to make innovations beyond these, or to think up anything outside the traditional material, in these areas or in *mousike* in general. If you look you will find that what was written or depicted there ten thousand years ago--and I mean ten thousand literally, not as a figure of speech--is neither better nor worse than what is made nowadays, but is done with the same art.'
'What you say is amazing.'
'It is, you will admit, a supreme expression of the aims of the lawgiver and the statesman, though you could find other things there that are bad. But as concerns music, it is true and note-worthy that it was possible in these matters for a bold man to lay down lasting laws prescribing melodies that possess a natural correctness. To do this would be a task for a god, or a godlike man, just as in Egypt they say that the melodies that have been preserved for this great period of time were the compositions of Isis. Thus, as I said, if one could somehow grasp the nature of correctness in melodies, one ought boldly to bring them under law and regulation. For pleasure and pain, in their constant pursuit of new music to indulge in, have little power to destroy a choric art that is sanctified, just by mocking its antiquity. In Egypt, at least, it does not seem to have been able to destroy it: quite the contrary.' (Barker, *Greek Musical Writings*, Vol.I, pp. 144-5)

Plato, *Laws* 799:

'Then does any of us have a better technique for the purpose than that of the Egyptians?'
'Which one do you mean?'
'That of dedicating all dancing and all melodies to religion. First, they should determine the festivals, putting together for the year a list of which festivals should be held at which times, in honour of which individual gods, which children of the gods, and which demi-gods. Next, they should determine which song ought to be sung at each of the sacrifices to the gods, and what sort of dancing should adorn the

condemned the notion of judgment by the will of the people, and he had no use for the democratic process.[26]

At any rate it is ridiculous for the mass of the people to suppose that they have an adequate understanding of what is harmonically and rhythmically good and what is not--those of them who have been drilled in singing to an accompaniment and stepping in rhythm, but do not grasp the fact that they do these things without understanding any of them. (Plato, *Laws* 670, in Barker, *Greek Musical Writings*, Vol. I, p. 155)

Rather the "best people" (i.e., the best educated, the most "musical") were to serve as judges of what is proper or incorrect in music, disdaining the will of the many.[27] By this assertion Plato revealed his true aristocratic colors. Plato also provided specific guidelines establishing the qualifications for judges and the

---

various sacrifices. These ordinances should first be made by certain persons; and then all the people should join in common sacrifice to dedicate them to the Fates and to all the other gods, consecrating each of the songs, with a libation, to the appropriate gods and other beings. If anyone brings forward other hymns or dances beyond these for any of the gods, the priests and priestesses, with the guardians of the law, will be acting with both religious and legal propriety in excluding him; and the man who is excluded, if he does not accept his exclusion voluntarily, will be liable for the whole of his life to prosecution for impiety by anyone who wishes.' (Barker, *Greek Musical Writings*, Vol. I, p. 158)

[26]Plato, *Laws* 659:

For under the ancient Hellenic laws it was not permitted to follow what is the present custom in Sicily and Italy, by which responsibility is given to the mass of spectators, and the winner is decided by show of hands: since by composing for the depraved pleasure of the judges they have made the spectators their own teachers, and it has corrupted the pleasures of the audience too. For they ought always to be listening to things that are better than their own characters, and so improve their standard of pleasure, whereas exactly the opposite happens to them as a result of what they do now. (Barker, *Greek Musical Writings*, Vol. I, p. 147)

[27]Plato, *Laws* 658-9:

'Even I agree with the majority to the extent of saying that music should be judged by the criterion of pleasure, but not just anyone's pleasure. I would say that the best music is probably that which delights the best people, those who are fully educated, and especially that which delights the one man who is outstanding in excellence and education. That is why we say that judges of these matters need to be good men, in that they need to possess moral wisdom of all kinds, but courage especially. A true judge should not take instruction from the audience and his own lack of education; nor should he knowingly perjure himself, under the influence of cowardice or timidity, and give his judgement insincerely, through the very mouth with which he called upon the gods when he was setting out as an adjudicator. For the judge takes his seat, or properly should, as a teacher, not a pupil of the spectators, and as one who will stand up against those who offer the spectators pleasure in an unfitting or incorrect way.' (Barker, *Greek Musical Writings*, Vol. I, p. 147)

44   Wiser than Despair

criteria for judging music.[28] (Among these is the stipulation that judges be men no less than 50 years old!). Though so little is now known about ancient Greek

---

[28]Plato, *Laws* 667-8:

'First of all, then, mustn't it be true of everything that is accompanied by any kind of delightfulness that its most important aspect is either this delightfulness itself, or some sort of correctness, or, thirdly, its usefulness? For instance, food and drink and nourishment in general carry with them, I would say, the sort of delightfulness that we would call pleasure: but their correctness and usefulness, what we regularly call the wholesomeness of the things that are offered us, this I suggest, is really the correctest aspect of them.'
'Certainly.'
'Learning, too, carries with it the sort of delightfulness that is pleasure, but what produces its correctness and usefulness, its goodness and excellence, is truth.'
'Yes.'
'What about the techniques of representation that produce likenesses? Isn't it true that if they fulfil this objective, the pleasure generated in association with them, if there is any, should most properly be called delightfulness?'
'Yes.'
'But correctness in things of this kind, to put it quite generally, would be produced by equality of quantity and quality, rather than by pleasure.'
'True.'
'Then the only thing that could be correctly judged by the criterion of pleasure is that which produces no usefulness or truth or likeness, nor indeed any harm, but is created only for the sake of that which follows along with the others, delightfulness, which would best be given the name 'pleasure' when none of the others accompanies it.'
'You mean just the harmless kind of pleasure.'
'Yes; and I say that when this pleasure does no harm or good worth mentioning seriously, it is also play.'
'Quite true.'
'Then shouldn't we say, on the basis of this discussion, that the last criterion by which any imitation should be judged is pleasure and false opinion, and neither should any equality be so judged? For it is not because of someone's opinion, or because someone finds no pleasure in it, that an equal thing is equal or a proportionate one proportionate: it is because of what is true, first and foremost, and not at all because of anything else. (Barker, *Greek Musical Writings*, Vol. I, pp. 151-2)

Plato, *Laws* 802:

The right way to organise the songs and dances is this. Among the musical works of the ancients there are many fine old compositions, and similarly dances for the body to perform, and no jealousy will be aroused by our selecting from these what harmonises fittingly with the constitution that is being established. Those chosen to assess these works and to make the selection would not be less than fifty years old; and whichever of the ancient compositions is adjudged adequate they are to select, while whatever is deficient or wholly inappropriate they must either discard completely or study more carefully and revise. They should get both poets and musicians to assist them, making use of their talents for composition, but not placing any reliance on their pleasures and desires, except in the case of a few such people. Thus by working through fully the intentions of the lawgiver, they will put together in closest correspondence to the sense of these intentions dancing, singing,

music that it is no longer possible to understand the practical applications for Plato's directions, it is nevertheless evident that they were precise and stringent. They had to be, for according to Plato, the result of a lack of control in music is political anarchy.[29] Plato's acerbic comments again reveal his aristocratic

---

and choric practices in general. Every disorganised musical activity becomes a thousand times better when it accepts organization, even if no musical sweetness is added: all such activities alike give pleasure. For when someone passes his life from childhood up to the age of steadiness and sense among temperate and ordered music, then when he hears the opposite kind he detests it, and calls it unfit for free men: but if he was brought up amid the sweet music that is generally popular, he says that the opposite kind to this is frigid and unpleasing. Thus, as we said just now, neither is better than the other in respect of pleasantness and unpleasantness: the difference lies in the fact that the one kind always makes those brought up in it better, the other worse. (Barker, *Greek Musical Writings*, Vol. I, p. 161)

[29]Plato, *Laws* 800:

Yet in our countries this is what happens, one may just about say, in virtually all cities. For whenever an official makes a civic sacrifice, there arrives immediately not one chorus but a crowd of them: they do not stand at a distance from the altars, but often close by, and they pour out every kind of blasphemy upon the sacred offerings, stretching the souls of the listeners with their words, their rhythms, and their most mournful *harmoniai*: and whichever chorus causes the sacrificing city to weep most bitterly, then and there, carries off the prize of victory. Shall we not vote to reject this custom? (Barker, *Greek Musical Writings*, Vol. I, p. 159)

Plato, *Laws* 700-1:

'Under the ancient laws, my friends, our common people were not masters of anything, but were in a sort of way voluntary slaves to the laws.'
'What laws do you mean?'
'Those, first of all, to do with the music they had then, if we are to describe the growth of the excessively liberated life from its beginning. In those days our music was divided into various types and forms. One type of song consisted of prayers to the gods, the name given to these being 'hymns'. There was another type, the opposite of the first, which one might best call 'lamentations': another consisted of paeans, and there was another, invented, I think, by Dionysus, known as the 'dithyramb'. To another class of song they assigned the name *'nomoi'* itself, adding the title 'kitharodic'. With these types and various others properly distinguished, it was not permitted to use one type of melody for the purposes of another. The authority responsible for knowing them, for judging them, once known, and for penalising anyone who disobeyed, was not the whistling (*syrinx*) or the uneducated (*amousoi*) shouts of the mob, as it is now, or clappings that signal applause: instead, it was the rule for those in charge of education themselves to listen in silence to the end, while for the children and their attendants, and for the mass of the people generally, there was the discipline of the stick to keep order. While these matters were organised like this, then, the mass of the citizens were [sic] content to be governed, and not to have the effrontery to adjudicate by their hubbub. But later, as time went on, there appeared as instigators of unmusical law-breaking composers who, though by nature skilled at composition, were ignorant of what is right and lawful in music. In a Bacchic frenzy, and enthralled beyond what is right by pleasure, they mixed lamentations with hymns and paeans with dithyrambs, imitated *aulos*

46 Wiser than Despair

contempt for the many; his ideas also brand his political scheme as utopian and incapable of being realized except in the most repressive autocracy.

Here in summary are Plato's primary ideas about music:

- Music is central to the creation and ordering of the universe; specifically, the ratios of musical intervals order the cosmos.

- The universe is characterized by a quality of interrelatedness (*harmonia*) that is highly evident in music.

- By making and hearing proper music, humans can integrate themselves into universal harmony; thus good music forms good people (the Doctrine of Ethos).

- Since music is a powerful force in the formation of good or bad character, its use must be carefully regulated.

- Music must always be subservient to the text that it should inevitably accompany; instrumental music per se should be banned.

- The seasoned philosopher is a more reliable judge of musical propriety and worth than the composer or performer.

- Musical continuity with long-established tradition is an unquestioned good; there should be no innovation, variety, or novelty in music.

- Musical practices that provide immediate sensual pleasure (e.g., virtuosity, levity) should be condemned.

- Musical change and decay are at the root of the deterioration and disintegration of the state; therefore, music must be strictly censored by the state's leaders, without regard for the wishes and tastes of ordinary citizens.

Although these ideas had many adherents, they were by no means universally accepted in antiquity. Aristotle in particular, whose mind was predisposed to a

---

songs with their *kithara* songs, and put everything together with everything else, thus unintentionally, through their stupidity, giving false witness against music, alleging that music possesses no standard of correctness, but is most correctly judged by the pleasure of the person who enjoys it, whether he is a better man or a worse. By creating compositions of these kinds and by choosing corresponding words, they inspired the masses with lawlessness towards music, and the effrontery to suppose that they were capable of judging it. As a result the audiences, which had been silent, became noisy, as if they understood what is good in music and what is not, and a musical aristocracy was displaced by a degenerate theatocracy. Now no doubt it would have been no very terrible thing if a democracy of free men had arisen just in the field of music: but in fact, from a starting-point in music, everyone came to believe in their own wisdom about everything, and to reject the law, and liberty followed immediately. Believing themselves knowledgeable, people became fearless, and fearlessness bred shamelessness. When boldness prevents one fearing the opinion of a better man, that amounts to depraved shamelessness: it is caused by a liberty that is too self-confidently grasped. (Barker, *Greek Musical Writings*, Vol. I, pp. 156-7).

Music in Ancient Greece   47

methodical, empirical approach, disagreed with many of them, especially those conceived along Pythagorean lines. Aristotle had no patience with Pythagorean /Platonic speculative numerology, such as is found in the *Timaeus*. In his *Metaphysics*, the exposition of his own ontology, he entirely rejected the notion of numbers as the basis of being. He also dismissed the idea that the movements of celestial bodies produce an actual sound, though (significantly) he did not reject the idea of a harmonically ordered, musical universe, a universe based on *harmonia*.

> The single harmony produced by all the heavenly bodies singing and dancing together springs from one source and ends by achieving one purpose, and has rightly bestowed the name not of 'disordered' but of 'ordered universe' upon the whole. And just as in a chorus, when the leader gives the signal to begin, the whole chorus of men, or it may be of women, joins in the song, mingling a single studied harmony among different voices, some high and some low; so too is it with God that rules the whole world. (Aristotle, *De Mundo*, Chap. VI, 399a)

That Plato had his detractors is, however, of secondary importance; what is essential is that his ideas on music were widely disseminated and heeded in pagan antiquity, and were incorporated into the classical educational curriculum, the proto-quadrivium. Because they were given such widespread credence, they were accepted to one degree or another by many important early Christian theologians (some of whom, e.g., St. Augustine, had extensive training in the classical curriculum) and thus passed into Christian theology.

The church by no means adopted all of Plato's ideas; it was far too unique and powerful an intellectual force simply to appropriate *in toto* any pagan thought system, no matter how distinguished or well established. Plato, for example, taught that harmony and rhythm must follow the words (*Republic* 398d), an idea widely pursued again only in the Renaissance; he conceived musicians as mouthpieces of the divine (*Ion* 533-5; note the similarity to the Old Testament prophetic ideal), an idea that has no counterpart in Christian theology; he, in common with other Greek philosophers, attributed specific characters to the various *harmoniai*, the Greek musical "modes" (*Republic* 398-9), a notion also reborn only in the Renaissance; and although he condemned the *aulos* (a double-reed instrument), he approved the use of certain instruments for purposes of accompaniment (*Laws* 669-70), while early Christian leaders overwhelmingly rejected their use in any way.

Yet the church adopted and adapted a majority of Plato's ideas on music, because the church's *attitude* toward music was fundamentally similar to his. Because of that similarity of outlook, it was natural that the church should find his writings congenial, and that it should seek to preserve and propagate his ideas. From all that has been said thus far, it should be evident that there is an ambiguity, a "love-hate relationship," inherent in Plato's view of music. On the one hand, he embraced the use of music as one of the cornerstones in shaping human character; on the other, he feared its power, and his suspicion led him to establish elaborate guidelines severely to circumscribe its influence. The Christian church inherited this tension, and it characterized its relationship to music for at least the first one and one-half millennia of its existence.

4

Music in the Early Church: The Patristic Era to Gregory the Great

The energizing force behind the spectacular growth of the early Christian church was the intensity, the centrality, and the uncompromising nature of its worship. Viewed in contrast with more modern Christian worship attitudes and practices, the rigor and fervor of early Christian worship clearly identifies it as cultic. The early church bore all the hallmarks of cult. Its believers were fully world-conscious humans. They lived in the constant presence of the spirit-world, the holy, the "other."[1] They considered visions and epiphanies a normal, vital feature of their lives, and indeed they looked forward to the imminent dissolution of the present world order with the coming of the kingdom of God, the *parousia*. The early Christian cult was as compelling and intense in every way as primitive cults (though with certain clearly recognizable differences).[2]

The cultic nature of the early church is unmistakable: early Christians understood themselves to be bound in a covenant relationship with God (though the renewed covenant as ratified by the death and rising of God's Son now required unconditional faithfulness.[3] Early Christians interpreted their personal significance primarily in terms of belonging to the Body of Christ, the fellowship of the faithful: in baptism they were given a new family name (no longer "Jane Doe", but "Jane of the Father, and of the Son, and of the Holy Spirit"), and some early Christians even went so far as to unite all their material possessions into a pool for the common good.[4] The basic shape of Christian cultic ritual was relatively quickly established, centering on a two-part liturgy: the liturgy of the catechumens (which developed from the Jewish synagogue liturgy of psalm-

---

[1] For further evidence of the interpenetration of the two worlds, spiritual and physical, in Christian domestic art of the fourth through seventh centuries, see Eunice D. Maguire, Henry P. Maguire and Maggie J. Duncan-Flowers, *Art and Holy Powers in the Early Christian House*.

[2] Some of these differences have already been discussed in the Prologue, pp. 10ff.

[3] See Prologue, p. 10.

[4] See the Book of Acts 2: 44ff; 4:32-35.

singing, prayer, and instruction) and the liturgy of the Eucharist (which paralleled scriptural accounts of the institution of the Lord's supper). When early Christians blessed and broke bread and drank wine, while at the same time repeating Jesus's words spoken at the Last Supper ("This is my body... This is my blood..."), the crucified and risen Christ came truly to be present in their midst. And finally, early Christians shared in the irresistible cultic urge to call on the best of human artistry to ornament their worship (though always as an act of love, praise, or devotion, never as a means of pleasing, placating or summoning God).[5] In the interest of validating their positions, some subsequent Christian sects have promoted a view of early Christian worship as uniformly prosaic, colorless, and austerely simple. The surviving evidence--early liturgies and artifacts from Christian liturgical celebrations (e.g., the paintings at the Christian church at Dura Europos in Syria, dating from the third century)--witnesses to the contrary. The ornamentation of Christian worship flourished--commensurate with the church's freedom to worship without persecution, its social stature, and its material wealth--until the rise of extreme Christian asceticism introduced the church to iconoclastic, anti-artistic ideas.

Since the earliest Christians were anchored in their Jewish heritage and felt no antipathy toward it, it was only natural that they should adopt Jewish cultic music as their own. And so early Christians adopted the psalms in their entirety for use in their cultic celebrations. Early Christian writers are of one mind in exhorting Christians to sing psalms, both in communal worship and at home.[6]

> In the churches there are vigils, and David is first and middle and last. In the singing of early morning hymns, David is first and middle and last. In the tents at funeral processions David is first and last. In the houses of virgins there is weaving, and David is first and middle and last. What a thing of wonder! Many who have not even made their first attempt at reading know all of David by heart and recite him in order.... Yet it is not only in the cities and the churches that he is so prominent on every occasion and with people of all ages; even in the fields and deserts and stretching into uninhabited wasteland, he rouses sacred choirs to God with greater zeal. In the monasteries there is a holy chorus of angelic hosts, and David is first and middle and last. In the convents there are bands of virgins who imitate Mary, and

---

[5]For example, with regard to the use of music in worship, pagan Roman belief credited music with being pleasing to the gods (see Quasten, *Music and Worship in Pagan and Christian Antiquity*, p. 1), an idea never encountered in early Christian writings (in which music is always a gift of God for human use). Common pagan belief also held that music would drive away demons and invoke the presence of the gods (see Quasten, pp 15-6;17). Although such ideas were prominent in ancient Judaism (as well as other primitive religions), they are only occasionally alluded to in Christian writings (and when St. Basil writes that "A psalm drives away demons, summons the help of angels" (Strunk, *Source Readings*, p. 65), his words seem to suggest something more figurative and poetic than exorcism or magic).

[6]See also St. Cyprian, *Epist. I ad Donatum* 16, trans. in Skeris, Χρομα Θεου, p. 46, and McKinnon, *Music in Early Christian Literature*, 94; St. Athanasius, *De Virginitate* 20, trans. in Routley, *The Church and Music*, p. 235; St. Ambrose, *Enarratio in Psalmum I*, 9, trans. in Sendrey, *Music in Ancient Israel*, p. 197, and McKinnon, *Music in Early Christian Literature* 276; as well as McKinnon 35, 89, 106, 115, 151, 164f., 253, 275 & 276.

Music in the Early Church 51

David is first and middle and last. ([Pseudo-]St. John Chrysostom (late fourth century), *De poenitentia*; trans. in: McKinnon, *Music in Early Christian Literature*, 195)

St. Basil's *Commentary on Psalm I*[7] is a noteworthy example in this regard; he can hardly contain his enthusiasm in praising the Psalms. Some sources[8] mention antiphonal or responsorial singing as the preferred manner of psalm performance: "The more diligent in prayer are wont to subjoin in their prayers the 'Hallelujah,' and such kind of psalms, in the closes of which the company respond" (Tertullian, early third century, *De Oratione* 27:17; trans. in Skeris, Χροµα Θεου, p. 40, and McKinnon, *Music in Early Christian Literature*, 78). St. Basil records that antiphonal and responsorial psalmody was practiced universally throughout Christian Africa and the Near East,[9] and Pope St. Celestin (422-32) introduced both types of psalmody into the Roman liturgy.[10]

Yet almost immediately Christians also began to create an indigenous cultic music.[11] The New Testament contains numerous fragments of early Christian hymns, some of which may have had a cultic function.[12] Most of the post-apostolic Christian writings contain similar hymnic passages; for example, the *Didache (Teaching of the Twelve Apostles)*, a manual on the Christian life and church order dating from c. 110, contains a hymnic eucharistic prayer.[13] And among the Christian writings found at Oxyrhynchus in Egypt (from the end of the third century) is a fragment of a hymn to the Holy Trinity, complete with musical notation.[14]

We know all too few specific details about the nature of early Christian music and musical practice. Since it was essentially music of the cult, however, the following features are generally accepted as being characteristic. Although musical style was severely circumscribed (for reasons yet to be explored), it tended to be more spontaneous and emotional than calculated and intellectual. It retained (for a time, at least) a considerable degree of spontaneity and ecstatic improvisation.[15] It was music not primarily for personal devotion, but for the corporate worshiping community. And it was almost exclusively vocal.

---

[7] Parts I & II trans. in Strunk, *Source Readings*, pp. 64-66.
[8] See also McKinnon, *Music in Early Christian Literature*, 80, 102, 111, 139, 170, 178, 184, 208, 218, 221, 223 & 224, 364.
[9] See Reese, *Music in the Middle Ages*, p. 63.
[10] Hayburn, *Papal Legislation*, p. 3.
[11] See Tertullian, *Apologeticum* XXXIX, 18, trans. in Skeris, Χροµα Θεου, p. 37, and McKinnon, *Music in Early Christian Literature*, 74; and Tertullian, *Ad Uxorem* II, 8, trans. in Skeris, p. 41, and McKinnon 80.
[12] For example, 1 Timothy 1:17 and 6:15-16; see Deiss, *Springtime of the Liturgy*, p. 30 (pp. 29-69).
[13] This hymn has become familiar in its English translation by F. Bland Tucker, "Father, we thank thee who hast planted Thy holy Name within our hearts," found in *The Hymnal of the Protestant Episcopal Church 1940* (New York: Church Pension Fund [1940]), number 195. See Deiss, *Springtime of the Liturgy*, pp. 73ff.
[14] For a description and transcription, see Dom Anselm Hughes, ed., *Early Medieval Music up to 1300*, pp. 4-5.
[15] Music may have accompanied prophetic utterance in the practice of *glossolalia*. On the other hand, there is no evidence that Christians induced a

To the degree that the Christian cult flourished and prospered, the various forms of art (including music) that grew out of it flourished with it. Indeed, as an inevitable concomitant of the cult, this artistic activity was one of the clearest signs of cultic vitality. Since it is not usual for cultic music to be intellectually or formally complex, however, it is unlikely that music created solely to fulfill the requirements of the cult would ever have developed the degree of intellectual substance and complexity evident in the ensuing growth of Christian art music. That development required the stimulus of theological ideas, undergirded by the power of myth.

The Christian cult was brought to life and has continued to be energized through the ages by a powerful nexus of Christian myths,[16] a "history of salvation." Since they understood themselves as the continuation of God's chosen people, Christians appropriated the entire salvation history of their Jewish forebears: the doctrine of creation (God created heaven and earth out of love, and found all creation to be good) and the mighty saving acts by which God chose his people, brought them out of slavery, provided them a land to dwell in, and granted them blessing and increase. To this prior salvation history they added the central doctrines of Christianity: the doctrine of the incarnation (in love God emptied himself out into a human body, becoming the human Jesus), the doctrine of Jesus's passion and resurrection (Jesus was crucified and after three days rose from the dead), the doctrine of the atonement (Jesus's death was the ultimate sacrifice that paid the price for human sin and made possible human oneness with God), and the doctrine of salvation (Jesus's resurrection is the pledge of eternal life for all who believe in him). It is the re-enacting, the re-presenting, of these myths (in order to allow believers to integrate themselves into salvation history) that has formed the substance of Christian liturgies (cultic celebrations) through twenty centuries. But, as we have already discovered, music plays no part in the central Jewish or Christian myths; it was only the later Christian acceptance of Greek creation mythology that provided the theological undergirding for the central role music came to occupy in the Christian liturgy.

Early Christian worship adopted much of its its form and practice from the Jewish synagogue service, to which it then added its own representation of the disciples' last meal with Jesus. It thus inherited its cultic music and musical

---

prophetic state by means of music, as happened in ancient Israel and in ancient Greece (see Plato, *Ion*, 533-5, in Barker, *Greek Musical Writings*, pp. 125-7), and as was common in pagan Roman cults (see Quasten, *Music and Worship in Pagan and Christian Antiquity*, pp. 36; 39.

[16]Mircea Eliade, the historian of religions, draws a distinction between myth, which he understands as primordial, and the central events of the Christian gospel, which are historical (*Myths, Rites, Symbols*, p. 35). Without questioning the validity of this distinction, we should observe that both the myths of more ancient religions and the gospel are intended to energize faith on a primal level, establishing the important features of reality together with a resulting worldview. The gospel also involves some sense of the primordial; in I Corinthians 15:45, for example, St. Paul contrasts the (primordial) man Adam with his successor Jesus Christ. Myths and the gospel exhibit broad fundamental similarities that reveal their close interrelation and set them both in contrast to the self-conscious worldview (see also Eliade, p. 78).

practice from Judaism, a matrix with an ancient, rich, and well-established musical heritage. The fundamental musical practice of the early apostolic church was thus Middle Eastern, semitic, Jewish, not Greek or Roman.

Christianity, however, grew and flourished in a pagan Graeco-Roman environment whose popular ideas about music were at odds with Christianity's, whose musical practice was debased and whose opinions of music and musicians were low. Unlike early Christianity, which from the beginning took a strong stance against the secular culture in which it found itself, there seems to have been no distinction between sacred and secular in pagan musical practice. Paul Henry Lang (*Music in Western Civilization*, p. 32) observes that "such a distinction was...unknown to the whole of antiquity, as theatrical performances formed a part of the religious service." The Christian writer Tertullian (A.D. c.160-c.220) confirms this fusion of theater and religion in pagan rites:

Let us pass on now to theatrical exhibitions, which we have already shown have a common origin with the circus, and bear like idolatrous designations--even as from the very first they have borne the name of "Ludi" [games], and equally minister to idols. They resemble each other also in their pomp, having the same procession to the scene of their display from temples and altars, and that mournful profusion of incense and blood, with music of pipes and trumpets, all under the direction of the soothsayer and the undertaker, those two foul masters of funeral rites and sacrifices. (Tertullian, *De Spectaculis* X 1/2; trans. in Skeris, Χρομα Θεου, pp. 37-38 and McKinnon, *Music in Early Christian Literature*, 75)

The Roman world inherited its musical practice from the Greeks[17] (who likewise recognized no distinction between sacred and secular in musical practice). Apparently, however, Rome was not fortunate enough to fall heir to Greek sensitivity and artistry. While Roman music was fundamentally indebted to Greek music, it was heavily influenced by the massive, exotic spectacles characteristic of the Middle East.[18] Roman music thus lost any pretense of the nobility promoted by Plato's view of music. Almost all ancient Roman writers who discuss music picture it as a degenerate art.[19] This decadence is reflected, for example, in a description of the proceedings at a musical contest, written by the Roman poet Horace (65-3 B.C.):

> Flutes, which were formerly made of a simple shinbone,
> Not, as now, brass-bound, with elaborate stops,
> Were then a subdued accompaniment to the chorus
> And sounded well when the benches were not too full
> --You could count the audience, who were not only few
> But sober, hard-working people, even chaste.
> When cities began to spread and the country grew bloated
> And holiday drinking began before the evening,
> The music grew less controlled and the noise was greater.
> What tastes could there be in an incoherent crowd
> Just finishing work, and only some of them honest?
> So movement and crude display spoiled the original art

---

[17] See Lang, *Music in Western Civilization*, p. 31.
[18] See Ibid., pp. 31-32.
[19] See Ibid., p. 32.

54 Wiser than Despair

> And the flute-player walked around in beautiful costumes;
> The instruments learned to make all kinds of noises
> The words were thrown round in a quite hysterical way.
> The stage propounded idiotic opinions
> Like fortune-tellers or bawds or pseudo-prophets.
> (Horace, *Ars Poetica*, 203-19; trans. by C. H. Sisson, p. 28)

Roman music found its *raison d'etre* in the amusement and pleasure of its listeners.[20] Thus the "bad music" condemned by Plato became the standard musical fare. The Roman public also placed a high premium on technical facility and virtuosity, which gave rise to petty jealousies and rivalries between performers.[21]

The early Church Fathers[22] thus encountered a pagan musical situation that they found intolerable, and they were presented with the dilemma of reconciling a heritage that was favorable to music (i.e., the practice of music in the Jewish Temple liturgy, supported by Old Testament scripture, and the enthusiastic adoption of Jewish psalms into the Christian cult) with a pagan environment whose music was abhorrent to them. On the level of musical practice, their solution was a rejection (often a violent one) of pagan practices and ideas, and an insistence on the strict separation of Christian and pagan customs.

At least three difficulties arise in trying to evaluate and interpret early Christian sources that refer to musical practice. (1) The written evidence is not extensive and often not conclusive. (2) It is not always easy or even possible to detect a source's context (its *Sitz im Leben*, to borrow a term from theological hermeneutics)--that is, what are the writer's musical background and standards? What is he reacting to: pagan practice or heretical Christian practice? (3) There is a certain ambiguity and contradiction between sources that exhibit minute variances of opinion--the inevitable result of a new institution "feeling its way." Nevertheless, the available evidence (sometimes vehement, occasionally amusing) allows us to draw a number of conclusions.

Christian writers unconditionally condemned pagan music, pagan musicians, and pagan beliefs about music:[23] "I have no mind to stand agape at a number of

---

[20] See Ibid.

[21] See Ibid., pp. 33-34.

[22] The expression "Fathers of the Church" (or at times the "Doctors [i.e., teachers] of the Church") refers to a large number of Christian theologians, preachers and writers who were active in the post-apostolic church through (approximately) the fifth century. Their sermons and writings--theological, moral, polemic, apologetic-- were highly influential, both on the growth and theological development of Christianity and on the decline of paganism. The period of theological ferment surrounding the work of these theologians (A.D. c.100-c.600 at the latest) is referred to as the patristic period.

[23] *Didascalia* V, 10/2 (early third century):

Even your very rejoicings therefore ought to be done with fear and trembling: for a Christian who is faithful ought neither to repeat an heathen hymn nor an obscene song, because he will be obliged by that hymn to make mention of the idolatrous names of demons; and instead of the Holy Spirit, the wicked one will enter into him. (trans. in Skeris, Χρομα Θεου, p. 33 and McKinnon, *Music in Early Christian Literature*, 241)

singers, nor do I desire to be affected in sympathy with a man when he is winking and gesticulating in an unnatural manner" (Tatian, A.D. c.160, *Address to the Greeks* 22-24; trans. in Skeris, Χρομα Θεου, p. 30, and McKinnon, *Music in Early Christian Literature*, 30). As Horace's censure of degenerate musical practices reveals, even some of the more thoughtful pagan writers in fact condemned the debased music that prevailed during their time, for the same reasons as their Christian contemporaries.[24] Christian theologians also rejected out of hand the idea that music pleases or placates God, vehemently (sometimes sarcastically) deriding pagan practices directed toward that end.[25]

The use of instruments among Christians was generally discouraged. The distaste for instruments became stronger and stronger as the church matured, probably in part as a reaction to the inevitable penetration of pagan practices into Christian life and worship. The later the source, the more likely it is to denounce the use of instruments. Thus Clement of Alexandria could write (A.D. c.200): "But if you want to sing and praise God to the music of the cithara or the lyre it is not blameworthy. You are imitating the righteous King of the

---

See also Tertullian, *De Spectaculis* X, 6-9 and XXV, 3, trans. in Skeris, Χρομα Θεου, pp. 38 & 39, and McKinnon, *Music in Early Christian Literature*, 76 & 77; Cyprian (or Novatian?), *De Spectaculis* VII 1-3, trans. in Skeris, p. 48, and McKinnon 92; and Arnobius, *Adversus Nationes* II, 42, trans. in Skeris, p. 49 and McKinnon 95; as well as McKinnon 46, 90, 91, 145, 149, 176, 182 & 183, 185, 240, & 263.

[24]See Quintilian, *Institutio Oratoria*, Book I, 10, trans. by H. E. Butler, pp. 31-32; Lucian of Samosata, *De Saltatione* 2, trans. in Quasten, *Music and Worship in Pagan and Christian Antiquity*, p. 126.

[25]Arnobius (early fourth century), *Adversus Nationes* VII, 32:

But let there be, as you wish, honour in wine and in incense, let the anger and displeasure of the deities be appeased by the immolation and slaughter of victims: are the gods moved by garlands also, wreaths and flowers, by the jingling of brass also, and the shaking of cymbals, by timbrels also, (and) also by symphonious (pipes)? What effect has the clattering of castanets, that when the deities have heard them they think that honour has been shown to them, and lay aside their fiery spirit of resentment in forgetfulness? Or, as little boys are frightened into giving over their silly wailings by hearing (the sound of) rattles, are the almighty deities also soothed in the same way by the whistling of pipes? and do they become mild, (is) their indignation softened, at the musical sound of cymbals? What is the meaning of those calls which you sing in the morning, joining (your) voices to the (music of the) pipe? Do the gods of heaven fall asleep, so that they should return to their posts? (trans. in Skeris, Χρομα Θεου, p. 50, and McKinnon, *Music in Early Christian Literature*, 96)

St. John Chrysostom (late fourth century), *In Psalmum* 7:15:

Just as [God] accepted sacrifices while not needing sacrifices - 'If I were hungry,' he says, 'I would not tell you' [Ps. 49:12] - but rather to lead men to honor him, so too does he accept hymns while not needing our praise, but rather because he desires our salvation. (trans. in McKinnon, *Music in Early Christian Literature*, 162)

Hebrews [i.e., David], who was well-pleasing to God[26] (Clement of Alexandria, *Paidagogos* 2, 4; trans. in Quasten, *Music and Worship in Pagan and Christian Antiquity*, p. 73, and McKinnon, *Music in Early Christian Literature*, 54). Later writers, however, were less permissive,[27] often branding the use of instruments in worship as a sign of human weakness. Strong rhythm, handclapping, and dancing were also condemned,[28] although admonitions against them indicate that they were at times practiced in Christian circles, as they are up to the present in the Coptic Christian Church in Ethopia. On the other hand, ecstatic expression continued to be tolerated (or even encouraged) for quite a long time,[29] though frequently with reservations (cf. St. Paul in I Corinthians 12-15).

The sound of jubilation signifies that love, born in our heart, that cannot be spoken. And to whom is such jubilation due if not to God; for He is the ineffable One, He Whom no words can define. But if you cannot speak Him into words, and yet you cannot remain silent, what else is left to you if not the song of jubilation, the rejoicing of your heart beyond all words, the immense latitude of the joy without limit of syllables. (St. Augustine, fifth century, *In Psalmum XXXII Enarratio* ; trans. in Pirotta, *Music and Culture in Italy*, p. 24, and McKinnon, *Music in Early Christian Literature*, 356)

It was only after the fourth century that the ecstatic element faded from the liturgy, suppressed perhaps in part because of its inherently divisive nature, in part because of its pagan associations.

World-conscious worship (the "cult") finds it natural and fitting to offer God the very best of which human minds and hands are capable. Thus when the elaborate, splendid worship of the Old Covenant (the Jerusalem temple, destroyed

---

[26]This passage, however, may not be expressing approval of actual musical instruments; see McKinnon, *Music in Early Christian Literature*, 54.

[27]St. John Chrysostom, (late fourth century), *De Elia et Jejunio* 55:

Marriage is accounted an honorable thing both by us and by those without [i.e., pagans]; and it is honorable. But when marriages are solemnized, such a number of ridiculous circumstances take place as ye shall hear of immediately: because the most part, possessed and beguiled by custom, are not even aware of their absurdity, but need others to teach them. For dancing, and cymbals, and flutes, and shameful words and songs, and drunkenness, and revellings, and all the Devil's great heap of garbage is then introduced. (trans. in Philip Schaff, *Nicene and Post-Nicene Fathers*, XII, p. 69)

See also St. Ambrose, *De Elia et Jejunio* 55, trans. in Routley, *The Church and Music*, p. 238 and McKinnon, *Music in Early Christian Literature*, 283; as well as McKinnon 51, 122, 160, 182, 187, & 264.

[28]See Cyprian (or Novatian?), *De Spectaculis* III, 1-3, trans. in Skeris, Χρομα Θεου, p. 47 and McKinnon, *Music in Early Christian Literature*, 90; Pseudo-Justin, *Quest. ad Orthod.*, 107 (Patrologia Graeca 6, 1353-55), trans. in Gelineau, *Voices and Instruments*, p. 152, n. 308.

[29]See also Tertullian, *De Anima* 9, trans. in Skeris, Χρομα Θεου, pp. 42-3, and McKinnon, *Music in Early Christian Literature*, 82; St. Cyprian, *De Dominica Oratione* 4, trans. in Skeris, p. 45; St. Augustine, *In Psalmum IC Enarratio* 4, trans. in Gelineau, *Voices and Instruments*, p. 26 and McKinnon 361.

in A.D. 70) was no longer a possibility for Christians, the maturing church began to develop indigenous practices to adorn its worship, practices that derived at first from the natural urge to adorn that which one loves, and later from the adoption of imperial court ceremonial. Even without the drift away from Judaism, that liturgical evolution would have been a natural development in early Christianity, because there was at first a continuity of attitude that did not fear or disdain ceremony, splendor, or elaboration in worship. It should have been inevitable that Christian cultic celebrations would (like Jewish ones) admit the striving for artistic excellence, the incorporation of objective quality (the result of investing rare and expensive materials and the labor of highly talented people in the adornment of worship), if for no other reason than to fulfill the desire to bring always more perfect, more beautiful gifts to lay before the manger and at the foot of the cross. The teachings of Jesus (Luke 7:37-50; John 12:1-8) are consistent with the Old Testament prophets' approach to this matter: a sincere faithfulness to the will of God is important above all else, but given that right intention, the desire to ornament, to bring one's best to worship, is laudable. This assumption comes under sustained attack only with the advent of Christian asceticism and monasticism, that despised outward elaboration and ornament and promoted simplicity and austerity. The suspicion of outward ornament and elaboration in worship has continued to surface regularly in subsequent Christian circles that have understood themselves to some degree to be at odds with the world instead of embracing it, that have put more emphasis on the temptations of the flesh than on the goodness of God's creation: for example, the medieval Cistercian monastic order or the more extreme reformers (Ulrich Zwingli, the English Puritans).

Already in the third century the complex of ideas and practices associated with the rise of Christian monasticism was beginning to modify the enthusiastic praise of singing among Christians. Early monasticism was marked by rejection of the world, asceticism, severe self-discipline, and a spirit of contrition and penance,[30] ideals that were adhered to until the influence of Irish and Scottish monks began to modify them beginning in the seventh and eighth centuries. Thus it was inevitable that the movement should be suspicious, if not hostile, to anything that might gratify the senses, including music.[31]

The same complex of attitudes and ideas that gave rise to Christian monasticism was also suspicious in general of artistry in any form as distracting the believer's concentration from things divine.[32]

---

[30] These ideals can indeed claim to be founded on scriptural teaching (e.g., Matthew 16: 24; Mark 8: 34; Luke 9:23; I Corinthians 7: 32-5); but as has so often been the case, one particular aspect of scripture was in this instance exalted at the expense of another, and equally valid ideas, ideas that should have remained in tension, lost the balance and perspective that should properly have been accorded to them.

[31] See Quasten, *Music and Worship in Pagan and Christian Antiquity*, pp. 94-96, 97.

[32] See also St. Jerome, *Ad Rusticum monachum* 15, trans. in McKinnon, *Music in Early Christian Literature*, 328; St. Jerome, *...epistulam ad Ephesios*, III, V, 19, trans. in McKinnon 333.

Even though the meaning of the words [of the Psalms] be unknown to you, teach your mouth to utter them meanwhile. For the tongue is made holy by the words when they are uttered with a ready and eager mind. Once we have acquired this habit, neither through free will nor through carelessness shall we neglect our beautiful office; custom compelling us, even against our will, to carry out this worship daily. Nor will anyone, in such singing, be blamed if he be weakened by old age, or young, or have a harsh voice, or no knowledge at all of numbers. What is here sought for is a sober mind, an awakened intelligence, a contrite heart, sound reason, and clear conscience. If having these you have entered into God's sacred choir, you may stand beside David himself...

Here there is no need for art which is slowly perfected; there is need only for lofty purpose, and we become skilled in a brief decisive moment. (St. John Chrysostom, fourth century, *Exposition of Psalm XLI* ; trans. in Strunk, *Source Readings*, pp. 69-70, and McKinnon, *Music in Early Christian Literature*, 168)

The attitudes characteristic of monasticism also led to the gradual exclusion of women from singing.[33] (Misogyny is characteristic of early eremitism and monasticism; witness the legend of the devil appearing to the hermit St. Anthony in the guise of a naked woman, a favorite subject of medieval religious paintings.) This tendency was already evident (though by no means universal) in the fourth century:[34] "Women are ordered not to speak in church, not even softly, nor may they sing along or take part in the responses, but they should only be silent and pray to God" (*Didascalia*, fourth century; trans. in Quasten, *Music and Worship in Pagan and Christian Antiquity*, p. 81). By the end of the patristic era, the exclusion of women from participation in corporate worship had become well nigh universal, in both eastern and western Christianity. The idea that women should not sing in the liturgy weakened only with the coming of the Renaissance. (The Protestant Reformers rejected it, and popular practice has gradually overcome it in the Roman Catholic Church.) On the other hand, the liturgical singing of boys was favored and promoted. This is already hinted at in documents from the fourth century and is closely linked with the growing practice of employing boys as lectors (i.e., those who chant scripture) in worship. Schools were soon established to educate these choirboy-lectors, and from one of them developed the famous Roman *schola cantorum*.[35]

Not all of the ideas represented above are mutually compatible, and their fundamental irreconcilability gave rise to an inevitable tension, an unavoidable ambiguity. The following passage perfectly captures that ambiguity. It is from the *Confessions* of St. Augustine, the most intimate disclosures of the early church's most brilliant and well-educated theologian, who in spite of reservations

---

[33]That is, in public worship attended by both sexes; cloistered women have always continued to sing in their services of worship.

[34]See also Isidore of Pelusium, *Epistle I*, 90, trans. in McKinnon, *Music in Early Christian Literature*, 121; Cyril of Jerusalem, *Procatechesis* XIV, trans. in McKinnon, 154; St. Jerome, *Against the Pelagians*, trans. in Quasten, *Music and Worship in Pagan and Christian Antiquity*, p. 82, and McKinnon, *Music in Early Christian Literature*, 334. Some fathers, however, express contradictory teachings; see: Ephraem Syrus, *Hymns of Eastertide*, II, 7-9, trans. in McKinnon 201; St. Ambrose of Milan, *Explanatio psalmi* I, 9, trans. in McKinnon 276.

[35]See Quasten, *Music and Worship in Pagan and Christian Antiquity*, pp. 89-91.

Music in the Early Church 59

exhibits here a broadminded tolerance and acceptance (dare we say, a suppressed passion?) for music:

> I used to be much more fascinated by the pleasures of sound than the pleasures of smell. I was enthralled by them, but you broke my bonds and set me free. I admit that I still find some enjoyment in the music of hymns, which are alive with your praises, when I hear them sung by well-trained, melodious voices, but I do not enjoy it so much that I cannot tear myself away. I can leave it when I wish. But if I am not to turn a deaf ear to music, which is the setting for the words which give it life, I must allow it a position of some honor in my heart, and I find it difficult to assign it to its proper place. For sometimes I feel that I treat it with more honor than it deserves. I realize that when they are sung, these sacred words stir my mind to greater religious fervor and kindle in me a more ardent flame of piety than they would if they were not sung; and I also know that there are particular modes in song and in the voice, corresponding to my various emotions and able to stimulate them because of some mysterious relationship between the two. But I ought not to allow my mind to be paralyzed by the gratification of my senses, which often leads it astray. For the senses are not content to take second place. Simply because I allow them their due, as adjuncts to reason, they attempt to take precedence and forge ahead of it, with the result that I sometimes sin in this way but am not aware of it until later.
>
> Sometimes, too, from over-anxiety to avoid this particular trap I make the mistake of being too strict. When this happens, I have no wish but to exclude from my ears, and from the ears of the Church as well, all the melody of those lovely chants to which the Psalms of David are habitually sung; and it seems safer to me to follow the precepts which I remember often having heard ascribed to Athanasius, bishop of Alexandria, who used to oblige the lectors to recite the psalms with such slight modulation of the voice that they seemed to be speaking rather than chanting. But when I remember the tears that I shed on hearing the songs of the Church in the early days, soon after I had recovered my faith, and when I realize that nowadays it is not the singing that moves me but the meaning of the words when they are sung in a clear voice to the most appropriate tune, I again acknowledge the great value of this practice. So I waver between the danger that lies in gratifying the senses and the benefits which, as I know from experience, can accrue from singing. Without committing myself to an irrevocable opinion, I am inclined to approve of the custom of singing in church, in order that by indulging the ears weaker spirits may be inspired with feelings of devotion. Yet when I find the singing itself more moving than the truth which it conveys, I confess that this is a grievous sin, and at those times I would prefer not to hear the singer.
>
> This, then, is my present state. Let those of my readers whose hearts are filled with charity, from which good actions spring, weep with me and weep for me. Those who feel no charity in themselves will not be moved by my words. But I beg you, O Lord my God, to look upon me and listen to me. Have pity on me and heal me, for you see that I have become a problem to myself, and this is the ailment from which I suffer. (St. Augustine, fifth century, *Confessions* X, 33; trans. by R.S. Pine-Coffin, pp. 238-9)

The evidence discussed up to now originated out of involvement with the actual practice of music; none of it is concerned with music's theoretical aspect. In their intense struggle with pagan music the Fathers of the church forged a specifically Christian conception of musical practice, a conception that bore a pronounced polemic and ascetic character. For succeeding centuries their authority created the status of dogma for their doctrines, and later writers continued to cite their teachings in support of attacks against inroads of secular musical practice.

In contrast to the teachings about music in practice, there was a second complex of ideas and attitudes toward music, proceeding from theoretical and aesthetic concerns. It originated in the Hellenistic matrix in which the early church grew to prominence. To be sure, Hellenism had already deeply influenced Judaism before the advent of Christianity (witness the Septuagint, the pre-Christian translation of the Old Testament into Greek). But the early church's decision that the gospel was intended for gentiles as well as Jews (Acts 10-11; 13 ff.) made it inevitable that Christian communities should come to include persons educated in, indeed formed by, Greek modes of thought. Some of these people (often the most learned and astute members of the community) became highly influential theologians (for example, St. Augustine, whose schooling as a youth was accomplished entirely within the classical, i.e., Greek, educational system). Perhaps the most obvious evidence of these men's influence was early Christianity's continuing involvement with gnostic language and ideas.[36] These thinkers could hardly avoid bringing Greek philosophical ideas about music to bear upon the formation of a Christian theological stance on music. As the patristic period emptied into the early Middle Ages, this process was stabilized by the adoption of classically-based treatises on music as the foundation of Christian views on music theory, notably those by Augustine, Cassiodorus, and Boethius. The Christian theoretical doctrine of music, then, was in essence neo-Pythagorean and Neo-Platonic. From it stemmed:
1. The idea of music as a science
2. A coarse remnant of the ancient doctrine of ethos
3. The purely arithmetic treatment of musical elements
4. The interpretation of music in a theological, metaphysical, and speculative[37] sense, leading to a preference for allegory, symbolism, and various sorts of hidden magical significance.[38]

---

[36]Gnosticism is the name given to a variety of systems of religious thought that were widespread in the Graeco-Roman world during the first centuries of the Christian era. Common to most of these systems was the belief that salvation was available only by the deliverance of the human spirit from its imprisonment in the world of the flesh; this deliverance could be accomplished by means of secret knowledge (*gnosis*). This knowledge was commonly imparted by a divine deliverer from the kingdom of light who enters the world in disguise, eluding the evil powers of darkness that enslave the world, and offers the knowledge that will free the human spirit to return to its eternal home. Although gnosticism is not Christian in origin, nor is it compatible with Christian theology (since it denies the goodness of creation and the real humanity of Jesus), its tenets and its language often proved superficially compatible with Christianity's. Thus the early Church Fathers considered it a particularly dangerous threat to Christian orthodoxy.

[37]The terms "speculative" and "speculation" are found frequently in medieval treatises on music. The words are meant to signify that the theories under discussion are based on tradition--and ultimately on divine revelation--rather than on positive knowledge or observation.

[38]See Abert, *Die Musikanschauung*, pp. 15-16.

Music in the Early Church

When the early church reached the point in its maturity at which it was capable of reflecting on music, Christian theologians began to attempt to reconcile Greek speculative ideas on music with Christian theology (a facet of the broader work of reconciling and integrating elements of a still-powerful and pervasive pagan mythology with Christian mythology). Most of the borrowed ideas were Pythagorean and Platonic in origin, but had undergone development and modification during the intervening centuries. The task of reconciliation was not as formidable as it might seem at first, however, since Pythagorean "philosophy" was by nature religious, and Pythagorean philosophers were as much religious mystics as philosophers. The distinction between religion and philosophy was more important to Christians than to their Greek predecessors: Plato and Aristotle used the terms interchangeably, and what Aristotle's disciples referred to as "first philosophy" Aristotle himself called theology.[39] Indeed, there is a certain compatibility--one might almost say sympathy--between certain aspects of Pythagorean philosophy and Christian theology. For example, the numerical perfection of creation and its origin (cf. the Timaeus legend, pp. 33-34 above) could hardly fail to strike a sympathetic note in Christians who would read in the apocryphal *Wisdom of Solomon* 11:21 (itself a product of Greek influence): "Sed omnia in mensura, et numero, et pondere disposuisti (For You have ordered all things by measure and number and weight)." One product of the reconciling activity was the creation of a number of "apologies," attempts by Christian theologians to convince the Graeco-Roman world of Christianity's validity, in part by preempting and "baptizing" pagan ideas, figures, and legends, interpreting them to demonstrate that they were at heart derived from Old Testament and Christian concepts. One of those apologies, for example, is the *Hortatory Address to the Greeks*, whose author, a second-century Christian, maintains that Moses is the ultimate source of everything that is good and true in Greek culture (thus furthering an argument begun by Jewish apologists of previous centuries). He claims that many important Greek figures, including Pythagoras and even Plato, had at one time or another visited Egypt and there imbibed the wisdom of the Jews.[40] Clement of Alexandria (second century) even

---

[39] Ellefsen, "Music and Humanism" (diss.), p. 16.

[40] Of particular interest in this apology is the so-called *Testament of Orpheus*, a passage in which Orpheus supposedly writes to his "son" Musaeus testifying to the truth of monotheism:
Pseudo-Justin Martyr (second century), *Hortatory Address to the Greeks* 15:

> I speak to those who lawfully may hear:
> All others, ye profane, now close the doors,
> And, O Musaeus! hearken thou to me,
> Who offspring art of the light-bringing moon:
> The words I utter now are true indeed;
> And if thou former thoughts of mine hast seen,
> Let them not rob thee of the blessed life,
> But rather turn the depths of thine own heart
> Unto the place where light and knowledge dwell.
> Take thou the word divine to guide thy steps,
> And walking well in the straight certain path,
> Look to the one and universal King--

accuses the Greeks of plagiarizing the miracles related in the Old Testament, and asks how one can refuse to believe in the latter while holding to the "prodigies of Hellenic mythology."[41]

Because so many early Christian theologians were products of the classical educational curriculum, they were convinced of its value and fostered its continuing influence. In his *Miscellanies* (Book 6, Chap. 10), for example, Clement maintains that in search of truth one should take from each preparatory subject whatever it can contribute toward knowledge of the truth; among the preparatory subjects he numbers dialectic, astronomy, geometry, arithmetic, and music.[42] In the third century, the Gnostic Christian theologian Origen recommended the same course of action:

> ...my desire for you has been that you should direct the whole force of your intelligence to Christianity as your end... I would wish that you should take with you on the one hand those parts of the philosophy of the Greeks which are fit, as it were, to serve as general or preparatory studies of Christianity, and on the other hand so much of geometry and astronomy as may be helpful for the interpretation of the holy Scriptures. The children of the philosophers speak of geometry and music and grammar and rhetoric and astronomy as being ancillary to philosophy; and in the same way we might speak of philosophy itself as being ancillary to Christianity. (Origen, *Letter to Gregory*, I; trans. in Skeris, Χρομα Θεου, p. 90)

There was one Greek doctrine that the church had already begun to adopt in the apostolic era: that of "spiritual sacrifice" (cf. "spiritual worship," in Paul's letter to the Romans, 12:1), together with its limitations on musical expression.[43] The doctrine was a development of Greek philosophy that rejected bloody sacrifice and other liturgical externals in favor of an entirely spiritual worship. Contemporary Jewish and Christian writers alike, under the influence of this

---

> One, self-begotten, and the only One,
> Of whom all things and we ourselves are sprung.
> All things are open to his piercing gaze,
> While He Himself is still invisible.
> Present in all his works, though still unseen,
> He gives to mortals evil out of good,
> Sending both chilling wars and tearful griefs;
> And other than the great King there is none,
> And mortal eyeballs in mere mortal eyes
> Are weak, to see Jove reigning over all.
> He sits established in the brazen heavens
> Upon His golden throne; under his feet
> He treads the earth, and stretches His right hand
> To all the ends of ocean, and around
> Tremble the mountain ranges and the streams,
> The depths, too, of the blue and hoary sea.
> (trans. in Skeris, Χρομα Θεου, pp. 26-28)

[41]Clement of Alexandria, *Miscellanies*, Book 6, Chap. 2; trans. in Skeris, Χρομα Θεου, p. 77.

[42]Ibid., Book 6, Chap. 10; see Skeris, Χρομα Θεου, p. 77.

[43]See Quasten, *Music and Worship in Pagan and Christian Antiquity*, pp. 51-60.

hellenistic doctrine, expressed their abhorrence of sensuous pagan cultic music. They lent their support to an unpretentious mode of worship, in particular rejecting the use of instruments and tending to allegorize their mention in the Old Testament. Such a repudiation of the external elements of worship could not help but have an effect on music. Although some writers urged the complete renunciation of music in the liturgy as the highest ideal, the early church adopted a more moderate stance, retaining a restrained mode of singing in worship and interpreting that singing as its "spiritual sacrifice."

The rejection of pagan cultic music, however, is not as surprising as the rejection of Jewish temple worship and its music. This represents a decisive change from the earliest period of Christian worship, during which Christians maintained their presence at worship in the Jerusalem temple. Already in the New Testament, however, the author of the Letter to the Hebrews (in accord with the doctrine of spiritual sacrifice) transformed the ancient Jewish doctrine of atonement by bloody sacrifice (Hebrews 9-10), by asserting that Christ's death, the ultimate and final bloody sacrifice, has supplanted any further animal sacrifice. As soon as Christianity moved beyond its earliest stage as a Jewish sect, then, Christians rejected the idea and practice of temple worship entirely, discarding at the same time its sensuous, emotional and spectacular character[44] and its use of instruments in the liturgy.[45] Thus, while Christian rejection of pagan customs discouraged the use of instruments in general, the doctrine of spiritual sacrifice eliminated them specifically from Christian worship. Christian writers often asserted that God had allowed the use of instruments under the old covenant merely as a concession to human weakness[46]: "Instruments were permitted to them [i.e., the ancient Israelites] out of regard for the weakness of their spirit, and because they had hardly emerged as yet from the cult of idols. Just as God allowed their sacrifices, so also He allowed their instruments, condescending to their weakness" (St. John Chrysostom, late fourth century, *In Psalmis* 149; trans. in Gelineau, *Voices and Instruments in Christian Worship*, p. 151, n. 305, and McKinnon, *Music in Early Christian Literature*, 173). No elements of temple worship were preserved in later Christian worship and ceremonial, while on the other hand a number of elements of the synagogue service have indeed survived up to the present day in traditional Christian liturgies. By repudiating the use of instruments in the liturgy, Christians actually aligned themselves more closely with Platonic tradition than with traditional Jewish attitudes and practices. In order to reconcile the apparent contradiction of the use of instruments in the Psalms and elsewhere in the Old Testament with the Christian repudiation of instrumental music, many early Christian theologians resorted to allegory, ascribing a purely vocal or spiritual significance to references to instruments in worship.[47]

---

[44] As has previously been mentioned, this character was again fully realized in Christian worship only with the adoption of Christianity as the official state religion and its gradual adoption of imperial Roman (specifically Byzantine) court ceremony.

[45] See Quasten, *Music and Worship in Pagan and Christian Antiquity*, pp. 62-64.

[46] See also Isidore of Pelusium, *Epistle II*, 176, trans. in McKinnon, *Music in Early Christian Literature*, 123, as well as McKinnon 174, 229-32, & 308.

[47] Clement of Alexandria (second century), *Paidagogos* II 4, 41, 4-5:

64 Wiser than Despair

If Christian writers and theologians were so suspicious of music (and especially of elaborate, artistic music-making), then how did music ever find an opportunity to develop and flourish in the church? The answer to this question is to be found in the increasing importance to Christian theology of certain elements of Greek mythology (and the doctrines that proceed from them) that accord music a role of central, indispensable significance. For example, the Pythagorean doctrine of world or cosmic harmony is present only by inference in the Psalms[48] and in Job 38:7[49] (the latter perhaps already influenced by the spread of hellenic ideas). The doctrine is also not in any way evident in the New Testament. The concept particularly appealed to classically educated Christian theologians, however, and it was expressed again and again in their writings, although recast in Christian terms.[50]

If then the world is a tuneful instrument struck rhythmically, I reverence the one who put it in tune and plucked the strings and sang the harmonious accompaniment, but not the instrument itself. The stewards of the games do not pass over the lyre-players

---

The Spirit, distinguishing from such revelry the divine service, sings, "Praise Him with the sound of trumpet;" for with sound of trumpet He shall raise the dead. "Praise Him on the psaltery; for the tongue is the psaltery of the Lord. "And praise Him on the lyre." By the lyre is meant the mouth struck by the Spirit, as it were by a plectrum. "Praise with the timbrel and the dance," refers to the Church meditating on the resurrection of the dead in the resounding skin. "Praise Him on the chords and organ." Our body he calls an organ, and its nerves are the strings, by which it has received harmonious tension, and when struck by the Spirit, it gives forth human voices. "Praise Him on the clashing cymbals." He calls the tongue the cymbal of the mouth, which resounds with the pulsation of the lips. (trans. in Skeris, Χρομα Θεου, p. 69, and McKinnon, *Music in Early Christian Literature*, 52)

See also Pseudo-Origen, *On Psalm 150*, 3-5, trans. in Skeris, Χρομα Θεου, p. 92, and McKinnon, *Music in Early Christian Literature*, 69; Eusebius of Caesarea, *Commentary on Psalm 92*, 2-3, trans. in McKinnon 206 and Skeris, p. 112, as well as McKinnon, 68, 101, & 169.

[48] See Spitzer, *Classical and Christian Ideas of World Harmony*, p. 25.
[49] Job 38:4-7:

> Where were you when I laid the earth's foundations?
> Tell me, if you know and understand.
> Who settled its dimensions? Surely you should know.
> Who stretched his measuring-line over it?
> On what do its supporting pillars rest?
> Who set its corner-stone in place,
> when the morning stars sang together
> and all the sons of God shouted aloud?

[50] See also Clement of Alexandria, *Exhortation to the Greeks* I, trans. in Strunk, *Source Readings*, pp. 62-63, and McKinnon, *Music in Early Christian Literature*, 44-45; Athanasius, *Oratio contra Gentes* 42, trans. in Skeris, Χρομα Θεου, pp. 94-5, and McKinnon 107; Eusebius of Caesarea, *Tricennial Oration* XII 11, trans. in Skeris, p. 117)

Music in the Early Church 65

in the contest and go and crown their lyres. If, as Plato says, this world is God's craft, then, marvelling at its beauty, I go to worship the craftsman. (Athenagoras, second century, *Plea for the Christians* 16; trans. in Skeris, Χρομα Θεου, p. 31, and McKinnon, *Music in Early Christian Literature*, 32)

Just as they embraced the idea of a harmonically ordered universe, a number of Christian theologians asserted that cosmic harmony is also transferred to and resides in humans. It is at this point that music comes to be related to Christianity under the third primary aspect of religion: ethos (behavior or morals).[51] From this point on, various Christian writers have continued to suggest that music has a formative effect (either positive or negative) on behavior and morals. Prophets in particular were said to harmonize with God.[52] Human harmony was conceivable only because of the redeeming work of Christ.[53] According to

---

[51] The Prologue has already explored how music figures into the first two primary aspects of religion: cult (worship) and myth (doctrine).

[52] Hippolytus (third century), *Treatise on Christ and Antichrist* 2:

For these fathers [i.e., the Prophets] were furnished with the Spirit, and largely honored by the Word Himself; and just as it is with instruments of music, so had they the Word always, like the plectrum, in union with them, and when moved by Him the prophets announced what God willed. For they spake not of their own power (let there be no mistake as to that), neither did they declare what pleased themselves. But first of all they were endowed with wisdom by the Word, and then again were rightly instructed in the future by means of visions. And then, when thus themselves fully convinced, they spake those things which were revealed by God to them alone, and concealed from all others. (trans. in Skeris, Χρομα Θεου, p. 102, and McKinnon, *Music in Early Christian Literature*, 86)

See also Pseudo-Justin Martyr, *Hortatory Address to the Greeks*, 8, trans. in Skeris, Χρομα Θεου, p. 26, and McKinnon, *Music in Early Christian Literature*, 28; Athenagoras, *Plea for the Christians* 7:9, trans. in Skeris, p. 30; cf. McKinnon, 216.

[53] Methodius of Olympus (third-fourth century), *Symposium* III, 7:

Two elements which are utterly contradictory to each other are life and death, corruption and incorruptibility. Life is evenness; corruption is unevenness. And justice and prudence are harmony, while injustice and folly are disharmony. Man himself, being between these two extremes, is neither absolute justice nor injustice; but placed midway between corruption and incorruptibility, to whichever he bends and inclines, he is said to turn to the nature of that which has gotten the upper hand of him. Inclining towards corruption he becomes corruptible and mortal; and incorruptible and immortal if he inclines towards incorruption... It follows, then, that man is not disharmony and unevenness, nor yet harmony and evenness. But when he took on disharmony, that is, transgression and sin, he became disharmonious and inacceptable; and when he took on harmony, that is justice, he became an harmonious and acceptable instrument, so that the Lord, Incorruptibility itself and the Conqueror of Death, might mix in harmony the resurrection with the flesh, and never again suffer it to be claimed by incorruption. (trans. in Skeris, Χρομα Θεου, p. 104)

See also Clement of Alexandria, *Exhortation to the Greeks* I, trans. in Strunk, *Source Readings*, p. 61, and McKinnon, *Music in Early Christian Literature*, 43.

66 Wiser than Despair

Clement of Alexandria, the divine harmony is the creator of Christian unity;[54] consequently, music from human lips was said to express and create unity and concord among Christians.[55]

The Greek doctrine of ethos per se (i.e., music cooperates in the formation of good human character) found little direct expression among early Christian theologians. The complex of ideas associated with the doctrine was, however, well represented. Thus a righteous man was compared to a beautiful hymn.

A beautiful hymn to God is an immortal man who is being built up in righteousness, and upon whom the words of truth have been engraved. (Clement of Alexandria, second century, *Protreptikos* X, 107:1; trans. in: Skeris, Χρομα Θεου, p. 63)

Sing to God, not with the voice, but with the heart... Although a man be *kakophonos* [i.e., unable to carry a tune/unmusical], to use a common expression, if he have good works, he is a sweet singer before God. (St. John Chrysostom, fourth century, *Exposition of Psalm XLI* ; trans. in Strunk, *Source Readings*, p. 70)[56]

A number of Christian writers drew the distinction between good and harmful music, denouncing the harmful.[57] It is no longer possible to ascertain precisely

---

[54]Clement (second century), *Protreptikos* I:9:

And truly, this pure song, the key-note of the whole and the harmony of all things, extending from the center to the extremities and from the ends to the middle, has arranged all things harmoniously, not according to Thracian music, which follows Jubal, but according to the fatherly will of God, which fired the zeal of David...We want to strive so that we, the many, may be brought together into one love, according to the union of the essential unity. As we do good may we similarly pursue unity.... The union of many, which the divine harmony has called forth out of a medley of sounds and division, becomes one symphony, following the one leader of the choir and teacher, the Word, resting in that same truth and crying out: "Abba, Father." (trans. in Quasten, *Music and Worship in Pagan and Christian Antiquity*, p. 67)

[55]St. John Chrysostom (fourth century), *Homilies* 5:

The psalm which occurred just now in the office blended all voices together, and caused one single fully harmonious chant to arise; young and old, rich and poor, women and men, slaves and free, all sang one single melody... Here the prophet speaks and we all reply, all of us echo his words... Together we make up a single choir in perfect equality of rights and of expression whereby earth imitates heaven. Such is the noble character of the Church. (trans. in Gelineau, *Voices and Instruments*, p. 82)

See also Ignatius of Antioch, *Ephesians* IV:1-3, trans. in Skeris, Χρομα Θεου, p. 22, and McKinnon, *Music in Early Christian Literature*, 21; Pseudo-Origen, *On Psalm 149:3*, trans. in Skeris, p. 92; St. Ambrose, *In Psalmum I Enarratio* 9, trans. in Routley, *The Church and Music*, p. 237, and McKinnon 276.

[56]Also trans. in McKinnon, *Music in Early Christian Literature*, 333, where it is ascribed to St. Jerome, *epist. ad Ephesios*.

[57]Pseudo-St. John Chrysostom (fourth century), *De Poenitentia* VI:

what bad characteristics these writers are condemning; but that is of little importance. Rather it is important to note that the distinction between bad/secular music and good/sacred music is one that goes back to a very early stage of Christianity.

Instruments were not only proscribed in worship, they were also said to promote moral decay.[58] Thus vocal music was considered unquestionably superior to instrumental: "No cithara, no flute, or any other musical instrument produces such a [lovely] sound, which one can perceive, than when those holy ones [the monks] sing in deepest silence and solitude" (St. John Chrysostom, fourth century, *In Epist. I ad Timoth.*, 4 Homilia, 14; trans. in Quasten, *Music and Worship in Pagan And Christian Antiquity*, p. 92, and in McKinnon, *Music in Early Christian Literature*, 187).

Even though the extreme dualism of body and soul as propounded by gnostic theologians was ultimately declared heretical, a milder form of the doctrine, the heritage of Greek philosophy, can be traced throughout the development of early and medieval Christian theology (especially that of ascetics). It is reflected in the assertion that the mind controls the senses as a musician controls a lyre.[59] For example, Gregory of Nyssa (fourth century) taught that the human soul is present everywhere in the body, "just as an artist is present in his musical instrument."[60] Just as a player draws different tones from different strings, the soul controls the various organs of the body.[61]

Thus does the devil stealthily set fire to the city. It is not a matter of running up ladders and using petroleum or pitch or tow; he uses things far more pernicious--lewd sights, base speech, degraded music, and songs full of all kinds of wickedness. (trans. in Routley, *The Church and Music*, p. 240)

See also Clement of Alexandria, *Paidagogos* II 4, 44, 4-5, trans. in Skeris. Χροµα Θεου, p. 71, and McKinnon, *Music in Early Christian Worship*, 51; Basil of Caesarea, *The Letters*, trans. in Weiss and Taruskin, *Music in the Western World*, p. 27, and McKinnon 140.

[58][Pseudo-]Basil of Caesarea (fourth century), *Commentary on Isaias*:

Of the arts necessary to life which furnish a concrete result there is carpentry, [which produces] the chair; architecture, the house; shipbuilding, the ship; tailoring, the garment; forging, the blade. Of useless arts there is harp playing, dancing, flute playing, of which, when the operation ceases, the result disappears with it. And indeed, according to the word of the apostle, the result of these is destruction. (trans. in McKinnon, "The Church Fathers and Musical Instruments" (diss.), p. 182)

[59]See St. Athanasius, *Oratio contra Gentes* 31, trans. in Skeris, Χροµα Θεου, p. 93.

[60]Quoted in Spitzer, *Classical and Christian Ideas of World Harmony*, p. 20.

[61]St. John Chrysostom (fourth century), *Exposition of Psalm XLI*:

Here [i.e., when singing the psalms] there is no need for the cithara, or for stretched strings, or for the plectrum, or for art, or for any instrument; but, if you like, you may yourself become a cithara, mortifying the members of the flesh and making a full harmony of mind and body. For when the flesh no longer lusts against the spirit, but has submitted to its orders and has been led at length into the best and

68   Wiser than Despair

The ideal music in the opinion of early Christian writers was calm and tranquil, settling the emotions rather than raising them[62] (in full acord with Plato's teaching; cf. Chap. 3, p. 38): "...if somewhere one who rages like a wild beast from excessive anger falls under the spell of the psalm, he straightway departs, with the fierceness of his soul calmed by the melody" (Basil of Caesarea, fourth century, *Homily on Psalm I*, 1; trans. in Strunk, *Source Readings*, p. 65). In a word, the musical ideal as conceived by the early Church Fathers was *noble*.[63]

Early Christian theologians also maintained the conservative attitude toward music that was characteristic of earlier Greek philosophers. Indeed, in that Christianity is historically based, it is inherently conservative; it is constantly reviewing its Old and New Testament roots--God's saving acts in history--since it has always regarded them as standards for recognizing authenticity in faith and doctrine. The early Church Fathers, however, did not limit their teachings by basing them entirely on the canon of scripture,[64] but predicated them on the idea that God continued to reveal his truth in the teaching authority of the church throughout its entire history, right up to the present. The teachings of preceding

---

most admirable path, then you will create a spiritual melody. (trans. in Strunk, *Source Readings*, p. 70, and McKinnon, *Music in Early Christian Literature*, 169)

[62]See Clement of Alexandria, *Paidagogos* 2:4, trans. in Quasten, *Music and Worship in Pagan and Christian Antiquity*, p. 68; St. Athanasius, *Epistola ad Marcellinum* 29, trans. in Skeris, Χροµα Θεου, p. 98, and McKinnon, *Music in Early Christian Literature*, 100.

[63]See also Chapter 3, p. 38. The use of the word *noble* in this context needs to be explained, since I use it from this point on to express a basic quality of church music. Other words can mean essentially the same thing, and might equally well be used to express the basic concept intended here. I have, however, chosen to use *noble*, and the following may help to clarify and defend this choice.

1. *heroic* is very close in meaning to *noble*, except that it might tend to suggest accomplishment achievable by only a few individuals.

2. *galant* is in fact identical in meaning to *noble*, but a.) it is not an English word, b.) it is already tied to a particular style of music, and c.) it may at times connote a certain degree of superficiality, especially to modern minds.

3. *dignified, stately, grand*, all comprise a part of the meaning of *noble*, but they lack the ethical dimension of the word, and that ethical dimension is very important in the history of ideas in church music.

4. *idealistic* is quite close to what I mean by *noble*, but it bears the connotation of arising from and belonging to a more recent, secular culture.

5. *noble* also clearly evokes the image of European titled aristocracy, and it is an undeniable fact that the concepts that underlie feudal courtly life have played a great role in shaping the history of church music. Not merely the notion of patronage, but chivalrous virtues, wisdom, moderation, the idea of a "gentleman" (as propounded in the sixteenth century by Baldassare Castiglione in his *Book of the Courtier*) are all basic presuppositions for Western art music as it evolved up through the nineteenth century, and this holds true for church music as well.

For a discussion of the idea of nobility or heroism in the broader context of myth, see Eliade, *Myths, Rites Symbols*, pp. 92ff.

[64]Indeed, that canon was created by the church, and not until the third or fourth century.

Fathers were regarded as extensions and elucidations of scriptural truth.[65] Accordingly, any "new" idea (i.e., any idea that was not obviously derived from previous Christian teaching and practice) had to be proved consonant with already existing tradition; if it could not be (or if it were proved not to be), then it had to be rejected. The early Church Fathers had established that the only music appropriate for Christian lips was the Psalms; consequently there could not be any variety or novelty in music.[66]

Although the attitudes explored above leave little doubt in this regard, Christian theologians expressly stated that the primary purpose of music is not to give sensual pleasure, but to sing and to hear the praises of God.[67] In

---

[65]The Roman Catholic Church continues to view its *magisterium*, or teaching office, in this way.

[66]Clement of Alexandria (second century), *Stromateis* VI 11, 89:4-90:2:

Music is then to be handled for the sake of the embellishment and composure of manners. To be sure, when drinking, we mutually encourage each other to psalmody by the exchange of pledges, soothing by song the eagerness of our desires, and glorifying God for the copious gift of human enjoyments, for His perpetual supply of the food necessary for the growth of the body and of the soul. But we must abominate extravagant music, which enervates men's souls, and leads to changefulness--now mournful, and then licentious and voluptuous, and then frenzied and frantic. (trans. in Skeris, Χρομα Θεου, p. 78)

St. John Chrysostom (fourth century), *Exposition of Psalm XLI*:

Inasmuch as this kind of pleasure [i.e., in music] is thoroughly innate to our mind, and lest demons introducing lascivious songs should overthrow everything, God established the psalms, in order that singing might be both a pleasure and a help. From strange chants harm, ruin, and many grievous matters are brought in, for those things that are lascivious and vicious in all songs settle in parts of the mind, making it softer and weaker; from the spiritual psalms, however, proceeds much of value, much utility, much sanctity, and every inducement to philosophy, for the words purify the mind and the Holy Spirit descends swiftly upon the mind of the singer. (trans. in Strunk, *Source Readings*, p. 68, and McKinnon, *Music in Early Christian Literature*, 165)

[67]Lactantius (fourth century), *Divine Institutions* VI, 21:

Therefore he who is anxious for the truth, who does not wish to deceive himself, must lay aside hurtful and injurious pleasures, which would bind the mind to themselves, as pleasant food does the body: true things must be preferred to false, eternal things to those which are of short duration, useful things to those which are pleasant. Let nothing be pleasing to the sight but that which you see to be done with piety and justice; let nothing be agreeable to the hearing but that which nourishes the soul and makes you a better man. And especially this sense ought not to be distorted to vice, since it is given to us for this purpose, that we might gain the knowledge of God. Therefore, if it be a pleasure to hear melodies and songs, let it be pleasant to sing and hear the praises of God. This is true pleasure, which is the attendant and companion of virtue. This is not frail and brief, as those which they desire, who, like cattle, are slaves to the body; but lasting, and affording delight without any intermission. (trans. in Skeris, Χρομα Θεου, p. 53)

particular, liturgical singing was not to provide sensual pleasure:[68] "...those who sing psalms at the altar shall not sing with pleasure but with wisdom; they shall sing nothing but psalms" (*Canons of Basil*, fourth century, Canon 97; trans. in Quasten, *Music and Worship in Pagan and Christian Antiquity*, p. 94).

An abhorrence for the sensual attraction of pagan music undoubtedly contributed to the attitude of early Christian writers toward the pleasurable aspect of music. Here again, however, the fundamental compatibility between Christian and earlier Platonic attitudes toward music is evident. As the church continued to confront and battle pagan practices, the assertion became unanimous that the pleasure offered by music was fundamentally only God's concession to those who were weak in spirit, a means of making the psalms and other sacred songs more palatable to them. God required music (in and of itself) as little as sacrifice; but as a means of rescuing the weak from error, God tolerated sacrifice and musical instruments under the old covenant. Such childish ways could not be permitted under the new covenant. But since music itself was too firmly rooted in scripture and practice to be eliminated, and the charm of music was too obvious to be denied, Christian leaders sought to curb its attractiveness by insisting that the songs of the church be performed in such a way as to place

---

See also Clement of Alexandria, *Paidagogos* II, 4, 40:1-2 - 41:1-3, trans. in Skeris, p. 68, and McKinnon, *Music in Early Christian Literature*, 51; St. Cyprian, *De Habitu Virginum* 11, trans. in Skeris, p. 44 and McKinnon 93; as well as McKinnon 30 & 150.

[68]St. Gregory the Great (early seventh century):

Sometime ago, in this Roman Church, over which Divine Providence wished to place me, an exceedingly reprehensible custom arose. Certain chanters chosen for ministry at the sacred altar and ordained to the order of deacons that they might be devoted to sacred music, were called to the office of preaching and almsgiving. Whence it happens for many that while enticing duties draw you to the sacred ministry, a righteous life fails to attract. And the chanter, the minister, angers God by his manners while pleasing the people with his voice. Therefore, I establish by this decree from the [Apostolic] Chair that the sacred ministers ought not to sing and they may perform the office of reading [i.e., chanting] the Gospel only during the solemnization of Masses: I decree that the psalms and other readings should be done by subdeacons, or if necessity requires it, by those in minor orders. (trans. in Hayburn, *Papal Legislation*, p. 5)

See also McKinnon, *Music in Early Christian Literature*, 98, 100, & 266. There is an occasional comment, however, that seems to approve of the spiritual pleasure derived from singing:
St. John Chrysostom (late fourth century), *De sanctis Bernice et Prosdoce* 3:

Hence in the beginning there was wailing and lamentation over the dead, but now there are psalms and hymnody. The Jews, in any case, mourned Jacob for forty days and Moses for a similar number; they grieved because death at that time was death indeed. Now, however, it is not so; rather there is an element of pleasure in the matter. For psalms are a sign of good cheer; as it is written, 'Is anyone among you cheerful? Let him sing psalms' [James 5:13]. (trans. in McKinnon, *Music in Early Christian Literature*, 192)

fundamental emphasis on the content of the text. Even more important, however, was their insistence that singers must examine the disposition of their souls as they sang. That disposition had to be such that the music evoked a *compunctio cordis*[69] (contrition of the heart) rather than any sensual pleasure.

As the restrictive pronouncements on music grew into an avalanche of opinion, blanketing the Christian landscape, they succeeded in producing a sort of de facto "censorship" that grew ever more forceful as church doctrine gained influence and control over popular thought processes. There is a sense in which one is compelled to admit that the church by and large succeeded where Plato failed in applying restrictions to music. Christian constraints were not as immediate or as complete as Plato might have preferred; the church had to work diligently for several hundred years to set them in place. Yet the church did succeed, in large measure, in stamping out non-Christian practices and in imposing its musical ideals on the populace of Christianized lands. By no means did the church succeed in eradicating all secular music, frivolous or "pleasurable" music--but it did manage to reduce it to a status of such insignificance that we know next to nothing about it for the ensuing one thousand years. There are a number of medieval tracts on music, but the only ones that describe secular music date from the later Middle Ages. It is as if early medieval writers on music were unaware that music existed outside the church. Peasants in their huts and lords in their manors must have continued to enjoy lilting tunes or dances, but by general consensus of opinion this music was of no account; it was the music of the church that mattered, that was "right." Any other sort of music was merely an unfortunate sign of carnal frailty, to be either winked at or excoriated (according to the disposition of the observer), but certainly not to be openly and unabashedly appreciated, acclaimed, and cultivated.

The impulse to make music rises fundamentally from the emotions. This is as true for music in the service of religion as for music in the service of human love, or sorrow, or exaltation. The church's influence, however, limited and severely inhibited the emotional range of music, both in the liturgy and in Christian life in general. (This fact is all the more curious since Christianity is potentially so emotional.) In attempting properly to understand and evaluate early Christian attitudes toward music, especially in light of the completely transformed and entrenched attitudes about music that prevail in our own time, it is important to consider what the sources do *not* say as well as what they do say. There is no mention (and certainly no praise) of music's power to rouse violent, strong emotions. About the closest the Church Fathers ever come to this is St. Basil's assertion that "a psalm brings a tear even from a heart of stone" (St. Basil, *Homily on the First Psalm* II; trans. in Strunk, *Source Readings*, p. 65). Nor is there ever a hint that music should be used to induce religious feeling. In fact, it is this very power of music to serve as a sort of "holy anaesthetic," paralyzing the rational mind, that St. Augustine deplored (see p. 59 above). Early Christian song may indeed have been calming, but it was also meant to be actively sung (or more accurately, prayed), rather than to be listened to. As a

---

[69]See Abert, *Die Musikanschauung*, p. 85. For a fuller explanation of the doctrine of contrition and penance and its effect on the early church's view of music, see Quasten, *Music and Worship in Pagan and Christian Antiquity*, pp. 94-98.

number of passages quoted above indicate, it required mental attentiveness, not mindless narcosis. The idea of religious background music would have been totally abhorrent to the early Christian church.

What sort of liturgical music would result from the restrictions imposed by the early church? Of necessity, it would be music characterized in the following ways: vocal, emphasizing the text (especially the Psalms); occasionally exhibiting an element of ecstasy (though increasingly carefully moderated); primarily objective, with a limited emotional range; rhythmically subtle; calm, tranquil, and noble; conducive to spiritual (as opposed to sensual) worship; exhibiting minimal variety or novelty; evoking minimal sensual pleasure. These characteristics correspond, of course, to ecclesiastical chants of all types, both Eastern and Western. They (the characteristics) became the ideals of Western sacred music, and later sacred-secular arguments are not conceivable without them as a basis. Other cultures (even those as close as ancient Greece and Israel) used instruments and dance in their religious rites; the church rejected them. Other cultures (e.g., ancient Greece and Rome) featured drama as a part of religious observances; drama per se entered the Christian church only at the dawn of the late Middle Ages. Other religions featured loud noises and other sensual elements in worship; Christianity shunned them. "Sacred" musical characteristics came to mean, for later ages, "consonant with the attitudes of the early Christian church toward music."

5

Integration and Transmission

At the beginning of the Middle Ages the church was poised to do something significant in the area of music:

- It had a vital, flourishing cultic life, with the practice of music firmly imbedded in it.

- It had laid the foundation for developing a mythology in which music had a central role.

- It had generated a viable means of continually celebrating and revivifying that mythology in cultic celebrations: the liturgical year.[1]

- It had established the impossibility of uncritically borrowing its entire musical practice from any external source, either Jewish or pagan, and had thus committed itself to establishing an indigenous musical tradition.

What the Western (proto-Roman Catholic) church yet lacked, though, was a definitive model for synthesizing the Greek philosophical tradition in music (which understood music as being of ultimate significance) with the Jewish, biblical theological heritage--in other words, a proof-text (or texts) that would legitimize the integration of musico-theological ideas into the gradually coalescing body of Christian myth. The church also lacked a means of propagating and transmitting to future generations the doctrines resulting from that integration. The synthesis it achieved in large measure through two seminal treatises: St. Augustine's *De musica* and Boethius's *De institutione musica*; the means of propagation and transmission it gained by means of the triumph of

---

[1] See: Talley, *The Origins of the Liturgical Year*.

broad scholarship over monastic asceticism and by schools, connected at first with monastic foundations and later with cathedrals.

ST. AUGUSTINE: *DE MUSICA*

The earliest Christian treatise on music is St. Augustine's *De Musica*,[2] written between A.D. 387 and 389. It immediately presents a number of problems to anyone who attempts to study it for musical purposes:

1. Both the language and the thought of the treatise are difficult to follow.

2. By Augustine's own admission it is incomplete, consisting of only the first six out of a projected twelve books. The six books that do exist are primarily introductory in nature and are concerned mostly with rules of prosody, the proper structure of Latin poetical forms according to antique meters. (Poetry was, of course, still declaimed by singing, and thus its study was inseparable from that of music.)

3. The treatise is very early, belonging in time more to the patristic than to the medieval church. Thus

4. the extent of its influence on later authors is not clear (and is accorded varying degrees of significance, depending on which modern scholar one is reading[3]), since it espouses the type of neo-Pythagoreanism and neo-Platonism that could just as easily be derived from other sources (e.g., Boethius).

In spite of the difficulties, the ideas the treatise introduces are crucial to the process of integrating pagan learning into a Christian theological approach to music. In these six books Augustine displays not only the extent to which his aesthetics were formed by the classical educational curriculum, but also the outlook, inherited from antiquity and perpetuated throughout the Middle Ages, that immutable and unquestionable truth is to be found in the corpus of

---

[2] There is a translation of the entire treatise by Robert C. Taliaferro in Vol. 2 of the *Writings of St. Augustine*. There is also an English synopsis done by W. F. Jackson Knight, and Book VI in English translation is included in Edward A. Lippman, ed., *Musical Aesthetics: a historical reader*, vol. I, pp. 21-67.

[3] Most modern texts on the history of medieval music do not even mention the treatise, apparently agreeing with Gustave Reese (*Music in the Middle Ages*, p. 52) that "Boethius and Cassiodorus produced writings that were to render them the two great intermediaries between ancient and medieval music." Indeed, scholars of the last century dismissed the treatise as a shoddy piece of work (see William R. Bowen, "St. Augustine in Medieval and Renaissance Musical Science", p. 29, and Robert J. Forman, "Augustine's Music: "Keys" to the Logos," pp. 17-8, both in La Croix, *Augustine on Music*). William Waite (*The Rhythm of Twelfth-Century Polyphony*, pp. 8, 29, 35-39), on the other hand, suggests that Augustine's thought may have heavily influenced the rhythmic modes of twelfth-century polyphony, and Nino Pirrotta (*Music and Culture in Italy*, p. 17), suggests that the treatise may be the source for the medieval system of church modes as well as the rhythmic modes.

traditional (i.e., Greek) learning. Augustine clearly considers music a science, and an important one. He holds that music is an expression of the formative power of number that underlies and orders all of creation. Music for him is a matter of mathematical law and order, in perfect harmony with all other facets of organized existence and subject to the same fundamental rules.

Augustine begins by defining music as "*ars bene modulandi*," a definition repeated by later Christian writers, for example, Cassiodorus (sixth century) and Isidore of Seville (seventh century). The definition may be translated literally as the "art [actually, "science"] of modulating well;" but that translation is likely to mean little to a modern reader, and so it is necessary to delve further into the Latin meaning. The crucial word is, of course, "*modulandi*." It has to do with order, and thus Erik Routley translates the definition as "the art of the well-ordered." [4] Otto von Simson, however, comes closer to Augustine's own precise definition of the term when he writes that "the science of good modulation is concerned with the relating of several musical units according to a module, a measure, in such a way that the relationship can be expressed in simple arithmetical ratios."[5]

Thus Augustine conceives of music in terms of mathematics, like Plato and other Pythagoreans. This becomes even more evident in the key words that Augustine uses throughout the treatise: for example, *numerositas*, the quality that good poetry and good music exhibit, by which the hearer may perceive that they are in agreement with universal truth (i.e., cosmic harmony); or *numeri*, the various means or faculties by which humans are enabled to apprehend that harmony. (There are five of them: in the sound itself, in hearing, in pronouncing, in memory, and in the intellect.) Augustine indeed subscribes to the idea that music is a means of apprehending cosmic truth and perfection through the number and measure inherent in it.

The laws of numbers are important to Augustine because only by their objective, mathematical certainty can we demonstrate the certainty of God--and by applying the numbers to a stretch of time [i.e., to quantitative poetic meter] he succeeds in making man conscious of himself as a being living in time. Man can find only in his soul the *numeri* testifying to the existence of God; numbers and their laws are higher than human reason. Music (and metrical poetry) is based on numbers and develops in time; how could music not bear witness to God? (Spitzer, *Classical and Christian Ideas of World Harmony*, pp. 28-29)

Of the five *numeri*, four are in the senses; these Augustine considers less dependable than the fifth *numerus*, the "judicial" (the ability to evaluate, to judge), which resides in the human intellect and which alone is absolute.

The source of pleasure in music Augustine calls *aequalitas* (another mathematical term), "symmetry" or "balance." It is possible for an approximate *aequalitas*, he says, to please the senses, but this is "shameful"--only the intellect can perceive and appreciate true *aequalitas*. Thus only by the exercise of reason and contemplation can one come to comprehend what is good in music. The refusal to engage in this exercise of reason and the satisfaction with

---

[4]Routley, *The Church and Music*, p. 57.
[5]Simson, *The Gothic Cathedral*, p. 21.

what is inferior Augustine attributes to the love of doing rather than knowing. That in turn proceeds from the ultimate sin of pride: trusting one's own powers and will over God's.

Augustine's dependence on antique thought is evident: the central role of mathematics in music, the primacy of the intellect, the superiority of the man of thought to the man of action. He expresses all of this, however, in theological terms that shift the concern for proper music from the earthly to the cosmic, and the condemnation of bad music from human dissoluteness to sin against divine law.

The same tension characteristic of Augustine's personal feelings toward music (Chap. 4, p. 59) upon reflection also becomes evident in his scholarly treatment of it. He unquestionably conceived of music as a gift of God, and a significant one at that, yet he believed it is very easy to misuse it, and the consequences of that misuse are grievous indeed. The passage quoted earlier from the *Confessions* might lead us to suspect that Augustine's view of music was puritanical.[6] Only by comparing that passage with the *De Musica* does it become possible to understand how Augustine (together with many other early Church Fathers) was fundamentally at odds with a puritanical attitude toward music. The puritanical suspicion of music resides entirely in its ability to seduce the senses. Augustine had to hold this suspicion in tension with an exalted philosophical and theological estimation of music that has no parallel in puritanical attitudes.

Augustine's *Six Books on Music* stand in the tradition of Pythagorean music theory. The resounding order of the cosmos, however, no longer rests in itself but is the work of the Divine Creator. It is God who has created the harmony and consonance in microcosm and macrocosm... If earthly music thereby becomes an image of the heavenly, its worth and honor are not lessened but rather infinitely heightened. (Söhngen, "Music and Theology," p. 3)

BOETHIUS: *DE INSTITUTIONE MUSICA*

There is general agreement among scholars that the *De Institutione Musica*[7] by Boethius (c.480-c.524) is fundamental to all subsequent medieval musical philosophy and theology. His description of the three levels of music--*mundana, humana, instrumentalis*--was adopted or modified by later writers up to the Renaissance. Even as late as the fifteenth century the German musical scholar Adam of Fulda disparaged unlearned musicians by accusing them of being ignorant of Boethius's statement in the twenty-fourth chapter of the first book of his *Institutione*: "the musician is one who contemplates...by reason."[8]

It must be said at the outset that Boethius's work produced no new ideas about music. This Roman politician and gentleman was no innovator. Rather, he

---

[6]The word is used here to denote an ascetic suspicion or outright rejection of art on moral grounds, characteristic of early Christian monasticism; see Chapter 4, p. 57ff.

[7]Calvin M. Bower has translated the treatise into English as *Fundamentals of Music*. Parts of Book I are also translated in Strunk, *Source Readings*, pp. 79-86.

[8]See Gerbert, *Scriptores ecclesiastici*, vol. III, p. 347.

synthesized and summarized the vast treasury of knowledge accumulated in antiquity (not only in music, but in other classical disciplines as well) and transmitted it to his successors. An enormously erudite scholar, Boethius was conversant enough with Greek learning to pass for a native Greek. We need only recall just how scarce antique treatises in the original Greek were during the Middle Ages, and we begin to understand how indispensable Boethius was for the survival and dissemination of the classical heritage. His introduction to the treatise[9] reveals his extensive dependence on neo-Pythagorean and neo-Platonic concepts.

Boethius bases his argument on the presupposition that music is number made audible, the idea expressed in the legend of Pythagoras and so often repeated by later writers. Music is beautiful to the human ear, not because it possesses any intrinsic perfection of its own, but because it reflects and demonstrates in sound the universal perfection of number. In this way, it is like anything else that is beautiful to the senses: the only reason a thing may be considered beautiful is because it reflects the perfection of number. (To grasp this idea is to understand the medieval conception of beauty.) The source of all beauty, all order, is God, who has created cosmic order and harmony (*musica mundana* in Boethius's terminology: the music of the universe). The world is a reflection of that beauty and order, as is human beauty (Boethius's *musica humana*--not merely physical beauty, but the perfect harmony of body and soul), and all of these beauties may be expressed mathematically in the form of numerical ratios. Those ratios in turn may be perceived by the ear as Boethius's *musica instrumentalis*, sounding music (both vocal and instrumental).[10]

Music possessed no beauty or perfection apart from its role as a reflection of cosmic order. Boethius held that the person best suited to judge and interpret perfection in music was not the practicing musician (the *cantor*, lit. "singer"), but the person who understands the ratios by which music imitates cosmic perfection (the *musicus*):

>...every art...considers reason inherently more honorable than a skill which is practiced by the hand and the labor of an artisan. For it is much better and nobler to know about what someone else fashions than to execute that about which someone else knows; in fact, physical skill serves as a slave, while reason rules like a mistress...
>Thus, there are three classes of those who are engaged in the musical art. The first class consists of those who perform on instruments, the second of those who compose songs, and the third of those who judge instrumental performance and songs...

---

[9]See Strunk, *Source Readings*, pp. 79f.
[10]In this regard, Albert Seay (*Music in the Medieval World*, p. 20) writes:

Thus it is that music stands as a way of depicting the beauty and perfection of God and his creations, the world and man. It is here that music achieves its real place in medieval philosophy, for as a microcosm in the macrocosm it can duplicate on a small scale the power of number inherent in the otherwise almost incomprehensible grand expanse about us.

The third class..., since it is totally grounded in reason and thought, will rightly be esteemed as musical. That person is a musician who exhibits the faculty of forming judgments according to speculation or reason relative and appropriate to music concerning modes and rhythms, the genera of songs, consonances. (Boethius, *De institutione musica*, Book I:34; trans. in Bower, *Fundamentals of Music*, pp. 50-51)

THE CONFLICT BETWEEN THE MONASTIC AND INTELLECTUAL IDEALS

Although Augustine and other early Church Fathers were supportive of the intellectual heritage of antiquity, the early Christian monastic movement was not. It not only had little use for music or the arts in general,[11] but it often rejected the pursuit of secular (i.e., non-biblical) knowledge as detrimental to the development of Christian piety and humility. Thus while the struggles of the early church were against the external pagan environment, the major conflicts of the early medieval church were internal: between those who rejected learning and scholarship and those who promoted it.

Traditionally historians have identified the distinguished Roman statesman and author Flavius Cassiodorus (c.485-c.580) as the champion of the latter position. Sometime after the year 554 Cassiodorus founded a monastery at his country home at Vivarium in Italy and undertook the direction of its principal activity, its scholarship, establishing a library and scriptorium with a small number of monks who copied manuscripts and translated Greek scholarly treatises into Latin. While it is not clear how much direct influence this scholarly activity, however intense and laudable it may have been, exerted on the future development of medieval monasticism, it seems certain that Cassiodorus's writings, especially his *Institutiones*, were an important step toward the eventual broad cultivation of learning that came to characterize the life of many medieval monasteries. Cassiodorus explicitly sanctioned the study of antique non-Christian learning, declaring it useful for the interpretation of profane matters found in the Bible.[12]

...the second book [of the *Institutiones*]...concerns the arts and disciplines of liberal letters...whatever will be found in the Divine Scriptures concerning such matters will generally be better understood because of previous knowledge. For it is agreed that in the origin of spiritual wisdom...evidences of these matters were sown abroad in the manner of seeds, which instructors in secular letters later most wisely transferred to their own rules. (Cassiodorus, Preface to the *Institutiones*; in Cassiodorus Senator, *An Introduction to Divine and Human Readings*, trans. L. W. Jones, p. 70)

The primary advocate of the earlier monastic attitude that rejected the study of non-Christian learning is usually identified as Pope Gregory the Great (reigned 590-604). Gregory seems not to have been the implacable foe of classical culture that some have made him; rather, he regarded it as subordinate to that higher

---

[11] See Quasten, *Music and Worship in Pagan and Christian Antiquity*, pp. 94-97.

[12] See also Cassiodorus, *Institutiones*, Book I, XXVII, "On Figures of Speech and the Liberal Arts," trans. as Cassiodorus Senator, *An Introduction to Divine and Human Readings*, trans. L. W. Jones, p. 127.

Integration and Transmission   79

quest for knowledge and wisdom whose goal is the knowledge of God.[13] Gregory was, however, a dedicated monastic, yearning for the ascetic life even when the course of events thrust him into the papacy. He admired Benedict of Nursia to the extent that he wrote a biography of this founder of organized Western monasticism. Gregory's writings, with their emphasis on superstition and miraculous happenings, breathe more the spirit of the incipient Middle Ages than the broad-minded tolerance and inquisitiveness of classical authors. He never learned Greek, and more important, he had an abiding suspicion of Greek culture, even an antipathy for it. He seems to have had no more love for music (either practical or speculative) than for any other branch of classical learning.

Gregory's biographer, John the Deacon (writing almost three centuries after Gregory's reign), credited him with the foundation of the Roman *schola cantorum* and the compilation of books of chant.

St. Gregory compiled a book of antiphons. He founded a *schola* which to this day performs the chant in the Church of Rome, according to his instructions. He also erected two dwellings for it, at St. Peter's and at the Lateran palace, where are venerated the couch from which he gave lessons in chant, the whip with which he threatened the boys, and the authentic antiphonal. (John the Deacon, *Life of Gregory the Great*, written 873-875; trans. in Van Dijk, "Papal Schola *versus* Charlemagne," p. 23)

Sources stemming from this one gave rise to the popular medieval belief that Gregory wrote the chant that bears his name while under divine inspiration (thus the manifold medieval representations of Gregory at a desk writing music, with the Holy Spirit in the form of a dove perched on his shoulder singing into his ear; Illustration 2). The preponderance of scholarly opinion suggests, however, that Gregory's involvement with the Roman *schola cantorum* (an institution that almost certainly pre-dates Gregory's reign) appears to have been more to organize and regulate it than to promote its activities, and that the compilation of chant books is more properly attributed to the reigns of other sixth- and seventh-century popes.[14] Later popes who were products of schools that Gregory established reflect the limited scope of those schools' curricula. Those popes evince an interest only in the most basic sort of education: grammar, the study of scripture, and music only insofar as needed for the conduct of the liturgy.

THE RESOLUTION OF THE CONFLICT

Although Cassiodorus's and Gregory's roles in the contest between the monastic attitude and the continuation of classical pagan learning are not entirely unequivocal, the tension between the two outlooks was very real. It persisted throughout the patristic period and beyond. Primary credit for the triumph of broad learning and scholarship in monasticism must be given to the Scottish and Irish monks, whose missionary activities in Western Europe during the seventh

---

[13] see Richards, *Consul of God*, pp. 27-29.
[14] see Ibid., pp. 124-5.

80   Wiser than Despair

Illustration 2:
Pope Gregory the Great receives chant from the Holy Spirit in the form of a dove.

Source: Ms.Clm 17403; courtesy of the Bavarian State Library, Munich, Germany.

and eighth centuries not only spurred the growth of Christianity, but also provided the intellectual basis for the Carolingian Renaissance. The struggle between Irish monastic cultivation of learning and art and the earlier monastic ideal is paradigmatic of the constant tug-of-war between liberal and restrictive attitudes that characterized most of the history of the church after the patristic period.

In about A.D. 590, the year of St. Gregory's elevation to the throne of St. Peter, the Irish missionary monk St. Columbanus and his companions took up residence in the kingdom of the Franks, in present-day France. Their missionary journey had been foreshadowed twenty-five years earlier by St. Columba (Columbcille), who had founded a monastic community at Iona, an island off the west coast of Scotland, in about 565. These two events mark the beginning of an Irish missionary effort that persisted throughout the seventh and eighth centuries. The reasons for this sudden missionary expansion are obscure; a passion for spreading the gospel surely figured into it, but the monks who forsook their homeland may also have been impelled by *Wanderlust*, by a thirst for learning that drew them closer to the sources of antique culture, and, later, by the depredations of the Norse raiders who wrought havoc in Ireland in the eighth and ninth centuries.

Even more surprising than this unexpected missionary thrust is the cultivation of a broad spectrum of learning and a love for classical writings that accompanied the Irish monks and became characteristic of life in the monasteries they founded. Again, the reasons for this are obscure; early Irish monasticism on its own native soil was characterized more by eremitism and self-abnegation than by the pursuit of knowledge. That the fifth-century pre-eminence of Irish bishops (beginning with St. Patrick) yielded in the sixth century to the supremacy of the monasteries with their powerful abbots may figure into the relatively sudden cultivation of letters. So may the fact that Ireland was the only Christian land that had never bowed under the yoke of imperial Rome, thus making the pagan matrix of antique learning less of a stigma for the Irish church. What can be said with certainty is that wherever the Irish monks gained a foothold on the continent, there scholarship flourished. Wherever they went, the Irishmen "were surrounded by an aura of superior learning."[15]

The Irish zeal for learning was sufficiently mature by the end of the sixth century to accompany the monks on their earliest missionary journeys. During the abbacy of St. Columba, Iona had a scriptorium of considerable importance. Scribes held places of honor in the monastic community; indeed, the care and skill lavished on manuscripts that survive from this milieu[16] bear witness to the importance of scribal activity. At an early date there grew up a distinct class of monks, the *fratres operarii* (working brothers) who undertook the manual labor necessary to operate the monastery, thus freeing the scholars to concentrate on their specialized labors. The Irish missionary effort and its attendant love of learning spread to northern England as well. Alcuin, the English cleric whose keen intellect spearheaded the Carolingian Renaissance, in all probability owed some part of his early education to Irish monks.

---

[15] Bieler, *Ireland*, p. 13.
[16] such as the Book of Kells, which may have been created in Iona's scriptorium; see Bieler, *Ireland*, p. 41.

The Irish monastic presence on the continent, however, is more adequately documented than that in Britain. After St. Columbanus's arrival in 590, the Irish spread very quickly across west-central Europe, evangelizing the populace and founding monasteries in Burgundy, Flanders, northern Italy, Switzerland, Bavaria, Franconia, and Lotharingia. The monastic houses they founded or populated--Luxeuil, Bobbio, St. Gall, Reichenau--were gradually absorbed into the administrative structure of the local church. Most of them eventually adopted the Rule of St. Benedict, relinquishing the rules they had imported from Ireland, and by recruiting monks from the native populations they wove themselves into the fabric of life in their adopted lands. In one way, however, they decisively transformed St. Benedict's intentions. The original intent of Benedict's rule was that the monks' study should serve only to further Christian piety, but in the Irish foundations scholarship and the cultivation of a broad spectrum of arts and letters became a central feature of monastic life. It was at this point that monasteries assumed their decisive role in the preservation, cultivation, and dissemination of culture (including, of course, that of pagan antiquity), led by men of genius--at first Irish (*Scotti*, as they are called in contemporary continental sources) and then pupils of the Irish intellectual pioneers. The schools in these monasteries flourished and ultimately became the fountainheads of the Carolingian Renaissance.[17]

Speculative theology again began to flourish, and musical speculation based on it blossomed as well. After a lapse of two centuries, the Boethian *musicus* once again lived and thrived, incarnated in the Irish scholar-monks and their pupils. As examples we may mention the Irishman Moengal (Marcellus) and his native pupils Tuotilo, Ratpert and Notker Balbulus at the monastery of St. Gall. The most important musical figure of this period, however, is Johannes Scotus Erigena or Eriugena (810-886), an Irish monk ("Eriugena" means "scion of Ireland") who together with his followers Remigius of Auxerre (841?-908?) and Regino of Prüm (860?-915) was responsible for the first important medieval contribution to the continued development of speculative musical philosophy/theology.

Erigena's scheme of the levels of music (based in turn on the thought of Dionysius the Areopagite and Martianus Capella) differs in its particulars from that described by Boethius. He posits only two kinds of music. The first is *musica naturalis*.

Natural music is that which is made by no instruments nor by the touch of fingers, nor by any touch or instigation of man: it is modulated by nature alone under divine

---

[17]Ludwig Bieler (*Ireland*, pp. 104 & 115) writes:

It is hardly an exaggeration to say that between 600 and 750 the Irish--first alone and later together with the Anglo-Saxons --constitute the decisive cultural factor throughout the territory of the future Carolingian Empire.... The so-called Carolingian Renaissance is not so much a revival of classical antiquity as a "renaissance" of late-antique Christianity, in particular of the age of the great Fathers of the Church. Speculative theology, which had been at a low ebb for two centuries, is resumed with a new vigour.

Integration and Transmission   83

inspiration, teaching the sweet modes, such as there is in the motion of the sky or in the human voice. (Regino of Prüm, *Epistola de harmonica institutione*, trans. in Bower, "Natural and Artificial Music," p. 21)

Natural music, then, is comparable to Boethius's *musica mundana* and *musica humana*. The other kind of music is *musica artificialis*, which Regino defines as music conceived and invented by human art and genius and produced by certain instruments. This second kind of music, then, is equivalent to Boethius's *musica instrumentalis*. (The term *artificialis* subsequently passed through various transformations in meaning and ultimately figured in the musical controversies that accompanied the shift in musical ideas resulting from the rise of humanism, discussed in Chapter 12 below). Despite the differences in terminology, it is clear that the schemes of Boethius and Erigena are fundamentally compatible: both are predicated on a musical hierarchy in which there is a kind of celestial music at the top and the sounding music produced by human activity at the bottom. For Erigena and his followers, the only way to comprehend *musica naturalis* was to begin with music that can be sensed, *musica artificialis*.

But to anyone wishing to have a knowledge of that art [i.e., music], it must be known that, though natural music is far superior to artificial music, no one can know the power of natural music except by the study of artificial. That is why no matter how much the learned discussion of our argument begins with the natural, we must end in the artificial, so that we can prove things invisible by things visible. (Regino of Prüm, *Epistola de harmonica institutione*, trans. in Bower, "Natural and Artificial Music," p. 22)

Erigena and his followers moved beyond Boethius, however, in asserting that *musica naturalis* (properly understood) was that kind of church music sung within the framework of the eight church modes. This was of great significance for the future development of church music, since it established that the method by which the church ordered its music here on earth was a reflection of divine order, of cosmic harmony--the rules governing church music *practice* proceeded directly from the mind of God.

Consequently the beauty of the whole universe is arranged according to an extraordinary harmony of things similar and dissimilar; it is coupled from diverse genera and forms, from different orders of substances and accidents into a certain indescribable unity. Just as the melody of organum consists of diverse qualities and quantities of sounds which, when heard separately, sound largely out of tune with themselves because they rise and fall in separate proportions, but, when heard together in singular modes according to the rational rules of the musical art, they render a certain natural charm; so the harmony of the universe is wedded together into a whole as subdivisions of nature are brought in accordance with the will of the creator, but these subdivisions seem to disagree with each other when examined individually. (Johannes Scotus Erigena, *De Divisione Naturae*; trans. in Bower, "Natural and Artificial Music," p. 28-29)

The above passage offers yet another reinforcement for the platonic idea that the theorist (here the theologian) is the true musical authority, the judge and guide for practicing musicians. It also contains what may be one of the earliest references to polyphony, suggesting that from its very beginning the practice of polyphony was closely linked with musical speculation.

MUSIC IN MEDIEVAL SCHOOLS AND UNIVERSITIES

The means by which the musical doctrines of writers such as St. Augustine, Boethius, and Erigena were propagated and transmitted to future generations of scholars and theologians were the schools that were a normal component of most medieval monastic houses. Such doctrines received all the more emphasis, since in these schools' curricula (derived from the classical educational curriculum of antiquity) music was grouped with disciplines that are today considered humanities: grammar, rhetoric, dialectic (the *trivium*) and arithmetic, geometry, and astronomy (which together with music made up the *quadrivium*, the intermediate studies that served as a preparation for philosophy and theology).

Instruction in music theory and practice (as well as in other arts and letters) was the responsibility of the monastic schools during the early Middle Ages, but after the tenth century it was increasingly taken over by the cathedral schools. Among the most prominent we might name those at the cathedrals of Chartres, Rheims, and Laon in France, Liège and Utrecht in the Low Countries, Freising and Cologne in Germany. These schools included in their curricula not only the preparatory studies of the *trivium* for younger boys, but also the higher disciplines of the *quadrivium*. The fundamental reason for the existence of the cathedral school (the *maîtrise*), however, came to be the rehearsal and performance of polyphonic liturgical music. This eventually evolved into the very *raison d'etre* of the school's existence.[18]

Although the *maîtrise* has survived in some form or another up to the present day, it remained the vital mainstay of musical practice at cathedrals and other large churches until the eighteenth century. The *Thomasschule* at Leipzig, over which J. S. Bach presided as cantor, was just such an institution. Haydn received his early training in the *maîtrise* of St. Stephen's Cathedral in Vienna-- though by his time the institution had so badly deteriorated that his general education was poor and his musical training both uneven and unpleasant. The Renaissance Franco-Flemish composers were all products of such schools (of which the *maîtrises* at Cambrai and Liège may be cited as leading examples). Of course, not all the graduates of these schools became professional musicians. Many matriculated at universities in other disciplines, and thus became leaders of society and culture in their day. The *maîtrise* as an educational institution therefore served to ensure not only the continuing central role of music in education and character formation (cf. the ancient Greek concept of *paideia*), but also an intelligentsia in medieval and Renaissance Europe that was both musically literate and inculcated with the doctrines of speculative music.

The cathedral *maîtrises* in turn gave birth to the earliest universities, and the cultivation of speculative music eventually shifted from the *maîtrise* to the uni-

---

[18]See Ellefsen, "Music and Humanism" (diss.), pp. 67-68.

versity.[19] Actually, both speculative and practical music found a place in the universities. Practical music-making assumed a significant role in university life in general, yet the very nature of the university demanded that it remain outside the university curriculum. Up until the end of the sixteenth century, however, musical speculation was retained as an integral part of that curriculum.[20]

The statutes of the philosophical faculty of the University of Leipzig in the fifteenth and sixteenth centuries mention among the books to be read the "*Musica* of [the fourteenth century philosopher and mathematician Jean de] Muris." The same is true in the venerable old universities of Vienna, Louvain, Heidelberg, Basel, Cracow, Tübingen, Greifswald, Königsberg, Padua, Bologna and Salamanca. The famous theoretician Salinas, active in Salamanca about 1577, wrote with pride on the title page of his work, *In Academia Salamanticensi Musicae Professor.* (Lang, *Music in Western Civilization,* p. 310)

The extraordinary longevity and vitality of the *quadrivium* as the central focus of the cathedral school curriculum and as the basis for university studies paralleled and supported the continued growth and evolution of church music theory, composition, and practice. The passing of the ancient curriculum in schools and universities also coincided with the beginning of the gradual decline of church music from a position of musical pre-eminence to its present place at the margin of musical life and activity.

---

[19]Nan Carpenter (*Music in the Medieval and Renaissance Universities*, p. 131) writes:

In general, by the end of the twelfth century the monastic schools no longer offered the scientific disciplines: until the rise of the universities, only in the schools of the great cathedrals did the encyclopedic studies find a place. As the medieval universities developed from the cathedral schools "when the intellectual enthusiasm of the Middle Ages began to flow in a distinct channel from its religious enthusiasm," the cathedral schools lost their best scholars and teachers, and the higher studies ceased to be taught. With the rise of the universities in the thirteenth century, it was left to these institutions to continue the tradition of the seven liberal sciences, music among them as an integral part of the mathematical quadrivium and as a living art.

[20]For a detailed history of this relationship, see Carpenter, *Music in the Medieval and Renaissance Universities.*

6

Interlude: Ecclesiastical Authority in Theory and Practice

As late classical antiquity evolved into the Middle Ages, an increasingly unstable political situation--in part the product of internal uncertainty in the wake of a constant succession of new emperors, in part due to external invasion by barbarian hoards from the north and the east--led to the gradual but inexorable disintegration of the weakened Roman Empire. In attempting to counteract the process of decay, emperors beginning with Diocletian in the third century began to divide the unwieldy Empire into the more manageable divisions of East and West. This led to a complete separation between the two halves at the death of the Emperor Theodosius in 395. The Eastern (Byzantine) Empire managed to maintain enough internal stability to survive until the late Middle Ages. The Western Empire, however, bore the brunt of the collapse. Therefore, although an increasingly christianized Western culture continued to respect and to make use of the cultural heritage of classical antiquity, it could do so only fragmentarily and at a great disadvantage. Its separation from the East deprived it not only of contact with the primary sources of ancient learning, but even of familiarity with Greek as a living language. Until the later Middle Ages, Western involvement with Greek philosophical achievements had to take place through the medium of (often faulty) Latin translations. In such troubled times, the Christian church offered the only semblance of security and permanence, and its monasteries the sole haven for scholarly pursuits.

The church, established as the state religion of the Roman Empire in the early fourth century, was led gradually to widen its control over all facets of human life and thought. As it began to fill in part the vacuum in temporal power left by the Empire's wane, the church's vitality and resolve, operating in tandem with the evolving medieval feudal system, gradually brought about a situation whose ramifications are almost unimaginable today in the New World and are rapidly becoming so today in Europe. Those ramifications are so sweeping that it would take an encyclopedia to catalog them. The modern mind cannot hope to understand them all, much less empathize with them. A partial list of the

88   Wiser than Despair

results of the changes will have to suffice to suggest how fundamentally different the medieval order was from presently prevailing conditions:

- Financial support for *all* church endeavors was derived from taxes and from endowments in the form of land and business enterprises. In no way, then, was the church dependent on popular opinion to support its activities or its intentions financially. In fact, it dictated in large measure what popular opinion would be.

- All facets of the church's life came to be controlled more and more by the feudal elite. The nobility, the aristocracy, really were conceived as "better people" than the peasants, and the great majority of people looked up to and admired them (or at least they admired the ideal of nobility). The higher clergy, and even the monks in important monasteries, were more and more frequently from aristocratic families; if they were not, training and social contact soon taught them the advantages of behaving as if they were. All activities in the church (including music) were geared to the learned ecclesiastical aristocracy.

- The medieval church continued and intensified the conservatism of the early church. From earliest times the Church of Rome had a reputation for conservatism; she clung stubbornly to long-established traditions and was extraordinarily cautious about any sort of innovation. Developments in all areas of Christian theology, including music, had to be interpreted as extensions or further explanations of already existing and established truth. In this context, the shreds of antique learning that were preserved came to assume a status almost as unassailable as Scripture.

- The church held a total hegemony over the spiritual dimension of life. Indeed, it was all-pervasive.[1] Other forms of religion (e.g., vestiges of earlier Celtic religions, or Judaism) were not simply repressed; they were increasingly inconceivable to the vast majority of the European populace. The church's ideals became more and more established until an intensely Christian spirit permeated every aspect of medieval life, affecting in particular all artistic endeavors.

    Difficulty of empathy, of genuinely entering into the mental and emotional values of the Middle Ages, is the final obstacle [to understanding them]. The main barrier is, I believe, the Christian religion as it then was: the matrix and law of medieval life, omnipresent, indeed compulsory. Its insistent principle that the life of the spirit and of the afterworld was superior to the here and now, to material life on earth, is one that the modern world does not share, no matter how devout some present-day Christians may be. (Tuchman, *A Distant Mirror*, p. xix)

- Medieval Christians were just as fully world-conscious as their early Christian forebears. The fundamental continuity of the spiritual and physical world was a perception shared in common by all from peasant to pope, from serf to scholar. Indeed, the collapse of civilization and the retreat of learning created a

---

[1] See Routley, *The Church and Music*, p. 75.

situation particularly favorable to a recrudescence of coarser forms of superstition and magic.

People [of the fourteenth century] lived close to the inexplicable. The flickering lights of marsh gas could only be fairies or goblins; fireflies were the souls of unbaptized dead infants. In the terrible trembling and fissures of an earthquake or the setting afire of a tree by lightning, the supernatural was close at hand. Storms were omens, death by heart attack or other seizures could be the work of demons. Magic was present in the world: demons, fairies, sorcerers, ghosts, and ghouls touched and manipulated human lives; heathen superstitions and rituals abided among the country folk, beneath and even alongside the priest and sacraments. (Tuchman, *A Distant Mirror*, pp. 54-55)

All manifestations of the supernatural were an accepted factor in scientific theory and investigation, and all were commonly viewed as belonging to the realm of religion. Thus the attribution of a supernatural function and power to music was nothing out of the ordinary; on the contrary, it conformed quite naturally to the prevalent view of the world and its operation.

- There was an almost total emphasis on God's radical transcendence, to the exclusion of his immanent, personal quality. (This latter aspect of the deity is understood today as having been represented by the mother figure of the Blessed Virgin and also by the saints.) God (together with His Son, Jesus Christ) was typically viewed as the righteous King, the terrible judge (cf. the sculpted scenes of the Last Judgment that adorn the tympana of medieval cathedral portals), the holy, incomprehensible, unapproachable One who could best be addressed through the medium of the intercession of the Blessed Virgin and the saints.

- The authority of the teaching office of the church (the *magisterium*) to determine theological and liturgical matters had come to be equivalent in force to the authority of Scripture. The church's liturgy, therefore, was splendid, ceremonial, and ritualistic in part because it was considered to be the divinely revealed earthly counterpart of the worship of God in heaven.[2] The liturgy

---

[2]cf. Cyril of Jerusalem (fourth century), *Mystagogical Catechesis* V, 6:

We call to mind the Seraphim also, whom Isaiah saw in the Holy Spirit, present in a circle about the throne of God, covering their faces with two wings, their feet with two, and flying with two, and saying: 'Holy, holy, holy is the Lord of hosts' [Isaiah 6:3]. Therefore we recite this doxology [i.e., the Sanctus] transmitted to us by the Seraphim, in order to become participants in the hymnody of the super terrestrial hosts. (McKinnon, *Music in Early Christian Literature*, 157)

What Giulio Cattin says about the hymns of the eastern church may also be applied to those of the medieval Western church:

...according to the *De caelesti hierarchia*, the work of the author known by the name of Dionysius the Areopagite [whose influence on Johannes Scotus Erigena has already been mentioned], an echo of the harmony and beauty of God is transmitted to the hierarchy of heavenly beings and thence to the earthly hierarchy of the Church.

(both Mass and Office) was not meant to be primarily personal (private prayer and meditation took care of that dimension of spirituality), but an earthly reflection of the angels' worship before the throne of God. Paradoxically, because liturgical words, music, and actions were so unquestionably significant, there was no need for the celebrant or singers to *make* them convincing by delivering them emotionally or rhetorically. Thus the medieval liturgy (as well as its music) was remote, impersonal, and objective, intended to mirror a heavenly, cosmic reality instead of an earthly one. There is no more forceful witness to this than the rise of the Cluniac monastic order, with its intricate, splendid (and interminable) liturgical ceremonies, its dazzling array of liturgical accoutrements, and its awesome mother church at Cluny, the largest in Christendom. The divine liturgy was considered primarily a courtly ceremony conducted day and night in homage to the omnipotent King of Heaven, held in "palaces" whose splendor no other buildings on earth could rival.

•Since the liturgy was considered to be not of earthly, but rather of heavenly origin, it became essential, indeed crucial that its conduct be as "perfect" as humanly possible. Ecclesiastical authorities therefore carefully regulated all aspects of it, including music--sometimes in ways that seem quite brutal to modern minds.

At Nocturns, and indeed at all the Hours, if the boys [child novices entrusted to the monastery from an early age] commit any fault in the psalmody or other singing, either by sleeping or such like transgression, let there be no sort of delay, but let them be stripped forthwith of frock and cowl, and beaten in their shirt only, with pliant and smooth osier rods provided for that special purpose. If any of them, weighed down with sleep, sing ill at Nocturns, then the master giveth into his hand a reasonably great book, to hold until he be well awake. At Matins the principal master standeth before them with a rod until all are in their seats and their faces well covered. At their uprising likewise, if they rise too slowly, the rod is straightway over them. In short, meseemeth that any King's son could scarce be more carefully brought up in his palace than any boy in a well-ordered monastery. (*Costumal of St. Benigne,* Dijon[3] (c.1050); trans. in Dent, "The Social Aspects of Music," pp. 190-1.)

In the later Middle Ages the emphasis on "perfection" of execution began at times to overshadow the idea that perfect praise is a matter of the heart, and some writers began to promote the notion that God is praised through perfect

---

The music of the hymns sung in Heaven is revealed by the seraphim to those (prophets and saints) who are gifted with divine inspiration, and from them it is handed on to the inspired musicians who are the composers of liturgical hymns. Therefore the Church's hymns are nothing else than heavenly canticles conveyed from one order of beings to the next as far as the earth, and made perceptible to the human ears of the members of the ecclesiastical hierarchy. (Cattin, *Music of the Middle Ages,* p. 24)

[3]Since the customary of this Benedictine abbey is dated prior to the rigors of the Cistercian monastic reform, this passage does not seem to reflect a degree of severity unusual for its time.

craftsmanship (i.e., "artifice") in the adornment of buildings and liturgies. In writing about the splendid west doors of his abbey church of St. Denis, for example, the twelfth-century French cleric Abbot Suger asserted:

> When--out of my delight in the beauty of the house of God--the loveliness of the many-coloured stones has called me away from external cares, and worthy meditation has induced me to reflect, transferring that which is material to that which is immaterial, on the diversity of the sacred virtues; then it seems to me that I see myself dwelling, as it were, in some strange region of the universe which exists neither entirely in the slime of earth nor entirely in the purity of Heaven; and that, by the grace of God, I can be transported from this inferior to that higher world in an anagogical manner.
>
> Whoever thou art, if thou seekest to extol the glory of these doors.
> Marvel not at the gold and the expense but at the craftsmanship of the work.
> Bright is the noble work; but, being nobly bright, the work
> Should brighten the minds so that they marvel, through the true lights
> To the True Light where Christ is the door.
> In what manner it be inherent in this world the golden door defines;
> The dull mind rises to truth through that which is material
> And, in seeing this light, is resurrected from its former submersion.
> (trans. in Panofsky, *Abbot Suger*, pp. 63-5, 47-9)

• The clergy controlled all music-making in the church; indeed, the clergy *made* all the music in church. By the tenth century the singing of the Ordinary of the Mass had been assigned to the *schola*, a choir normally constituted of clergy who were trained in music, that replaced the singing by the people. Therefore tensions between clergy and musicians could in no wise be compared to those of later centuries, when the exercise of church music came again to be entrusted to the laity.

• In the wake of the widespread acceptance of the humanist attitude, it has become axiomatic that music theory follows practice. This has not always been the case, however. Indeed, by now it should be obvious that during the Middle Ages, under the influence of a Christian neo-Platonic theology of music, music practice followed theory and was carefully controlled by it. Adam of Fulda (fifteenth century) spoke for the entire Middle Ages:

> Truly the author of nature and not man made the consonances which are implanted in nature, for the consonances existed before they appeared to men. For this reason, we take great pains to inquire into these consonances. (Adam of Fulda, *De Musica* III, 368[4])

• "Musicality" meant something quite different than it does today. The idea of musicality is not always and everywhere the same. Basic concepts regarding music are not always in agreement, and thus the music and musical practices that these concepts produce are not always compatible or even mutually

---

[4]In Martin Gerbert, *Scriptores ecclesiastici de musica sacra potissimum*, vol. III, p. 368; trans. in Oskar Söhngen, "Music and Theory: A Systematic Approach," p. 4.

comprehensible. Indeed, musicality is as manifold and diverse as human personality and culture.[5] Thus it cannot be assumed that earlier Christians understood "musicality" in any way as twentieth-century Christians (much less non-Christians) understand it.

> ...we should never forget that music in the Middle Ages was intended not as an appeal to man's subjective irrationality but as an objective reminder of laws ultimately inaccessible to the human mind. (Spitzer, *Classical and Christian Ideas of World Harmony*, p. 36)

The observations offered above are fragmentary and fall far short of forming a complete picture. They may, however, help to suggest some of the ways the prevailing situation affected music-making in the medieval church.

---

[5] cf. Sachs, *Wellsprings of Music*, pp. 218-9.

7

The Golden Age of Musical Speculation

The legitimacy of reinterpreting Greek philosophical ideas to serve a Christian theology of music was well established by the end of the patristic period (ca. A.D. 600). That theology continued to undergo further development for the next thousand years or more. Treatises written toward the end of the Middle Ages, during the fourteenth and fifteenth centuries, betray a gradual loss of momentum in the Græco-Christian synthesis as a vital, evolving nexus of interrelated ideas. Yet even this slackening did not signal the end of the synthesis's vitality, for the revival of interest in ancient learning, a fundamental characteristic of early Renaissance humanism, brought in its wake a renewal of musical speculation.[1] That rebirth lent a new vitality to ancient doctrines that was not entirely spent until the mid-eighteenth century.

A survey of the ideas that figured most prominently in medieval speculation can be conveniently divided into four categories: the idea of cosmic harmony, the Christian adaptation of the Greek doctrine of ethos, the idea of music as a science, and the proliferation of number symbolism.

COSMIC HARMONY

Pythagorean cosmic harmony, also referred to as world harmony or expressed figuratively as the music of the spheres, became a central concept for medieval philosophy/theology. It was transferred from its pagan matrix almost without alteration, the only difference being that now the creator of cosmic harmony was God as revealed in Jesus Christ. Boethius captured the concept in his projection of *musica mundana,* the harmony of the celestial spheres (the macrocosm), in contrast to *musica humana,* the harmony inherent in the human body and its

---

[1] See Toulmin, *Cosmopolis,* p. 39.

relation with the soul (the microcosm) and to *musica instrumentalis*, music that actually sounds on earth. Pope Gregory the Great identified the Greek music of the spheres with the angelic choirs.[2] The seventh-century Christian writer Isidore of Seville asserted that nothing in the universe should be without music: "Thus without music no discipline can be perfect, for there is nothing without it. For the very universe, it is said, is held together by a certain harmony of sounds, and the heavens themselves are made to revolve by the modulation of harmony" (Isidore of Seville, *Etymologiarum* III:17; trans. in Strunk, *Source Readings*, p. 94). Centuries later Honorius of Autun (c.1075-1156) represented God the Creator as playing on a "world cithara": "Summus opifex universum quasi magnam citharam condidit in qua veluti varias chordas ad multiplices sonos reddendos posuit [the all-high creator constituted the universe as a great cithara, in which he placed as it were various strings vibrating in multiple sounds]" (Honorius of Autun; quoted in Spitzer, *Classical and Christian Ideas of World Harmony*, p. 35). The musical classifications of Boethius (and others, such as Erigena) were restated and reinterpreted in numerous late medieval treatises (for example, the *Ars musica* of the thirteenth-century theorist Gill de Zamora[3]). Boethian doctrines (allied with number symbolism) both underlie and pervade Dante's *Divine Comedy*[4] (early fourteenth century), and the teachings of St. Catherine of Siena (1347-1380) also presume the doctrine of world harmony.[5]

This thoroughgoing Christianization of a pagan idea occupied theologians for at least a thousand years. The three sources by which the myth of the music of the spheres was directly bequeathed to medieval Christianity were a Latin translation of Plato's *Timaeus* by Chalcidius (fourth century A.D.), a fragment of the same translated by Cicero in his *Dream of Scipio,* and a neo-Platonic commentary on Cicero by the fourth-century writer Macrobius. Here is the passage as found in Cicero:

"What is this large and agreeable sound that fills my ears?"
"That is produced," he replied," by the onward rush and motion of the spheres themselves; the intervals between them, though unequal, being exactly arranged in a fixed proportion, by an agreeable blending of high and low tones various harmonies are produced; for such mighty motions cannot be carried on so swiftly in silence; and Nature has provided that one extreme shall produce low tones while the other gives forth high. Therefore this uppermost sphere of heaven, which bears the stars, as it revolves more rapidly, produces a high shrill tone, whereas the lowest revolving sphere, that of the moon, gives forth the lowest tone; for the earthly sphere, the ninth, remains ever motionless and stationary in its position in the centre of the universe. But the other eight spheres, two of which move with the same velocity, produce seven different sounds--a number which is the key of almost everything. Learned men, by imitating this harmony on stringed instruments and in song, have gained for themselves a return to this region. (Cicero, *Somnium Scipionis* ; trans. in Hollander, *The Untuning of the Sky*, pp. 29-30)

---

[2]See Spitzer, *Classical and Christian Ideas of World Harmony*, p. 35. Dante expressed a similar thought in his *Divine Comedy: Purgatory* XXX, 92-94.
[3]See Cattin, *Music of the Middle Ages*, p. 187.
[4]See Hopper, *Medieval Number Symbolism*, pp. 136ff.
[5]See Spitzer, *Classical and Christian Ideas of World Harmony*, p. 39.

The Golden Age of Musical Speculation   95

The three sources mentioned above served as the basis for subsequent philosophical and theological speculation.[6] The music of the spheres became one of the most frequent subjects for pictorial representation, even into the Renaissance and beyond.[7] A woodcut (see Illustration 3), from Hartmann Schedel's *Liber chronicarum* (1493), provides one such illustration of the concept of cosmic harmony. In it God is shown sitting above the planetary spheres of the universe, surrounded by angels (several of whom are playing musical instruments) and the four winds.

There is a temptation to view the Renaissance as a bold rejection of medieval ideals (for example, the ideal of a harmoniously ordered universe) in favor of more modern ways of thinking. Yet even though new currents were indeed forming during the fifteenth and sixteenth centuries, there was a fundamental continuity in the prevailing worldview of the Middle Ages and the Renaissance.[8] The Renaissance rejected the Middle Ages by ignoring medieval speculative accretions and vaulting back to newly rediscovered sources from antiquity, but it did not repudiate the cosmic worldview or its attendant musical beliefs and attitudes.[9] The traditional cosmic worldview, though increasingly ignored, questioned, or rejected, continued in some measure to occupy the attention of theorists[10] (and to energize practical artistic developments as well) throughout the Renaissance and even into the eighteenth century. It became extinct as a vital artistic force only with the widespread adoption of new ideals and attitudes in the eighteenth century (the Enlightenment).

The running argument as to whether the planets actually made sound (albeit inaudible to human ears) as they revolved, or whether their music was only

---

[6]See Klibansky, The Continuity of the Platonic Tradition, pp. 28-29.

[7]Kathi Meyer-Baer's book, *Music of the Spheres and the Dance of Death: Studies in Musical Iconology*, provides a comprehensive overview of this tradition of illustration.

[8]See Lang, *Music in Western Civilization*, p. 196; Tillyard, *The Elizabethan World Picture*, pp. 1-6.

[9]As Spitzer writes (*Classical and Christian Ideas of World Harmony*, p. 115):

With the Renaissance, the cosmos has been widened and the landscape of humanity broadened, but the infinite roof of the sky that encompasses the *gran teatro del mundo* has not lost its connection with the microcosmic soul of man: the greater sky is still but an image of the greatness of the human heart possessed of God.

[10]See Gary Tomlinson, *Music in Renaissance Magic*, especially pp. 61ff. and pp. 71 ff.

96 Wiser than Despair

Illustration 3:
Cosmic harmony.

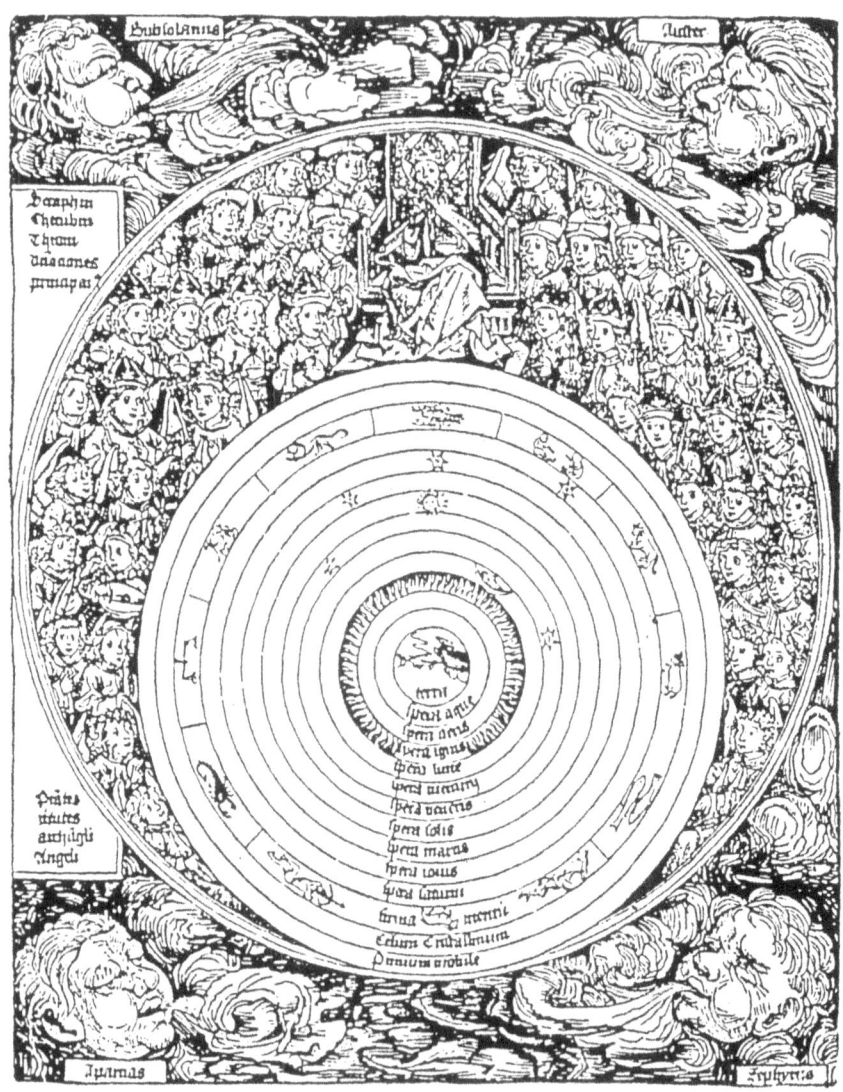

Source: Hartmann Schedel, *Buch der Chroniken* (1493).

mental and never acoustic, bears witness to the continuing vigor of the doctrine of cosmic harmony.[11]

Accordingly the movements of the heavens are nothing except a certain everlasting polyphony (intelligible, not audible) with dissonant tunings, like certain syncopations or cadences (wherewith men imitate these natural dissonances), which tends towards fixed and prescribed clauses [i.e., cadences]--the single clauses having six terms (like voices)--and which marks out and distinguishes the immensity of time with those notes. Hence it is no longer a surprise that man, the ape of his Creator, should finally have discovered the art of singing polyphonically [*per concentum*], which was unknown to the ancients, namely in order that he might play the everlastingness of all created time in some short part of an hour by means of an artistic concord of many voices and that he might to some extent taste the satisfaction of God the Workman with His own works, in that very sweet sense of delight elicited from this music which imitates God. (Johannes Kepler, *The Harmonies of the World*, 1619, p. 1048)

The renewed interest in musical speculation as a result of Renaissance humanism is evident in the number of treatises from the fifteenth century onward that feature discussions of world harmony prominently. Influential treatises throughout the Renaissance and well into the seventeenth century continued to interpret the cosmic worldview (as well as the interrelationship of music and number). These treatises include:

--Marsilio Ficino (1433-1499), *De rationibus musicae*; *Commentary on Timaeus* (both published in 1576)
--Franchinus Gaffurius, *Practica musicae* (1496)
--Gioseffo Zarlino, *Le Istitutioni Harmoniche* (1558)
--Robert Fludd, *Utriusque cosmi...metaphysica, physica atque technica histories* (1617-1624) and *Monochordum mundi symphoniacum* (1622-1625)
--Michael Praetorius, *Syntagma musicum* (1615-1619)

---

[11]Michel de Montaigne (*Essais*, 1580):

The bodies of its circles, being solid smooth, and in their rolling motion, touching and rubbing against another, must of necessity produce a wonderful harmony: by the changes and entercaprings of which, the revolutions, motions, cadences, and carols of the asters and planets, are caused and transported. But that universally the hearing senses of these low world's creatures, dizzied and lulled asleep...by the continuation of that sound, how loud and great soever it be, cannot sensibly perceive or distinguish the same. (trans. Florio, 1603; quoted in Crofton & Fraser, *Dictionary of Musical Quotations*, p. 140:7)

Thomas Stanley (*History of Philosophy*, 1655-1662):

Pythagoras (saith Censorinus) asserted, that the whole world is made according to musical proportion, and that the seven planets...have a harmonious motion...and render various sounds, according to their several heights, so consonant, that they make most sweet melody; but to us inaudible, by reason of the greatness of the noise, which the narrow passages of our ears is not capable to receive. (Quoted in Crofton & Fraser, *Dictionary of Musical Quotations*, p. 140:13)

98   Wiser than Despair

--Johannes Kepler, *Harmonices mundi* (1619)[12]
--Marin Mersenne, *Traité de l'harmonie universelle* (1627)
--Athanasius Kircher, *Musurgia universalis* (1650)

The retrospective speculative tendencies represented in these treatises were fruitful the longest in Northern Europe, especially in England and German-speaking lands. In England, neo-Platonic concepts are especially evident in drama and poetry.

> Ring out, ye crystal spheres,
> Once bless our human ears,
> If ye have power to touch our senses so;
> And let your silver chime
> Move in melodious time,
> And let the bass of heaven's deep organ blow;
> And, with your ninefold harmony,
> Make up full consort to the angelic symphony.
>
> Such music (as 'tis said),
> Before was never made,
> But when of old the sons of morning sung,
> While the Creator great
> His constellations set,
> And the well-balanced world on hinges hung;
> And cast the dark foundations deep,
> And bid the weltering waves their oozy channel keep.
> (John Milton, *Hymn on the Morning of Christ's Nativity*, 1645)

> From harmony, from heavenly harmony,
>   This universal frame began:
> When nature underneath a heap
>   Of jarring atoms lay,
> And could not heave her head,
> The tuneful voice was heard from high,
>   "Arise, ye more than dead!"
> Then cold, and hot, and moist, and dry,
>   In order to their stations leap,
>   And Music's power obey.
> From harmony, from heavenly harmony,
>   This universal frame began:
>   From harmony to harmony
> Through all the compass of the notes it ran,
> The diapason closing full in Man.
>
>   GRAND CHORUS
>
> As from the power of sacred lays
>   The spheres began to move
> And sung the great Creator's praise
>   To all the Blest above;

---

[12]See Stephenson, *The Music of the Heavens*, pp. 3ff.

The Golden Age of Musical Speculation

> So when the last and dreadful hour
> This crumbling pageant shall devour,
> The trumpet shall be heard on high,
> The dead shall live, the living die.
> And Music shall untune the sky!
> (John Dryden, *A Song for St. Cecilia's Day*, 1687)

In German-speaking lands, musical speculation frequently appeared in the writings of music theorists and of philosophers: for example, Praetorius, Kepler, and Kircher (already mentioned above), but later figures as well, such as Andreas Werckmeister (1645-1708).[13] Only in the first half of the eighteenth century did the neo-Platonic viewpoint finally yield in Germany in favor of a more modern, "enlightened" attitude.[14]

THE DOCTRINE OF ETHOS

The ancient Greek doctrine of ethos, as propounded by Plato and others, was built on the premise that music (that is, the right kind of music) is a decisive agent in the formation of good human character. Medieval writers did not mention this doctrine as such, any more than early Christian theologians. Those who did allude to it presented it in the negative, depicting sin (human disobedience against God) as disharmony. Johannes Scotus Erigena, for example (following the ideas of the third-century writer Plotinus), depicted human wickedness as a dissonance introduced into harmony, a dissonance that is, however, the assurance of the ultimate triumph of goodness and harmony and a sign of the inevitable return of humanity to its harmonious origin (since the end of the world will be as its beginning). Even if they did not explicitly mention the doctrine of ethos, subsequent authors assumed it by affirming the complex of ideas surrounding it. Indeed, the curricula of the monastic schools and the cathedral *maîtrîses* were in a sense institutional embodiments of the doctrine of ethos.

The transfer of cosmic harmony into the human harmony that exists between soul and body is fundamental to Boethius's philosophical system, and was taken for granted by all subsequent philosopher-theologians as an integral part of the

---

[13]See Irwin, *Neither Voice nor Heart Alone*, pp. 43ff, p. 115.
[14]Lang, *Music in Western Civilization*, p. 440:

> Beginning with [Johann] Mattheson the philosophical conceptions and empirical leanings of the Enlightenment began to displace entirely the many medieval survivals still extant in earlier baroque musical thought. In his very first work, *Das Neu-Eröffnete Orchestre* (1713), the tendency to turn to the educated music lover instead of to the professional musician is apparent. The ideal of the Enlightenment, the universally cultured man, the *homme galant*, becomes the addressee of dissertations. The aim is no longer to justify new theoretical findings by reconciling them with ancient musical doctrines or to introduce musicians into the art and science of musical composition, but to enable the educated person to "form his tastes, understand the technical terms, so that he can discuss this noble science with understanding." With this begins an entirely new era of musical thought.

doctrine of universal harmony. Macrobius's comment on the final sentence of Cicero's *Dream of Scipio* (quoted above) makes this explicit:

> Every soul in the world is allured by musical sounds so that not only those who are more refined in their habits, but all the barbarous peoples as well, have adopted songs by which they are inflamed with courage or wooed to pleasure; for the soul carries with it into the body a memory of the music which it knew in the sky, and is so captivated by its charm that there is no breast so cruel or savage as not to be gripped by the spell of such an appeal. (Macrobius, *Commentary on the Dream of Scipio*, p. 195)

By imitating in their *musica instrumentalis*, their practical music, the ideal order of world harmony, human beings (the microcosms) could in some small way tune themselves to the *musica mundana*, could order themselves in harmony with the music of the spheres (the macrocosm), and thus could regain the prior good state of their souls before they were marred by sin.

> The discipline of music is diffused through all the actions of our life. First, it is found that if we perform the commandments of the Creator and with pure minds obey the rules he has laid down, every word we speak, every pulsation in our veins, is related by musical rhythms to the powers of harmony. Music indeed is the knowledge of apt modulation [cf. St. Augustine]. If we live virtuously, we are constantly proved to be under its discipline, but when we commit injustice we are without music. The heavens and the earth, indeed all things in them which are directed by a higher power, share in this discipline of music, for Pythagoras attests that this universe was founded by and can be governed by music. (Cassiodorus (sixth century), *Institutiones* 5:2; trans. in Strunk, *Source Readings*, p. 88)

The revival of musical speculation during the Renaissance not only revitalized the idea of cosmic harmony,[15] but also gave new impetus to ideas related to the doctrine of ethos.[16] Unlike medieval treatises, however, theoretical writings from the fifteenth century onward show considerable interest in the doctrine itself. As the quotation below from Shakespeare attests, it grew beyond the solitary preserves of philosophy and theology and became embedded in the consciousness of

---

[15] See Finney, "Harmony or Rapture in Music," pp. 390-1.
[16] Cf. William Shakespeare, *Sonnet VIII, Merchant of Venice*, V,1; John Milton, *At a Solemn Music, Arcades* (lines 61ff.); John Dryden, *A Song for St. Cecilia's Day*, 1687.

the rising middle class.[17]

---

[17]After 1500 references to the Doctrine of Ethos, both explicit and implicit, multiply exceedingly. Here are several further examples:

Leonardo da Vinci (1452-1519), *Notebooks*:

Do you know that our soul is composed of harmony
(trans. in Crofton & Fraser, *Dictionary of Musical Quotations*, p. 74:9)

John Donne (1572-1631), *Hymn to God my God, in my Sickness*:

Since I am coming to that holy room,
Where, with thy Choir of Saints for evermore,
I shall be made thy music; as I come
I tune the instrument here at the door,
And what I must do then, think now before.

John Donne, *Sermons*, Vol. II, no. 7, p. 170:

God made this whole world in such an uniformity, such a correspondency, such a concinnity of parts that it was an Instrument, perfectly in tune: we may say, the trebles, the highest strings were disordered first; the best understandings, angels and men, put this instrument out of tune. God rectified all again, by putting in a new string, *semen mulieris*, the seed of the woman, the Messias: And onely by sounding that string in your ears, become we *musicum carmen*, true musick, true harmony, true peace to you.

Andreas Werkmeister, *Musicalische Paradoxal-Discourse* (1707), pp. 24-25:

Since we now see that God has created and ordered everything in harmony, we can also know and discover to some degree why humans are delighted by music. In the first place, all consonances are basically proportional numbers [i.e., ratios] that are closest to unity and balance, as are the motions of meter (*mensur*) and beats. For everything that is closest to unity is clearer, more orderly and more pleasing than that which tends toward plurality and irrationality, which create confusion. Now since music is an orderly and clear phenomenon (Wesen), and thus nothing other than a model (Formular) of the order of God's wisdom, then a human being, if he is not a wild beast, must indeed naturally (billig) be moved to rejoice when the order and wisdom of his gracious Creator are introduced by means of such sounding numbers into his hearing and consequently into his heart and soul. This is all the more so, because a human bears the image of God within, and thus can more readily comprehend the wondrous unity of God's wisdom, for likenesses are fundamentally attracted to each other. Boethius also says this in the preface to his *Musica*, where he writes: *Amica est similitudo ; dissimilitudo odiosa, et contraria* [likenesses are compatible, while dissimilarities are mutually offensive and repulsive]. Furthermore, a human also has in his soul and external limbs the likeness of the musical proportions. ...When a human perceives these in sounds, then they harmoniously represent to him his image, for him to take delight in. These musical proportions have the power recorded by St. Augustine in his first book of *De Musica*, Chap. 13: *Nam et illi, qui hos numeros noverunt, sentiunt eos in plausu et saltatione etc.* [for those who encounter these numbers feel them in the beat and in the dance]. This then gives rise to orderliness. Thus the late Mr. Luther also says, "Anyone who loves music is of good stuff, and

> ...how sour sweet music is,
> When time is broke and no proportion kept!
> So is it in the music of men's lives.
> And here have I the daintiness of ear
> To check time broke in a disorder'd string;
> But for the concord of my state and time
> Had not an ear to hear my true time broke.
> I wasted time, and now doth time waste me;
> For now hath time made me his numbering clock.
> (William Shakespeare (1564-1616), *Richard II*, V, 5)

Music, as the audible earthly representation of cosmic harmony, was accorded enormous formative power over human minds. Numerous writers of the Renaissance, for example, Ficino, Gaffurius, and Zarlino, expounded on music's power to order and rectify the human soul or spirit.[18] By the seventeenth century the resurrected doctrine of ethos was even being used as a defense of church music.[19]

A few medieval writers echoed the Greek theory that specific musical modes affect human behavior in different ways.[20] On the whole, however, the

---

adept at all things; anyone who despises it is a coarse clod." Such contempt arises from a confused spirit that is not anchored and formed according to the harmonic ratios in the order of its wise Creator.

Isaac Watts (1674-1748):

> When I with pleasing wonder stand,
> And all my frame survey,
> Lord, tis thy work, I own thy hand
> Thus built my humble clay.
>
> Our life contains a thousand springs,
> and dies if one be gone.
> Strange that a harp of thousand strings
> Should keep in tune so long.
> (as printed in Billings, *The Continental Harmony*, 1794, pp. 52-54)

[18] See Gaffurius, Dedication to *Practica musice* (Milan, 1496), trans. in Palisca, *Humanism in Italian Renaissance Musical Thought*, p. 19; Baldassare Castiglione, *Il Cortegiano*, 1528 (trans. by Sir Thomas Hoby, 1561), quoted in Strunk, *Source Readings*, p. 282. See also Finney, "Harmony or Rapture in Music," p. 391.

[19] Sir Thomas Browne, *Religio medici*, 1642:

Whosoever is harmonically composed delights in harmony, which makes me much distrust the symmetry of those heads which declaim against all church music. (Quoted in Crofton & Fraser, *Dictionary of Musical Quotations*, p. 32:10)

See also Finney, "Harmony or Rapture in Music," p. 392.

[20] Boethius, *De institutione musica*, Introduction to Book I:

Hence Plato prescribes that children not be trained in all modes, but only in those which are vigorous and simple. This rule must be most carefully adhered to, for if henceforth anything should somehow be altered ever so slightly...after some time it

The Golden Age of Musical Speculation 103

correlation between church modes and human emotional states does not seem to have been an important one for medieval musicians. It was the renewed interest in ancient Greek modal theory during the Renaissance that revived that aspect of the Doctrine of Ethos.[21] Whereas modality seems to have been of only marginal concern to composers of polyphonic music through the mid-fifteenth century, after that time the connection between the mode of a piece and the sense of its text became important. For example, grave, serious texts were often set to music in the dorian mode, sorrowful texts in the phrygian, and joyful texts in the lydian.

The renewed emphasis on the doctrine of ethos ensured that music remained linked, as earlier, with human nobility.[22] The theme of "nobility" continued to underlie the creation of music despite changes in style and attitude.[23] Even when the Baroque dissolved into the frivolities of the Rococo, the word "galant" (for example, in the expression "Stil galant") was still intimately bound up with the concept of nobility (though now a bourgeois nobility, not an aristocratic one). As a result, gravity and majesty remained important ideals from the fifteenth through eighteenth centuries, especially for sacred music.[24]

Of the manifold effects credited to music, the one that was emphasized was its ability to tame and order the mind. In accord with antique and early Christian

---

will make a considerable difference and will sink through the ears into one's character. (trans. in Boethius, *Fundamentals of Music* (trans. in Bower, p. 4))

John (c.1100):

Music has different powers according to the different modes. Thus, you can by one kind of singing rouse someone to lustfulness and by another kind bring the same man as quickly as possible to repentance and recall him to himself. (trans. in Babb, *Hucbald, Guido and John on Music*, p. 136).

[21]Palisca, *Humanism in Italian Renaissance Musical Thought*, p. 12:

The modes were fascinating to Renaissance musicians not simply because they were a link to a noble ancient past but because they were thought to unlock the powers of music over human feelings and morals. Plato in the *Republic* and *Laws*, Aristotle in the *Politics*, works previously unknown except to a very few, could now be read in printed Latin translations, and they spoke eloquently of the emotional and moral or ethical effects that could be wrought by a musician through the proper choice of mode. Gaffurio, and those who, like Glarean, followed him, by equating the modern and ancient modes, associating the effects of the latter with the former, thereby transferred these powers, theoretically at least, to the modern modes.

[22]See Pierre de Ronsard, Dedication to King François II, in *Livre des Mélanges*, 1560, trans. in Strunk, *Source Readings*, p. 287.
[23]See Marco da Gagliano, Preface to the opera *La Dafne*, 1608, trans. in Weiss & Taruskin, *Music in the Western World*, pp. 176-7; Claudio Monteverdi, Foreword to *Madrigali guerrieri ed amorosi*, 1638, trans. in Strunk, *Source Readings*, p. 413; Christoph Bernhard (1627-1692; pupil of Heinrich Schütz), trans. in Weiss & Taruskin, p. 188.
[24]See Thomas Morley, *A Plain and Easy Introduction to Practical Music*, 1597, quoted in Strunk, *Source Readings*, p. 274; Pietro Cerone, *El melopeo y maestro*, 1613, trans. in Strunk, p. 236.

doctrines, medieval writers asserted that music calms human emotions,[25] and there is less mention of music's power to excite them. The treatises do not suggest that the majority of learned people valued music for its ability to express or arouse strong emotional states; rather, the ideal music was calm, tranquil, and noble (though this ideal might not always have been sought or attained in practice). This certainly holds true for church music, but even secular music was affected by chivalry and courtly virtues that promoted the noble, permanent values of life. Although there was plenty of barbarity and brutality in the earlier Middle Ages, the records that have survived from this period imply an approval of the doctrine of ethos by their admiration for a lifestyle characterized by grave, majestic nobility. (If the early Middle Ages cannot be praised for its vitality, it can at least be respected for its even, steady tenor of life, for its love of balance, symmetry and that most noble of antique Roman virtues, *gravitas*.)

Furthermore, it was a common assumption that music operates on people to influence (mostly to calm) their feelings and behavior, rather than to express feelings.[26] Various authors attributed to music the power to embolden warriors, to calm the feelings, and to restore balance to troubled minds. Those statements were tacit admissions that music has an effect on human emotions. Yet St. Augustine in his *Confessions* (Chapter 4, p. 59) seems to have been the only early theologian who squarely confronted that fact. For the medieval church, music's proper construction and use was paramount, and that was unquestionably a matter of intellectual understanding and discipline. Feelings were for medieval clerics entirely an interior affair, a matter of the disposition of the heart, which was to be controlled in turn by the mind. Music's addressing the mind (to impart universal order) was considered far more important than its ability to affect the emotions.[27]

---

[25] See Isidore of Seville, *Etymologiarum*, trans. in Strunk, *Source Readings*, p. 94; Guido of Arezzo, *Micrologus*, trans. in Babb, *Hucbald, Guido and John on Music*, pp. 69-70.

[26] John (c.1100):

It should not pass unmentioned that chant has great power of stirring the souls of its hearers, in that it delights the ears, uplifts the mind, arouses fighters to warfare, revives the prostrate and despairing, strengthens wayfarers, disarms bandits, assuages the wrathful, gladdens the sorrowful and distressed, pacifies those at strife, dispels idle thoughts, and allays the frenzy of the demented.

Thus one reads of King Saul in the Book of Kings that when possessed by an evil spirit, he was soothed by David's singing to the harp, but when David stopped he was as tormented as ever. Likewise, a certain madman is said to have been freed from insanity by the singing of the physician Asclepiades. It is also recounted of Pythagoras that he recalled a certain licentious youth from his disordered passion by the ordered quality of music (*musica modulatione*). (trans. in Babb, *Hucbald, Guido and John on Music*, p. 136)

See also Boethius, *De institutione musica*, Introduction to Book I, trans. in Strunk, *Source Readings*, pp. 79-86.

[27] Another curious circumstance that furthered the emotionally neutral character of early medieval church music was the general European lack of interest in a strong rhythmic drive. Rhythm is, of course, one of the most sensual, emotional elements in music. This characteristic extends even to medieval secular music; in comparison with

The Golden Age of Musical Speculation 105

This is not to say that Christian doctrine succeeded in draining all emotional content from medieval and Renaissance church music. Rather, the emotions that early church music (and much early secular music as well) arouses are predicated on and circumscribed by years of familiarity with its style and careful training of the listener's ear to distinguish subtle features and to comprehend complex forms and textures. Such emotions are filtered through memory and conditioned by long experience, and thus they lose a degree of immediacy, which is compensated for by their depth and degree of refinement. They are unlikely to be evident to the casual listener or observer. Indeed, the person who harbors them is likely to prefer that they remain interior, outwardly imperceptible. Furthermore (and this is important), an emotional response to such music need by no means be the only response, nor even the primary one.

MUSIC AS A SCIENCE

The insistence that music should primarily address the mind rather than the emotions, together with its exalted role as a reflection of cosmic harmony and order, tended to create for it a unique status in the Middle Ages, separate from the other arts. True, music at that time was regarded as one of the seven *artes liberales*.[28] The *artes* did not involve technical mastery and practice, however, as we today conceive "the arts," but rather philosophical examination and understanding. Thus music was understood as a "science" or "knowledge" (the actual meaning of the Latin term *scientia*). It was primarily something to be understood rather than to be done or experienced. Segregating music from the other arts in this manner unquestionably gave it a privileged position, but it also caused it to develop in a very different direction than it otherwise might have.

The reason for considering music from a scientific point of view, for separating it from other "arts" (in the modern sense of the term) is discussed in the *Scholia enchiriadis* (ninth/tenth century) which, with its parent work the *Musica enchiriadis*, is perhaps the most important of the early medieval musical treatises (as well as the first extensive discussion of polyphony). The *Scholia* manifests its Pythagorean derivation by identifying number as the unifying factor underlying all creation: number is the key to knowledge, to understanding cosmic order. Music was immensely significant because it was a primary way of apprehending number (cf. St. Augustine's definition of music as the "ars bene modulandi," Chap. 5, p. 75).

Music, like the other mathematical disciplines, is in all its aspects bound up with the system of numbers. And so it is by way of numbers that it must be understood... Music is entirely formed and fashioned after the image of numbers. And so it is number, by means of these fixed and established proportions of notes, that brings about whatever is pleasing to the ear in singing. Whatever pleasure rhythms yield, whether in song or in rhythmic movements of whatever sort, all is the work of

---

other cultures, medieval European percussion instruments were crude and limited in variety (see Sachs, "Primitive and Medieval Music: A Parallel," pp. 46-47).

[28]The disciplines that were included in the educational curriculum inherited from antiquity: the trivium (grammar, rhetoric, and dialectic [logic]) and the quadrivium (arithmetic, geometry, music, and astronomy).

number. Notes pass away quickly; numbers, however, though stained by the corporeal touch of pitches and motions, remain. (*Scholia Enchiriadis*, ninth/tenth century; trans. in Weiss and Taruskin, *Music in the Western World*, pp. 38 & 40)

For the author of the *Scholia*, music existed as a primary source of universal knowledge and as a way to explain the workings of the cosmos; for that reason it is a science, not an art. The *Scholia* reveals why speculative thinking played such a prominent role in music: music in all its practical forms was understood not as an isolated means of expression operating under its own precepts, but as an integral part of universal harmony.[29] Practical music, *musica instrumentalis*,

---

[29]*Scholia Enchiriadis*:

(Disciple) How is Harmony born of Arithmetic as from a mother; and what is Harmony, and what Music?
(Master) Harmony we consider a concordant blending of unequal sounds. Music is the theory of concord itself. And as it is joined throughout to the theory of numbers, as are also the other disciplines of Mathematics, so it is through numbers that we must understand it.
(D) What are the disciplines of Mathematics [i.e., of number]?
(M) Arithmetic, Geometry, Music, and Astronomy.
(D) What is Mathematics?
(M) Doctrinal science.
(D) Why doctrinal?
(M) Because it considers abstract quantities.
(D) What are abstract quantities?
(M) Those which being without material, that is, without corporeal admixture, are treated by the intellect alone. In quantities, moreover, multitudes, magnitudes, their opposites, forms, equalities, relationships, and many other things which, to speak with Boethius [*De Institutione Arithmetica*, I, i], are by nature incorporeal and immutable, prevailing by reason, are changed by the participation of the corporeal and through the operation of variable matter become mutable and inconstant. These quantities, further, are variously considered in Arithmetic, in Music, in Geometry, and in Astronomy. *For these four disciplines are not arts of human invention, but considerable investigations of divine works; and by most marvelous reasons they lead ingenious minds to understand the creatures of the world; so that those who through these things know God and His eternal divinity are inexcusable if they do not glorify Him and give thanks* [italics mine].
(D) What is Arithmetic?
(M) The discipline of numerable quantities in themselves.
(D) What is Music?
(M) The rational discipline of agreement and discrepancy in sounds according to numbers in their relation to those things which are found in sounds.
(D) What is Geometry?
(M) The discipline of immobile magnitude and of forms.
(D) What is Astronomy?
(M) The discipline of mobile magnitude which contemplates the course of the heavenly bodies and all figures and considers with inquiring reason the orbits of the stars about themselves and about the earth.
(D) How is it that through numerable science [i.e., arithmetic] the three other disciplines exist?
(M) Because everything comprehended by these disciplines exists through reason formed of numbers and without numbers can be neither understood nor made known.

The Golden Age of Musical Speculation

was always located in the shadow of cosmic music, *musica mundana*; it had no independent significance or existence of its own. Speculation therefore was not imposed on music. Instead, it was an integral part of it.[30] This attitude had an astonishingly long lifespan:[31]

It is proportion that beautifies everything, this whole universe consists of it, and music is measured by it, which I have endeavored to observe in the composition of these few airs.
(Orlando Gibbons, Dedication to *The First Set of Madrigals and Motets*, 1612; quoted in Crofton & Fraser, *Dictionary of Musical Quotations*, p. 69:17)

Equality of measure is indeed to be preserved, lest the harmony be impaired or confused; for to sing without rule and measure is to offend God himself, who arranged all things by number, weight and measure, as Plato said [sic!]. (Michael Prætorius, *Syntagma musicum* III, 1619, p. 79)

Music is a secret exercise in arithmetic of a soul unaware that it is counting; for it [the soul] does many things in confused or unconscious perceptions that it is unable to note with distinct apperception. In fact, they are in error who think that nothing happens in the mind of which the mind itself is not conscious. The mind, then, even if it does not realize it is counting, still senses the effect of this unconscious counting, whether it be pleasure at consonances or annoyance at dissonances, recoiling from them. Indeed it is from many "insensibilities' coming together that pleasure arises.
(Leibniz, Letter #154, 1712)

Since music was understood as a science, medieval writers staunchly affirmed the attitude that had its genesis in Plato (Chapter 3, pp. 39-40), and was translated into its medieval form by Boethius (Chapter 5, pp. 77-78): the *musicus* (the

---

For how can we learn what a triangle or quadrangle is, and the other concerns of Geometry, unless we already know what three and four are?
(D) In no way.
(M) Of what use is it in Astronomy to know the theory without knowing number? Whence do we know the risings and settings, the slowness and velocity of the wandering stars? Whence do we perceive the phases of the moon with its manifold variations, or what part of the zodiac is occupied by the sun or moon or any other planet you will? Is it not that as all things are set in motion by certain laws of number, without number they remain unknown?
(D) It is indeed.
(trans. in Strunk, *Source Readings*, pp. 134-5)

Thus chant and early polyphony may best be understood as a sonorous (and indispensable) ornament to the text, just like medieval manuscript illuminations and illustrations: a way of enshrining the text in a marvelous sonic reliquary whose tonal structure was patterned on the form and order of creation.

[30]Bukofzer, "Speculative Thinking," p. 167.
[31]cf. Portnoy, *Music in the Life of Man*, p. 10. Lang (*Music in Western Civilization*, p. 726) notes that Lorenz Mizler, who founded the Association for Musical Science in 1738 (of which J. S. Bach later became a member), was "still a scientist who considered philosophy and mathematics the most important prerequisites to music."

musical philosopher who understood the "why" of music) was superior to the *cantor* (lit. "singer," the music performer--either vocal or instrumental--who understood the "how").[32] The *musici* were unavoidably aristocrats addressing themselves to a small, knowing circle. Indeed, theologians vented their ire in particular on secular musicians who ignored the principles of speculative music and strove for popularity by providing music solely for human pleasure.[33]

> Musicorum et cantorum magna est distantia:
> Isti dicunt, illi sciunt quae componit Musica.
> Nam qui facit quod non sapit diffinitur bestia.
> ('Twixt the students of *musica* and the practising singers there lies a great gulf: the latter sing, the former know what *musica* consists of. For he who does what he doesn't understand is no more or less than an animal.) (Guido of Arezzo (tenth century), *Regulae Musicae Rhythmicae*, lines 1-3; trans. in Cattin, *Music of the Middle Ages*, p. 158)

In the later Middle Ages the term *musicus* could be construed as applying to a theorist as well as to a philosopher/theologian. The "professional" composer, however, was unknown. Those who composed polyphonic music were not normally scholars by profession, but members of some music-making establishment, either noble or ecclesiastical. But since composing was not a full-time occupation, and since it required so much intelligence and erudition to master the necessary skills to do it, it was inevitable that some composers should become polymaths: Leonin was a canon of Notre Dame Cathedral in Paris as well as a poet of some note;[34] Philippe de Vitry was a diplomat at the French royal

---

[32]cf. John (c.1100), trans. in Babb, *Hucbald, Guido and John on Music*, pp. 104-5.

[33]Honorius of Autun (eleventh-twelfth century):

Can a minstrel be saved? No; minstrels are ministers of Satan. They laugh now, but God shall laugh at them on the last day. (trans. in Crofton & Fraser, *Dictionary of Musical Quotations*, p. 4:7)

Marchetto of Padua, *Lucidarium*, 1309-1318:

A musician is defined, according to Boethius, as one who has the ability to make judgements concerning modes and rhythms and concerning the varieties of cantilena in accordance with the speculation and reason of the science of music. For every art or discipline naturally holds reason in higher regard than the skill which is exercised by an artist's hand and in his work. For the musician learns the possibility and rationality of musical proportions and makes judgements in accordance with this and not only by the sound. The singer is, as it were, an instrument of the musician, on which instrument the artist or musician performs, putting into practice that which he already knows by reason. Therefore the musician is to the singer as the judge to the crier; for the judge issues a decree and orders that it be announced by means of the crier. There is the same relation between musician and singer; for the musician learns, feels, discerns, chooses, decrees and disposes everything that touches upon the science; and he commands that it be put into practice by the singer as though by his own messenger. (trans. in Gallo, *Music of the Middle Ages*, p. 111)

[34]See Wright, "Leoninus, Poet and Musician," p. 31.

court and then bishop of Meaux; Guillaume de Machaut (more famous in his day as a literary figure than as a composer) served as secretary to John of Luxembourg, king of Bohemia; John Dunstable wrote books on astronomy and may well have been a church canon as well as an official in the service of the duke of Bedford; and Guillaume Dufay was an official at Cambrai Cathedral as well as a chaplain at the Burgundian court. Composers of polyphonic music moved in aristocratic circles,[35] and their art was not only aristocratic but even secret[36] (just as elements of Gothic architecture were kept secret). Even when the Boethian distinction of *cantor* versus *musicus* faded into obsolescence during the fifteenth and sixteenth centuries, the aristocratic ideal of secrecy in musical composition and performance persisted in the concept of *musica reservata*, an expression whose exact meaning is now obscure, but whose aristocratic, secretive connotation is unmistakable. Ultimately, early polyphony was meant more to be sung than to be listened to;[37] to appreciate complex polyphony fully, one needs to know it thoroughly, and best of all, to sing it.

In spite of the esoteric, erudite, and aristocratic character of their work, medieval composers were seldom accorded the same musical respect as the *musici* . Only after the fifteenth century is it possible to detect any change in the assumption that a composer's work was a handicraft rather than an art (in the modern sense of the term). Fulfilling the role of a servant (often highly valued, but nevertheless a subordinate) to the church or to a noble court, the composer always plied a trade, occupied a post. The idea of the independent artist had not yet been born, and "art for art's sake" was inconceivable.

NUMBER SYMBOLISM

Even a casual reading of the New Testament gospels or epistles will reveal that esoteric numerology is quite at odds with their simplicity and directness. The fondness that many of the early Church Fathers showed for symbolic numbers was not based on Scripture, but was primarily a result of numerology's pervasive influence in the culture of late classical antiquity. The first several centuries of the Christian era were especially dominated by an exaggerated sort of number mysticism, evidences of which may be found in the writings of Philo, Plutarch, and various neo-Platonists (both pagan and Christian).[38] Christian theologians perpetuated the Greek reverence for number, and with it the symbolic meanings acquired by various numbers. Although some Christian apocryphal writings (e.g., the Shepherd of Hermes and the Clementine Recognitions) concern themselves with numerology, the acceptance of the Book of Revelation (which is full of arcane numbers) into the biblical canon made number symbolism a

---

[35] See Salmen, *Social Status*, p. 19.
[36] See Gallo, *Music of the Middle Ages*, pp. 8-9.
[37] Pirotta, *Music and Culture in Italy*, p. 371:

It has often been stressed that medieval polyphony addresses itself not to an audience but to the church or monastic choir that is the agent of the celebration. It is, therefore, listened to, so to speak, from the inside.

[38] Hopper, *Medieval Number Symbolism*, p. 50.

respectable pursuit for subsequent Christian theology. The sources for the numerology contained in these and other writings were ancient and various: primitive number lore, Babylonian astrology, Pythagoreanism, and even the Old Testament.

St. Augustine in particular spoke of the mysteries of number in general and the hidden significance of particular numbers; his involvement with number symbolism gave it the ultimate stamp of approval for later writers. It pervades not only the pages of his *De musica*,[39] but many of Augustine's other writings as well. Augustine is fully in line with earlier Platonic doctrine in that he understands numbers to reflect absolute truth: "...there is a relation of numbers which cannot possibly be impaired or altered, nor can any nature by any violence prevent the number which comes after one from being the double of one" (*On the Morals of the Manicheans*, XI, 24; trans. in Hopper, *Medieval Number Symbolism*, p. 78). In fact, the writings of Augustine are among the most comprehensive sources for information about pagan neo-Pythagorean number theory.[40] Thus both Christian and non-Christian teachings conspired to render number symbolism a central feature of musical speculation. As Vincent Hopper writes (p. 89), "The penetration of number consciousness into the Middle Ages was inevitable from the sheer circumstance that there was literally no reservoir of knowledge or inspiration on which this period could draw which was not impregnated with number philosophy."

Building on the number symbolism of late classical neo-Pythagoreans (especially Nicomachus, fl. c. A.D. 100), Christian writers such as St. Augustine assigned an allegorical significance to each number. These attributions played an important role in allegorical explanations of music (and eventually they came to be applied to musical form and structure as well). For example:

3: is the perfect number; the first number with a beginning, a middle and an end; the sum of the values of the two preceding numbers; the fundamental source of all moral good; the Holy Trinity.

4: represents the quadrivium; the elements; general directions (north, south, east, west); seasons; virtues; kinds of beings (angels, demons, animals, plants); musical concordances.

7: represents the harmony of the seven planets; strings of the lyre; days of the week; tones of the scale; graces of the Holy Spirit.[41]

Symbolism like this is apt to be regarded today as naive and arbitrary. Only when it is viewed in light of both the importance of number for medieval thought processes as well as the medieval reverence for tradition is it possible to comprehend just how profoundly significant and determinative it was.

As subsequent writers contributed to speculative number theory, the edifice created by number lore became vast and complex. A prime example of this

---

[39] See Robert J. Forman, "Augustine's Music: "Keys" to the Logos," in La Croix, ed., *Augustine on Music*, pp. 19ff.
[40] Hopper, *Medieval Number Symbolism*, p. 79.
[41] Lang, *Music in Western Civilization*, p. 56. For a detailed account of ancient number symbolism, see Hopper, *Medieval Number Symbolism*, pp. 2-88.

The Golden Age of Musical Speculation

complexity at the height of the later Middle Ages is the extensive system defining the significance of symbolic numbers devised by the enormously influential musical philosopher-theorist Jean de Muris (d.1351). In order to make the subject more comprehensible, Hermann Abert reduced this description to the following diagram.[42]

Number	Music	Church
1	music	church
2	mundana/humana naturalis/instrumentalis authentic modes/plagal modes	Old and New Testaments contemplative life/active life love of God/love of neighbor
3	contratenor bassus, tenor, contratenor altus percussion instruments, wind instruments, stringed instruments beginning, ending, middle	contrite heart, confession of mouth, work of satisfaction faith, hope, love Father, Son, Holy Spirit
4	first, second, third and fourth modes 4 lines of the staff	wisdom, temperance, fortitude, justice the 4 Evangelists
7	final tones note names intervals of the tenor (within the mode)	Office hours Sacraments gifts of the Holy Spirit
8	modes (from 4 finals)	beatitudes (from the 4 virtues)
9	intervals locations on the staff	orders of angels lessons, responds, psalms (in the office of Matins)
10	staff lines	Commandments of God
19	intervals (within the gamut)	the various degrees of believers

After the fifteenth century the increasingly complex and arcane number symbolism that grew out of medieval musical speculation tended to be superseded in humanist circles by a return to an emphasis on more basic Pythagorean ratios of musical intervals. Yet number symbolism continued to surface sporadically for several centuries thereafter, perhaps finding its final expression as late as the works of J. S. Bach.

---

[42]*Die Musikanschauung des Mittelalters*, p. 191.

8

Speculation and Musical Practice

> "Composers,...while they defended their art as a representation of world symmetry and proportion, or as a symbol of the divine, made no application, as far as has been noted, of metaphysical ideas to the music they composed." (Finney, "Harmony or Rapture in Music," p. 388)

> "To the minds of the men of the Renaissance musical consonances were the audible tests of a universal harmony which had a binding force for all the arts. This conviction was not only deeply rooted in theory, but also--and this is now usually denied--translated into practice." (Wittkower, *Architectural Principles*, p. 126)

Which of these two statements are we to believe? Their apparent contradiction is evidence of the confusion about the role that speculation played in musical composition. A number of factors complicate any attempt to correlate speculation with musical practice: (1) The literary sources of information are few in number and often vague--the best evidence is usually provided by analyzing pieces of music. (2) The techniques of composing were traditionally secret ones, and musical scores often disclose their secrets grudgingly. (3) Speculation is by nature mystical, not rational (in the modern sense of the term); it is not empirical, but arrived at through intuition and revelation. Its practical applications, therefore, are often vague and arbitrary. (4) Speculation has never been uniform. Although much was shared in common, assumptions and emphases differed from writer to writer and century to century. Thus it is fruitless to try to construct any rigid system of correspondences between speculation and practice. There is always a danger of reading more into these matters than the evidence will support. Nevertheless, there are some reasonably clear indications that musical speculation did not remain the exclusive property of philosophers and theologians, but had a role in determining the composition of church music. In the early Middle Ages that role was a loose one, but it grew ever more specific as polyphony became the central focus of Western European music. It is not mere coincidence that the *Scholia enchiriadis* (c. 900), perhaps the earliest treatise on the new art of polyphony, interpreted (and thus defended) the new practice entirely in terms of the Pythagorean consonant ratios.[1]

ECCLESIASTICAL CONSERVATISM

Why did the writer of the *Scholia enchiriadis* think it necessary to defend the new practice at all? The answer to that question reveals an important attitude that underlay all Christian musical speculation. We have already noted the conservative attitude characteristic of the church in earlier centuries (Chap. 4, p. 68; Chap. 6, p. 88). That attitude became a hallmark of the society that had the church at its center. Jacob of Liège, admittedly a conservative among conservatives, wrote c.1330: "...just as it is profitable and praiseworthy to imitate things well done by the ancients, so it is pleasant and commendable to approve things well said by them" (*Speculum musicae*, Prohemium to the Seventh Book; trans. in Strunk, *Source Readings*, p.180). The medieval mind was predisposed to value continuity with long-established tradition as an unquestioned good, and to retain and respect the heritage of ideas from the past, interpreting new ideas as extensions of already existing ones (and thus allowing no contradiction of tradition). Any new ideas or practices that could not be reconciled with tradition had to be rejected out of hand.[2]

One manifestation of this pervasive conservative attitude was the practice of writing new treatises as *scholiae* (glosses or commentaries on older writings). Manfred Bukofzer, among others, has suggested that this practice was applied to practical music as well as speculative, since tropes as well as early polyphony (written on a pre-existent *cantus firmus*) are best regarded as glosses or commentaries on earlier material[3] (i.e., the original chant melodies that were obligatory and indispensable in the doing of the liturgy). This is not to assert that the practice of polyphony was in itself a specifically Christian invention. Yet on the other hand, the church's acceptance of polyphony was absolutely conditional upon its integration into the tradition of musical speculation. Polyphony could never have flourished in the church without precisely that sort of theological support that is evident in the *Scholia enchiriadis* and subsequent treatises.[4]

Once the practice of polyphony had been sanctioned and had become established in the church, then it became in turn a part of "tradition," assuming

---

[1] The relevant portions of the *Scholia enchiriadis* are translated in Strunk, *Source Readings*, pp. 136-8.

[2] In this regard, Paul Henry Lang writes (*Music in Western Civilization*, p. 38):

The "true," the "good," and the "beautiful" did not have to be invented and shaped into form again and again, because the "ancients" had created these elements once and for all; the problem was to acquire the knowledge of these elements and to practice and propagate them.

[3] Bukofzer, "Speculative Thinking in Medieval Music," pp. 172-3.
[4] See Ellefsen, "Music in Humanism" (diss.), pp. 36-7.

Speculation and Musical Practice 115

the same sacrosanct character as other traditional elements.[5] In the case of polyphony, this became evident as early as the fourteenth century, in the bull *Docta sanctorum* issued by Pope John XXII in 1324.[6] The stated purpose of the bull was to forbid a number of liturgical and musical excesses that the pope (as well as others) deemed improper. It is a particularly interesting document at this juncture, however, because in it the pope designated polyphony as especially suitable for solemn feasts. He thus implied that it was somehow 'more special' than ordinary, everyday monophonic chant.

> We do not intend to forbid the occasional use--principally on solemn feasts at Mass and at Divine Office--of certain consonant intervals superposed upon the simple ecclesiastical chant, provided these harmonies are in the spirit and character of the melodies themselves, as, for instance, the consonance of the octave, the fifth, the fourth, and others of this nature; but always on condition that the melodies themselves remain intact in the pure integrity of their form, and that no innovation take place against true musical discipline... (Hayburn, *Papal Legislation...*, p. 21)

Thus a formerly new practice was not only accepted as a part of tradition, but because it was so evidently based on traditional musical doctrine[7] and hallowed by long usage, it actually came to be considered tradition's crowning achievement.[8]

Even when the authority of earlier Christian writers began to diminish with the advent of humanism, respect for the heritage of Greek and Roman antiquity preserved the reverence for Greek speculative musical theory. As late as the early seventeenth century both Giovanni Maria Artusi and Claudio Monteverdi appealed to Plato's authority in defense of their (diametrically opposite) opinions.[9] At this late stage, a conservative (if not reactionary) attitude was a trademark of the various Christian churches; among the fruits of this conservatism we may note the Jesuit Athanasius Kircher's *Musurgia universalis* (1650), which contains an exhaustive summation of musical speculation, and Prince-Abbot Martin Gerbert's important works: *De cantu et musica sacra* (1774), treating earlier music for the Mass, offices, psalms and hymns, and

---

[5]The integration of polyphony into musical speculation may have been further aided by the fact that polyphony is conceptually sympathetic to medieval Christian attitudes: it is inherently orderly, unifying two or more independent entities, and thus accords well with a monistic, neo-Platonic worldview in which the tension of opposites is in process of being resolved into unity. As the twentieth-century French theologian Father Joseph Gelineau observes,

> ...polyphonic singing can be acknowledged as a beautiful sign or symbol of the liturgical community itself; for this is a unity in diversity, a single choir made up of diverse persons (*Voices and Instruments*, p. 143).

[6]Trans. in Hayburn, *Papal Legislation*, pp. 20-21.
[7] Note that the pope is careful to cite the Pythagorean consonances to support his statements.
[8]Cf. Bukofzer, "Speculative Thinking," pp. 173-4. The same process is evident in the acceptance of Gothic as the universal Christian architecture of western Christendom; see Simson, *The Gothic Cathedral*, p. xx.
[9]See Strunk, *Source Readings*, pp. 404, 407, & 413.

regional chant traditions; and *Scriptores ecclesiastici de musica sacra*, a comprehensive collection of primary sources on medieval church music and music theory.

THE SPECULATIVE CONCEPTION OF BEAUTY

Sometime between the years 816 and 836, a gift arrived at the monastery of St. Gall, intended for Gozbert, its abbot. In all likelihood it came from Haito (763-836), sometime bishop of Basel and abbot of the monastery at Reichenau.[10] It was a large sheet of parchment (still preserved in the St. Gall monastery library) on which was drawn the plan of an ideal monastery: ideal not merely in its scope (more complete and extensive than any known monastic complex of the period), but in its detail, its balance of parts and cunning arrangement, and even in its perfect proportions.[11] Gozbert was indeed engaged in planning the rebuilding of St. Gall at this time, but Haito's gift was not intended to instruct him in the practical aspects of monastic construction. Rather, Haito's letter that accompanied the plan suggests a different purpose for the gift:

I have sent you, Gozbert, my dearest son, this modest example of the disposition of a monastery, that you may dwell upon it in spirit...and know my love toward you; think not that I laboured at this design because we believed that you had need of instruction, but rather believe that we drew it through love of God out of fraternal affection, for you to study only... (trans. in Braunfels, *Monasteries of Western Europe*, p. 46)

In accordance with long-standing neo-Platonic tradition, Haito sent Gozbert not a practical plan, but an *ideal*, something to hone and focus his thinking for the practical tasks in which he was engaged. The plan teaches us nothing specific about medieval music, of course; but it is a parallel to the emerging practice of music governed and perfectly ordered by ideal precepts, music that was intended not primarily to delight the ear or to reflect and arouse human emotions but to form and conform the intellect to numerical (universal, cosmic) perfection. It is a striking piece of evidence that both ecclesiastical architecture and music were significant not primarily as works of art, but as a means of incarnating and communicating cosmic harmony.[12] The medieval mind judged a work of art to

---

[10] See Braunfels, *Monasteries of Western Europe*, p. 38.

[11] A. Reinle has suggested that the plan is based on numerical ratios derived from the Golden Mean. See A. Reinle, "Neue Gedanken zum St. Galler Klosterplan," in *Zeitschrift für Schweizerische Archäologie und Kunstgeschichte*, Vol. XXIII, 1963-64; summarized in Braunfels, *Monasteries of Western Europe*, pp. 45-46.

[12] Cf. Simson, *The Gothic Cathedral*, p. 51:

The medieval experience and philosophy of beauty...are not exclusively or even primarily derived from sense impressions. It is even doubtful that we may speak of medieval aesthetics, if we define aesthetics as the autonomous philosophy of beauty. To the medieval thinker beauty was not a value independent of others, but rather the

Speculation and Musical Practice   117

be beautiful not because it delighted the senses or affected the emotions, but to the degree that its form was perceived to reflect universal harmony.[13]

As a result of this attitude, writers showed little interest in the pleasure music affords and conversely a great concern for accuracy and precision. The *musici* insisted that exact musical intonation must take precedence over that which merely pleases the ear.

> Ordinary singers often fall into the greatest error because they scarcely consider the force of tone and semitone and of the other consonances. Each of them chooses what first pleases his ear or appears easiest to utter or to pronounce, and with many melodies a great error is made in the mode. ([pseudo-]Odo of Cluny, tenth century, *Enchiridion Musices* ; trans. in Strunk, *Source Readings*, p. 110)

Under the pressure of that attitude, the ecstatic element in music, tolerated and even encouraged in the early church and preserved to some extent in the melismatic singing of the eastern churches, was alternately neglected and regulated until it all but disappeared. The element with the closest affinity to the ecstatic that survived in Western chant was the *jubilus*, a florid melisma on the final syllable of the Alleluia sung before the reading of the Gospel. Its diffuse melody became increasingly perilous to sing, however, since improvisation was increasingly restricted in favor of exact reproduction. It appears that in part from the need to render precisely such textless melodies there arose the practice of troping, fitting new para-liturgical texts to the music as an aid to memory. This was in all probability the origin of the *sequentia cum prosa*, an art form that eventually broke free from its parent chant and became the primary focus of creative energy in medieval music and poetry before the rise of polyphony. Together with the regulation of the ecstatic element, then, came a decline of improvisation and an emphasis on the exact transmission of the musical tradition, parallelled and undergirded by the development of music notation.[14]

THE RISE OF POLYPHONY

During the early Middle Ages there was general agreement that music spoke primarily and most appropriately to the mind, but this intellectual emphasis was not unambiguously evident in musical practice. Only an overall restrained

---

radiance of truth, the splendor of ontological perfection, and that quality of things which reflects their origin in God.

[13]As Nino Pirotta writes:

No human rational process can ever be totally free of emotional elements... But it is in the nature of the Gothic artist, in his *modus essendi*, to identify his faith with his passion, and his passion with the hard-won conquest of a rational truth. ("Dante Musicus," in *Music and Culture in Italy*, p. 19)

[14]Early polyphony also seems to have begun by being improvised, but likewise became subject to the growing tendency toward stricter regulation; see Seay, *Music in the Medieval World*, p. 80.

quality and (perhaps) a preference for certain intervals betrayed its presence. The church's influence on music had mostly a negative force, in that by being anti-sensual and anti-emotional it repressed those elements of music that had to do with feeling and that might have tended to eclipse rational processes. When musical developments began to focus on polyphony, however, then music began to exhibit most clearly those mathematical and formal qualities that reflect its dependence on speculation. Thus it is the repressive attitudes of the Church Fathers and their reactions to pagan musical abuses and excesses that seem to have been the most influential factors in determining musical practice during the first millennium of the Christian era. Only with the rise of polyphony in the eleventh and twelfth centuries did the speculative ideas inherited and transformed from antiquity begin to play a positive role in determining the course of music composition.

The eleventh and twelfth centuries enjoyed a renewed economic and political stability, making possible what some scholars have characterized as a European cultural renaissance. A number of features that typify modern culture first appeared at this time, for example, the rise of cities as independent commercial and cultural centers, and the foundation of universities. Massive, fortress-like romanesque church architecture gave way to the expansive lightness of gothic tracery and flying buttresses. The arts also entered an era of creative ferment; to realize this, we need only consider the appearance of the *Nibelungenlied*, the *chansons de geste*, the poetry of the Troubadours and Trouvères, liturgical dramas, and, of course, the first major stage in the history of polyphony, the School of Notre Dame.

Music research to date has provided only a fragmentary picture of the role that speculative musical ideas played in the twelfth-century cultural renaissance. The introductory chapters of Otto von Simson's book, *The Gothic Cathedral*,[15] offer a more complete view of the context of musical speculation at this time, as well as the extent of its influence. Simson deals extensively with Pythagorean musical interval ratios as a prime factor in the conception of the gothic architectural ideal. Like the music of the period, gothic architecture was understood as a symbol of the kingdom of God on earth. Its precisely calculated (but usually secret) geometric structure was intended to be a representation of ultimate reality. Such a structure was by no means a matter of artistic intuition; it could only be computed on the basis of "science:" a thorough comprehension of perfect, eternal, "divine" geometric principles, principles best manifested in music. The proportions employed in gothic architecture faithfully reflected the eternally valid Pythagorean consonant ratios as revealed in music. Both the *organa* of Leonin and Perotin and the cathedral for which they were created, Notre Dame of Paris, were intended to be earthly representations of divine order and "numerosity," "models" of the medieval universe.

Because musical speculation had established that the Pythagorean perfect intervals, the intervals with the simplest, "purest" ratios--the *diapason* (octave: 2:1), *diapente* (fifth: 3:2), and *diatesseron* (fourth: 4:3)--were those that most accurately reflected cosmic harmony, those intervals had already become for

---

[15]Especially pp. xv-xx, 4-6, 8, & 13-43. In order to understand the application of Simson's ideas to music, one must substitute "music" for "architecture," "cathedral," or "church" whenever the author is speaking about ideas or concepts.

Speculation and Musical Practice 119

practicing musicians the consonant intervals,[16] helping to determine pivotal notes in the developing modal system. With the rise of polyphony, however, this element of speculation entered into a much closer relationship with practice. The function that the Pythagorean "pure" intervals assumed in the twelfth-century polyphonic developments associated with the Cathedral of Notre Dame in Paris is among the earliest unambiguous indications that musical speculation had a decisive influence on early polyphony.[17] The unison, fourth, fifth and octave play pivotal roles in the harmonic structure of Leonin's and Perotin's *organa*, constituting both the opening and the final, cadential intervals of musical phrases (Illustration 4).

Illustration 4:
Leonin, organum *Alleluia: Nativitas*.

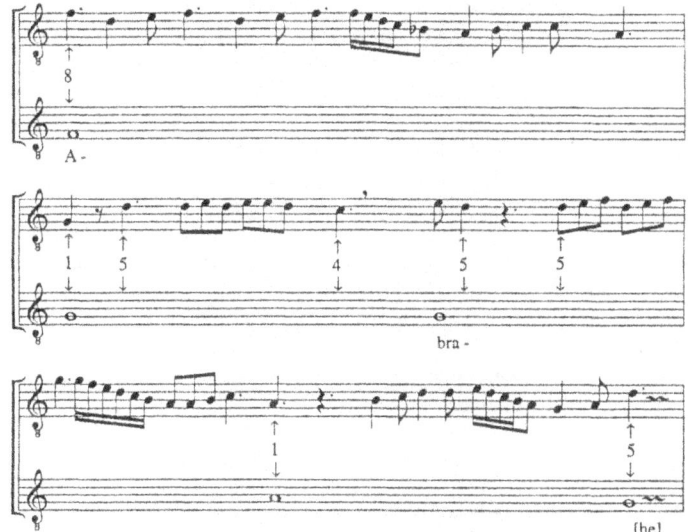

Source: Waite, *The Rhythm of Twelfth-Century Polyphony*, p. 200.

---

[16]The third, on the other hand, a primary consonance for modern ears, was considered a dissonance--not because of its sound, but because in Pythagorean theory its ratio (81:64 in the case of the major third) is obviously far from pure; see Spitzer, *Classical and Christian Ideas of World Harmony*, p. 37.

[17]Manfred Bukofzer arrives at the same conclusion ("Speculative Thinking," pp. 173-4):

While the patristic writers interpreted music in a vague manner as an imitation of the *musica mundana*, the *Musica enchiriadis* argues in a more convincing way. The comparison of polyphony with the universal harmony is more consistent, since on both sides real harmony is implied, viz., tones sounding simultaneously. Polyphony deserves to be called the image of universal harmony, rather than monody.

120 Wiser than Despair

In succeeding centuries the unison, fifth, and octave continued to play that role in the gradual evolution of polyphony, while the interval of the fourth retained its hallowed position in musical theory long after musical practice had transformed it into a dissonance. Even the more progressive fifteenth-century composers trod warily when it came to tampering with the Pythagorean consonances. The third became firmly established as a consonant interval in compositional practice around the middle of the fifteenth century, but for more than a half century thereafter composers shrank from using it in the final chords of pieces. In the final *clausula* from the "Agnus Dei II" of Josquin's *Missa Pange Lingua* (Illustration 5), observe how the music cadences to a complete triad and then resolves the third to the tonic, leaving a perfect Pythagorean consonance as the final sound of the work. Even a century after the acceptance of the third as a consonance, some conservative composers still ended their works with pure Pythagorean intervals (though they, of course, used the interval of a third freely within their compositions). Note, for example, the final *clausula* of the Responsory for the first Sunday of Advent, "Ecce dies veniunt" (Illustration 6), composed in the early 1540s by the Lutheran bishop and musician Balthasar Resinarius and printed by Georg Rhau in 1543. Not until the mid-sixteenth century did Gioseffo Zarlino (in the First Part of his *Istitutione Harmoniche* of 1558) legitimize the use of the third as a consonance--by interpreting it in terms of Pythagorean numerical ratios.

One of the most puzzling features of early polyphony is its departure from the earlier Christian insistence that the text be the central focus of attention instead of the music. By inordinately lengthening the notes of the chant *cantus firmus*, melismatic organum inevitably obscured the text of the chant on which it was based. Subsequent developments in polyphony seem to pursue goals other than textual clarity. A number of comments in contemporary writings corroborate a cavalier attitude toward the sacred texts.[18]

After the music has been made and fixed, then take the words which are to go into the motet and divide them into four segments; and divide the music into four corresponding segments; and put the first segment of the words over the first segment of music as best you can, and proceed in this way all the way to the end. Sometimes it will be necessary to stretch many notes over few words in order to make the setting come out right, and sometimes many words must be squeezed into a small amount of

---

[18] Jacob of Liège, *Speculum musicae*, c. 1330:

In a great company of judicious men, when motets in the modern manner were being sung, I observed that the question was asked, what language such singers were using, whether Hebrew, Greek, Latin, or some other, because it could not be made out what they were saying. Thus, although the moderns compose good and beautiful texts for their songs, they lose them by their manner of singing, since they are not understood (trans. in Strunk, *Source Readings*, p. 190)

Desiderius Erasmus, early sixteenth century:

Modern church music is so constructed that the congregation cannot hear one distinct word. (trans. in Crofton & Fraser, *Dictionary of Musical Quotations*, p. 31:15)

Illustration 5:
Josquin des Prez, "Agnus Dei II," *Missa Pange Lingua*

Illustration 6:
Balthasar Resinarius, Responsory "Ecce dies veniunt."

Source: Georg Rhau, 1543.

time. Just fit it together any way you can. (Aegidius of Murino, *Tractatus cantus mensurabilis*, c.1400; trans. in Weiss & Taruskin, *Music in the Western World*, p. 67)

This subordination of the text would seem to be a flagrant offense against the church's devotion to tradition. An explanation for it may lie in a paradox: an extreme emphasis on one aspect of Christian tradition (i.e., musical number and proportion) seems to have overwhelmed and devaluated another aspect (i.e., the supremacy of the text). The "sacredness" of a piece of music may have come to reside more in its actual musical structure, its reflection of numerical, mathematical perfection, than in its text. An emphasis on words reappeared in the Renaissance, but for reasons of musical expressiveness (stimulated by the rise of humanism) apparently quite at odds with earlier Christian attitudes. The neglect of words in favor of musical form may help to explain some (to modern minds) curious features about early polyphony: (1) the superimposition of sacred and secular texts; (2) careless or nonexistent text underlay, reflected in Aegidius's instructions above and abundantly evident in manuscript sources; and (3) the increasingly frequent use of instruments in the church. Although investigations into expenditures at such important musical centers as Cambrai Cathedral and the Sistine Chapel suggest that vocal performance was still an ideal during the fifteenth and sixteenth centuries, instruments began to make increasingly frequent appearances in the performance of church music, either sounding *colla parte* or actually substituting for voices.[19] The gradual introduction of instruments into the church (in tacit defiance of the time-honored ban against them) and the growing emphasis on them may also have been spurred on by other influences: contact with Near Eastern cultures during the Crusades or a general trend toward secularization during the fourteenth century. But these circumstances do not suffice to explain how "heathen" instruments came to be allowed to perform sacred songs; the departure from the earlier ideal of text supremacy seems to provide a more adequate explanation for this.

We have learned from the previous chapter that musical speculation did not cease with the coming of the Renaissance. In order fully to comprehend the scope of its influence on musical practice during and after the sixteenth century, however, we must again refer not to musical scholarship, but to a modern writing on Renaissance architecture. Rudolf Wittkower's book *Architectural Principles in the Age of Humanism*[20] reveals both the degree to which musical ideas continued to be determined by the concept of cosmic or world harmony and also the way in which cosmic musical harmony and proportions were applied to Renaissance architecture: "...man-created harmony was a visible echo of a celestial and universally valid harmony" (Wittkower, p. 8). Renaissance painters also applied musical proportions to their art.[21]

---

[19]For documented instances of instrumental participation in the Mass during the fourteenth and fifteenth centuries, see Fallows, "Specific information on the ensembles for composed polyphony, 1400-1474," p. 127, n. 42.

[20]Especially pp. 1-3, 7-10, 27-30, & 117-26.

[21]Charles Bouleau documents this application in detail in his book, *The Painter's Secret Geometry*: see in particular pp. 81-87.

In addition to the traditional Pythagorean ratios, some Renaissance artists and craftsmen began to experiment with other speculative proportional formulas as determining factors in formal construction (formulas that had already begun to attract attention during the later Middle Ages). For example, luthiers seem to have explored (albeit secretly) a wide range of geometrical and numerical proportions, including the Golden Section (also known as the Golden Ratio or Golden Mean), Fibonacci numbers, root proportionals and the *Vesica piscis*.[22] A situation similar to that of the luthiers appears to exist in the works of fourteenth- and fifteenth-century composers, notably the Masses and motets of the Burgundian school and early Franco-Flemish masters. Because musical speculation was so inextricably interwoven with the traditional worldview, however, and because it seems to have been only marginally affected by humanistic ideas,[23] its presence in musical compositions of this period is probably best understood as a final surge of medieval artistic energy (indeed, in its inordinate intensity, as a sort of *fin de siècle* burst of musical mannerism).

The fifteenth century seems to have been a time of particularly intense and wide-ranging involvement with speculative ideas, and it is becoming increasingly evident that composers at times brought such ideas to bear on musical composition. The same problems hamper an understanding of their application, however, as inhibit our understanding of their relationship to medieval music: no written evidence, a paucity of sources, and the problems inherent in dealing with the products of an irrational, mystical approach to knowledge and learning. Furthermore, modern scholarship in this area is still in its early stages; much fourteenth- and fifteenth-century music has yet to be "decoded" from this perspective. The evidence presently available, however, suggests that speculative ideas were involved in the structural formation of some of the most significant musical compositions of this era.

If (as musical speculation asserted) music is scientific, based on mathematics, and if its basic purpose is to symbolize cosmic order, then musical composition must be considered not so much a matter of feeling or intuition as an intellectual process. The resulting musical works are, then, more manifestations of intellect, of formal shape and technical procedure, than of emotion. Therefore it is not surprising that those fifteenth-century composers who subscribed to speculative ideas adhered to the intellectual emphasis in music composition that was characteristic of the Middle Ages. Recent research by an array of scholars, establishing the existence of numerical formulas as hidden organizing factors in the construction of certain Renaissance motets and Masses (the correlative of proportional structure in architecture, painting, and instrument-making), is only the most sensational indication that speculative ideas governed musical composition. The more obvious manifestations of the scientific generation of musical composition have always been recognized, though their grounding in musical speculation has not always been adequately acknowledged: isorhythm, riddles, canons, augmentation and diminution, inversion, retrograde and retrograde inversion, imitation and motivicity, parody and paraphrase techniques. All of these procedures manifest a thrust toward order and control as well as the

---

[22]See Coates, *Geometry, Proportion and the Art of Lutherie*, pp. 15ff.

[23]Paul Henry Lang (*Music in Western Civilization*, p.184) in fact labels this era and its musical style as Neo-Gothic.

Speculation and Musical Practice 125

dominance of the intellectual (the knowing) over the sensual (the feeling). The following are random examples of these techniques; in each instance, there are other examples that could serve equally well.

- **Isorhythm:**[24] (This procedure flourished throughout the fourteenth century, enjoying a final burst of creativity during the early fifteenth.) John Dunstable (c.1383-1453) - Motet "Veni Sancte Spiritus." The entire motet may be divided into three major parts, each having a successively faster tempo. Each part is subdivided into two isorhythmic halves. The two *taleae* of the tenor in each part (corresponding to the two halves) are stated three times in progressive ratio diminution of 3:2:1.

- **Riddles**: Guillaume Dufay (c.1400-1474) - Mass "L'Homme armé," Agnus Dei III. The cantus firmus (derived from the popular song *L'Homme armé*) does not appear in the manuscript sources. In its place stands the verbal "canon" [rule or instruction]: *Cancer eat plenus et redeat medius* (Let the crab proceed full and return half). From this cryptic instruction the performers are to deduce that the cantus firmus is to be sung in retrograde (thus the "crab") in full note values, and immediately thereafter in its normal form at half note values.

- **Canon**: Johannes Ockeghem (c.1420-1495) - Missa Prolationum. Only two voices of this Mass are notated, and from them the other two must be derived. The two derived voices are to be performed in canon with the given ones, resulting in a double canon. The sections of the Mass from the Kyrie to the Osanna form a cycle of canons at intervals progressing from unison to octave. The Benedictus and Agnus Dei I reintroduce the interval of the fourth, and the Agnus Dei II and III, the fifth. (Thus the "purest" intervals recur at the end.) With the exception of the Christe, the interval of the canon is indicated by the position of the time-signatures on the staves and wherever possible (i.e., unison, third, fifth, seventh) by the position of the clefs.

- **Augmentation and diminution**: Dufay - Missa "Se la face ay pale." In this Mass setting Dufay organizes the tenor *cantus firmus* in a proportional system involving both augmented and diminished note values in addition to the normal ones.[25]

---

[24] See also Bukofzer, "Speculative Thinking," pp. 178-80; Ficker, "Formprobleme," pp. 211-13.

[25] Reese, *Music in the Renaissance*, p. 70:

...Dufay applied the proportional system to his tenor, thereby modifying its rhythm according to a series of possibilities of a semimathematical order. With this system a given tenor may, in the course of an extended work, appear in normal basic time values, in diminished or augmented values, in duple or triple measure, etc. If the tenor is to reappear from one end of the Mass to another without changing anything but its "proportions," it need be written only once--in *integer valor* (i.e., with normal time-values)--the requirements for its various modifications being indicated by verbal canons.

•**Inversion, retrograde and retrograde inversion**: Jacob Obrecht utilized these procedures in composing several of his Mass settings.[26]

Regarding the music that resulted from such procedures, Paul Henry Lang says:

> This complicated, erudite art reminds us that the real meaning of the verb *componere*, from which we take our term for musical composition, is merely "to put together"; and indeed this phase of musical history is usually prefaced by the reprobative epithet, "the canonic artifices of the Netherlanders." But besides enormous technical skill, these works show inspired imagination and taste; to overlook these qualities is tantamount to calling Bach's *Art of Fugue* a collection of contrapuntal exercises. (*Music in Western Civilization*, p. 188)

The medieval mind, on the other hand, would likely have expressed this same sentiment in the exactly opposite fashion: "These are works of inspired imagination and taste (attributes that make them to some degree sensuously attractive), properly expressed in their enormous technical skill, their artifice (that which makes them perfect expressions of cosmic order)."

NUMBER SYMBOLISM

Musical scholarship has yet to meet the challenge of establishing a correlation between number symbolism and musical practice before the twelfth century. The exclusive use of triple meter in the rhythmic modes of twelfth-century polyphony seems to be the earliest clear instance of number symbolism's

---

[26]Todd, "Retrograde" p. 51:

Several of the approximately twenty-five Masses definitely ascribed to Obrecht offer examples in which the cantus firmus is ordered according to a precalculated plan similar to our modern notion of serialism. In these works the cantus firmus, in addition to being heard in its original form, is also stated in retrograde, arranged in inverted order, or, by combining the two properties, presented simultaneously in an inverted and retrograde fashion. On occasion Obrecht employs transposition, either of the original cantus firmus--which is, of course, consistent with the increasing theoretical recognition of modal transposition at this time--or of a derivative version of the cantus firmus. Often these elaborations are concisely effected by verbal canons without notating in full the new form of the cantus firmus. However, if the canon calls for especially elaborate changes, then the new, derived cantus firmus may be written out to ensure proper execution. For example, the *Et incarnatus* of the *Missa Graecorum*, which survives in a single printed source (Petrucci's *Misse Obreht* [sic] of 1503), requires extensive adjustment of the cantus firmus by means of a canonic inscription. To avoid possible error, Petrucci provides both the canon and its realization. Four other Masses of Obrecht that illustrate canonically produced techniques of retrograde, inversion, or retrograde-inversion are *L'Homme armé, De tous bien plaine, Fortuna desperata,* and *Petrus Apostolus.*

Speculation and Musical Practice 127

influence on musical practice.[27] Christians of course held the number 3 in reverence because of its association with the doctrine of the Trinity; but in fact the number 3 had already been assigned manifold mystical meanings and had enjoyed special veneration from remotest antiquity.[28] Graeco-Christian number symbolism regarded it as the pre-eminent and perfect number, and thus it was unavoidable that 3 should be incorporated in some fashion into a musical style so permeated by number doctrines. Since it could not figure into the harmonic canon, it manifested itself in the rhythmic system of Notre Dame organum, the rhythmic modes.[29] Indeed, the very idea of an unyielding rhythmic regularity (as typified by the rhythmic modes) bespeaks a sort of orderliness that accords well with the doctrine of cosmic harmony. The fact that this regularity is quite likely the result of a conscious application of speculative principles is yet another bit of testimony to the degree to which the intellect was pre-eminent in the development of polyphony.[30]

In spite of the introduction of binary meter into mensural music during the *Ars Nova*, the fourteenth century continued to regard triple meter as perfect.[31] *Musici* such as Jean de Muris in his *Ars novae musicae*[32] (1319) engaged in elaborate discourses interpreting ternary perfection. If binary meter were to be used in church music, it had to be reconciled with Christian tradition; later in the treatise cited above De Muris attempts to do just that.[33] Even such a progressive figure as the fifteenth-century composer and author Johannes Tinctoris attempted a theological justification for binary meter, almost as an aside, in his *Proportionale musices*: "But, after the fullness of time, in which the greatest of musicians, Jesus Christ, in whom is our peace, in duple proportion made two natures one, there have flourished in His church many wonderful musicians..." (Tinctoris, c.1476; trans. in Strunk, *Source Readings*, p. 194).

The influence of number symbolism is especially striking in some Masses and motets that are constructed according to hidden geometrical or proportional formulas, a result of the fifteenth century's intense interest in neo-Pythagorean (neo-Platonic) speculation and number lore. The mathematically determined architecture of such works is not normally evident from listening to them or from casually examining them; it reveals itself only upon painstakingly meticulous mathematical analysis. The esoteric, intellectual structures of such works are in part the heritage of the Middle Ages and in part the result of the renewed interest in the learning of antiquity spearheaded by humanists. In either case, the activity can be understood as one aspect of the heightened interest in

---

[27]William Waite (*The Rhythm of Twelfth-Century Polyphony*, pp. 8, 29, 35-39) suggests that St. Augustine's *De musica* may have been the major influence behind the creation of the rhythmic modes.
[28]See Chap 7, p. 110, as well as Hopper, *Medieval Number Symbolism*, pp. 4-8, 73-74.
[29]See Bukofzer, "Speculative Thinking," p. 177.
[30]The exclusive use of triple meter in early polyphony is all the more striking, in that triple meter is rarely encountered in the music of other cultures; see Sachs, *Wellsprings of Music*, p. 114; Merriam, *African Music in Perspective*, pp. 78, 88.
[31]See Gallo, *Music of the Middle Ages*, pp. 29-30.
[32]Translated in Strunk, *Source Readings*; see in particular p. 173.
[33]see Strunk, *Source Readings*, pp. 175ff.

128   Wiser than Despair

music as a vehicle for symbolic meaning that prevailed during the fifteenth and sixteenth centuries.[34]

1. Guillaume Dufay - motet "Nuper rosarum flores." This motet was composed in 1436 for the dedication of the Cathedral of Florence, Italy, concurrent with the completion of the great dome designed by and executed under the direction of Filippo Brunelleschi. Charles Warren has suggested that Dufay wrote the motet in consultation with the architect, in order to be able to structure the music according to the numerical ratios Brunelleschi employed in constructing the dome and the cathedral.[35] In particular, this structure involved the Pythagorean ratios 6:4:2:3. Craig Wright, on the other hand, has advanced a competing theory, claiming that there is no correlation between motet and cathedral proportions; rather the motet's formal plan is based on the dimensions of the Old Testament Temple of Solomon as described in I Kings 6: 1-20, as well as the number 7, symbolic of the Virgin Mary.[36] In either event, almost every aspect of the motet's structure seems to be determined by symbolic numbers.

2. Johannes Ockeghem. Marianne Henze has posited an elaborate series of proportional relationships that determine the structure of a number of Ockeghem's Mass settings, for example, *Missa Caput, Missa L'Homme armé, Missa De plus en plus,* and *Missa Ecce ancilla domini.*[37] Not only do structural features such as the number of lines and number of repetitions of the cantus firmus appear to be mathematically generated, but in some cases even hidden text meanings are realized in proportional relationships.[38]

   Edward Lowinsky has proposed that Ockeghem's canon for thirty-six voices on the text "Deo gracia[s]" is governed not by musical-technical considerations, but by the composer's desire to make it a reflection of the angels' music in praise of God.[39]

---

[34]Cf. Elders, *Studien zur Symbolik in der Musik der alten Niederländer,* as well as *Composers of the Low Countries,* Chap. 3, pp. 49-86.
[35]Warren, "Brunelleschi's Dome and Dufay's Motet."
[36]Wright, "Dufay's *Nuper rosarum flores"*
[37]Henze, *Studien zu den Messenkompositionen Johannes Ockeghems.*
[38]Henze, pp. 192-4.
[39]Lowinsky, "Ockeghem's Canon" p. 157:

...technique was the least of Ockeghem's concerns in composing this canon...the canon was merely the instrument needed to carry out an idea. The idea that prompted Ockeghem to such an extraordinary enterprise had been for many centuries an integral part of the Christian mystical vision; it went back in part to the Neoplatonic, in part to the Jewish prophetic tradition, notably to Isaiah and Ezekiel, and was nourished by various ancient mythologies as well. It was the concept of the heavenly music of the angels sung in praise of God.
Ockeghem's motet, the number of its parts, the canonic construction, and its whole technique can be explained in terms of the angelic music it was designed to echo.

Speculation and Musical Practice   129

3. Antoine Busnois (d. 1492) - motet "In hydraulis." The text of this motet alludes to the Pythagorean proportions, proportions that are realized as the tenor repeats its motive (consisting simply of three notes: D-C-C) at the fifth and octave above. Furthermore, the motet displays pitch and durational palindromic symmetry.[40]

According to Richard Taruskin, Busnois' Missa "L'Homme armé" exhibits an elaborate system of isorhythmic proportional durations.[41]

4. Jacob Obrecht (c.1450-1505) - Missa "Sub tuum praesidium." In the course of preparing the score of this Mass for publication, the editor, M. van Crevel, became aware of the mathematical organization of the cantus firmus. In his own words:

Soon it became apparent that I had hit upon a hidden cosmos of mathematical relations and proportions interweaving the outer cyclic structure of the Mass throughout. The discovery of this underlying structure, the gradually deepening penetration into what I should like to call--paradoxical as it may seem--its crystalline complexity, and, finally, the spreading of its manifold and ever extending ramifications over other realms: it was an overwhelming experience. (Van Crevel, Foreword to Jacobus Obrecht, *Opera omnia* : Missae VI. Sub tuum presidium, p. XVIII)

---

[40] See Higgins, "*In hydraulis* revisited," p. 76.
[41] Taruskin, "Antoine Busnoys," pp. 269-70:

[An] elaborately worked-out quasi-isorhythmic structure...is one of this Mass's most distinctive characteristics...
...we are dealing here with a most elaborate array of Pythagorean durational "harmonies," analogous to those of the consonances. Unity is represented by the closing sections of all five movements, which are of identical length: eighteen tempora... The octave and fifth are represented by the durations of the opening sections, which reduce to 1:3:2. The closing Agnus Dei, with its internal durational ratio of 4:3:2, sums up the perfect consonances, much as would the final harmony of any fifteenth-century Mass or motet, including this one. Even the whole tone, which Pythagoras measured along with the octave, fifth, and fourth in the famous legend of the smithy and the hammers, is represented in the Kyrie, which, in terms of notated tempus, displays the *epitritum* proportion (4:3), but with respect to actual durations measured in terms of the original perfect breve...displays the epogdoon (9:8). (I am using here the terminology of the text in Busnoy's own motet *In hydraulis*.)
There is only one movement that has four composed sections: the Sanctus (as notated, that is, disregarding the repetition of the Osanna). Busnoys seized this unique opportunity to sum up the whole Pythagorean harmonic complex as represented in the legend of the four hammers: to wit, 12:9:8:6. Arranged in the form of two successive and equivalent ratios (which is how Busnoys arranged them if we count the second, concluding, Osanna rather than the first), they constitute the so-called Golden Proportion (12:9=8:6), representing the division of the octave by the arithmetic mean 9 and its reciprocal, the harmonic mean 8. Two fourths (8:6 and 12:9, reducing to 4:3), two fifths (9:6 and 12:8, reducing to 3:2) and the tone (9:8) are all enclosed within the octave (12:6).

In the Foreword to his edition (in the chapter entitled "Secret Structure," pp. XVII-XXV) he proposes the existence of a complex and comprehensive mathematical edifice, founded on the organization of the cantus firmus, encompassing the Pythagorean interval ratios in both simple and compound forms, the Golden Ratio, Fibbonaci series, and other symbolic numerology.

5. Heinrich Isaac (c.1450-1517) - motet "Quis dabit aquam capiti meo." In her dissertation on Isaac and number symbolism, Sarah Funkhouser advances the theory that both the textual and musical aspects of this and other motets are constructed according to the Golden Mean.[42]

6. Josquin des Prez (c.1440-1521) - motet "Illibata Dei virgo nutrix." Richard Sherr contends that both the tenor and also other levels of structure in the second part of this motet reflect the Pythagorean proportions 1:1, 2:1, 3:2, 4:3 and 9:8.[43]

Even if scholars were ever able to identify all of the works constructed according to hidden mathematical principles, these works would in all probability still constitute only a limited percentage of the entire corpus of late medieval and early Renaissance polyphony. Yet the fact that such works exist at all is the surest proof for the existence and the persistence of Christian speculation's practical relationship to music composition. Some of the instances of mathematical symbolism cited above may in the course of time prove to be exaggerated or even false. It is inevitable that the case for musical number symbolism will at times be carried too far. Yet there remains a core of examples whose authenticity seems beyond a reasonable doubt. This core will grow as further analysis uncovers other examples of symbolic mathematical structure, because the ideas of mathematical construction and number symbolism in medieval and Renaissance music correspond so perfectly to the basic conception of music prevalent in those eras.

---

[42]Funkhouser, "Heinrich Issac and Number Symbolism" (diss.), pp. ii- iii:

The importance of symbolic numbers--an all-pervasive concept in the Renaissance--is corroborated by this study of symbolism in Heinrich Isaac's motets *Quis dabit capiti*, *Quis dabit pacem*, *Virgo prudentissima*, *Sancti Spiritus*, and *Imperii proceres*... All components of each composition--tactus, notes, words, syllables and letters--were considered both vertically and horizontally with respect to large form, sections, phrases and textual units. Additionally, symbolic aspects of word painting and *soggetto cavato* were investigated...
The analysis shows that not only did Isaac use numbers symbolically but indeed they were a motivating, structural force in his compositional technique. Number symbolism pervades every work analyzed. The golden mean proportion is consistently found to be the structural basis of these motets and was further utilized by Isaac to stress important words of the text. In *Quis dabit capiti*, the golden sections are identical both in Isaac's motet and Poliziano's poem, a remarkable achievement.

[43]See Sherr, "*Illibata Dei virgo nutrix*," p. 439 and Table 2, p. 440.

Speculation and Musical Practice   131

Speculation's last significant penetration into the realm of musical practice seems to have been in Germany during the seventeenth and early eighteenth centuries,[44] culminating in the music of J. S. Bach. From its earliest days, German Lutheran Protestantism approved and supported the practice of complex art music as a fitting way to praise God in worship (see Chap. 9, pp. 138-40). Such music maintained a close relationship to Lutheran liturgical life throughout the sixteenth and seventeenth centuries. Indeed, seventeenth-century central Germany (through the time of Bach's childhood), a bastion of conservative Lutheran orthodoxy, seems to have been one of the last places where Christian life and worship flourished free from the serious incursion of more modern, self-conscious modes of thinking,[45] and exhibited all of the constitutive features of cult (in its Protestant, Lutheran form):[46]

- An uncontested, vital Christian mythology to support and energize worship.
- A high degree of religious and cultural solidarity (a minimum of religious and cultural pluralism).
- The cultivation of a style of worship based almost wholly on world-conscious attitudes--traditional, splendid, and zealous in its pursuit of elaboration (especially musical elaboration) as an appropriate expression of Christian devotion to God.[47]

It was also in German-speaking lands that the tradition of musical speculation survived the longest--right up into the eighteenth century, the threshold of modern times (see Chapter 7, pp. 99). In addition to the treatises that preserved the tradition of Christian cosmic harmony, there are scattered hints that it also survived (albeit tenuously) in compositional practice, and that Bach's cultivation of it does not represent an isolated phenomenon. For example, Mattheson reports that Buxtehude in his seven keyboard suites sought to portray the nature and character of the planets,[48] and in each of the four sections of Buxtehude's *Passacaglia in d minor* (BuxWV 161) the seven-note theme appears seven times.[49]

The evidence for Bach's adherence to the traditional cosmic worldview and his use of symbolic numbers as determining factors in his musical compositional process is still subject to debate and skepticism, for precisely the same reasons that cloud this issue for earlier eras: the speculative tradition was largely a secret one, and most of the evidence is found not in the form of verifiable written

---

[44]See Irwin, *Neither Voice nor Heart Alone*, p. 115.

[45]See Craig, *The Germans*, pp. 26-30 (esp. pp. 29-30).

[46]For a detailed discussion of the intense cultic activity characteristic of Leipzig during and after Bach's tenure as the *Thomascantor*, see Stiller, *Johann Sebastian Bach and Liturgical Life in Leipzig* (especially pp. 31-33):

...the church life and the liturgical life in Leipzig appears to have remained completely inaccessible to the spirit of the Enlightenment far into the 18th century. In fact, that life seems to have experienced a very impressive late flowering. (p. 32)

[47]See Schweitzer, *J.S. Bach*, pp. 69-71.
[48]Mattheson, *Der vollkommene Kapellmeister*, p. 130.
[49]See Wurm, "Christus Kosmokrator," pp. 263ff. In the same article, Wurm also finds number symbolism to be the basis of J. S. Bach's *Prelude and Fugue in C Major*, BWV 547.

statements but in the musical scores themselves. The extra-musical evidence that Bach had any sympathy for the traditional worldview is essentially circumstantial:

1. Indications such as "J.J." (*Jesu juva*: Jesus, help) or "S.D.G." (*Soli Deo Gloria*: To God alone the Glory) at the head of many of his manuscript scores, as well as marginal notes in Bach's own hand in his copy of the Calov Bible,[50] suggest that Bach's faith and thought were in essential conformity with that of his time and place.[51]

2. Bach lived in the same milieu as several of the important figures in late Baroque musical speculation: Werckmeister, Leibniz (who lived in Leipzig, though before Bach took up residence there), and Mizler (also a resident of Leipzig; Bach was inducted as the fourteenth member of his Association for Musical Science in 1747). A treatise on mystical number symbolism, Caspar Heunisch's *Haupt=Schlüssel über die hohe Offenbarung S. Johannis*, is known to have been in Bach's library.

3. Bach's definition of figured bass in his *Generalbasslehre* (borrowed largely from F. E. Niedt's *Musikalische Handleitung* of 1700) is as follows: "Figured bass is a most perfect foundation for concerted music that is played with both hands... in order to produce a pleasing harmony for the glory of God and the permissible delight (*Ergötzung*) of the spirit; like all music, the final purpose and end of figured bass ought also to be none other than the glory of God and the re-creation (*Recreation*) of the spirit." (Neumann & Schulze, eds., *Bach-Dokumente*, Vol. II, p. 334) The word *Ergötzung* in modern German means "amusement, entertainment, delight." Bach's equating it with the word *Recreation*, however, suggests that he may have understood it to some degree in its earlier sense, in which both *Ergötzung* and *Recreation* are best perceived as related to the Latin *recreare*: to re-create, make anew; to restore, cause to recover; recover one's spirits.[52] This in turn suggests that Bach might have understood music's purpose in some measure in terms of the ancient Doctrine of Ethos.

4. Intelligent listeners have perceived the serious, profound, intellectual character of much of Bach's music,[53] as well as its formal unity.

---

[50]See Leaver, *J. S. Bach and Scripture: Glosses from the Calov Bible.*

[51]Support for this supposition may be found in Petzoldt, *Johann Sebastian Bach: Ehre sei dir Gott gesungen: Bilder und Texte zu Bachs Leben als Christ und seinem Wirken für die Kirche.* See also Irwin, *Neither Voice nor Heart Alone*, p. 142.

[52]See Irwin, *Neither Voice nor Heart Alone*, p. 144.

[53]It was not only Bach's contemporaries that sensed this quality; listeners from subsequent eras have recorded the same sort of reaction to Bach's music:
Johann Wolfgang von Goethe (on hearing Bach's organ works):

It is as though eternal harmony were conversing with itself, as it may have happened in God's bosom shortly before he created the world. (trans. in Crofton & Fraser, *Dictionary of Musical Quotations*, p. 12:1)

Speculation and Musical Practice   133

If ever a composer showed polyphony in its greatest strength, it was certainly our late lamented Bach. If ever a musician employed the most hidden secrets of harmony with the most skilled artistry, it was certainly our Bach. No one ever showed so many ingenious and unusual ideas as he in elaborate pieces such as ordinarily seem dry exercises in craftsmanship... His melodies were strange, but always varied, rich in invention, and resembling those of no other composer. His serious temperament drew him by preference to music that was serious, elaborate, and profound. (C.P.E. Bach & J. F. Agricola, *Obituary of...Johann Sebastian Bach*, 1754; trans. in David & Mendel, p. 222)

Indeed, it was that profoundly learned character that brought Bach's music adverse criticism, even in his own lifetime.[54] It is this intellectual quality (more than the specifically Christian texts) that continues to make Bach's church music more at home in the church than in the milieu of the concert hall, where demands of virtuosity and histrionics are placed on it that it was never meant to live up to. If virtuosity is present in Bach's music, it always seems directed toward a different purpose than astonishing the listener with technical skill.[55]

It is the research into Bach's use of number symbolism, however, that has perhaps offered the most convincing evidence of his involvement with the traditional cosmic worldview. The pioneer in this research was Martin Jansen, whose article on number symbolism in Bach's passion settings created a sensation when it was published in the 1937 *Bach-Jahrbuch*.[56] Jansen offers manifold evidence that Bach relied heavily on number symbolism as a basic structural device in creating the Passions, especially the St. Matthew Passion. Subsequent writers have vastly expanded Jansen's pioneering work, perhaps at times carrying their speculation to excess, but nevertheless providing many intriguing examples of number symbolism as a constitutive feature of Bach's compositional technique.[57]

Frederic Chopin, in a letter to Delphine Potocka:

Bach is like an astronomer who, with the help of ciphers, finds the most wonderful stars. (trans. in Crofton & Fraser, p. 30:9)

[54]See Johann Adolph Scheibe, "Letter from an able Musikant Abroad" (1737), trans. in David & Mendel, *Bach Reader*, p. 238.
[55]Cf. Lang, *Music in Western Civilization*, p. 514.
[56]Jansen, "Bachs Zahlensymbolik, an seinen Passionen untersucht."
[57]See Smith, "J. S. Bach the Symbolist."

9

The Reformation

The successful challenge that the sixteenth-century Reformers mounted against the church's universal authority formed one of the fundamental preconditions for the emergence of the self-conscious worldview (brought to fulfillment in the Enlightenment). Yet none of the Reformers ever intended to create a new worldview. In the first place, they were not a new phenomenon; they were only the final "successful" chapters in a history of attempts at reform that reached far back into the Middle Ages. And they were all at heart conservatives--actually it would be more correct to say that many of them were reactionaries, since their teachings (including those on music) represented a desire to return to ancient New Testament ideals.[1] Paul Henry Lang characterizes the Reformation as a "true renewal of medieval earnestness and self-denial" (*Music in Western Civilization*, p. 168). The Reformation did not give birth to any radically new ideas or attitudes about music. Rather, it represents largely the reassertion of ancient attitudes and principles, now redistributed along denomination lines.

---

[1] Paul Henry Lang (*Music in Western Civilization*, p. 200) writes:

Formalistic history writing has erroneously considered Renaissance and Reformation as a joint phenomenon marking the advent of the modern era, independence of thought, freedom and truth displacing the bigotry and coercion of the medieval spirit. But the two movements do not run parallel. The Reformation has a popular character; the Renaissance is courtly, aristocratic, learned, and at times snobbishly exclusive. The earnest and severe religiousness of the adherents of the Reformation is in contrast with the indifference of the humanists.

JOHN CALVIN

Calvin, the father of the Reformed tradition, expounded at length on his views on music in the Foreword to the 1543 edition of the *Geneva Psalter*.[2] The early Church Fathers who wrote on music would have found no reason to disagree with them in any way; indeed, they would have greeted them with enthusiastic approbation. Calvin cited Plato and various Church Fathers to support his fear that human pleasure in music can easily lead to dissoluteness or effeminacy. He advocated musical censorship, proposing to allow only religious music to be sung, in particular the Psalms. Concerning the melodies appropriate for use in psalm-singing, Calvin recommended that they be characterized by moderation, gravity, and majesty.

ULRICH ZWINGLI

Zwingli, leader of the Reformation at Zurich, Switzerland, represents perhaps the most extreme Reformation position on music.[3] A highly intelligent and educated man, Zwingli was by all accounts a gifted and skillful musician, both instrumental and vocal. His fanatic zeal for reform, however, together with his peculiar interpretation of New Testament Scripture, led him to the conviction that music should have no place in public worship, and thus he proscribed not only musical instruments (including organs, which were dismantled and removed from churches influenced by his teachings), but also singing of any sort. Even congregational singing was banned in Zurich for seventy-five years. Zwingli's attitude echoes fourth-century monasticism's violent rejection of music.[4]

Both Zwingli's and Calvin's ideas on music were in accord with the restrictive teachings already propagated by the early church, with one important difference: neither of them showed any evidence of belief in cosmic harmony. They did not denounce the complex of ideas associated with that belief; they simply ignored it, because it was outmoded and irrelevant to their thought. Thus both of these Reformers contributed to the resurgence (in a new guise) of an attitude that has been known ever since their time as Puritanism.

PURITANISM

The term *Puritanism* refers specifically to a movement that arose during the sixteenth century in the Church of England, opposing the traditional forms of worship and religious customs that had survived the English Reformation,[5] and

---

[2]Translated in Strunk, *Source Readings*, pp. 346-8.
[3]Charles Garside's book *Zwingli and the Arts* provides a comprehensive discussion of Zwingli's attitude toward music and the arts.
[4]Cf. in particular Quasten, *Music and Worship in Pagan and Christian Antiquity*, pp. 94-97.
[5]In particular, Puritanism uncompromisingly rejected any religious practice suggesting that a desired result could be effected merely by the performance of a given act or acts (i.e., the concept of *ex opere operato*).

favoring simpler, more austere worship practices. Insofar as the term connotes an attitude, however, puritanism was not confined to England; related attitudes, together with their inevitable rejection and persecution of elaborate church music, prevailed in some parts of Germany, Holland, and Switzerland as well. But in England (and then in the English-speaking New World) its influence was felt longest and most profoundly. Among its first acts, the seventeenth-century English Commonwealth dissolved cathedral and collegiate choirs, destroyed church organs, and banned any sort of church music except the simplest congregational singing: "The use of musical instruments may also add some little advantage to singing, but they are more apt to change religion into air and fancies, and take some of its simplicity, and are not so fitted for edification" (Jeremy Taylor, *Ductor dubitantium*, 1676; in Crofton & Fraser, *Dictionary of Musical Quotations*, p. 32:15). English Puritan pronouncements on music simply rephrase ancient ideas; they reveal how closely Puritan attitudes resemble those of the early church (in particular the attitudes of early monasticism). The puritan suspicion of music and the fear that it might distract attention from the Word of God were echoes of the same fears St. Augustine voiced in his *Confessions* (Chapter 4, p. 59), but by ignoring ideas of world harmony, the puritan attitude did not exhibit the tension (characteristic of earlier ages) that forced a rapprochement with music. Thus, while seventeenth-century English Puritans were often quite fond of music-making at home, and practiced a simple but honest sacred music in worship, later generations reviled musical pursuits as idle sensuousness or simply as a waste of time.

Music is almost as dangerous as gunpowder; and it maybe requires looking after no less than the press, or the mint. 'Tis possible a public regulation might not be amiss. (Jeremy Collier, *A Short View of the Immorality and Profaneness of the English Stage*, 1698; in Crofton & Fraser, *Dictionary of Musical Quotations*, p. 113:11)

Cautions are necessary with respect to Musick and Painting; the fancy is often too quick in them, and the Soul too much affected by the Senses... How can chaste Minds delight in the Languishments of wanton Poetry, made yet more languishing by the Graces of Musick. What great or noble is there in the dying Notes of foreign Strumpets and Eunuchs?... Should Christians squander away so many precious Hours in Vanity, or take Pleasure in gratifying a Sense that has so often been a Traitor to Virtue? (*The Ladies' Library, written by a Lady*, pub. Richard Steele, 4th ed., 1732, I, p. 16; in Lang, *Music in Western Civilization*, p. 518)

Although the passages quoted above probably refer to secular music (and specifically to the opera), they reveal the sort of suspicion of sensual pleasure in music that could not help but perpetuate a negative attitude toward elaborate church music as well.

MARTIN LUTHER[6]

As a theologian and reformer, Luther's interest in music was primarily practical in nature. He believed, of course, that music was a gift of God best employed to praise the Giver; but Luther held that music benefited human hearers as well. He adhered to the idea that music forms good character (the Greek Doctrine of Ethos): music governs the feelings of the heart; it quiets and cheers the soul; it produces "fine and skillful people."[7] Yet there is something quite remarkable about the attitude he expressed toward music--indeed, one might almost say revolutionary: the traditional ecclesiastical suspicion of music is totally absent, and in its place stands a love, an open, warm acceptance of music in all forms.[8] "[After] the Word of God, the noble art of music is the greatest treasure in this world"[9]--these are hardly the words of one who sympathized with the early church's position on music. In fact, Luther consistently placed as much emphasis on the Old Testament in his writings on music as on the New (see Chapter 2, p. 24). Oskar Söhngen goes so far as to say that "for Luther all music is "spiritual," that is, theologically relevant. There is for him no secular music in the strict sense, only degenerate music."[10]

> Music is a beautiful and lovely gift of God which has often moved and inspired me to preach with joy. St. Augustine was afflicted with scruples of conscience whenever he discovered that he had derived pleasure from music and had been made happy thereby; he was of the opinion that such joy is unrighteous and sinful. He was a fine pious man; however, if he were living today, he would hold with us. (Martin Luther; trans. in Buszin, "Luther on Music," p. 89)

> I rejoice to let the 79th Psalm [O God, the heathen are come] be sung as usual, one choir after another. Accordingly let one sweet-voiced boy step before the desk in his choir and sing alone the antiphon or tract *Domine, ne secundum*. After him let another boy sing the other tract, *Domine, ne memineris*; and then let the whole choir kneeling sing *Adjuva nos, Deus*, just as we sang it in the Popish Feasts, for it sounds and looks very devotional (Denn es seer andechtig laut und sihet). (Martin Luther, *Exhortation to Prayer against the Turks*, 1541; Luthers Werke, Bd. 51, p. 607; trans. in Lang, *Music in Western Civilization*, p. 280)

Luther showed his unabashed fondness for all types of music by declaring himself in particular a lover of polyphony. For him, complex art music had as much place in the praise of God as simple congregational song.[11]

---

[6]There are several collections of Luther's most important writings about music, translated into English: Walter E. Buszin, "Luther on Music," and Carl F. Schalk, *Luther on Music: Paradigms of Praise*. Vol. 53 of *Luther's Works* makes available everything Luther wrote related to music, but contains other material as well.

[7]Buszin, "Luther on Music," p. 8; Schalk, *Luther on Music*, p. 34.

[8]Cf. Martin Luther, Preface to the *Burial Hymns* (1542), trans. in *Luther's Works*, vol. 53, pp. 327-8.

[9]Preface to Georg Rhau's *Symphoniae jucundae* (1538), trans. in Buszin, "Luther on Music," p. 5.

[10]See Söhngen, "Music and Theology: A Systematic Approach," p. 13.

[11]Martin Luther, *Harmoniae de passione Christi* (1538):

That Luther adhered in some measure to the medieval neo-Platonic worldview and its accompanying conception of music is evident from his writings.[12] Yet Luther never promoted the ideas that grow from that worldview, since he was at heart a pragmatist. His pragmatic attitude is evident in his motto, "*Nos interim omnia probabimus, quod bonum est tenebimus*" ("Meanwhile we shall try all things, and what is good we shall retain;" from the *Formula missae*, 1523, derived from I Thessalonians 5:21). Luther was more interested in the gifts music brought to Christian life and worship, and in particular to the spread of the Gospel,[13] than in speculation.

Luther represented a judicious balance of traditional Christian and more popular, progressive attitudes. He embodied this balance (as well as the contradictions that result from it) in his very personality, and the church that rose in his wake continued to embody it for the following two centuries. Although his involvement with music extended only superficially to speculation, his sympathy for the medieval worldview allowed room for tolerance of and interest in speculative inquiry in the church that issued from his reforming work.[14] Lutheran musical practice, however, did not suffer under the repressive aspects of patristic or neo-Platonic doctrine. Thus as the Lutheran Church evolved in Germany, the practice of music blossomed freely in all forms, based on a love of the art and its gifts, and not necessarily on speculative premises. The favorable

---

Finally, however, when the attempt is made to improve one's natural ability, to develop and unfold it completely, we can perceive, astonished, but cannot comprehend the boundless and perfect wisdom of God revealed in His wonderful gift of music. Outstanding in this art is this, that while one voice continues to sing its *cantus firmus*, other voices at the same time cavort about the principal voice in a most wonderful manner with praise and jubilation, adorning the *cantus firmus* with most lovely movements; they seem to present a kind of divine dance so that even those of our day who have only a most limited amount of sentiment and emotion gain the impression that there exists nothing more wonderful and beautiful. Those who are not moved by this, are, indeed, unmusical and deserve to hear some dunghill poet or the music of swine. (trans. in Buszin, "Luther on Music," p. 82)

[12]Martin Luther, Preface to Georg Rhau's *Symphoniae iucundae* (1538):

...looking at music itself, you will find that from the beginning of the world it has been instilled and implanted in all creatures, individually and collectively. For nothing is without sound or harmony [lit. "sounding number": Nihil enim est sine sono, seu numero sonoro]. (trans. in *Luther's Works*, Vol. 53, p. 322; cf. *Martin Luthers Werke*, Bd. 50, pp. 368-9)

Letter from Martin Luther to Kaspar Zeuner, February 9, 1543:

If one preserves that principal and pre-eminent uniformity and agreement, which is in doctrine, the reconciliation of outwardly dissimilar ceremonies will be easy; just as, for instance, if there be health in mind and body, the diversity of operations in the various members will create no discord in the body, but rather a beautiful concord out of the various voices, as in music. (*Martin Luthers Werke*, Bd. 10, p. 260)

[13]See Söhngen, "Music and Theology: A Systematic Approach," p. 14.
[14]See Irwin, *Neither Voice nor Heart Alone*, pp. 43ff.

consequences of this open attitude toward music, both for German Protestant church music and for the general practice of music in Germany, are matters of record. Luther's taste and support for learned art music found sympathetic approval among the German people, and the history of German Protestant church music for two centuries after Luther is triumphant testimony to the noble, responsible exercise of free choice in musical style and performance. The potential for abuse inherent in the freedom to base music on personal taste instead of divine precept became evident only after the seventeenth century, when clergy and musicians no longer exercised that freedom so responsibly. What Friedrich Blume has observed about the Lutheran liturgy also holds true for its music: "...the history of the Lutheran service is justly called a history of its decline." (*Protestant Church Music*, p. 5).

THE COUNTER-REFORMATION

The official Roman Catholic response to the various reformation movements was the Council of Trent, which met between 1545 and 1563, establishing a direction for Catholic policy and practice that was to endure for the next four centuries. Viewed superficially, the Council's deliberations regarding church music simply restated past ecclesiastical attitudes and teachings. The preliminary report[15] from September 10, 1562, was ratified by the Council in summary form on September 17, 1562:

So that the house of God should truly appear to be rightly called a house of prayer, compositions in which there is an intermingling of the lascivious or impure, whether by instrument or voice, and likewise every secular action, idle and even profane conversation, strolling about, bustle, and shouting must be ousted from the churches. (trans. in Hayburn, *Papal Legislation*, p. 28)

---

[15]That report reads as follows:

All things should indeed be so ordered that the Masses, whether they be celebrated with or without singing, may reach tranquilly into the ears and hearts of those who hear them, when everything is executed clearly and at the right speed [i.e., the priest should avoid speaking too quickly or softly]. In the case of those Masses which are celebrated with singing and with organ, let nothing profane be intermingled, but only hymns and divine praises. If anything is to be sung with the organ from the sacred services while they are in progress, let it be recited in a simple clear voice beforehand so that no one will miss any part of the eternal reading of the sacred writings. The whole plan of singing in musical modes should be constituted not to give empty pleasure to the ear, but in such a way that the words may be clearly understood by all, and thus the hearts of the listeners be drawn to the desire of heavenly harmonies, in the contemplation of the joys of the blessed. Those things which are established for the celebration of the Masses should be observed in them and also in the other sacred services, so that those things which are performed in a sacred manner may be understood with greater reverence, piety and faith. (trans. in Hayburn, *Papal Legislation*, p. 27)

The Reformation   141

The Council censured abuses and the inroads of secular practices, reaffirmed the tranquil nature of church music, dismissed pleasure in music, and reasserted the supremacy of the sacred text. Yet (though some bishops would have favored such a move) the Council did not forbid polyphony, which was by now a long-established, time-hallowed tradition in church music. Such a move was stalled, among other things, by the exemplary practice of music at Council liturgies. Otto Cardinal Truchsess, bishop of Augsburg and one of the most influential figures of the Council, arranged for the Council to commission his choirmaster, the Franco-flemish musician Jacobus de Kerle, to compose a number of works to be sung at the Council's worship, the so-called *Preces speciales*. De Kerle's work, written in a sober and moderate style with a balance of polyphony and homophony, elicited general commendation from the churchmen who were present, mollifying the suspicions of those predisposed because of previous excesses to reject polyphonic singing. The Council fathers encountered intervention by extra-conciliar forces, as well.

> There are some other [proposed] articles about which we think that we must speak with you. Among these is the last of the third section, which states: "sentimental chants must be outlawed, and in our churches we must maintain grave music which is more fitting to the ecclesiastical simplicity."
> We will not approve removing ornate chants [i.e., polyphony] completely from our services, because we believe that so divine a gift as music can frequently stir to devotion the souls of men who are especially sensitive to music. This music must never be banned from our churches. (Ferdinand I, Emperor of Spain, in a letter to the fathers of the Council, dated August 23, 1563; trans. in Hayburn, *Papal Legislation*, p. 28)

If the Council did not forbid polyphony, however, neither did it anywhere make allusion to neo-Pythagorean or neo-Platonic doctrines or to speculative ideas of world harmony to support its position on music. By this late date, such ideas were much contested and already beginning to pass out of fashion. They survived into the seventeenth century in the writings of some Roman Catholic clerics (notably Athanasius Kircher), but the Counter-Reformation's wholehearted acceptance of extroverted, sensual Baroque art forms (especially as promoted by the missionary-minded Jesuits) helped hasten the neglect and demise of musical speculation by placing emphasis on music's ability to excite an emotional piety rather than on its ability to engage the intellect.[16]

Although the actions of the Council regarding church music undoubtedly had an effect on specific abuses at particular places (notably at St. Peter's Basilica in Rome), in the long run artistic change and evolution--forces beyond church control--had as much to do with bringing about the ideals of simplicity and text supremacy as did the Council's decrees. The era of decisive Christian influence on music was moving to a close, and subsequent papal decrees repeatedly bear witness to the limited success of attempts to keep secular influences at bay.

---

[16]Cf. Lang, *Music in Western Civilization*, pp. 315ff.

10

The Decline of Musical Speculation

Only in the later Middle Ages did signs appear to indicate that the momentum of traditional Christian attitudes and viewpoints on music had begun to lose energy. Neo-Platonic speculation was challenged by the rediscovery of Aristotelian philosophy[1]--through contact with Islamic scholarship--which denied the existence of any music of the spheres or any role at all for music in speculation, and (more importantly) emphasized systematic scientific observation over speculation. Platonic systems of thought tend to comprehend and organize the particular with reference to the universal (universally valid principles, normally those established by revelation and hallowed by long tradition); in other words, they understand what is seen by means of what is unseen. Aristotelianism tends to comprehend the universal (to derive universally valid principles) by observing and analyzing the particular; in other words, it understands what is unseen by what is seen. Early Christianity, being predisposed to experience and to interpret the world solely in terms of divine revelation, had an innate attitudinal affinity to Platonism.[2] Aristotelian modes of thought did not suddenly replace neo-Platonic attitudes; in fact, the later Middle Ages witnessed various attempts to reconcile the two. These attempts were all doomed to failure, however, since the two proceeded from fundamentally irreconcilable attitudes.

One of the earliest casualties of the growing defection from Plato to Aristotle was the idea of a music of the spheres. Already at the beginning of the Renaissance the composer and theorist Johannes Tinctoris could write: "Concords of sounds and melodies, from whose sweetness, as Lactantius says, the pleasure of the ear is derived, are produced, then, not by heavenly bodies, but by earthly instruments with the cooperation of nature" (Johannes Tinctoris, *Proportionale musices*, c.1476; trans. in Strunk, *Source Readings*, p. 198). The new ideas inevitably contributed to the de-sacralization of musical science by divorcing it from metaphysical speculation.

---

[1] See Ellefsen, "Music and Humanism" (diss.), pp. 37-45.
[2] Cf. II Corinthians 4:18.

Aristotelian philosophy, however, was not the only new current that challenged the supremacy of neo-Platonic musical speculation. The enormous increase in musical activity outside of the church during the later Middle Ages offered examples of other kinds of music, less oriented toward the intellect, more sensually attractive, more emotionally expressive. Although much of the music of the troubadours and trouvères, for example, is serious and elevated in tone, it is unmistakably permeated by an ardent, sensuous eroticism interwoven with the chaste pursuit of an unattainable love. Later secular songs, such as those of the goliards, are unabashedly erotic, if not lewd (e.g., the *Carmina burana*, c.1300). This new sensuality is not a flat contradiction of world-consciousness, since world-conscious humans normally understand human sensuality--like everything else--as dominated by the sacred. (Indeed, for many world-conscious people there is nothing that is not under that domination.) But by diverting attention from the realm of the divine to focus it on human concerns and pursuits (thus hastening the de-sacralization of the world), such artistic activities inadvertently helped to weaken a specifically Christian worldview.

The tension between various attitudes toward music must have become especially intense during the fourteenth century, a period whose insecurity, decay, and disintegration helped hasten the demise of a unitary Christian world view. That tension fairly bristles in these lines from a poem by Guillaume de Machaut: "And music is a science, whose purpose is to make people laugh and sing and dance."[3] The popularization of music, especially among the upper classes, meant that more music was being made than ever before.[4] Yet at the same time, paradoxically, the age-old presumption that poetry was to be sung was for the first time brought into question: the poetic works of the troubadours and trouvères were intended to be sung, but those of Petrarch and Chaucer probably were not. Furthermore, music (other than dance music) no longer perforce had to have a text--for example, Machaut's instrumental piece *Hoquetus David*.

Despite the tenacity of the traditional worldview in some quarters, the process of de-sacralization accelerated after the fourteenth century. In the realm of ideas about music, the increasing impotence of traditional ideas manifested itself in the growing muddle of thought associated with music's effects on human beings; the complex of ideas on this topic became increasingly turgid and impotent.[5] The Renaissance tendency to abandon medieval (i.e., specifically Christian) speculation in favor of the learning of pagan antiquity doubtless contributed to the confusion of ideas, and thus had a weakening effect on speculation in general. The practical problems and controversies that began to affect church music composition and performance as they were influenced by new developments, however, afford a clearer picture of the passing of old attitudes and ideas. Roman Catholic papal and conciliar decrees that censure the invasion of de-sacralizing musical practices[6] are undeniable witnesses to the fact that such incursions were common. These decrees did not ordinarily address theological and philosophical issues, but reacted only to practical abuses with juridical

---

[3]Trans. in Lang, *Music in Western Civilization*, p. 162.
[4]Ibid., pp. 165-66.
[5]See Finney, "Harmony or Rapture in Music," p. 391.
[6]See: Hayburn, *Papal Legislation*, pp. 78, 87-88, 99-101.

The Decline of Musical Speculation 145

proscriptions. Their effectiveness was in any event only local and of brief duration.

After the fourteenth century, the rejection of various aspects of musical speculation became increasingly frequent and widespread.

Music, in the practice, hath been well pursued, and in good variety; but in the theory, and especially in the yielding of the causes of the practice, very weakly; being reduced into certain mystical subtilities of no use and not much truth. (Francis Bacon, *Sylva sylvarum*, 1626; in *The Works of Francis Bacon*, §.100)

Most contemporary treatises on music, however, did not bother to confront or deny traditional ideas; they simply disregarded them, often opening with several perfunctory paragraphs to prove that their authors were aware of them, and then proceeding forthwith to the "more important" matters of musical practice or theory. Just such a treatise is the *Discourse on Ancient Music and Good Singing* (c.1580) by Giovanni de' Bardi, a prominent figure in the Florentine Camerata. After a paragraph on the powers of music, Bardi continues: "But I should go far afield and beyond my intention if I were to give to music and all its marvels the praise that is their due, for my sole intention is to show you, as clearly as I can, how it is to be treated in practice" (trans. in Strunk, *Source Readings*, p. 293).

There were further concrete signs of the disintegration of the old worldview as it pertained to music. One was the decline of the *maîtrise* during the sixteenth and seventeenth centuries,[7] hastened by a new style of church music (largely derived from opera and dance) that was intended primarily for solo performance. Thus Dietrich Buxtehude's cantatas, often considered to be choral works, are actually intended for performance by soloists,[8] and Joshua Rifkin has argued that even J.S. Bach's cantatas are to be performed with one singer to a part.[9] The period after the English Commonwealth marked the nadir of English cathedral and collegiate choral foundations[10] (restored only in the nineteenth century under the aegis of the Oxford and Ecclesiological Movements).

By abolishing minor orders and choral benefices, the Reformation effected the disappearance of clergy from Protestant choirs. After the fifteenth century, ever-increasing demands for musical proficiency and specialization aided their departure from Roman Catholic choirs, thus ensuring that musicians would henceforth be subordinates, never equals in determining what was appropriate for the conduct of the liturgy: "A singer need not be in holy orders but must be a man of honor and of good repute... (*Constitutiones capellae pontificiae*, 1545; trans. in Stevenson, *Spanish Cathedral Music in the Golden Age*, p. 27).

In the course of completely reorganizing their course of studies at the end of the sixteenth century, universities began to drop speculative musical philosophy from their curricula. Thereafter practicing musicians often assumed a prominent

---

[7] See: Fellerer, *History of Catholic Church Music*, p. 113; Blume, *Protestant Church Music*, p. 321.
[8] See: Snyder, *Dieterich Buxtehude*, pp. 360-6.
[9] Rifkin, "Bach's 'Choruses'--Less Than They Seem?," pp. 42-44.
[10] See Long, *The Music of the English Church*, pp. 285-7; also Hutchings, *Church Music in the Nineteenth Century*, pp. 98-101.

role in the life of the university, but they were not regular members of the faculty. Music scholarship thus disappeared from universities until the late nineteenth century, when it returned (with a completely different emphasis) as musicology. For a number of reasons, then, the advent of humanism and the embryonic self-conscious worldview signaled the relentless decline and rejection of musical speculation. More and more, old ideas were bypassed and forgotten.

Concurrent with the wane of musical speculation (during the fifteenth and sixteenth centuries), ideal principles of sacred music became thoroughly established:[11] severe, ascetic, serene, balanced, intellectual, evoking contemplation and mental involvement rather than outward emotional excitement. This is seen nowhere more clearly than in the Counter-Reformation's quasi-official sanction of the Palestrina style.[12]

...music would have come very near to being banished from the Holy [Roman Catholic] Church by a sovereign pontiff, had not Giovanni Palestrina found the remedy, showing that the fault and error lay, not with music, but with the composers, and composing in confirmation of this the Mass entitled *Missa Papae Marcelli*. (Agostino Agazzari, *Of Playing upon a Bass with all Instruments and of their Use in the Consort*, 1607; trans. in Palestrina, *Pope Marcellus Mass*, p. 28)

Until the end of the sixteenth century there was a minimum of conflict between these ideals and new views and practices, since the secular musical ideal remained by and large grave and majestic as well.[13] With the coming of the seventeenth century, principles of sacred music began to lose their unique identity as they were inundated by new ideas and practices, in particular the influence of opera and dance on almost all aspects of music-making. Even then, they were vigorous enough to maintain the shell of their old identity in the Baroque *stile antico*. By the middle of the eighteenth century, however, specifically Christian music ideals and practices had been thrust to the periphery and dismissed. Overwhelmed by the force of new ideas and attitudes, conservative, retrospective elements within the churches (that might have fought for the perpetuation of traditional ideals) were at first paralyzed and could only react feebly and defensively. Thus the intense sacred/secular conflict that still figures into today's arguments about church music did not arise until the advent of the nineteenth-century retrospective ecclesiastical revivals: the Oxford and Ecclesiological Movements in England, the *Kirchenagenden* in Germany, and the work of the monks at the Abbey of St. Pierre de Solesmes in France.

Curiously enough, distant echoes of the cosmic worldview's ideas about music have survived even into the twentieth century:
1. In language (in words whose roots still have both a musical as well as a personal or ethical meaning): harmony, harmonious; temper, temperament,

---

[11] Even though the music of this period does not exhibit uniform style characteristics (Dunstable's music is not stylistically identical with Palestrina's), the underlying principles governing the music did not change except when and to the degree that they were affected by extra-Christian influences.

[12] For further discussion of this matter in historical context, see Palestrina, *Pope Marcellus Mass*, ed. Lockwood, pp. 3-36.

[13] See Blume, *Protestant Church Music*, p. 29.

The Decline of Musical Speculation   147

temperance, temperate, intemperate, temperamental; consonant, dissonant; concord; rational (originally meaning in "tune" with the Pythagorean ratios).
2. in isolated (often poetic) statements by well-known public figures:[14]

One of the trumpets asked Bodanzky in dispair: "I'd just like to know what's beautiful about blowing away at a trumpet stopped up to high C!" This gave me an insight at once into the lot of man, who likewise cannot understand why he must endure being stopped to the piercing agony of his own existence, cannot see what it is for, and how his screech is to be attuned to the great harmony of the universal symphony of all creation. Bodanzky answered the unhappy man very logically: "Wait a bit! You can't expect to understand it yet . . . When all the rest come in, you'll soon see what you're there for." (Gustav Mahler, in a letter to Alma Mahler, September 10, 1908; trans. in Mahler, *Gustav Mahler*, p. 253)

But ideas born of the old worldview no longer have a widespread or coherent intellectual base. At best, they are a poetic echo of times past. At the worst, the ethical powers of music are often left to be propounded by what might euphemistically be called "the fringe," writers who assure us (on the basis of questionable "experiments" and "tests") that music will provide immediate benefit to our (or our children's) physical, mental, and spiritual well-being, that it is a panacea to improve coordination, concentration, memory, vision and hearing, and to alleviate stress. Or, conversely, certain kinds of music (again for nebulous reasons) are proclaimed degenerate, inciting to moral and social collapse: "These Beatles are completely anti-Christ. They are preparing our teenagers for riot and ultimate revolution against our Christian Republic" (Reverend David Noebel, sermon to his congregation in Claremont, California; quoted in Crofton & Fraser, *Dictionary of Musical Quotations*, p. 115:6). Not the least of the consequences of the final demise of the cosmic worldview, therefore, is that we cannot truly understand or sympathize with the music of the past, especially with the past music of the church.[15]

Thus we arrive at the present, having briefly traced the transformation of a culture (Western European) that was steeped in the awareness of cosmic harmony into one that now for the most part considers it a quaint relic (if indeed it is aware of it at all).

---

[14]See also E.T.A. Hoffmann, *Beethoven's Instrumental Music* (1813), trans. in Strunk, *Source Readings*, p. 779; Hindemith, *The Craft of Musical Composition*, pp. 12-13.
[15]See Lowinsky, "The Goddess Fortuna in Music," p. 77.

11

The Gifts of Christian Musical Speculation

The period from the fourteenth to the eighteenth centuries witnessed the decline and end of the church's hegemony over music.[1] The future course and shape of Western art music had in large part, however, already been determined by music's long subservience to the church and its ideas. The technical procedures and devices born of those ideas, though now shorn of their original cosmic, metaphysical significance, continued to serve as the fundamental structural material of Western European art music: procedures such as canon, imitation, thematic inversion, augmentation, diminution (thematic development in general)--and indeed, the very practice of polyphony itself.

As you listen to a Mass setting by Josquin des Prez or a motet by J. S. Bach, it is instructive to reflect on just what odd musical phenomena these greatest monuments of Western art music are. They are unlike music of any other culture: a painstakingly complex, highly intellectual music that can only truly be appreciated after a lifetime of experience, study, and performance. To realize fully how unnatural (how "artificial") such polyphonic works are, direct your mind for a moment outside the realm of music. Which of the other arts exists primarily in time (as does music) instead of in space (e.g., painting, sculpture, architecture)? Beside music, the arts that exist primarily in time are literature, poetry and drama.[2] It is within the realm of possibility that each of these arts could also have developed polyphonically instead of monophonically. That is, they could have evolved procedures of composition and performance that feature two or more trains of thought uttered simultaneously, trains of thought that the reader or listener would be expected to follow and comprehend simultaneously. Indeed, there are some operas that feature moments of text delivery in just this way, but such immensely complex artifice is very much a fringe phenomenon in

---

[1] See Routley, *The Church and Music*, pp. 163-4.
[2] Dance is unique in that it exists equally in time and in space.

the literary arts. Music, on the other hand, at one point in its development chose to pursue this "artificial" tangent, and to make polyphony (with all its attendant intellectual artifice) not a fringe phenomenon, but the normative way to make music. The course that it chose has determined the development of music ever since.

It would be an exaggeration to claim that Christian speculation gave birth to polyphony; no doubt it was an idea whose time had come, and it might well have appeared in some form or another, regardless of Christian theology. But it is not overstating the case to assert that the development of polyphony as we know it is inconceivable without the formative influence of Christian speculation. There are those who hold that the church impeded the advance of music;[3] the evidence presented thus far ought to contribute to a more balanced, fair view of the matter. Christian ideas shaped the progress of music constantly, decisively and positively, long after the rising tide of ideas not generated by Christian thought wrested music from the church's control.

Consider for a moment elements of certain works by Beethoven (surely a composer beyond the domination of the church): the fugal sections in the second movement (*Marche funebre*) and the Finale of the Third Symphony (in E flat, opus 55--the *Eroica*); or the combination of complex fugal writing with sonata structure in the Finale of the String Quartet, Opus 59 (Razumovsky), No. 3 in C; or the augmentation, retrograde, inversion, and stretto in the *Hammerklavier* Sonata, Opus 106, in B flat. Why all these abstruse polyphonic devices? Why this painstaking emphasis on form: balance of sections, key areas, themes? Surely Beethoven could have reached his listeners' feelings by a far more direct route. (We need only compare it with a work such as Ravel's *Bolero*, or with any piece of late twentieth-century popular music!) The answer is that Beethoven was writing in a lofty, noble musical "language" whose "vocabulary" was partially determined by the musical conventions of his time, and partially by the force of his own musical personality--but whose "grammar" and "syntax" (and thus a part of whose content) were in large measure an inheritance from ideas determined by Christian speculative theology. Indeed, it does not seem to be an exaggeration to say that the Western (i.e., European) notion of unity achieved by formal balance and cohesion as a primary determinant of musical quality or "greatness" is inconceivable without the underlying shaping force of Christian metaphysical speculation.[4]

Polyphony is often cited as the major distinction of Western European art music. The development of complex formal structures could also be singled out for this honor. The attitude toward music that lies behind these accomplishments is, however, a more fundamentally distinctive and decisive characteristic of Western art music: music has a profound intellectual dimension;

---

[3]For example, Bloch, *Essays on the philosophy of music*, pp. 2-3.

[4]Are balance and clarity of formal articulation (particularly evident in music of the Classic period) the result of Christian speculation, or are they products of classicism via the Enlightenment? The question probably cannot be answered. Perhaps one could say that Enlightenment ideals were favorable to the continued development of this aspect of previous musical tradition. At any rate, it is clear that the ordered character of Classical music is not a break with past musical theory and practice, but an intensification of it.

it speaks to the mind as well as the emotions. No other culture has nurtured such a deep ingress of music into the domain of the intellect. A number of reasons for this singularity could be advanced: societal demands, native genius, or simply blind chance. In the final analysis, none of them is as convincing as the influence of metaphysical, speculative Christian theology. It is not an accident that music's intellectual component began to recede simultaneously with the retreat of the church's hegemony. Viewed against the background of primitive music and the music of other cultures, Christian art music appears as something unnatural, "artificial"--a glorious aberration that has left an indelible impress on all Western art music following it, up to and including the present.

Here the tale might end. We have finished tracing the birth, growth, and decay of a complex of ideas (inherently religious, and then Christian by adoption) that shaped and energized music in Christian civilization and that produced splendid fruit even in its decline. The story cannot end here, however, for the Christian church is still a living organism, and the practice of Christian music-making continues up to the present day. It operates not in the matrix in which it once flourished, though, but in a foreign and rather unsympathetic one.

On the level of practice, the development of music may be understood as an ever-evolving continuum. Even startling novelties, such as the advent of organum or of monody, may upon closer inquiry be seen to have their roots in already established practices. On the level of ideas, however, the situation is different. The foregoing chapters have traced the evolution of a complex of ideas grounded in the world-conscious worldview. By the end of the Middle Ages that worldview had begun to disintegrate. Simultaneously, a vigorous new complex of ideas began to flourish, ostensibly rooted at first in the spirit of antiquity, but in reality radically discontinuous with older modes of thought: self-conscious, non-Christian, and increasingly anti-religious. That complex of thought has developed into the modern secular worldview, which focuses on human life and achievement, on the world here and now, and which dismisses or ignores the existence of any dimension of reality beyond the world of the senses. Such a thoroughgoing transformation of human thought and awareness could hardly help but produce new ideas and attitudes about music; the rise of those new ideas and attitudes could in turn hardly help but have a gradual yet profound effect on musical practice.

The process has been rather like shifting a house from an old foundation to a new one. The house (music) is still the same, but what is holding it up is quite new and different. The new foundation has allowed the present occupants (us) new liberties, new opportunities. Accordingly, some of the occupants have embarked on a far-reaching campaign of redecoration that has either relegated the former scheme to the closets or has transformed it so as to be increasingly unrecognizable in comparison with what it once was. The occupants who have spearheaded the redecoration are, of course, delighted with the results, but there are others with a greater or lesser degree of attachment to the former furnishings. They have begun at times to feel somewhat ill at ease, and to wonder if the transformation has so radically altered the house that it will no longer allow either memory of or appreciation for the former one.

The task of the ensuing chapters, then, is to trace the birth and development of the new ideological foundation, and to investigate what the consequences of its coming have been, both for music in general and more specifically for the music of the Christian church. Before forging ahead, the reader may find it helpful to page again through Chapter 1, the Prologue, in order to refresh the memory of the old ways of thinking before embarking on the new.

12

Humanism

The movement that is widely understood as having initiated the growth of the self-conscious worldview is known as humanism. The term has a broad range of meanings and implications. Originally denoting the pursuit of learning based on literary works of classical antiquity, it came eventually to signify an interest in the human sphere in contrast to the medieval preoccupation with otherworldly concerns. Humanism, then, was essentially extra-Christian in origin and in orientation, arising from ideas outside the realm of established Christian theology and piety. Until the late sixteenth century, however, the church did not oppose or interfere with the progress of the new movement,[1] for humanism, properly speaking, was not fundamentally at odds with Christianity or the church.[2] Learned church circles were in fact often overtly sympathetic to humanist ideals, and some of the leading early humanists were churchmen (Cardinal Pietro Bembo, for example, or Ulrich Zwingli).

Indeed, humanism was based to a degree on the same classical ideals as the traditional medieval worldview. There was a fundamental difference in scope between humanism and the Middle Ages, however: the Renaissance bypassed the learning of the church-dominated Middle Ages and vaulted directly back to the sources of learning from pagan antiquity.[3] Humanists criticized more and more sharply those aspects of culture that seemed to be products of the intervening

---

[1] When the Roman Catholic Church finally did intervene (e.g., in the Council of Trent), the result was twofold: the hastening of the advent of a more outwardly pious Baroque art, and the acceleration of the process of rupture between Christianity and humanism.

[2] See Toulmin, *Cosmopolis*, pp. 24-5.

[3] See Vicenzo Galilei, *Dialogo della musica antica e della moderna* (1581), trans. in Strunk, *Source Readings*, pp. 302-3; see also Palisca, *Humanism in Italian Renaissance Musical Thought*, p. 6.

"dark ages" and thus incompatible with a proper understanding of classical ideas. (One of the targets for their fire was of course elaborate, abstruse polyphony.[4])

An increased cultivation of music in the secular sphere accompanied the earliest stirrings of humanism, not primarily because music embodied cosmic perfection, but because it was entertaining and pleasing to listen to.

> For they [i.e., Binchois and Dufay] have found a new way
> of making fresh harmony
> in loud and soft music,
> with feints and rests and shifts.
> They have assumed the English manner
> and follow Dunstable,
> and so a marvelous delight
> makes their music joyful and engaging.
> (Martin Le Franc, *Le champion des dames*, c.1441)[5]

Even clownish music, so thoroughly condemned by Plato, found a receptive audience.[6]

Sixteenth-century writings provide the first hints that art should be considered a matter of inspiration, not of learning. It had of course always required talent and intelligence, but now the element of genius began to be accorded more weight than knowing the rules. What we today call "art" was throughout the Middle Ages considered handicraft, and the person who engaged in it was normally held to be merely an artisan. This is one reason why posterity has preserved the names of very few medieval practicing musicians (*cantores*), in contrast to the more respected *musici*. The humanist movement began to recognize what previously would have been unthinkable: that individual creativity is essential to art,[7] that the artist has a creative soul to which he must remain faithful.

---

[4] See Giovanni de' Bardi, *Discourse on Ancient Music and Good Singing* (c.1580), trans. in Strunk, *Source Readings*, pp. 293-4; see also Palisca, *Humanism in Italian Renaissance Musical Thought*, p. 17.

[5] For the manuscript source of this poem, see Reese, *Music in the Renaissance*, p. 12, n.46.

[6] Thomas Morley (1597):

The last degree of gravity (if they have any at all) is given to the *villanelle*, or country songs, which are made only for the ditty's [i.e., text's] sake, for, so they be aptly set to express the nature of the ditty, the composer (though he were never so excellent) will not stick to take many perfect chords of one kind together, for in this kind they think it no fault (as being a kind of keeping decorum) to make a clownish music to a clownish matter. (quoted in Strunk, *Source Readings*, pp. 275-6)

[7] Adrian Petit Coclico, *Compendium musices* (1552):

Josquin did not judge everyone capable of the demands of composition. He felt that it should be taught only to those who were driven by an unusual force of their nature to this most beautiful art, since he asserted that many works had been beautifully composed, and only one man out of thousands could compose anything like them, let alone better. (trans. Seay, p. 16)

The recognition of individual creativity, then, was one innovative idea. A second, no less momentous, idea was that music should be written and indeed prized for its ability to express and to move human "passions." (Used in this sense, the word is synonymous with "emotions.") Our own age assumes this notion so completely that it comes as something of a shock to realize that the earliest unambiguous records of it in Western European art music date from the sixteenth century,[8] and that it became axiomatic only in the seventeenth century.

...having in mind those inflections and accents that serve us in our grief, in our joy, and in similar states, I caused the bass to move in time to these, either more or less, following the passions. (Jacopo Peri, Foreword to the opera *Euridice*, 1601; trans. in Strunk, *Source Readings*, p. 374)

The basis of music is sound; its aim is to please and to arouse the affections. (René Descartes, *Compendium musicae*, 1618; trans. in Weiss & Taruskin, *Music in the Western World*, p. 189)

Whereas in the Middle Ages music was regularly praised for its ability to calm emotions, now there was increasing praise for its power to move or excite them. Music was somewhat slower than the other arts in showing signs of this new development, perhaps due to its central role in the traditional worldview and to the continued influence of speculative theology. The first signs of serious attempts to express emotion were related to the rebirth of the old idea that words should rule the music, but with a new twist: music was no longer to remain simply an unobtrusive, emotionally neutral ornament to the text, but was now to cooperate in intensifying the human emotions inherent in the words.[9] The new idea that music should express the feeling evoked by the words seems to have begun (at first very subtly) in the motets of late fifteenth-century Francoflemish composers, but by the second quarter of the sixteenth century its development had shifted to the Italian madrigal, first reaching maturity in certain madrigals by Cipriano de Rore,[10] whom Claudio Monteverdi later recognized as the originator of the *seconda prattica*,[11] the new, progressive dramatic style. It continued to develop primarily in secular forms for most of the sixteenth century, belatedly re-entering church music in the early seventeenth century (in Monteverdi's *Vespers* of 1610, for example, or in Heinrich Schutz's *Cantiones sacrae* of 1625). The new emphasis on the dominance of the text, however, by no means altered the notion that the ideal church music should be characterized by gravity, majesty, and nobility, for even though humanist thought was

---

[8]For an early instance, see Jacques Descartes de Ventemille, as quoted in *Solitaire second ou prose de la musique* (1555), in Weiss & Taruskin, *Music in the Western World*, pp. 159-60.

[9]See Gioseffe Zarlino, *Istituzioni armoniche* (1558), trans. in Strunk, *Source Readings*, pp. 256-7; Mazzone de Miglionico, Dedication of the *First Book of Madrigals* (1569), trans. in Weiss & Taruskin, *Music in the Western World*, p. 143; Agostino Agazzari, *Of playing upon a bass* (1607), trans. in Strunk, pp. 430-31; see also Palisca, *Humanism in Italian Renaissance Musical Thought*, pp. 13-14.

[10]"O sonno", for example, or "De le belle contrade"

[11]In the Preface to the *Scherzi musicali* of 1607.

beginning subtly to undermine the traditional concept of man as a noble servant of God, it was replacing it with the image of man as a noble being in his own right.[12]

The central figure in initiating the innovation--music that consciously sought to express the emotion of the words--seems to have been Josquin des Prez (c.1440?-1521). His musical personality and compositions (like J. S. Bach's) mark one of those remarkable moments when intellect and emotion find a perfect equilibrium.[13] Josquin's mastery of intellectual, formally complex music techniques and procedures is uncontested.[14] Yet the Renaissance theorist Glarean praised Josquin's motet *Planxit autem David* for quite different reasons.

...throughout the motet, there is preserved what befits the mourner, who is wont at first to cry out frequently, then to murmur to himself, turning little by little to sorrowful complaints, thereupon to subside or sometimes, when passion breaks out anew, to raise his voice again, shouting out a cry. All these things we see most beautifully observed in this composition, as will be evident to the attentive reader. Nor is there in it anything unworthy of its author; by the gods, he has everywhere expressed the passion in a wonderful way. (Heinrich Glarean, *Dodecachordon*, 1547; trans. in Strunk, *Source Readings*, pp. 226-7)

In Josquin's late works such as the motets *Planxit autem David*, *Tu pauperum refugium*, and *Huc me sydereo*, intellect and emotion fuse to create artistry of the finest, rarest sort, artistry so far ahead of its time that it took several generations of composers to digest and appropriate its advances. Glarean, who recognized

---

[12]Giovanni Pico della Mirandola, "*Oratio de dignitate hominis*" (1486):

O sublime generosity of God the Father! O highest and most wonderful felicity of man! To him it was granted to have what he chooses, to be what he wills. At the moment when they are born, beasts bring with them from their mother's womb, as Lucilius says, whatever they shall possess. From the beginning or soon afterwards, the highest spiritual beings have been what they are to be for all eternity. When man came into life, the Father endowed him with all kinds of seeds and with the germs of every way of life. Whatever seeds each man cultivates will grow and bear fruit in him. If these seeds are vegetative, he will be like a plant; if they are sensitive, he will become like the beasts; if they are rational, he will become like a heavenly creature; if intellectual, he will be an angel and a son of God. And if, content with the lot of no created being, he withdraws into the centre of his own oneness, his spirit, made one with God in the solitary darkness of the Father, which is above all things, will surpass all things.

Who then will not wonder at this chameleon of ours, or who could wonder more greatly at anything else?

[13]This balance in his work was already recognized during the Renaissance: Heinrich Glarean, *Dodecachordon* (1547):

...our Josquin...now advances with impetuous and precipitate notes, now intones his subject in long-drawn tones, and, to sum up, has brought forth nothing that was not delightful to the ear and approved as ingenious by the learned. (trans. in Strunk, *Source Readings*, p. 221)

[14]See Sparks, *Cantus Firmus in Mass and Motet*, pp. 237-8

Josquin's genius, nevertheless could not fully fathom the depth of the new dimension Josquin brought to music, even a quarter of a century after his death.[15]

Music designed in some measure to express human emotion was, of course, destined to appeal to a much wider constituency than aristocratic speculative compositions. The shift to the new attitude about music was thus paralleled and aided by the rise of music printing and publishing at the beginning of the sixteenth century, a development that was by nature oriented toward human convenience and mass consumption.

Word or text painting can have an intellectual dimension, but since it was often applied during the Renaissance to affective words and texts, it bordered on and often penetrated the sphere of the emotional. Composers became amazingly skillful at depicting a great range of emotional states--sorrow, cruelty, bitterness, rage, joy, wonder, surprise--by melodic turns, rests, harmonic devices, varying musical textures and, on the whole, a tendency toward more immediately memorable melodic and rhythmic motives. A major factor in the emotional appeal of word painting was these composers' choice of affective texts to set to music. The predilection for such texts appeared during the late fifteenth century, and it subsequently became more and more pronounced. The preoccupation of early seventeenth-century opera composers with the dramatic story of Orpheus and Euridice shows how habitual it came to be. This held true primarily for secular music, but church music, too, often employed religious texts of fervent, emotional intensity: for example, Josquin's "Planxit autem David,"[16] or "Audi coelum" from Monteverdi's *Vespers* of 1610, or Heinrich Schütz's "O bone, O dulcis, O benigne Jesu" from the *Cantiones Sacrae* of 1625.

Probably the most striking evidence for the new attitude toward music was the proliferation of instruments in worship, a complete reversal of traditional Christian liturgical practice. Instruments of course lent greater range, power and sonority to church music, and thus more striking emotional impact. (One need only experience the delayed entry of the instrumental ensemble in Giovanni Gabrieli's motet "In ecclesiis" to comprehend this.) Although some church enclaves (e.g., the Sistine Chapel in Rome or, later, the churches of the Reformed movement) preserved a strict unaccompanied practice, the use of instruments in festive liturgical events was by no means uncommon in the Renaissance. Giannozzo Manetti's moving description of the dedication of

---

[15]Glarean, *Dodecachordon*:

If this man, besides that native bent and strength of character by which he was distinguished, had had an understanding of the twelve modes and of the truth of musical theory, nature could have brought forth nothing more majestic and magnificent in this art; so versatile was his temperament in every respect, so armed with natural acumen and force, that there is nothing he could not have done in this profession. But moderation was wanting for the most part and, with learning, judgment; thus in certain places in his compositions he did not, as he should have, soberly repress the violent impulses of his unbridled temperament. Yet let this petty fault be condoned in view of the man's other incomparable gifts. (trans. in Strunk, *Source Readings*, p. 220)

[16]David's lament over Jonathan, in II Samuel 1:17-27.

Florence's Cathedral, Santa Maria del Fiore,[17] in 1436 (the occasion of the premiere of Dufay's motet *Nuper rosarum flores* ; see Chapter 8, p. 128) preserves one man's rapturous account of the effect they produced. Iconographic evidence also reveals the use of instruments in liturgical events (Illustration 7). By the end of the seventeenth century the consistent use of instruments in larger churches had become the norm, both for Roman Catholics and Lutherans. The best known examples of this are Bach's Leipzig cantatas and the Mass settings of Haydn and Mozart.

In spite of obvious divergences, old and new ideas were clearly not always mutually repulsive or even exclusive. On the contrary, they continued to interact in curious ways. After 1600 the majority of composers' works exhibited both progressive and conservative tendencies, at times in the same piece and often not even clearly distinguishable. This observation becomes ever more true the closer one gets to modern times. A certain amount of tension between old and new was inevitable and indeed highly fruitful. A clear reflection of the friction between them can be seen in the transformed meaning of the word "artificial." Until the seventeenth century, it meant "full of artifice, good workmanship" (an encomium).[18] Composing music was understood as a work of devotion, a reverent reflection on and imitation of the divine order of creation. It therefore mirrored the complexity and perfection of the divine artifice evident in that creation.

...a song that is well and artificially made cannot be well perceived nor understood at the first hearing, but the oftener you shall hear it, the better cause of liking you will discover, and commonly that song is best esteemed with which our ears are most acquainted. (foreword to William Byrd's *Psalmes, Songs, and Sonnets*, 1611)

By the eighteenth century, "artificial" had come to mean "feigned, affected, unnatural" (an epithet).

In the past, the style of concerted music was altogether unlike today's. In melody, in harmony, and in form it differed greatly from what is being written now. Melody was neither as free nor as natural, and consequently less lively and flowing. More attention was paid to working out a full texture. Music thus artificially and laboriously fashioned could not hope to embody the affections the way today's music does. (Johann Adolph Scheibe, *Der critische Musicus* (1737-40); trans. in Willheim, "Johann Adolph Scheibe" (diss.), pp. 103-4)

---

[17]Trans. in Guillaume Dufay, *Opera omnia*, vol. II, p. xxvii.
[18]See Pietro Aron, *Il toscanello in musica* (1523), trans. in Weiss & Taruskin, *Music in the Western World*, p. 112; Baldassare Castiglione, *Il cortegiano* (1528; trans. 1561), quoted in Strunk, *Source Readings*, p. 284; Thomas Morley, *A Plain and Easy Introduction to Practical Music* (1597), quoted in Strunk, p. 275.

Illustration 7:
A sixteenth-century celebration of the Mass, sung with instrumental accompaniment

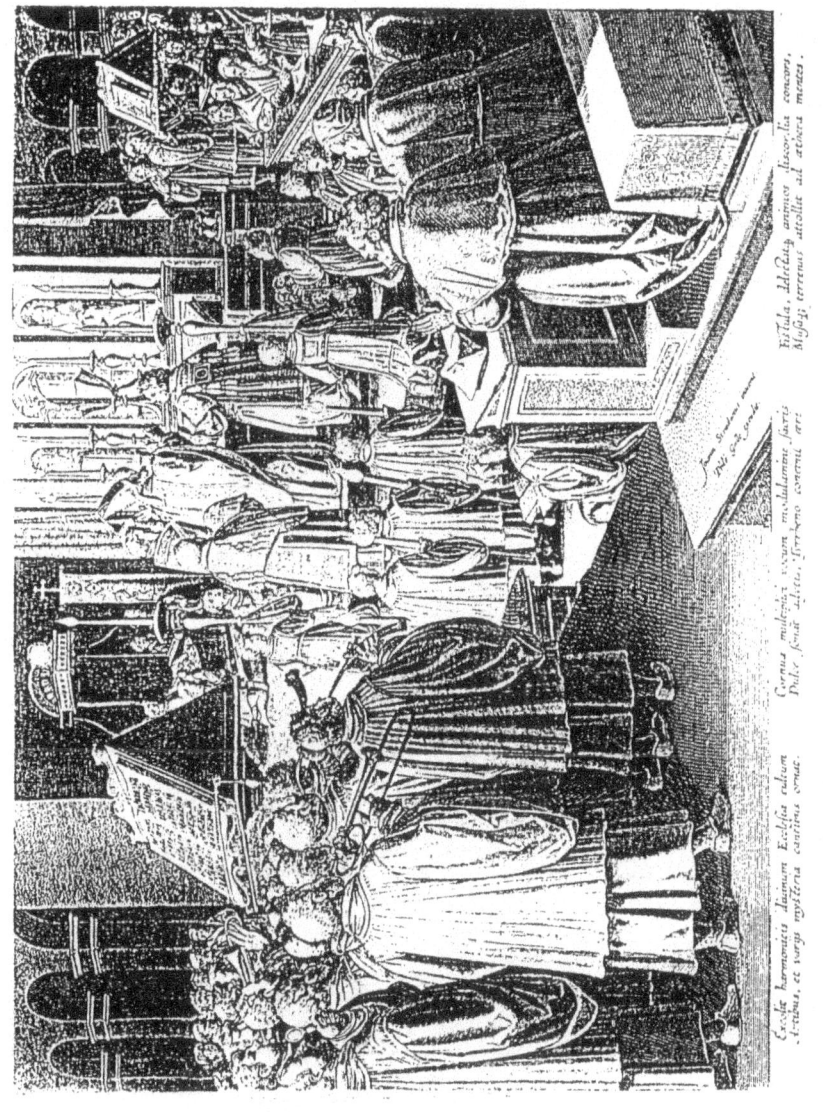

Source: Philipp Galle, *Encomium musices*, c.1590, plate 17.

13

The Self-Conscious Revolution

In his book *The Ethnomusicologist*, Mantle Hood contrasts the extremes of world-consciousness and self-consciousness (though he does not use those terms) in his comparison of the society of Bali in Indonesia with that of the United States.[1] The entire comparison is well worth reading because it brings into sharp focus not only the fundamental differences between the two cultures, but also their sharply divergent attitudes toward the arts. Here are the salient points of his argument:

The island of Bali, to the best of my knowledge, has more artists per capita than any other society. Here, where religion pervades every aspect of living, the creation and performance of music, dance, various forms of theater, sculpture, painting, and decoration are such an indispensable part of religious devotion that the arts, too, have become a way of life. Within the communal organization of Balinese society, the artist and his products are regarded as absolute essentials in the functioning of the community. Almost every performance or creation in the field of the arts is considered a kind of religious offering in which the dancer, the musician, or the carver is fulfilling all or part of his communal obligations... There is no word in the Balinese language for "art"; the arts are such an organic part of living that there appears to be no need for such an abstraction...

A deep commitment to the arts can also be seen at the national level. The central government of Indonesia has a ministry of education and culture and maintains cultural offices throughout Java and Bali as well as many of the Outer Islands. There is governmental support of conservatories devoted to training in the traditional arts as well as several academies that provide opportunities for graduates of the conservatories in advanced training and research in the arts. The traditional arts are programmed constantly by the national radio and are part of the curriculum in the public schools. From the poorest villager to the political elite, from the military to the university faculty, from the businessman to the students of elementary and secondary schools, there is a knowledge of and often direct involvement in the arts.

---

[1] pp. 9-16.

162 Wiser than Despair

...Viewed as a total society, the United States regards the arts as nonessential, low on its scale of values... The poet, the painter, the musician, the dancer, the writer, the actor manage a tolerable acceptance as nonessential members of an affluent society. Modern plumbing, electricity, and the full range of modern appliances, including hi-fi and television, are considered essential parts of the average man's household. He is a rare man indeed who foregoes any one of these items in order to afford a painting or sculpture or monetary contributions to the local civic symphony...

Possession of a first and a second automobile has high priority over direct support of the arts...

...within the federal government there is no "ministry of culture." ...the National Endowment for the Arts and the National Endowment for the Humanities are a token response, with token budgets, to the hue and cry from some intellectual minorities that there is a gross imbalance between support of the arts and humanities and support of the sciences...

In summary, aside from a certain entertainment and commercial value, the arts in the United States are regarded as nonessential recreation or as ornamentation befitting an affluent mode of life. (Hood, *The Ethnomusicologist*, pp. 15-16; 12-15)

The low priority that U.S. society accords the "doing" of the arts is a widely recognized phenomenon. What is especially interesting about Hood's analysis is the intimate interdependence he senses between religion and art.[2] He seems to be suggesting on the one hand that when religion thrives, so does artistic activity, and on the other, that a dimming of religious consciousness (note that Hood never mentions religion in the United States) may leave the arts to languish.

A superficial assessment of the situation indeed seems to challenge this statement. How can we speak of "a dimming of religious consciousness" in the United States? Religion (specifically Christianity) in the United States is big business: churches have sprung up on every corner, television evangelists enjoy audiences numbering in the millions, and a majority of the population professes some belief in God. A more thorough examination of the transformation of religious consciousness in modern industrial society is called for, however, in order adequately to address the question. That examination will reveal just how accurate Hood's appraisal of the situation may be. To understand the

---

[2]In his book *Notes Towards the Definition of Culture* (especially in Chapter 1, "The Three Senses of Culture"), T.S. Eliot explores the interrelatedness of religion and culture:

"...no culture can appear or develop except in relation to a religion...(p. 27); "We may go further and ask whether what we call the culture, and what we call the religion, of a people are not different aspects of the same thing; the culture being, essentially, the incarnation (so to speak) of the religion of a people" (p. 28); "...there is an aspect in which we can see a religion as *the whole way of life* of a people, from birth to the grave, from morning to night and even in sleep, and that way of life is also its culture." (p. 31)

Understanding culture in this way, as the collective behavior (together with the resulting artifacts) of a society engaged in acting out (symbolizing) its most deeply held and cherished (though perhaps unarticulated) shared beliefs and convictions, seems to be the best way to make sense of the evident etymological relationship between the words "cult" and "culture."

The Self-Conscious Revolution 163

transformation from the world-consciousness that prevailed through the Middle Ages to the self-consciousness that is the hallmark of the modern age, it is necessary to return to the seventeenth and eighteenth centuries to explore the roots of modern life and thought.

In *Cosmopolis: The Hidden Agenda of Modernity* (p. 23), Stephen Toulmin asks

> ...if the modern world and modern culture did not have two distinct origins, rather than one single origin, the first (literary or humanistic phase) being a century before the second. If we follow this suggestion, and carry the origins of Modernity back to the late Renaissance authors of Northern Europe in the 16th century, we shall find the *second*, scientific and philosophical phase, from 1630 on, leading many Europeans to turn their backs on the most powerful themes of the *first*, the literary or humanistic phase. After 1600, the focus of intellectual attention turned away from the humane preoccupations of the late 16th century, and moved in directions more rigorous, or even dogmatic, than those the Renaissance writers pursued.

If Toulmin is right (and I believe he is), then the first phase of the modern worldview is the humanistic one explored in the last chapter. What was humanism's effect on religion? If we take into account only the sixteenth century, then humanism's effect on theology or on popular religion was relatively limited and superficial. (Sixteenth-century humanism was, after all, the province of only a few scholars and intellectuals.) Humanism's first real effect on religion did not become manifest until the seventeenth century with the rise of pietism,[3] the intensely personal and individualistic approach to religion that emphasized human guilt and personal conversion and prized religious feeling over intellectual understanding. Pietism's grounding in humanism is not immediately obvious; it becomes manifest only with the realization that the precondition for pietism is a focus on human concerns, in contrast to the earlier

---

[3]The absence of a capital letter is intentional; in using the term, I intend to signify not merely Pietism as a specific movement in sixteenth- and seventeenth-century Protestant Germany, but the shift to a radically personal orientation in religious experience (rooted in late medieval affective piety, but now set adrift from the liturgy) that has been characteristic of all branches of Western Christianity since the seventeenth century. Other Protestant manifestations of this phenomenon include the Moravian (*Unitas Fratrum*) and Methodist movements and the hymns of the Wesleys. In Roman Catholicism, the transformation was manifest in the reorientation toward an ardent personal piety (among both clergy and laity), becoming more and more evident during the latter part of the sixteenth century in the wake of the Counter-Reformation, which replaced the widespread religious apathy and indifference characteristic of the pre-Reformation church. This personal piety is mirrored in certain elements of Jansenism, as well as in a growing devotion to the rosary, the Sacred Heart of Jesus and the Immaculate Heart of Mary. Its influence may be traced most clearly, however, in the appeal to the senses and emotions that is evident in seventeenth-century Roman Catholic religious art and architecture. Baroque painting, sculpture, architecture and music transformed the medieval Mass from a majestic, contemplative ceremony into a soul-stirring, sensually overwhelming spectacle. In doing so, they did not merely express the reality of Christian faith and piety, but attempted to awaken and intensify it; thus they tended to focus attention on personal feeling, rather than on solidarity with the cult, as primary evidence of human relationship with God.

primary focus on the self-effacing praise of and obedience to God. Although pietism as a specific movement faded after the eighteenth century, the fundamental reorientation of the Christian religion toward a preoccupation with its human dimension has grown[4] until by the twentieth century it has become by far the predominant characteristic of popular Christian religious thought and expression. (Some Eastern Orthodox churches remain an exception to this.) A glance through any modern hymnal will confirm the truth of this observation: hymns from the eighteenth century to the present are largely expressions of personal religious feeling and experience, and these hymns from the last three centuries comprise by far the bulk of any modern hymnal (and most assuredly one hundred percent of popular hymnody).[5] The primary effect that humanism has had, both on Christian theology and on faith in practice, is a shift of focus from God's transcendence to God's immanence, from God's holiness and unapproachability to God's intimate nearness, kindliness, and friendliness. Since the eighteenth century, Christians have grown more and more interested in what God in Christ has done for each individual human at the expense of emphasizing what the individual is compelled, for the sake of God's great love, to do for God in Christ.[6]

Toulmin's second phase, beginning in the early seventeenth century and gaining momentum throughout the eighteenth, is the phenomenon we know as the "Enlightenment." The term is a comprehensive one, connoting a vast complex of ideas and attitudes that gradually effected fundamental changes in almost all dimensions of human existence. It is usually linked with the eighteenth century, since many of its tenets became firmly established in the minds of the educated public during that time. Many of its characteristic thought patterns, however, were already evident in the writings of seventeenth-century authors, and the process of transformation that it set into motion does not seem even at the present time to have run its course completely.[7] In brief, the Enlightenment was characterized by

1. The enthronement of reason as the primary guiding principle in human thinking
2. An empirical approach to scientific problem-solving: observation, research and experimentation replaced intuition and revelation as the primary methods of establishing truth. This approach shaped modern science, which by the

---

[4]Particularly influential in that growth were nineteenth-century liberal Protestant theology (e.g., the work of Friedrich Schleiermacher) and the evangelical revival movements of the eighteenth and nineteenth centuries.

[5]To bring the contrast between earlier and later modes of thought into sharper focus, compare the relative prominence of first-person singular pronouns in the medieval hymn, the *Te Deum*, with those in the modern hymn "How Great Thou Art." (Both of these are hymns to God's transcendent majesty.)

[6]There is, of course, a significant amount of emphasis in the Bible on what God has done for us, but it is never seen as an end in itself, only as the impetus for an ever more perfect, self-giving worship in which total attention is focused on the praise of and obedience to God.

[7]The process is far advanced in first- and second-world countries; but it is worth keeping in mind that in many Third-World countries large segments of the population remain either untouched or only marginally affected by Enlightenment thought.

The Self-Conscious Revolution 165

twentieth century had gained ascendancy (both in the popular imagination and in governmental support) over the older disciplines of the arts and humanities.

The constant progress of ideas and attitudes first promoted during the Enlightenment has indeed been the major force in forging the self-conscious worldview (see Chapter 1, pp. 1-3).

Since the Enlightenment wrought sweeping changes in how humans viewed themselves in relation to their world or universe, no dimension of human existence has been more fundamentally affected by Enlightenment ideas and attitudes than religion. The Enlightenment was at heart a denial of the mystical, spiritual dimension of existence. Leading thinkers were disposed to consider religion, especially the Christian religion, as superstition, and in criticizing, indeed, ridiculing it they hastened the evaporation not only of superstition, but also of spirituality.[8] This is particularly evident in eighteenth-century attempts to promote "rational religion." There had always been isolated individuals, of course, who doubted the existence or the power of the spirit-world, but never had there been a frontal assault on religious belief such as that of eighteenth-century Europe (as well as the fledgling United States of America). For a coterie of intellectuals, the seventeenth century had brought the demise of the spirit-world, but in the eighteenth century it died for increasingly large numbers of the new bourgeoisie as well. What had been so real, so palpable to the great mass of humanity since before recorded history now began to vanish with ever-increasing rapidity. One result of this transformation is the continuing exodus of people from the church and from any contact with religious tradition. But the transformation has had its effect within the church, as well: intelligent believers since that time have had to contend with self-centeredness constantly gnawing around the edges of faith, a self-centeredness that is encouraged by an environment both subtly and overtly hostile to traditional religion. In spite of subsequent attempts to revive spirituality among the masses, no one now living in the developed world has escaped the effects of the transformation. They may be detected today, for example, in evangelical Christianity's tendency (evident in the mid-twentieth century) to segregate religion from community issues (politics or social concerns), in liberal Christianity's lack of attention to spiritual formation in seminaries, in Protestantism's general neglect of the sacramental dimension of worship, and in the widespread (though sometimes subtle) aversion in all branches of Western Christianity (including post-Vatican II Roman Catholicism) to the element of mystery, together with the prosaic, literal character of worship such an aversion produces.

At this point we need to refer back to the Prologue of this book and remind ourselves that music's central place in religious experience derives from its indispensable role in two aspects of religion: cult and myth. How were these two aspects affected by humanistic and Enlightenment ideas and attitudes? Cult, by its very definition, is concerned with the relationship between humans and a greater, more powerful being whose will takes precedence over human affairs and concerns, whose commands humans must follow. The cult places God at the absolute, unrivaled center of consciousness. When the consciousness of God as

---

[8]See Spitzer, *Classical and Christian Ideas of World Harmony*, pp. 75-76.

the center is dislodged by a focus on the human self as the center of interest and concern, then the cult is inevitably transformed. The sixteenth-century humanists testify that a burgeoning self-awareness does not preclude a lively sense of world-consciousness,[9] and thus does not oppose the idea of cult. Yet in examining the scope and tendencies of the history of Western ideas since the rise of humanism, it is hard to escape the conclusion than an inexorable progress toward a total self-consciousness has largely crowded out the former world-consciousness.[10] To the degree, then, that humanist ideals have found a sympathetic reception in recent Christian belief and theology, they have vitiated the traditional power of the cult. In the modern world, Christian cultic celebration struggles against humanist ideals in two ways. First, it must constantly resist being pushed into the background in the face of the church's concern with present (admittedly overwhelming) human distress and displacement. Second, to the degree that it reorients the focus of worship from God's transcendence to God's immanence and from self-effacing praise of God to human edification, modern cultic celebration (even at its most authentic) constantly skirts the edges of a prosaic sentimentality.

The Enlightenment, however, went far beyond the humanistic benign neglect of world-consciousness; it dismissed cultic activity as irrational, superstitious mumbo-jumbo, retaining from the teachings of Jesus only their high ethical standards and their sense of responsibility for other human beings. Thus while humanism fundamentally reoriented the Christian cult from within, Enlightenment thought attacked it from without. The effects of humanist and Enlightenment thought have combined to produce a fundamental transformation of Christian cultic celebration in the modern world.

Cult inevitably involves the notions of covenant, solidarity, ritual, sacrament, and ornament. As the Prologue asserts (p. 5), the position of the first two Commandments (Exodus 20:3-4) relative to the entire set of ten shows just how central the practice of the cult was to the covenant between Yahweh and the Israelites. The idea of covenant presumes an unshakeable belief in the omnipotence of God and God's ability to act in the world. The various Enlightenment conceptions of God (e.g., Deism, divine subservience to reason and natural law) tended to limit that belief; such conceptions could not help but dilute the immediacy of the idea of covenant.

Human solidarity (being first and foremost a part of a people, tribe, or family) was eroded by the emphasis (growing ever since the sixteenth century) on humans as first and foremost individuals. Carried to its ultimate, this emphasis might suggest that each person should pursue primarily only what is in his or her own self-interest. In fact, however, it has more often been expressed in terms of asserting and securing each person's right to "life, liberty and the pursuit of happiness," in realizing each person's human potential, in celebrating the uniqueness of each human's personality. There is, of course, nothing to

---

[9] Prominent figures that come to mind in this regard include the Dutch scholar Desiderius Erasmus (1466/69-1536), John Calvin's adversary Bishop Jacopo Sadoleto (1477-1547), the English statesman and author Sir Thomas More (1478-1535), and Martin Luther's protégé Philipp Melanchthon (1497-1560).

[10] See Evans-Pritchard, "Religion and the Anthropologists," p. 44.

censure in these objectives; nevertheless, they tend to disengage individuals from the larger community.[11]

Ritual and ceremony, the primary hallmarks of world-conscious cultic celebrations, have been more fundamentally affected by the transformation of thought than any other feature of cult. Modern thought, while acknowledging their existence (and sometimes their usefulness), is in fact at a loss to explain their significance for human life. The Enlightenment tended to regard religious ritual and ceremony at best as something vaguely suspicious or embarassing and at worst as something childish or barbaric. That opinion is perpetuated in self-conscious humanity's attitudes toward ritual; indeed, modern humanity is nowhere more "self-conscious" than when participating in it. The modern age has largely neutralized the power of ritual and ceremony by trivializing it, by relegating it to the raw enthusiasm of sports events and the pseudo-rituals of beauty pageants and parades. To the degree that they are self-conscious, humans tend to feel uncomfortable with religious ritual, to ridicule it, even to fear it. They may resist participating in it, and try to play down or to eliminate the ceremonial element in events of profound religious or communal significance, even when the solemnity of the occasion might support a certain ritual formality.

Sacrament--the means by which humans perceive the in-breaking of the spirit-world into the world of appearances--is likewise incomprehensible to the fully self-conscious human. That in-breaking is normally accompanied by a sense of awe in the presence of the holy. To the extent that self-conscious modes of thought have invaded cultic celebration, they have sought to disguise the element of transcendent awe and mystery, and have thus fostered a prosaism in modern worship, in both a literal and a figurative sense: there is more emphasis on prose than on poetry, and the worship that results runs the danger of being over-literal, wordy, over-clock-conscious, and lacking in spontaneity. Since the most vivid signs of God's presence among humans almost invariably involve the cooperation of acts and words, sacramental consciousness begins to fade when worship places a strong emphasis on words while at the same time neglecting actions (more "saying" than "doing"). In the process, words that once were charged with mysterious awe tend to lose their power and become commonplace.[12]

The rise of self-conscious modes of thought has ushered in the idea that to want splendid, costly accoutrements for worship--buildings, works of art, elaborate music--is inappropriate,[13] especially in a world wracked with human poverty, suffering and deprivation.[14] The human dislocation caused by the

---

[11]They have also contributed substantially to the insularity, alienation, and loneliness that have grown to epidemic proportions in modern, self-conscious society.

[12]Jews in ancient times, for example, would not even utter the divine name, Yahweh, substituting "Lord" (Elohim) or another name for it; there is no such awe for the word "God" or for any other word in modern religion.

[13]See White, "Church Choir: Friend or Foe."

[14]The contrast between world-conscious and self-conscious attitudes toward costly ornament in worship is epitomized in the recent controversy over the building of the new Roman Catholic Basilica of Our Lady of Peace in Yamoussoukro, Ivory

nineteenth-century Industrial Revolution has only intensified the idea, and so it has become widespread (both within and without the church) in the twentieth century. One in fact senses at times a certain embarassment about delighting in the finest gifts of the human imagination, almost as if it were childish to think that we should worship God by creating beautiful, elaborate things. Instead of wanting to give God the best, most elaborate gifts possible, some modern humans have come to believe that God is better served with simple praise:[15]

> He tends the pines and the sparrows,
> He knows us and all our ways;
> He is the source of our life and love,
> Thank him with simple praise.
> (Jack Miffleton, "Give Thanks and Remember")

The radical reorientation of Christian worship informed by the ideas just outlined is nowhere more clearly seen than in comparing the characteristics of medieval worship with those of modern worship:

Medieval Worship	Modern Worship
cosmic, 'eternal'	human-scale, 'humanistic' (i.e., organized around human concerns)
formal, ceremonial	personal, intimate, anti-formal
objective	subjective
mysterious, poetic	reasonable, prosaic
aristocratic, hierarchical	popular, democratic
often conducted in vast, resonant spaces	often conducted in low-built spaces with dry acoustics

The transformation of attitudes and approaches to cultic celebration inevitably had a profound effect on the attitudes toward and the practice of music in worship. Music finds its most congenial home in cultic celebrations as an integral part of ritual and ceremony; divorced from these, it runs the danger of taking on the aspect of a performance. A decline of sacramental consciousness weakens music's propensity to intensify the encounter with the holy. A suspicion of ornament sows doubt on the appropriateness of any elaborate music

---

Coast, Africa, a gift from the country's president, Felix Houphouet-Boigny. The basilica cost $150 million to build, and garnered widespread criticism from first- and second-world countries as a poignant example of extravagance and misplaced priorities in a poor country where the money might have been used for countless more pressing human needs. The building has drawn almost no criticism, on the other hand, from citizens of the Ivory Coast, who tend to view the accomplishment with pride as a natural and fitting expression of religious fervor.

[15]Consider, for example, the well-known "Simple Song" from Leonard Bernstein's *Mass*.

in worship. And a loss in human solidarity leads to a loss of consensus as to what music is fitting or desirable for worship.

The Christian cult was born out of and was supported by a powerful complex of myths (see Chap. 4, p. 52). The self-conscious worldview, in dismissing the power of myth as divine revelation, inevitably construes myth as a species of fairy-tale or a kind of naïve self-deception (that is in fact the present understanding of the term in the minds of most modern humans). The modern mind automatically interprets as a relic of the past anything that presents myth as a powerful expression of reality; that is why Tolkien's creation myth quoted above in the Prologue sounds "ancient," even though it was crafted in the twentieth century. Nineteenth-century biblical criticism[16] called into question the accuracy and validity of the Scriptures (the touchstone of Christian mythology), and twentieth-century theology has seen attempts, by the German theologian Rudolf Bultmann and others, to "demythologize" the Christian faith so as to make it comprehensible to modern minds. Popular Christian faith in the modern age, on the other hand, in that it is primarily concerned with present Christian experience, tends not to challenge its salvation history, but rather to ignore it, and thus runs the danger of cultural "amnesia," a forgetting of its roots. In contrast to earlier myths that formed the foundation on which Christian art music flourished, music does not figure prominently or positively in any of the attitudes and presumptions that have taken the place of myths in the self-conscious worldview (for example, evolution, or faith in the empirical scientific method). Thus, while there is ample support for music in worship, both from Scripture and from the natural human fondness for musical expression, Christians (to the degree that they subscribe, consciously or unconsciously, to modern thought processes) have no particular reason to value elaborate art music in worship.

How can we speak of "a dimming of religious consciousness" in the United States? Everything that has been said above begins to answer that question. As we asserted in the Prologue, the majority of the world's people (and especially modern Christians in the first and second worlds) instinctively react positively to elements of both the world-conscious and self-conscious worldviews. Therefore, while religion is an all-consuming way of life in Bali, it is accorded varying degrees of importance in the United States, depending on where a given person stands in the spectrum of belief characteristic of a modern, pluralistic society. At the most, it is a dimension of existence in constant tension with modern life and thought; at the least, it is a curious, suspect remnant of an antiquated worldview.

To the degree that modern Christians subscribe to modern modes of thought, the transformation of cult and myth described above (together with its effects on music in worship) is inescapable. And since almost all Christians in the modern world accept modern thought to some degree, the tension between conflicting priorities is inevitable in the worship of many branches of the modern Christian church. That tension is significant for contemporary church music in that it is symptomatic of the enormous cultural and intellectual chasm that divides and

---

[16] See Evans-Pritchard, "Religion and the Anthropologists," p. 34.

alienates the church of today from the church of the past[17]--the church that provided the treasury of music and musical ideas that forms the tastes and ideals of perceptive church musicians, and that these musicians still cherish and foster. If the rudimentary practice of music as it existed in the early church had continued to prevail, then church music today would in all probability be a relatively insignificant branch of music history and practice, demanding only limited technical skill and musicianship, unlikely to excite widespread admiration or enthusiasm. In fact, however, the works of the great composers of the church from Dunstable to Bach continue to find admirers and performers among musicians and music lovers, both inside and outside the church, and the characteristics of music established as a result of Christian theology and the worldview it promoted have been and by and large continue to be decisive in the determination of quality in art music (including sacred art music). On the one hand, there is this systemic memory of the towering accomplishments of the old order, a living memory that still informs musical composition and performance. On the other hand, there is the modern world, in which that music (and everything it stands for) is at times enigmatic or even repellent. When all the facts are considered, it becomes clear that church music in our time is one of the primary arenas in which the tension between the conflicting world-conscious and self-conscious worldviews continues to be worked out on a daily basis.

---

[17]What C. S. Lewis says in his essay "De Descriptione Temporum" is interesting in this regard. He argues that the lapse of Western civilization into a post-Christian ethos is a more traumatic cultural change than the shift from paganism to Christianity in the fourth century: "Christians and Pagans had much more in common with each other than either has with a post-Christian. The gap between those who worship different gods is not so wide as that between those who worship and those who do not." (In *They Asked for a Paper: Papers and Addresses*, p. 14)

14

The Enlightenment and Music

The preceding chapter explored the ways in which self-conscious modes of thought transformed cult and myth, and the effect that transformation had on the church and its music. The era during which this happened, the Enlightenment, also saw a far-reaching transformation of ideas and attitudes about music itself, and that, of course, had consequences for church music as well. Up to the Enlightenment, Christian ideas and attitudes had been major factors in determining the progress of music. As a result of the Enlightenment, leadership in musical creativity rapidly began to shift to the secular sphere. In order to understand developments in church music from this point on, then, it is necessary first to explore the most influential ideas behind secular musical culture, since the secular influenced (indeed, largely determined) the religious.

The phenomenon of music posed a knotty problem for Enlightenment thinkers, since it does not accord particularly well with reason, nor is its practice particularly amenable to the empirical scientific method. Therefore any number of (often conflicting) views and attitudes toward music surfaced during the Enlightenment. We need examine, however, only those that proved to have implications for church music. Some of those views have alternately gained and lost popularity during the course of time and with the coming and going of various "isms," but most are still current to some degree, at least in popular thinking.

1. *Music embodies, expresses and excites human emotion, feeling, passion.*[1]
An "enlightened" public was largely convinced that this was music's main purpose.

>...just as modulation [i.e., melody] is, as it were, a universal language of sensations intelligible to every man, so the art of tone wields the full force of this language wholly on its own account, namely, as a language of the affections, and in this way, according to the law of association, universally communicates the aesthetic ideas that are naturally combined therewith... [this] may be brought mathematically under certain rules...But mathematics, certainly, does not play the smallest part in the charm and movement of the mind produced by music. (Immanuel Kant, *Critique of Judgment*, 1790, p. 536)

This attitude toward music's purpose, clearly articulated during the Enlightenment, continued to prevail throughout the Romantic period[2] and, although contested by some twentieth-century composers, continues to be held by a (probably rather large) segment of the population.

> I get an audience involved because I'm involved myself--if the song is a lament at the loss of love, I get an ache in my gut.... I cry out the loneliness. (Frank Sinatra, quoted in Whitcomb, *After the Ball*, 1972, p. 203)

> [Of musicians] Our business is emotion and sensitivity--to be the sensors of the human race. (Dame Janet Baker, interview in *The Observer*, 1982; quoted in Crofton & Fraser, *Dictionary of Musical Quotations*, p. 112:9)

Since the Enlightenment, subjective tendencies have grown increasingly prominent in musical composition, resulting in an ever-expanding range and variety of sensual effects and devices that heighten emotional intensity. Some of these devices, first fashioned during the latter half of the eighteenth century, became clichés in the works of subsequent periods and are still current in today's concert hall repertory: for example, the "Mannheim crescendo" (a long, inexorable orchestral crescendo to a thundering *fortissimo*), rapidly sweeping, florid runs (especially by violins), or the simulation of a heartbeat by the low strings.

The pursuit of the subjective was an important factor in the eventual rise of the instrumental ensemble as the major performing medium for art music.[3] This

---

[1] See Pier Francesco Tosi, *Observations on the Florid Song* (1723; trans. 1743), quoted in Weiss & Taruskin, *Music in the Western World*, p. 259; Roger North, *The Musicall Gramarian* (1728), quoted in Crofton & Fraser, *Dictionary of Musical Quotations*, p. 58:11; C.P.E. Bach, *Versuch über die wahre Art das Clavier zu spielen* (1753), trans. in Weiss & Taruskin, pp. 271-2; J. F. Reichardt, *Briefe eines aufmerksamen Reisenden* (1774), trans. in Strunk, *Source Readings*, p. 703.

[2] See, for example, Arthur Schopenhauer, *The World as Will and Idea* (1819), pp 330-46, especially pp. 330 & 338; Richard Wagner, *Drei Operndichtungen nebst einer Mittheilung an seine Freunde* (1852), trans. in Weiss & Taruskin, *Music in the Western World*, p. 375; Franz Liszt, *Berlioz and his "Harold" Symphony* (1855), trans. in Strunk, *Source Readings*, p. 849;

[3] See E.T.A. Hoffmann, *Beethoven's Instrumental Music* (1813), trans. in Strunk, *Source Readings*, p. 775.

The Enlightenment and Music 173

happened by the early nineteenth century, and thereafter choral music has consistently assumed a status secondary to instrumental music.[4] Instruments not only offered greater range and dynamic intensity than voices, but they also provided greater potential for speed and virtuosity as well; they were thus more apt for expressing strong emotional states. Furthermore, the listener's emotional response to instrumental music is potentially more uninhibited and personal, since it is not conditioned by the concrete meaning of the text (as in vocal music).

2. Music provides entertainment and diversion.

Dramatic intensity, bold rhetoric, heroism, and the expression of lofty ideals characterized the seventeenth-century (Baroque) ideal. The early eighteenth-century Rococo, on the other hand, having become sated with the Baroque's larger-than-life pomposity, sought only to entertain; its hallmarks were intimacy, wit, grace, and polish. The notion that music's purpose is to entertain, though it encountered stiff opposition from later romantic spirits, continued to be in vogue long after the eighteenth century: "I consider music as a very innocent diversion... I do not mean, however to assert that we can be justified in devoting too much of our time to music, for there are certainly other things to be attended to" (Jane Austen, *Pride and Prejudice*, 1813, p. 105). That music was considered diverting, however, by no means implied that it should be calming. Music need not be grave; on the contrary, it might well be stimulating.[5] Some critics even approved of music with a comic or clownish element,[6] though others (appealing to "good taste" and decorum) scorned musical trickery.

But as the imitating the Cock, Cuckoo, Owl, and other Birds; or the Drum, French Horn, and the like; and also sudden Shifts of the Hand from one Extremity of the Finger-board to the other, accompanied with Contortions of the Head and Body, and all such other Tricks rather belong to the Professors of Legerdemain and Posture-masters than to the Art of Musick, the Lovers of that Art are not to expect to find any thing of that Sort in this Book. (Francesco Geminiani, *The Art of Playing on the Violin*, 1751, Preface, p. 1)

---

[4]From the nineteenth century on, for example, the major professional musical ensemble in a given city has almost invariably been a symphony orchestra, not a choir.

[5]This holds just as true in subsequent eras as in the Enlightenment; for example, Frederick Delius, "At the Crossroads" (1920):

In an age of neurasthenics, music, like everything else, must be a stimulant, must be alcoholic, aphrodisiac, or it is no good. (quoted in Morgenstern, *Composers on Music*, p. 322)

[6]Charles Burney, *The Present State of Music in France and Italy* (1771):

The overture [to Paesiello's comic opera *Trame per amore*], of one movement only, was quite comic, and contained a perpetual succession of pleasant passages. (quoted in Strunk, *Source Readings*, p. 691)

174 Wiser than Despair

3. *The best kind of music is characterized by constant variety.*
Musical practice embodied this idea long before the eighteenth century, and writers on music certainly expressed it.

> ...you must in your music [i.e., the madrigal] be wavering like the wind, sometimes wanton, sometimes drooping, sometimes grave and staid, otherwhile effeminate; you may maintain points and revert them, use triples, and show the very uttermost of your variety, and the more variety you show the better shall you please. (Thomas Morley, *A Plain and Easy Introduction to Practical Music*, 1597; quoted in Strunk, *Source Readings*, p. 275)

The eighteenth century, however, intensified it and made it an absolute virtue,[7] a status it has maintained until the present day.

> Everyone will recognize that every musical sound carries with it an incrustation of familiar and stale sense associations, which predispose the hearer to boredom, despite all the efforts of innovating musicians. We futurists have all deeply loved the music of the great composers. Beethoven and Wagner for many years wrung our hearts. But now we are sated with them and derive much greater pleasure from ideally combining the noises of streetcars, internal-combustion engines, automobiles, and busy crowds than from re-hearing, for example, the "Eroica" or the "Pastorale." (Luigi Russolo, *A Futurist Manifesto*, 1913; trans. in Slonimsky, *Music Since 1900*, p. 1298)

The overabundance of this new element helps to explain why certain works in the *Empfindsamer Stil* by C.P.E. Bach and other pre-classical composers sound "quirky" to some modern ears. Around the middle of the eighteenth century, extreme variety in dynamics, rhythmic movement, and texture, together with unexpected pauses, startling chords, and other harmonic surprises, became the fashion in musical composition. The best composers of following generations then learned to moderate the element of variety in their music, in general by seeking the greatest variety in those aspects of music that appeal primarily to the senses or emotions (memorable melody, rhythm, color, change in dynamics),

---

[7]Niedt, *Musicalischer Handleitung* (1721), pp. 2-3:

The sense of hearing can find no greater entertainment than in the variation of many pitches, songs and melodies; of this the ear can never get enough. On the other hand, there is nothing less tasteless and vexing than constantly having to listen to the same old pitches and melodies (Leyern). It is an undeniable consequence of this that for the pleasant enjoyment of intelligent ears nothing is more suited than the artificial (künstlich) and uncontrived variation of musical sounds. Therefore the greatest charm rests in part in variety, whether with the human voice or on various instruments.

See also Jacob Adlung, *Musica mechanica organoedi* (written ca. 1725-1730), p. 165; J. J. Quantz, *On Playing the Flute* (1752), Chap. XII, §.24; C. W. von Gluck, Dedication to *Alceste* (1769), trans. in Strunk, *Source Readings*, p. 674; the acceptance of this ideal was another reason for the growing preference for instrumental music over vocal.

The Enlightenment and Music   175

while at the same time striving for the greatest unity in those aspects of music that appeal primarily to the intellect (form and structure).

4. *Individuality and originality are virtues in musical composition and performance.*

> Music! The Calm of life, the cordial bowl,
> Which anxious care can banish from the soul,
> Affliction soothe, and elevate the mind,
> And all its sordid manacles unbind,
> Can snatch us from life's incidental pains,
> And "wrap us in Elysium with its strains!"
> To cultivated ears, this fav'rite art
> No *new* delight was able to impart;
> No Eagle flights its votaries durst essay,
> But hopp'd, like little birds, from spray to spray.
> At length great HAYDN'S new and varied strains
> Of habit and indiff'rence broke the chains;
> Rous'd to attention the long torpid sense,
> With all that pleasing wonder could dispense.
> Whene'er Parnassus' height he meant to climb,
> Whether the grand, pathetic, or sublime,
> The simply graceful, or the comic vein,
> The theme suggested, or enrich'd the strain,
> From melting sorrow to gay jubilation,
> Whate'er his pen produc'd was Inspiration!
> (Charles Burney, *Verses on the Arrival of Haydn in England*, 1791; quoted in Weiss & Taruskin, *Music in the Western World*, pp. 313-4)

First rising to prominence during the Enlightenment, this notion has only grown more absolute with the passing of time.

> The creator should take over no traditional law in blind belief, for this would make him view his own creative endeavor, from the outset, as an exception contrasting with that law. For his individual case he should seek out and formulate a fitting individual law, which, after the first complete realization, he should annul, that he himself may not be drawn into repetitions when his next work shall be in the making. (Ferruccio Busoni, "Sketch of a New Aesthetic of Music", 1906; trans. in Debussy *et al.*, *Three Classics in the Aesthetic of Music*, p. 88)

It is instructive to reflect on just how diametrically opposed this is to earlier ideas. The earliest non-pejorative references to originality in music that I can find were written by Johannes Tinctoris at the beginning of the Renaissance, c.1475.

> ...at this time the supply of our music has undergone such a remarkable increase that it seems to be a new art; of which new art, so to call it, the foundation and origin is reported to have been among the English, the chief of whom was Dunstable. (Johannes Tinctoris, Prologue to the *Proportionale musices*, c.1475; trans. in Gallo, *Music of the Middle Ages*, p. 126)

Further, although it seems beyond belief, there does not exist a single piece of music, not composed within the last forty years, that is regarded by the learned as worth hearing. (Tinctoris, *Liber de arte contrapuncti*, 1477; trans. in Strunk, *Source Readings*, p. 199)

The rise of this idea conflicted with the traditional conservative Christian stance, that required a conscious integration of the new into the old.[8] Conservatism came to be a sign of backwardness in music, and an increasingly rapid turnover in musical styles and popular musical postures became the order of the day. From the Romantic period onward, however, an ever greater individuality on the part of the composer threatened to create a breach between composer and public. Music critics began to sense this already in the early nineteenth century, in the works of Beethoven.[9]

5. *The gauge of music's excellence is popular acclaim; the public is the best judge of good music.*[10]

...the most beautiful thing is that which is equally admired by the people and by the learned or by all the connoisseurs. Then, after this, I should admire more that which is generally admired by all the people. Finally, that which is admired by all the learned. (J. L. Le Cerf de La Viéville, *Comparaison de la Musique Italienne et de la Musique Française*, 1705; trans. in Strunk, *Source Readings*, p. 497)

Born with the Enlightenment, this idea still controls today's music market. Many post-Enlightenment composers and other musicians have railed against it, however, both in the nineteenth and twentieth centuries.

...people don't like beauty because it's a nuisance and doesn't accommodate itself to their nasty little souls. (Claude Debussy, in a letter to Pierre Louÿs, February 6, 1900; trans. in *Debussy Letters*, pp. 110-111)

...the composer would do himself and his music an immediate and eventual service by total, resolute, and voluntary withdrawal from this public world to one of private performance and electronic media, with its very real possibility of complete elimination of the public and social aspects of musical composition. (Milton Babbitt, "Who Cares If You Listen?," 1958, p. 126)

---

[8] See Lang, *Music in Western Civilization*, p. 440.

[9] The following passage is taken from a review of the first public performance of Beethoven's Symphony No. 3 (*Eroica*), April 7, 1805:

His music could soon reach the point where one would derive no pleasure from it, unless well trained in the rules and difficulties of the art, but rather would leave the concert hall with an unpleasant feeling of fatigue from having been crushed by a mass of unconnected and overloaded ideas and a continuing tumult by all the instruments. (trans. in Forbes (ed.), *Thayer's Life of Beethoven*, p. 376)

[10] See J. J. Quantz, *On Playing the Flute* (1752), Chapter XI, §.7; Chapter XVIII, §.51.

The Enlightenment and Music 177

"Good taste" was a *sine qua non* of music in the Enlightenment; bluntly stated, it turned out to be equivalent to popular acclaim[11] (albeit by *cognoscenti*). This idea accorded well with the notion that music should express and arouse emotion, since what the majority of the public demanded--and still demands--is music of feeling. Music produced to suit the taste of the new public at large resulted in an enormous rise in music's popularity, with a concomitant meteoric growth in all facets of the new music industry. This growth was clearly reflected in the increasing number of people who were trained to play keyboard instruments.[12] (There are indications that the easy availability of broadcast and recorded music is bringing this era of ubiquitous keyboard training to a close, especially in the United States.)

6. *The best kind of music is "natural" and unlearned--an anti-intellectual attitude toward music.*

With the passing of the old worldview and the disappearance of number as the controlling force in the universe, there was no longer any need or rationale for complex polyphony, except that it was traditional. And, of course, the progressive mindset was far less interested in tradition than in originality and innovation. Thus sympathy for learned, abstruse, "artificial" music evaporated in favor of music that was simple and immediately appealing,[13] that flowed "from the heart." This attitude has continued to be well represented in succeeding centuries.[14]

The Enlightenment favored music that was "natural" and "simple";[15] this proved to mean "predominantly homophonic, with memorable melodies constructed in periods." The word "artificial" had by now entirely lost its earlier meaning (see Chap. 12, p. 158) and signified only "feigned, affected, unnatural:" "...*art* is not an *artificial* product--... the need of art is not one willfully induced, but rather one native to the natural, genuine, unspoiled human being" (Richard Wagner, *Das Kunstwerk der Zukunft*, 1850; trans. in Strunk, *Source Readings*,

---

[11]See Joseph Addison, *The Spectator* (1709-13), as quoted in Lang, *Music in Western Civilization*, p. 515; J. D. Heinichen, *Der General-bass in der Composition* (1728), quoted in Weiss & Taruskin, *Music in the Western World*, pp. 255-6.

[12]Arnfried Edler, "The Organist in Lutheran Germany" (in Salmen, *Social Status*, p. 67):

It was not until the end of the 17th, and above all, the 18th centuries that, in many circles, it was considered essential to a proper upbringing to be able to play a keyboard instrument.

[13]See J.A. Scheibe, *Der critische Musicus* (1737-1740), quoted in Weiss & Taruskin, *Music in the Western World*, p. 257; Georg Feder, "Decline and Restoration," in Blume, *Protestant Church Music*, p. 324.

[14]See V. V. Stasov, "Our Music," (1882), quoted in Weiss & Taruskin, *Music in the Western World*, p. 391; Conversations between Claude Debussy and Ernest Guiraud, quoted in Weiss & Taruskin, p. 418.

[15]See J. A. Scheibe, *Der critische Musicus* (1737-1740), quoted in Weiss & Taruskin, *Music in the Western World*, p. 256; C. W. von Gluck, Dedication to *Alceste* (1769), quoted in Strunk, *Source Readings*, pp. 674-5; J. F. Reichardt, *Briefe eines aufmerksamen Reisenden* (1774), trans. in Strunk, pp. 700-1.

p. 879). Criticism and neglect of complex polyphonic textures was accompanied by a decreasing need for listeners (especially amateurs) to hear and comprehend counterpoint,[16] a condition that is still widely prevalent today, exacerbated by the ubiquity of background "mood music" in offices, factories, and public places that encourages careless listening habits.

The performance of music--its actual sound--began to be considered more important than music theory, much less music philosophy;[17] correspondingly, in the popular mind innate musical talent and aptitude came to be considered in the end primary and self-sufficient, beyond requiring systematic musical training: "...a musician and a poet are born. You must think back, whether from tender years you have felt yourself impelled to this study by a certain natural impulse, and whether it has befallen you to be intensely moved by the delight of harmony" (J.J. Fux, *Gradus ad Parnassum*, 1725; trans. in Strunk, *Source Readings*, p. 536).

7. *Music is subject to examination and evaluation from the viewpoints of reason and of scientific empiricism.*

We may judge of music only through the intervention of hearing, and reason has authority in it only in so far as it agrees with the ear; at the same time, nothing can be more convincing to us than their union in our judgments. Our nature is satisfied by the ear, our mind by reason; let us then judge of nothing excepting through their co-operation. (J.-P. Rameau, *Traité de l'Harmonie*, 1722; trans. in Strunk, *Source Readings*, p. 567)

The doctrine of ethos, since it was based entirely on speculation, came under severe attack.[18] Enlightenment writers denied that music had any divine nature; there was nothing mystical or supernatural about it--or about anything else, for that matter. For example, David Hume, the great eighteenth-century empirical philosopher, argued that the artist is the source of his own creative power, a creator in his own right; experience teaches the artist how to shape musical material into coherent musical compositions--in this the conception of music is no different that that of a scientific idea.[19] Musical analysis became predominantly theoretical, not philosophical. The philosophy of music, after centuries of increasing neglect, was finally relegated to being a subcategory of music aesthetics. Philosophical ideas on music played (and continue to play) little or no role in the training of composers and performers.

---

[16]Cf. Zoltan Kodály, in *La Revue Musicale* (1921), quoted in Crofton & Fraser, *Dictionary of Musical Quotations*, p. 42:15.

[17]See J.P. Rameau, *Le Nouveau Systémé de Musique Théorique* (1726), quoted in Crofton & Fraser, *Dictionary of Musical Quotations*, p. 1:2; Leopold Mozart, in his *Versuch einer gründlichen Violinschule* (1756; trans. in Strunk, *Source Readings*, p. 599) says, "Everything turns on good performance--everyday experience confirms this rule."

[18]See John Milton, *Areopagitica* (1644), quoted in Weiss & Taruskin, *Music in the Western World*, pp. 189-90.

[19]See Portnoy, *Music in the Life of Man*, p. 11.

8. *The social status of the musician was low during the Enlightenment.*
The seventeenth and eighteenth centuries comprised the era of absolutist rulers, in which court patronage demanded subservience and servility: "It is a sad thing always to be a slave, but Providence wills it to be so, poor wretch that I am!" (Joseph Haydn, Letter to Marianne von Genzinger, June 27, 1790; in Haydn, *Gesammelte Briefe und Aufzeichnungen*, p. 243) Moreover, music was widely considered to be primarily for feeling and diversion, neither of which was accorded much importance in the eyes of reason.

...though it speaks by means of mere sensations without concepts, and so does not, like poetry, leave behind it any food for reflection, still [music] moves the mind more diversely, and, although with transient, still with intenser effect. It is certainly...more a matter of enjoyment than of culture--the play of thought incidentally excited by it being merely the effect of a more or less mechanical association--and it possesses less worth in the eyes of reason than any other of the fine arts. (Immanuel Kant, *Critique of Judgment*, 1790, pp. 535-6)

The passage that follows this statement in the *Critique of Judgment* suggests that Kant's disinterest in music colored his philosophical evaluation of it. His ideas, however, and the ideas of those who thought like him in this regard, helped to contribute to the nonessential status that music occupies in modern life and thought.

THE ENLIGHTENMENT AND CHURCH MUSIC

The established churches (Roman Catholicism and the traditional Reformation bodies) crumpled under the onslaught of Enlightenment ideas. These churches came under relentless attack: from philosophers;[20] from governments (monasteries were secularized and church lands and privileges were confiscated; church and state were separated, resulting in a temporary loss of tax support for the church); and from outright revolts (the French Revolution). The churches tried to conform to the greatest degree possible to the spirit of the times, and in doing so they forfeited much of their internal substance and self-identity. For example, Pope Clement XIV disbanded the Jesuits, the Roman Catholic Church's primary missionary arm, in 1773 (they were re-established in 1814 by Pope Pius VII), and Lutheran liturgical practice went into a steep decline. Religion was gradually transformed into an ethical humanitarianism.[21] All of the established churches were ill at ease with anything smacking of "enthusiasm" (i.e., fanaticism), meaning, among other things, anything to do with the mysterious or supernatural. Under both physical and intellectual attack, beleaguered, confused, and inwardly weakened, the churches by and large had no time, money, or sympathy for excellence in church music. It was simply relegated to the background in most places. The effect on church music was devastating.

---

[20]See Evans-Pritchard, "Religion and the Anthropologists," p. 30.
[21]See Feder, "Decline and Restoration," in Blume, *Protestant Church Music*, pp. 334-5.

...all the *musici* in the churches at present are made up of the refuse of the opera houses, and it is very rare to meet with a tolerable voice upon the establishment in any church throughout Italy. The virtuosi who sing there occasionally, upon great festivals only, are usually strangers, and paid by time. (Charles Burney, *The Present State of Music in France and Italy*, 1771; quoted in Strunk, *Source Readings*, p. 690)

Even a perfunctory perusal of the Enlightenment's ideas on music presented above will confirm that all of them are to some degree at odds with the traditional views they gradually supplanted. Some of the ideas merely denied the old worldview and its ideas about music. Others contradicted, subtly or not so subtly, the very essence of Christianity, its worship and its music. Given the prevailing climate of opinion in the eighteenth century, it was inevitable that music should cast off its traditional subservience to the church.

In the Middle Ages it was a question of accepted obedience, now [i.e., in the Enlightenment] of independence. The artist...began to spell himself with a capital A and to say, not without stridency, that he took orders from nobody. Thus absolute music becomes "absolute" in a new sense; not only is it free from the associations of words and dance-forms, but it is free from any connection with the institutions of Church or of Court. (Routley, *The Church and Music*, p. 164)

In adhering to Lutheran orthodoxy and its liturgical framework for his music, J. S. Bach was clearly an anachronism, and his loyalty caused him much discomfiture. Other composers of his generation, who were more in tune with the spirit of their age and who thus enjoyed greater contemporary prestige (e.g., Telemann, Graun, Handel), wrote a great deal of church music, but much of it only set religious texts, having already cast off its mooring in the liturgy (i.e., in the cult). Handel's oratorios, for example, were often written on religious themes and used biblical texts, but their home was rightly the concert hall and not any church or cultic celebration. Neither the Lutheran Church nor the Anglican had any place for them in their traditional liturgies.

As a result of Christian worship's reorientation in the direction of eliciting and satisfying human emotional expression (i.e., pietism), church music came to be seen primarily as a means of edification[22] (i.e., of inducing a vague religious feeling and a sense of spiritual uplift). Piety, generally understood as a matter of the heart rather than the intellect, called for a type of church music that shunned intellectual artifice and attempted to speak simply and directly to worshipers' emotions. One product of this idea was the decline of the German Lutheran chorale[23] and the elaborate art forms based on it. Another product was the growth of the spiritual song, both Roman Catholic and Protestant. (In North America, the popularity of this genre grew enormously with the influence of Great Awakening revivalism.)

Choral foundations connected with cathedrals and other large churches had long been deteriorating; now many of them disintegrated or were dissolved.[24]

---

[22]Ibid., p. 323.
[23]See Lang, *Music in Western Civilization*, p. 701; Feder, "Decline and Restoration," in Blume, *Protestant Church Music*, p. 336.
[24]See also Feder, "Decline and Restoration," in Blume, *Protestant Church Music*, p. 312.

The Enlightenment and Music   181

The invasion of Italy by the armies of republican France, in 1796, followed as it was by an almost total destruction of the power, and dissipation of the riches of the Church; by the suppression of monasteries and hospitals, and the sale of the lands destined for their support, destroyed at once the schools which educated the young and the retreats which fostered the adult musician. (from *The Harmonicon*, 1831; quoted in Weiss & Taruskin, p. 347)

Figural (i.e., elaborate concerted) music inevitably declined in quality and quantity: "By 1785 a writer could state that many cities had already done away with operatic church music (i.e., in cantata style), and that the choirs sang at most only four-part chorales, motets, hymns, and arias, to the accompaniment of organ and wind instruments" (Feder, "Decline and Restoration," in Blume, *Protestant Church Music*, p. 333). Secular elements, indeed entire secular works, were adopted or adapted into church music.[25] In some established Protestant churches the specifically Christian content of texts also evaporated. Papal decrees during this period bear witness to the distress and disarray in traditional Roman Catholic circles at the invasion of secular musical practices (see Chap. 10, p. 144). Some areas of Europe maintained a stronger practice of church music than others, notably Lutheran Saxony and Thuringia,[26] Bavaria, Austria, and German-speaking Roman Catholic lands. But all of these were gradually affected by a decline in the quality of works performed and by the increasing adoption of secular ideals and practices, especially those of the Classic and Romantic opera--as the Masses of Haydn and Mozart already show, glorious music though they may be.

The churches' accommodation to secular ideals and practices may be traced clearly in their gradual (sometimes grudging) acceptance of instruments (other than organ and bells) for use in worship. It is particularly interesting to trace the uneasiness in the Roman Catholic Church as it wrestled with the widespread introduction of instruments into the liturgy,[27] since its early tradition stood so diametrically opposed to it, and since papal and conciliar decrees offer such a vivid witness to its progress.

---

[25]Ibid., p. 325-6
[26]Ibid., pp. 319ff.
[27]See Hayburn, *Papal Legislation*, pp. 97 & 103, 136-8, 229, 331, 353; Abbott, ed., *The Documents of Vatican II*, "The Constitution on the Sacred Liturgy," Article 120.

15

Romanticism and Music

Enlightenment views conspired to rob music of any ethical dimension. Under their weight music might well have reverted to the status it held in Roman antiquity (see Chap. 4, pp. 53-54). Has music any deep significance, any profound positive value for humans, or is it just what the eighteenth-century music critic and historian Charles Burney says it is?[1] "Music is an innocent luxury, unnecessary, indeed, to our existence, but a great improvement and gratification of the sense of hearing" (Charles Burney, *A General History of Music*, Vol. I, p. xvii). Enlightenment views on music offer no adequate answer to this question. Music expresses feeling (is that good or bad?). Music provides entertainment (but entertainment is in itself ethically neutral). The answer formulated at the end of the eighteenth century, with the rise of the Romantic ideal, remained valid through the nineteenth. It was predicated on an old idea whose lineage we have traced from antiquity: *music is bound up with human nobility*[2].

---

[1] In all fairness to Burney, it must be said that he never intended to denigrate the art of music; he was reacting to the English Puritanical view (supported and intensified by Enlightenment attitudes) that music is an insidious and enervating waste of time. Nevertheless, a statement such as his could not have been made (and need not have been made) before the Enlightenment.

[2] See Charles Burney, *The present State of Music in France and Italy* (1771), quoted in Strunk, *Source Readings*, p. 692; C. W. von Gluck, Letter to the Editor of the "Mercure de France" (1773), trans. in Strunk, p. 682; J. F. Reichardt, *Briefe geschrieben auf einer Reise nach Wien* (1810), trans. in Strunk, p. 739; Hector Berlioz, *Rossini's "William Tell"* (1834), trans. in Strunk, pp. 809 and 819; Franz Liszt, "Concerning the Situation of Artists and Their Condition in Society" (1835), quoted in Weiss & Taruskin, *Music in the Western World*, p. 366; Hector Berlioz, Report to a newspaper (1851), trans. in Weiss & Taruskin, p. 353; Robert Schumann, *Davidsbündlerblätter* (1853), trans. in Strunk, pp. 844-5; Eduard Hanslick, review of Brahms's First Symphony (1876), quoted in Weiss & Taruskin, p. 404.

184   Wiser than Despair

[The author, one of the earliest of the German romantics, is speaking here about Joseph Berglinger, his personification of the noble, sensitive musician composer] ...when the music was over and he left the church, he thought himself made purer and more noble. (W. H. Wackenroder, "The Remarkable Musical Life of the Musician Joseph Berglinger," from *Herzensergiessungen eines kunstliebenden Klosterbruders*, 1797; trans. in Strunk, *Source Readings*, p. 753)

Unlike many other older ideas, this one had persisted undiminished in some circles into the Enlightenment, despite newer ideas that might have contradicted it. The concept of nobility in music was increasingly secularized--"humanized," "un-baptized," if you will; it lost its former specifically Christian connotation. But it was filled with new meaning by a series of composers (all of whom may be considered in some sense Christian) who perfected a type of music first envisioned in the Renaissance, a music that expressed and indeed embodied the noblest sentiments and aspirations of humanity--humankind in a state of perfect harmony. We could cite as examples almost any of the major works of great composers beginning with Haydn: specific examples might include Haydn's *Creation* (a sacred work), or Mozart's *Magic Flute* (a secular work). Beethoven's music is, of course, the very embodiment of human nobility; more than any other person, Beethoven was responsible for transforming the concept into something entirely personal and subjective.[3]

It is a remarkable paradox that the very age that witnessed the downfall of the

Illustration 8:
Franz Liszt in Concert

Source: Titlepage of *Berlin, wie es ist...und trinkt*, 1842, Heft 14, by Adam Brennglas.

---

[3]See Lang, *Music in Western Civilization*, pp. 750-1.

old view of the world and its music produced some of the most harmonious, orderly music imaginable. This could only happen because assumptions and practices generated by older ideas were anything but dead in music; they continued to exist in fruitful tension with the new. It is curious that the two great classical periods in music history, periods in which a perfect balance of intellectual and emotional elements was achieved, have occurred at the times when fundamentally new worldviews were assailing old, established ones: the High Renaissance, when humanism vied with the medieval worldview, and the Classical period, when the struggle between the religious and secular worldviews was at its height. Indeed, the very idea of the "classical" in music is best understood as the balance of intellectual and emotional elements (see Chap.14, pp. 174-5). The victorious struggle for unity that characterizes the works of the greatest classical composers--formal procedures associated with the classical sonata, key relationships, motivic unity, passages of imitative polyphony--represents the continuation of old ideals.[4]

Thus by the time the Classic period was giving way to the Romantic, the void created by the disappearance of musical speculation was filled by music as 1) *the noble creation* 2) *by noble humans* 3) *for noble humans*.

1. *The noble creation*: music itself became a quasi-religion.[5]

...there must be a growing number of persons...to whom...it [i.e., Beethoven's Ninth Symphony] is religious music, and its performance a celebration rather than an entertainment. I am highly susceptible to the force of all truly religious music, no matter to what Church it belongs; but the music of my own Church--for which I may be allowed, like other people, to have a partiality--is to be found in Die Zauberflöte and the Ninth Symphony. (George Bernard Shaw, *Music in London*, p. 275)

2. *By noble humans*: composers (in particular Beethoven) came to be popularly regarded as the perfect embodiment of human nobility, or even as superhuman, quasi-divine beings.[6]

The whole so-called Romantic School...is far nearer to Bach in its music than Mozart ever was; indeed, it has a thorough knowledge of Bach. I myself make a daily confession of my sins to that mighty one, and endeavor to purify and strengthen myself through him...to my mind Bach is unapproachable--he is unfathomable. (Robert Schumann, Letter to Keferstein, January 31, 1840; trans. in Morgenstern, *Composers on Music*, p. 152)

The public also granted the same sort of adulation to virtuoso performers, for example, Paganini and Liszt, that they accorded great composers (Illustration 8). The idea of great music as the creation of the misunderstood, sensitive,

---

[4]"Classical music" (from Bach to Brahms) is probably best understood as the final fruits of the accumulated creative energy of a worldview already in the midst of disintegration; see Chap. 11 above.

[5]See also W. H. Wackenroder, "The Remarkable Musical Life of the Musician Joseph Berglinger" (1797), trans. in Strunk, *Source Readings*, p. 753; Hermann Abert, "Geistlich und Weltlich in der Musik," p. 99.

[6]See Salmen, *Social Status*, pp. 267-9.

suffering musical genius[7] began to challenge the notion of judging music by popular acclaim. Beethoven's moody, morose personality and rough manners contributed much to this new conception of the composer.[8]

3. *For noble humans.* The rise during the later eighteenth century of a sizeable middle class broadly characterized by elevated ideals and a new seriousness of purpose set the tone for the entire nineteenth century.[9] Sobriety and dignity (some might say "stuffiness") reigned, along with Queen Victoria of England, into the early twentieth century. Frivolity as the characteristic of a culture passed out with the Rococo and did not recur until the generation after World War I (the "Roaring Twenties" in the United States, the era of the Weimar Republic in Germany).

Romanticism retained and even intensified a number of Enlightenment ideas regarding music, notably the conception of music as feeling. Romanticism gradually pushed the subjective, emotional element in music to its limit. (To the extent that it was successful in doing this, it disregarded the intellectual dimension of music and thus began to disturb the unity and balance characteristic of the Classic era preceding it.) Accordingly, it dismissed the empirical scientific or rational approaches to music in favor of a vague humanitarian mysticism:[10] "Nothing is more inadequate than theorizing in music; there are laws, to be sure, mathematically determined laws, but these laws are not the music, only

---

[7]See Wackenroder, "The Remarkable Musical Life of the Musician Joseph Berglinger" (1797), trans. in Strunk, *Source Readings*, pp. 752-3.

[8]In his *Briefe geschrieben auf einer Reise nach Wien* (1810), J. F. Reichardt records the following observations about Beethoven:

It gave me great pleasure to see the excellent Beethoven not only on hand but much made of, the more so since he has in mind and heart the fatal hypochondriac delusion that everyone here persecutes and despises him. To be sure, his stubborn outward manner may frighten off some of the jolly good-natured Viennese, and many of those who acknowledge his great talent and merits may perhaps not employ sufficient humanity and delicacy to so offer the sensitive, irritable, distrustful artist the means of enjoying life that he may accept them gladly and also take satisfaction in them as an artist. It often pains me to the quick when I see this altogether excellent and splendid man gloomy and unhappy, although I am at the same time persuaded that it is only in his willful mood of deep discontent that his best and most original works can be produced. Those who are capable of appreciating these works ought never to lose sight of this or to take offense at any of his outward peculiarities or rough corners. Only then are they true, genuine admirers of his. (trans. in Strunk, *Source Readings*, pp. 736-7)

See also E.T.A. Hoffmann, *Beethoven's Instrumental Music* (1813), trans. in Strunk, *Source Readings*, pp. 777-8.

[9]See Lang, *Music in Western Civilization*, p. 719. As examples, we might cite any of the founding fathers of the United States of America.

[10]See Wackenroder, "The Remarkable Musical Life of the Musician Joseph Berglinger" (1797), trans. in Strunk, *Source Readings*, p. 754; E.T.A. Hoffmann, *Beethoven's Instrumental Music* (1813), trans. in Strunk, *Source Readings*, pp. 780-81.

its prerequisites.... The essence of music is revelation, it is impossible to explain it" (Heinrich Heine, *Letters on the French Stage*, ninth letter (1837); trans. in Heine: *Selected Works*, p. 115). Romantic essays on music often express no truly coherent, logical ideas; frequently, they are visionary emotional outbursts, expressed with an ardor akin to a rousing sermon (this holds true especially for the writings of Liszt and Wagner)--vehicles perfectly suited to the demands of a bourgeois audience.

The noble, emotional subjectivity of Romanticism, when it filtered down to the (increasingly large and important) popular (middle-class) level, often fell prey to shallowness, domesticity, and sentimentality.[11] These terms aptly describe much of nineteenth-century bourgeois culture as well as its music. In the German and Austro-Hungarian Empires this culture is referred to as Biedermeier; in England and the United States it is called Victorian.[12]

ROMANTICISM AND CHURCH MUSIC

The nineteenth century was the era of Romanticism, particularly in music. It was also the period in which Christianity began to reassemble and regroup its forces after its first disastrous encounter with Enlightenment ideas. Romantic views and attitudes thus had a considerable amount to do with the churches' struggles for revival and with the ideas about music that these struggles promoted. The Romantic era was by and large favorably disposed to religion in general and Christianity in particular; a certain dimension of the Romantic attitude seemed to vibrate in sympathy with medieval Christian ideals. It was not the speculative, constructivist aspect of medieval thought that was reborn and that thrived, however, but the mystical, the other-worldly, the visionary.[13] Religion as espoused by romantics was frequently an unorthodox, emotional, highly personalized form of Christianity; in it the composer found a place, elevated to the level of a demi-god.[14]

---

[11]See Lang, *Music in Western Civilization*, pp. 805-7.

[12]The music identified with that bourgeois culture is only today beginning to be replaced in some churches with music influenced by the twentieth-century mass media.

[13]Thus the nineteenth-century gothic revival in architecture attempted to recreate the feel and ambience of medieval buildings, but showed little interest in employing the geometric ratios that determined the form of many medieval cathedrals. In the realm of the visual arts, Friedrich von Schelling in his *Philosophy of Art* (*Philosophie der Kunst*; 1807) writes of the moral character of great art, and develops at length the theme that art reflects the harmony of nature and the universe (without being specific as to how art is able to do it). This does not seem to be a deliberate resurrecting of the medieval vision of art. Rather, it is something more subtle: a fascinating instance of Romantic empathy with the medieval worldview. But whereas in the Middle Ages the concept was concrete and specific, in Schelling's writing it is idealized and poetic.

[14]There is, for example, a painting entitled *Liszt am Flugel* (*Liszt at the Piano*), done in 1840 by Josef Danhauser, now in the possession of the Staatlichen Museen Preussischer Kulturbesitz, Berlin. In it Franz Liszt plays the piano, surrounded by an entranced assembly of notables including Gioacchino Rossini, Niccolò Paganini,

Two characteristic attitudes of Romanticism strongly imprinted themselves on nineteenth-century ecclesiastical revivals and thus had an enormous impact on church music. The first was *historicism*, a respect and a longing for the past, in particular for the Middle Ages. Because the church was the central institution during the Middle Ages, this affinity for the medieval particularly affected nineteenth-century religion. Historicism was not at heart an objective, scientific inquiry, but rather a spiritual and artistic movement. It gave birth to the nineteenth-century gothic revival and to the renewed interest in music of past ages. The second attitude was *aestheticism*, the worship of beauty as an end in itself. Aestheticism in relation to Christianity led to equating the beautiful with the divine.[15] While both of these attitudes are well documented as influential movements in the churches during the nineteenth century (and well into the twentieth), it should be noted that neither of them was or is well grounded biblically or theologically. Thus when they came to be scrutinized by the more dispassionate, prosaic twentieth century, both of them appeared to be like the proverbial house built on sand.

Attempts at ecclesiastical revival in the wake of the Enlightenment followed two general directions:

1. The traditionally liturgical churches (Roman Catholic, Lutheran, Anglican) centered their revivals around a renewal of their historic liturgies--in effect an attempt to reassert the centrality of cultic celebration for Christian faith and life. Solesmes eventually took the lead for Roman Catholicism; the Lutheran revival was marked by the issuance of ever more historically based *Kirchenagenden*, or orders of worship;[16] the Anglican revival was led by the Oxford and Ecclesiological Movements. It was in these attempts at liturgical revival that the romantic characteristics of historicism and aestheticism were most clearly evident. They were marked by a strong reassertion of the by-now hallowed ideals of church music (see Chap. 10, pp. 146), and by a renewed and intensive cultivation of Gregorian Chant and Renaissance polyphony (especially Palestrina[17])--though now conditioned by a spirit of quietism: "Protestant church music must take care to remain within the venerable bounds of a distinctly prayerful mood. Under no circumstances should it express passion; it must exude divine calmness and peaceful consecration" (Julius Smend, c.1900; quoted in Blume, *Protestant Church Music*, p. 390). The traditional churches increasingly designated early music (or music conceived to some degree in the spirit of earlier styles, e.g.,

---

Victor Hugo, Alexandre Dumas, Aurore Dudevant (George Sand), and Countess Marie d'Agoult. Liszt faces a window, which frames a giant white bust (idol?) of Beethoven, in stark relief against a stormy sky.

[15]Reverend R.T.F. Brain, 1960:

As Healey [Willan, a leading early twentieth-century Canadian Anglo-Catholic church musician,] sees it, the liturgical worship of God is the consecration of beauty, and the spirit of the liturgy speaks to us of the holiness of beauty as well as of the beauty of holiness. (quoted in Wagner, "The Holiness of Beauty: Healey Willan as Church Musician," p. 1)

[16]See Blume, *Protestant Church Music*, pp. 377-8.
[17]Ibid., pp. 326f.

motets of Anton Bruckner such as "Christus factus es" or "Locus iste") as the music most proper for Christian worship. It was only during this period, and in circles concerned with the restored vitality of Christianity, that the opposition and tension between sacred (i.e., early music or the revival of early styles) and secular (i.e., music in a contemporary style) became heated and confused.

The restoration of church music of the past,[18] therefore, was largely initiated and conditioned by forces outside of the church (that is, historicism and aestheticism). Church music had lost its place as leader and had to be content to follow the trends set by contemporary secular music.[19] That secular musical ideas should condition the practice of church music was inevitable, given the continued disunity, internal weakness, and confused self-image of Christianity (despite sporadic internal revivals). Churchmen often ignored music or took it for granted; church musicians were largely ill-prepared and poorly paid.[20] To be sure, the situation was better in certain areas and churches, but this must be attributed to a peculiar affection for church music on the part of the populace in those regions, rather than to any vital theological conception of music's role in worship.

2. The newer evangelical churches (e.g., Baptist and Methodist), building on seventeenth- and eighteenth-century pietism, attempted to win back Christian losses by vigorous efforts at revival already begun during the eighteenth century, emphasizing emotional preaching leading to individual conviction of sin, repentance and conversion. While the roots of these movements were in Europe, most of their energy was generated in the United States. In its eagerness to use music as a tool in its missionary effort, evangelical Christianity was very receptive to new developments and ideas in music, especially devices that intensified music's emotional impact. This often led to the sort of exploitation of music that Eric Routley describes so well in his book, *The Church and Music* (pp. 179-80).[21]

The vice of Victorian music is often said to be "sentimentality," and if sentimentality is emotional content backed by no solid truth, a show of feeling with no intention of consequent honesty, the description is an accurate one. Hence, at any rate, came the

---

[18]It is worth noting in passing that the worship of many churches in England and Germany is today still largely characterized by the performance of choral church music of the past.

[19]See Georg Feder, "Decline and Restoration," in Blume, *Protestant Church Music*, p. 376.

[20]Concerning the situation in Germany at this time, Georg Feder says:

Most clergymen lacked any understanding of church music, and few church musicians understood liturgical requirements. In general, the church required no higher accomplishment of musicians than being able to beat time for the liturgical choral singing and to start or accompany the singing of the chorale. Pay was correspondingly low. A reorganization of the profession of church music, demanded periodically during the entire 19th century, never took place. (from "Decline and Restoration," in Blume, *Protestant Church Music*, p. 388)

[21]For the complete discussion of this topic, see Routley, *The Church and Music*, pp. 165-80; 186-91.

multitudinous drawing-room and salon music of the later Victorian era, and this music was "tool-music" at two levels: it was music composed and published in order to help the business of music-making along, and in that sense a tool; and it was music composed in order to create irresponsible emotion and an unreal sense of well-being, and in that sense also a tool.

But this music, the secular music of the salon, was not the final degradation. It remained for the church to debase music to the limit. For music designed to create mere natural emotions such as sorrow or pity, or peace of mind has at any rate what a celebrated broadcaster calls "animal content." But the hack-music of the church..., music designed to produce not natural emotion but (save the mark) religious emotion--this was music at its lowest ebb.

It is important to recognize that there was often no strict dividing line between the two directions (popularly termed "high church" and "evangelical"). Various aspects of both mixed and mingled in many churches during the nineteenth century, and continue to do so even today. It is crucial to emphasize that neither direction produced a broad-based, comprehensive, coherent theological explanation of the significance and function of music in relation to the church. Music (for that matter, all the arts) had become a theological orphan. In fact, no important theological movement, either in the nineteenth or twentieth century, has concerned itself in any profound way with the significance of harmony, order, or beauty in Christian life or cult.

16

The Twentieth Century

The advance of views associated with the Enlightenment in Europe coincided with the demise of the last remnants of the neo-Platonist Christian worldview. The final result of this transformation is modern society, egalitarian, pluralistic, and technophile--a phenomenon that has been intensified by the comprehensive cultural interchange that has taken place during this period. A significant percentage of people in traditionally Christian lands now no longer consider themselves Christian, or even religious. In place of a unified worldview there is now a multitude of worldviews--and a correspondingly vast muddle of ideas about music.[1] In music, as in so many other realms, the modern age is an age of contradictions.

---

[1] Roger Sessions, "Music in Crisis: Some Notes on Recent Musical History," p. 63:

Perhaps the most obvious symptom of the present crisis [in music] is its "confusion of tongues"--the result of nearly a century of musical development before the Great War [World War I]. What took place during this period was a gradual disassociation of the musical consciousness of Europe (rather, of the Occident) into a multitude of various components.

Virgil Thomson, "On Being American" (New York *Herald Tribune*, January 25, 1948):

The fact is, of course, that citizens of the United States write music in every known style. (Thomson, *A Virgil Thomson Reader*, p. 305)

Ernst Krenek, *Horizons Circled*, p. 74:

...our period seems to show a bewildering array of completely heterogeneous musical styles.

192 Wiser than Despair

There is no music in nature, neither melody or harmony. Music is the creation of man. He does not reproduce in music any combination of sounds he has ever heard or could possibly hear in the natural world. (H.R. Haweis, *Music and Morals*, p. 18)

My music is always the voice of Nature sounding in tone. (Gustav Mahler; quoted in Engel, *Gustav Mahler*, p. 73)

[of Elvis Presley] A weapon of the American psychological war aimed at infecting a part of the population with a new philosophical outlook of inhumanity... to destroy anything that is beautiful, in order to prepare for war. (East German newspaper, c.1958; trans. in Crofton & Fraser, *Dictionary of Musical Quotations*, p. 115:3)

God gave me a voice. If I turned against God, I'd be finished. (Elvis Presley; quoted in Crofton & Fraser, p. 118:11)

Furthermore, those who express ideas about music frequently do not articulate them clearly; often ideas and attitudes can be identified only by extrapolating from modern musical practice. In fact, the vacuum created by the total disappearance of the old worldview has made any consensus about the meaning and significance of music impossible.[2] One senses at times a reluctance to speak or think about music in philosophical or theological terms. If there ever was such a thing as a "neat package" of ideas and influences, it is now completely eradicated by a profusion and confusion of ideas, attitudes, and presuppositions.[3] In this potpourri, one thing is certain: church music is on the fringe of modern musical creativity. It sets no trends; it only follows trends established by the surrounding culture.

The ideas and attitudes toward music in general that have most affected twentieth-century church music seem to be the following.

1. A reaction against romantic emotional excesses, coupled with a renewed formal rigor and emotional restraint in musical practice[4] (in comparison with late Romantic music). This attitude is especially apparent in the rise of neo-classical and neo-baroque music with their re-introduction of older formal techniques and processes. In church music, it is most clearly reflected in the works of the composer Hugo Distler and his disciples.

---

[2]Symptomatic of this lack of consensus is the fact that the New Groves Dictionary of Music and Musicians contains no entry for "Music"; to survey the differing conceptions, one must consult the entry "Aesthetics of Music."

[3]Extreme cultural pluralism (together with its inevitable byproduct, extreme musical pluralism) is arguably the primary reason that the era of "great music" or "classical music" has come to an end, since the one essential precondition for it no longer prevails. That precondition is a unified worldview, a cultural solidarity on the part of a given society that shares visions and aspirations as to what is worthwhile and ideal and noble. That solidarity establishes an *a priori* unanimity among great numbers of people as to the underlying standards by which "great music" may be identified and judged. The last "great composer" (in the line of composers of Western art music) may well have been Benjamin Britten (1913-1976).

[4]See Igor Stravinsky, *Chronicles of my Life* (1936), quoted in Weiss & Taruskin, *Music in the Western World*, pp. 461-2.

The Twentieth Century   193

2. The call for individuality and originality, inherited from the Enlightenment and the Romantic, has become radical and absolutely uncompromising:[5] "I remember seeing, a few years ago, a newspaper report about one of the international music festivals headlined: "So-and-so Festival--No New Breakthrough."... It is regrettable that a new style is not allowed to mature and to unfold its potentialities" (Ernst Krenek, *Horizons Circled*, p. 89). This attitude confronts contemporary church musicians as they come into contact with the world of modern secular music, but they stand bewildered by its demand, since it is is incompatible with both the popular stance of modern worship (see Chap. 13, p. 168) and with the inherently conservative bias of Christian art.[6]
3. A renewed aristocratic attitude in twentieth-century art music:[7] "If it is art it is not for all, and if it is for all it is not art" (attr. Arnold Schönberg; quoted in Crofton & Fraser, *Dictionary of Musical Quotations*, p. 116:12). A wide gulf normally separates new art music (as it is now practiced in conservatories and universities, where many church musicians are trained) from the popular music of the marketplace. Church music is compelled to exist and to function suspended in the middle of that chasm.
4. The seemingly unassailable popular norm of major and minor modes and scales. The Classical and Romantic symphonic repertoire remains dominant in concert halls, and thus potent in musical life. As a result, common-practice tonal music is still well established and appreciated in limited (though culturally influential) circles. Other kinds of contemporary music have to some degree expanded the pitch and chordal vocabulary of the common practice, but without threatening its sovereignty in any significant way.

There are other factors as well that, although they have begun to affect the European church music scene, are most clearly evident in the United States and in Third-World Christian church music:
5. The increasing public taste for stimulating, rousing, sensuously rhythmic music, paralleled by the growing influence of music of non-European cultures, especially music with African roots (e.g., jazz) that is propulsive, syncopated, and rhythmically vivacious.
6. The belated rise of nationalism in music, a nineteenth-century phenomenon only recently evident in church music. Its influence is felt particularly in Third-World countries, whose indigenous music was formerly often suppressed by Christian missionaries. Many countries in Africa and Asia are now producing church music in native styles (e.g., the African *Missa Luba*), and recently this music has begun to be introduced into worship in the United States and (to a lesser degree) in Europe.

---

[5] See also Gatens, "What does the Avant-Garde Controversy Mean," p. 84. It has become a matter of course for composers (and other artists as well) to feel compelled to explain in words what they intend by their works, since the solidarity in presuppositions and values (indeed, any widely shared worldview) that would permit immediate and widespread comprehension does not exist.

[6] In this regard, see Gatens, "What does the Avant-Garde Controversy Mean," p. 85.

[7] See Ortega y Gasset, *Dehumanization of Art*, pp. 7 & 12.

7. The consumerist attitude toward music, fueled in part by a consumer-oriented society and in part by the meteoric rise of the popular music industry: publishing, recording, mass media. The mass media, being largely dedicated to the pursuit of monetary gain achieved by the production of ephemeral, disposable, but immediately appealing and highly seductive music, have promoted a principle of an infinite variety of surface events (musical effects and colors) within extraordinarily limited fundamental musical parameters. The resulting music perfectly constitutes the musical pole opposite that of earlier church music: it is fundamentally popular, almost entirely sensual in its appeal, and it possesses a minimum of musical intellectual content. Propelled by self-conscious humanity's apparently insatiable appetite for being entertained, it has produced ever more intense forms of emotional expression, with a corresponding increase in the illusion of sincerity (made possible in large measure by what Eric Routley calls "the factitious intimacy of the microphone"[8]). It is marked to an increasing degree by mechanization: drum machines, accompanimental sound tracks replacing live musical accompaniment, electronic amplification, electronically produced imitations of the sounds of acoustical instruments, and the rise of recordings and tapes--all serving as substitutes for individual participation in the arts. Whatever may be said in mass-media music's favor, it has had the unfortunate effect of obliterating folk music and inhibiting community singing in general wherever the mass media are easily accessible,[9] and of transforming music into a vicarious, consumer-oriented, and nonparticipatory experience.

The twentieth century has experienced an artistic tendency that profoundly reflects its fundamental "dis-ease,"[10] and that has brought further discomfort to church music: an attitude of pessimism that has gradually eroded the idea that music (or any of the arts) primarily represents human nobility. Every other era in Western civilization has been fascinated by the concept of nobility; the major artistic currents of the twentieth century, on the other hand, have either been indifferent to it or repelled by it: "Music in our time is granted little opportunity for glorification and flooding people with illumination. The flames of Hiroshima have gone beyond all that" (Hans Werner Henze, *Essays*, p. 115 (1963); trans. in Crofton & Fraser, *Dictionary of Musical Quotations*, p. 115:5). In this tendency, the twentieth century is diametrically opposed to the Enlightenment, which propounded an optimistic view of the human condition. That sense of optimism continued through the nineteenth century and into the early twentieth. It fueled the great Protestant missionary effort during the 1800s, and it was still evident in early twentieth-century hymn texts that foresaw the imminent establishment of a just Christian social order (Illustration 9).

---

[8]Routley, *Twentieth Century Church Music*, p. 156.
[9]See Portnoy, *Music in the Life of Man*, p. 89; Sachs, *Wellsprings of Music*, p. 4.
[10]The hyphen is intentional.

Illustration 9:
Hymn, "Where cross the crowded ways of life," by F. Mason North

Source: The Methodist Hymnal, 1905, No. 423.

Classic and some Romantic (i.e., common-practice) art music, in that it reflects this basically optimistic spirit in its purposive metrical drive, its consistent resolution of dissonance to consonance, and its pronounced formal coherence, was and still is widely perceived as purposeful and life-affirming, and therefore fundamentally consonant with the Christian stance toward life, even though the music is secular in origin.

The Enlightenment gave birth to another ideal, a "non-heroic" ideal: the heroic commoner who is unaware of his or her nobility or only gradually comes to discover it--a hero-in-spite-of-himself (cf. Rousseau's "noble savage"). This ideal continues to resound in such varied twentieth-century works of art as J.R.R. Tolkien's *The Hobbit* , the films of Charlie Chaplin, the writings and music of Charles Ives,[11] and Aaron Copland's *Fanfare for the Common Man.* It is different from the medieval ideal (e.g., the adulation of the "nobility" as a social class and the glorification of the learned *musicus*), but it is still undeniably "heroic" and by no means incompatible with Christian belief.[12]

The twentieth century has begun to witness a radically new artistic phenomenon: the glorification of the "anti-hero," the most vehement expressions of which are the doctrines of nihilism and the cult of the absurd, with their sinister implications for societal, civilized living. This tendency explores and even celebrates the selfish, sinister, macabre, violent, perverted, depraved, criminal, and insane, based on the presumption that life is fragmented and characterized by cynicism, human alienation, incoherency, frustration and boredom, regret and unfulfillment. It can be seen most clearly in certain films and in a sector of the popular music scene with its addiction to drugs and its repudiation of long-established Judaeo-Christian moral and social values. The tendency has even crept into some twentieth-century Christian poetry and hymn and song texts that sarcastically deride the cruelty and religious indifference of nominally Christian societies and their complacency in the face of social injustice.

> When Jesus came to Golgotha they hanged Him on a tree,
> They drove great nails through hands and feet, and made a Calvary;
> They crowned him with a crown of thorns, red were His wounds and deep.
> For those were crude and cruel days, and human flesh was cheap.
>
> When Jesus came to Birmingham they simply passed Him by,
> They never hurt a hair of Him, they only let Him die;
> For men had grown more tender, and they would not give Him pain,
> They only just passed down the street, and left Him in the rain.
>
> Still Jesus cried, "Forgive them for they know not what they do."
> And still it rained the wintry rain that drenched Him through and through;
> The crowds went home and left the streets without a soul to see,
> And Jesus crouched against a wall and cried for Calvary.
> (Geoffrey Anketel Studdert-Kennedy (1883-1929), "Indifference", in
> *The Best of G.A. Studdert-Kennedy*, p. 150)

---

[11]See Charles Ives, *Memos*, quoted in Weiss & Taruskin, *Music in the Western World*, p. 425.

[12]Indeed, the figure of Jesus can be understood as an archetype of the "non-hero."

It was on a Friday morning That they took me from the cell,
And I saw they had a carpenter To crucify as well.
You can blame it on to Pilate, You can blame it on the Jews,
You can blame it on the Devil, It's God I accuse.
It's God they ought to crucify Instead of you and me,
I said to the carpenter A-hanging on the tree.

You can blame it on to Adam, You can blame it on to Eve,
You can blame it on the Apple, But that I can't believe.
It was God that made the Devil And the Woman and the Man,
And there wouldn't be an Apple If it wasn't in the plan.
It's God they ought to crucify Instead of you and me,
I said to the carpenter A-hanging on the tree.

Now Barabbas was a killer And they let Barabbas go.
But you are being crucified For nothing, here below.
But God is up in heaven And he doesn't do a thing:
With a million angels watching, And they never move a wing.
It's God they ought to crucify Instead of you and me,
I said to the carpenter A-hanging on the tree.

To hell with Jehovah, To the carpenter I said,
I wish that a carpenter Had made the world instead.
Goodbye and good luck to you, Our ways will soon divide.
Remember me in heaven, The man you hung beside.
It's God they ought to crucify Instead of you and me,
I said to the carpenter A-hanging on the tree.
(Sydney Carter, "Friday Morning," 1959, in *Songs of Sydney Carter*,
Book 2, p. 7)

In music this tendency has its roots in the nineteenth century (cf. the program of Berlioz's *Symphonie Fantastique*), but it came into its own in twentieth-century works such as Schönberg's *Pierrot Lunaire*, Alban Berg's *Wozzeck*, and Strauss's *Salome* (to cite some well-known examples). By no means all twentieth-century works are in sympathy with this tendency; many (perhaps the majority) maintain either a neutral or a life-affirming stance. But the twentieth century's most characteristic works, works such as Krzysztof Penderecki's *Threnody for the Victims of Hiroshima* (1960) or Randall Thompson's *Alleluia* (through tears[13]), bear the unmistakable anguish that comes with a deeper

---

[13]Benser and Urrows, *Randall Thompson: A Bio-Bibliography*, p. 26: "[In June 1940 Serge] Koussevitsky asked him for a choral piece, a 'fanfare' to be performed as part of the opening exercises of the new Berkshire Music Center... But for Thompson, a fanfare was not possible: France had fallen. He struggled to find some suitable expression for his and the world's anguish at that moment, and later wrote [in a letter to Lydia P. Veazie, July 25, 1977]:

I recall that Louis Baille referred to it in speaking to me as being a very sad piece, and he was absolutely right. The word "Alleluia" has so many possible interpretations. The music in my particular Alleluia cannot be made to sound joyous. In fact, it is a slow, sad piece, and...here it is comparable to the Book of Job where it is written, "The Lord gave and the Lord has taken away. Blessed be the name of the Lord."

realization of the potential dimensions of human inhumanity. And those works that do exhibit a pronounced "anti-heroic" bias have often attracted more attention (or notoriety), especially in view of the twentieth century's demand for radical originality. Of course, the works named at the beginning of this paragraph have texts that make it clear they are not intended to sympathize with any Christian worldview. But what about their music? Are there some musical styles that are in some sense incompatible with Christianity, that essentially lend themselves better to the expression of other worldviews, such as pessimism and nihilism? Christian theology has not yet begun to confront the question of musical (or any other artistic) styles in any satisfactory way.

As we have already noted, the twentieth-century church and its music are at the periphery of musical life; thus any new influences on church music now come almost entirely from the secular culture surrounding it. Two movements within the churches, however, have also had a significant impact on church music.

1. The continued emphasis in some churches on an emotional, subjective mode of worship (often driven by the imperative to evangelize), now coupled with and intensified by the infiltration of devices and techniques from rock-and roll and other popular music and its accompanying entertainment industry, based on the implicit assumption that the end justifies the means, and that "results" are more important than musical integrity.[14]
2. The Liturgical Movement, manifested most clearly in Roman Catholic liturgical changes after the Second Vatican Council, is a twentieth-century attempt to restore the centrality of the cult to the formation of Christian faith and life, based on careful study of the worship of the early Church.[15] In an attempt to foster a mutually supportive community of faith with the church's liturgy at its center, the Liturgical Movement has insisted on the intelligibility and accessibility of forms of worship[16] and has stressed popular participation. These emphases have imparted a renewed vitality to all forms of congregational participation in music, but they have sometimes proved to be at the expense of art music.

---

[14]See Johansson, *Music and Ministry*, pp. 56-7.

[15]In the words of a pioneer of the movement, Dom Albert Hammenstede:

One applies the name "Liturgical Renewal" to those...efforts which [have] as their object the nurture of a spiritual life among clergy and laity centered about the cultic mysteries. Thus it would on the one hand form a more lively and integral participation in worship and on the other it would teach us consistently to extend our experience of God's grace within the liturgy also to the execution of the daily tasks of our calling. (Report at the fourth *Tagung für Christliche Kunst*, Freiburg im Breisgau, 1924; quoted in Koenker, *The Liturgical Renaissance*, p. 13)

For a detailed exploration of the various dimensions of the movement, see E. B. Koenker's *The Liturgical Renaissance in the Roman Catholic Church*.

[16]The cultivation of intelligibility has at times left worship vulnerable to the post-Enlightenment tendency to downplay the element of awe and mystery, contributing to a prosaic dullness.

...we should mention briefly the role of singing in the liturgy. This is something which the Liturgical Movement has stressed, particularly in its rediscovery of the congregational singing of psalms. We, as the people of God, are a people who sing. Singing by the entire congregation is an expression of both our unity and our love. We all know, however, some of the pitfalls of the tyranny of church music over the people. Walter Lowrie quotes provocatively that 'the greatest impediment to the propagation of the Gospel is the choir, the choirmaster, and the organ'. The Liturgical Movement has, however, shown us one way out of the difficulty. The answer is not to do away with the choir; the choir must simply be used in a different manner. It must be a resource for congregational singing and not a substitute. (Shands, *The Liturgical Movement and the Local Church*, pp. 132-3)

In particular, the insistence that the choir is not of the clergy, but is a section of the people, has promoted the idea that the choir's basic role is to support and adorn congregational singing, not to perform complex art music.[17] In parishes where worship has been guided and fostered by astute, sensitive men and women, the influence of the Liturgical Movement has been a welcome corrective to a formerly excessive emphasis on the performance of art music by trained musicians, and has even led to a new and creative synthesis. On the other hand, in the hands of those less sensitive to music, it has served as a pretext for disparaging and dismissing the use of art music in the liturgy as elitist and inappropriate.

CHURCH MUSIC AND EGALITARIANISM

No secular artistic ideal, however, and no movement within the churches continues in the final analysis to exert as powerful or determinative an effect on twentieth-century church music as the ideological matrix in which most of the Western churches exist. All of the lands in which church music now flourishes are imbued to some degree or another with what is perhaps the Enlightenment's most profound contribution to civilization: the modern democratic ideal: "We hold these truths to be self-evident, that all men are created equal, that they are endowed by their Creator with certain unalienable Rights, that among these are Life, Liberty and the pursuit of Happiness" (The United States Declaration of Independence, 1776). As noble and admirable as it is, the egalitarian democratic ideal has presented the fine arts, and especially church music, with an immense challenge. For whereas world-conscious societies implicitly recognize (and even cultivate) a hierarchy of human quality and "gifted-ness" (for good or ill), egalitarian, self-conscious societies are inherently suspicious and ill-at-ease with such distinctions; a powerful egalitarian consensus works at leveling them.

Egalitarian democracy in relation to the church presents a paradox: its development is inconceivable without Jesus's insistence on the equal worth of each individual before God, yet it is largely antithetical in form and spirit to the historic development of the Christian Church and its art. This has become particularly apparent in the twentieth century at the fountainhead of egalitarian ideals, the United States. With regard to the fine arts, the original "enlightened"

---

[17]See Gelineau, *Voices and Instruments in Christian Worship*, pp. 85; 87-88.

200 Wiser than Despair

notion, stemming from a typically eighteenth-century optimism, was to raise standards by educating the musically illiterate masses. Thus the great art of the past and present (including that of the church) would become accessible to and appreciated by all: "Music must be made popular, not by debasing the art, but by elevating the people" (Henry Cleveland, *National Music*, 1840; quoted in Crofton & Fraser, *Dictionary of Musical Quotations*, p. 116:5).

There are various indications that, for music, this ideal is not being realized as easily or quickly as its proponents might have hoped.[18] One of these indications is the uncontested hegemony of a debased popular music (Illustration 10): "...it's the same old story: drag them in and give them a show. The more vulgar it is, the better they like it" (Liberace, speaking of the hotels in Las Vegas, Nevada; quoted in Palmer, *All You Need Is Love*, p. 95).

Illustration 10:
Listeners' recorded music preferences in the United States in 1986.

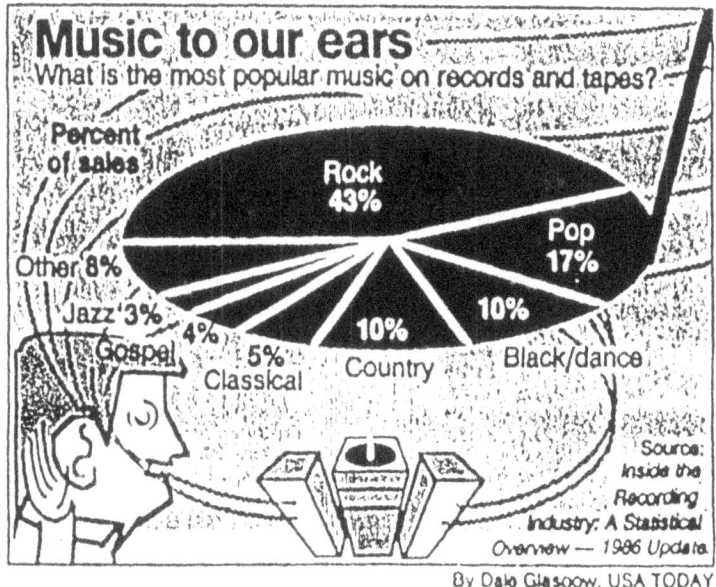

Copyright 1986, USA TODAY.   Reprinted with permission.

Art music still flourishes almost entirely in places that are holdovers from the old order: universities, elite schools, circles of long-established wealth and privilege.

---

[18]See Lang, *Music in Western Civilization*, pp. 1027-8.

A second indication is the decline of musical patronage.[19] The old ideal implicitly promoted financial as well as moral support for the artist (including, of course, the church musician).

Kings, princes and lords must support music: it is indeed fitting and proper that potentates and regents regulate the use and propagation of the fine arts. While some private citizens and common people are willing to finance the cultivation of music and love it, they are not able to shoulder its maintenance and cultivation.
Duke George, the landgrave of Hesse, and Duke Frederick, the elector of Saxony, maintained a choir and a *Kantorei* ; at the present time such organizations are being maintained by the Duke of Bavaria, by Emperor Ferdinand and Emperor Charles. One reads in the Bible that pious kings supported, maintained, and gave salaries to singers. (Martin Luther, from a table talk, c. 1536; trans. in Buszin, "Luther on Music," pp. 91-92)

The image of the neglected, misunderstood composer, on the other hand, is one that has arisen since the Enlightenment.

The splendid enterprise in Donaueschingen is something I have long admired: this enterprise that is reminiscent of the fairest, alas bygone, days of art when a prince stood as a protector before an artist, showing the rabble that art, a matter for princes, is beyond the judgment of common people. (Arnold Schönberg, Letter to Prince Egon Fürstenberg [1924], in response to an invitation to conduct the composer's "Serenade" at the Donaueschingen Music Festival; trans. in *Arnold Schoenberg Letters*, p. 108)

In some Western European countries, tax dollars still assume an important role in supporting church music (either directly or indirectly). In the United States, except in those rare situations where a congregation's endowment is sufficient to underwrite the cost of its music program, church music and musicians are financed by congregational giving and are thus answerable to the many, representing all shades of artistic taste and inclination.
A third and final indication is the low level of musical literacy (especially in the United States):[20] "A musical education is necessary for musical judgment.

---

[19]Not in terms of actual dollars, but in relation to total available wealth. In this regard, see Mantle Hood's comparison of the culture of Bali with that of the United States, found in Chapter 13 above.

[20]In his book, *Frames of Mind: The Theory of Multiple Intelligences*, pp. 108 & 109, Howard Gardner writes:

In Europe during the early years of the century, there was a fair amount of interest in the development of artistic abilities in children, including the growth of musical competence.... For reasons that one could speculate about, this interest rarely crossed the Atlantic...
Except among children with unusual musical talent or exceptional opportunities, there is little further musical development after the school years begin. To be sure, the musical repertoire expands, and individuals can sing songs with greater accuracy and expressivity. There is also some increase in knowledge about music, as many individuals become able to read music, to comment critically upon performances, and to employ musical-critical categories, such as "sonata form" or "duple meter." But whereas, in the case of language, there is considerable emphasis in the school on

What most people relish is hardly music; it is rather a drowsy revery relieved by nervous thrills" (Santayana, *The Life of Reason*, p. 51). The problem of musical illiteracy is exacerbated by the ubiquitous atmosphere- or background-music--Muzak--that encourages people to ignore musical sounds, that teaches them *not* to listen. Musical ignorance is characteristically accompanied by a philistine confidence of ignorance that further impedes musicians' ability to teach and to communicate musically:[21] "She [Zuleika] was one of the people who say 'I don't know anything about music really, but I know what I like.'... People who say it are never tired of saying it." (Max Beerbohm, *Zuleika Dobson*, 1911, pp. 155; 157) Musical literacy, of course, has a direct bearing on the adequacy of the musical resources with which church musicians work, particularly since the vast majority of church music is performed by volunteers.

At the end of the twentieth century, the modern democratic ideal is undergoing a fundamental transformation as it submits to the influence of an international, radically capitalistic economic cartel. The cartel is unconcerned with either the world-conscious or the self-conscious worldview; it centers entirely on productivity and profit. It is fostering a homogeneous, antipluralistic, consumer-oriented society, driven largely by the pursuit of material prosperity. That society is by definition "bureaucratic, technocratic and meritocratic;"[22] it focuses on administration, especially of people, in the quest for ever greater organization and efficiency. The cultural and artistic consequences of this new society--how it symbolizes its new allegiances and passions--are as yet unclear in society and in the church. On the surface of things, however, there is little reason to suppose they will be any more sympathetic than those of Enlightenment egalitarianism, either to religion or to the arts.

---

further linguistic attainments, music occupies a relatively low niche in our culture, and so musical illiteracy is acceptable.

[21] In his book *Church Music*, p. 71, Archibald Davison writes: "Assumed omniscience in matters musical is so common that we accept it as one of the painful phenomena of our society."

[22] Barber, "Jihad Vs. McWorld," p. 62.

17

Questions

Looking objectively at the present situation, there are a number of indications that the practice of church music has stabilized or actually improved since the eighteenth- and early nineteenth-century decline in the the wake of the Enlightenment:
1. Special schools for training church musicians have been founded in Europe and America, and there is a plethora of workshops and training courses for church musicians.
2. The liturgical renewal in the latter half of the twentieth century has rekindled an interest in promoting congregational singing among Protestants as well as Roman Catholics.
3. Church choirs have been established or re-established. Some have become extraordinarily competent (e.g., the English cathedral choirs) and have helped to revive an appreciation for the treasury of Christian music through their excellence in performing it.
4. A number of minor masters have directed the majority of their compositional output toward use in Christian worship, for example, Hugo Distler, Herbert Howells, and Leo Sowerby.
5. A number of first-rate scholarly books have been written on subjects pertaining to church music, for example, works by Julian, Zahn and Bäumker, Blume and Fellerer, Gelineau, Routley.[1]

Ironically, however, all this activity in church music has given rise to scant theological reflection as to its purpose. The impulse for the activity may grow out of love for God, for the church and its heritage, and for the music itself, but

---

[1] John Julian, A Dictionary of Hymnology (1907); Johannes Zahn, Die Melodien der deutschen evangelischen Kirchenlieder (1889-1893); Wilhelm Bäumker, Das katholische deutsche Kirchenlied in seinen Singweisen (1886-1911); Friedrich Blume, Die evangelische Kirchenmusik (1931); Karl Gustav Fellerer, Geschichte der katholischen Kirchenmusik (1972); Joseph Gelineau, Voices and Instruments in Christian Worship (1964); Erik Routley, The Church and Music (1967) and others.

it seems not to arise out of any generally acknowledged theological position, either articulated or implied, that makes sense of the value and purpose of this music for present-day Christians or Christian worship in the present. Behind the considerable activity in church music, then, a crisis has been steadily building, fueled by the lack of any theological underpinning for the church's musical enterprise. What are the signs of this crisis?

1. There is little, if any, theological investigation of the history or purpose of church music (or indeed, of the other arts in the church) in seminaries. This situation has produced a clergy largely ignorant and unappreciative of the practice, theory, or value of church music, and it has produced a corresponding unrest among church musicians. This is especially true in the United States.

> On October 27, 1987, representatives from [various religious denominations] and their related music associations attended the fourth annual interdenominational consultation hosted by the American Guild of Organists (AGO) in New York. The consultation was called to discuss the shortage of church musicians (reflected in an increasing number of vacant organ benches and plummeting enrollment in schools of sacred music) and working conditions in churches...
>
> The Rev. Walter Funk, National Chaplain of the AGO, greeted the delegates by stating that "psalms, hymns and spiritual songs are serious business." Representatives of the Guild reported that a recent survey of the two hundred seminaries which are members of the Association of Theological Schools indicates that a majority have virtually no requirements in worship or music for their graduates. Not only do future pastors have little seminary education in worship and music, but, stated Funk, "the gulf between pastors and musicians is firmly fixed in the seminary curriculum." (Staff notes: "Religious denominations asked: will you worship with music in the year 2000?")

2. There are large and ever-widening differences in the practice of church music,[2] differences that are largely irreconcilable and that have made a point of contention out of what ought to be one of the major signs and causes of Christian peace and unity.
3. There is a reluctance on the part of many worshipers to entering heartily into congregational singing.
4. There is a lack of any widely held objective criteria that establish propriety or quality in church music.

In the face of the perplexity and tension that the crisis causes, an occasional twinge of anxiety for the future on the part of musically sensitive church musicians is hardly surprising.

> I have a very real concern for the future of our profession as organists, choral directors and church musicians. At a time when our young artists are achieving the stature that we have heard in the [American Guild of Organists' Young Artists'] competition and our organbuilders are producing more beautiful instruments than ever, there is a strong trend in our society toward a stance that is anti-intellectual and looks for simplistic answers.

---

[2]Compare, for example, the traditional practice of church music in Europe and America with the practice of some evangelical churches, or with that of the Church Growth Movement/Entertainment Evangelism.

We must face the fact that the bulk of the musical literature with which we deal is intellectual and is certainly not simplistic.

Actually, it is not for our profession that I fear. I fear a world in which the heritage of beauty that we know and proclaim has disappeared. (Hansen, "President's Address to the AGO National Meeting")

The uneasiness vented here is the inevitable product of living in a time in which there are no longer any "answers" in church music; there are only questions. In such an age, the best that anyone who loves the music of the church can hope to do is to try to ask the right questions. In what I hope is a step in that direction, the last pages of this closing chapter will be given over to formulating and exploring six questions.

In what sense, if any, can the arts be considered profoundly significant for modern society? Educators and arts advocacy groups, when confronted with a question such as this one, will immediately protest that the arts are indispensable to a healthy society, that a culture without art is unthinkable. Mantle Hood's comparison of the culture of Bali with that of the United States in Chapter 13, however, gives us pause to consider. Since self-conscious societies are so fundamentally different from pluralistic, world-conscious societies, surely the significance of the arts is very different as well, and it is not at all clear what that significance is. The "doing" of the arts in the United States is more peripheral to the lives of "the masses" than in any other known culture, past or present; government spending to support artistic creativity is miniscule and under constant attack; the arts play only a token role in school curricula; and most popular "artistic" expressions (with the exception of popular dancing) are nonparticipatory. Consider, for example, the disappearance of community singing (whether in the family or in some larger communal gathering) in self-conscious cultures. Community singing is surely a "popular" art form (in contrast to forms of fine art), accessible to anyone who wishes to participate in it. World-conscious humans sing (both alone and in community) seemingly instinctively, because they perceive themselves as part of a greater whole from which they gain life and blessing. Self-conscious humans seem by and large to resist any urge to sing,[3] preferring to be part of an audience passively listening to a (professional) singer. Singing has traditionally been understood as a primary sign (and a primary instrument in the creation) of human health, wholeness and integration, together with everything that flows from these things: well-being, self-contentment, and joy. Yet there are great numbers of seemingly well-integrated, healthy self-conscious humans to whom it would never occur to join in any sort of community singing, and who on the surface seem none the worse for it. Are self-conscious humans too inhibited to sing with others, or do they simply have no need to sing together; or no need to sing at all? Other examples could be cited in this regard in addition to community singing: for example, communal dancing, or the artistic dimension of ritual and ceremony.

In the summer of 1991 I visited, with my family, the Epcot Center near Orlando, Florida. Epcot promotes itself as the "world of tomorrow;" it is full of

---

[3] See Marty, "Don't Sing," p. 1151.

technological wonders, it captures one's imagination with the promise of an exciting, adventurous future. As I wandered through its exhibits, I could not help but reflect that the technological world of the future promises no significant role for music (or any of the other arts, for that matter). Music at Epcot serves commercial purposes--it publicizes products and services; it provides a shallow kind of entertainment; and it masks that most odious of commodities in the late twentieth century: silence. Yet in his book *Music and Ministry: A Biblical Counterpoint* (p. 97), Calvin Johansson writes that

> ...music explores the mysteries of the essences of life: tension and release, struggle and conquest, movement and stillness, sound and silence, growth and decline, affirmation and rejection, life and death, and so on... These essences affect man in everyday life but are hidden from him, for they are truths to be known and felt in the unguarded moments of living. The composer takes these essences, these truths of life, puts them into another context, and returns them to man for his edification. One finds in music a great ability to deal with these hidden mysteries. For one thing, the processes of musical composition are...life processes. One only needs to hear the music to note its struggles, its consequences, its still moments, the tensions, the climaxes, its unity and diversity. Life is there. Sound in motion is life in motion. It somehow stirs man to his depths and he is moved, transported to the heavenly realm, and given a new vision of life.

Is music really that profoundly meaningful for human living? Epcot Center, the world of tomorrow, would not lead you to believe so. Is there reason to suspect that, in spite of the significant number of influential voices that disparaged the arts, the era of Christian dominance (in its world-consciousness) was inherently favorable to artistic expression, and that, on the other hand, in spite of the significant number of voices that support the arts, post-Enlightenment, self-conscious cultures are inherently inimical to artistic expression? Is art, which is so profoundly natural a phenomenon in world-conscious societies, alien in some fundamental way to the self-conscious worldview?

Perhaps, however, such questions arise out of too limited a conception of art. After all, in the broadest sense of the term, art is anything fashioned by human imagination and cunning (art is the opposite of nature). Elsewhere (Chapter 13, note 2) I have suggested (based on some observations by T. S. Eliot concerning the definition of culture) that culture is perhaps best defined as the collective behavior (together with the resulting artifacts) of a society engaged in acting out (symbolizing) its most deeply held and cherished shared beliefs and convictions. If that definition is true, then in order to recognize what art is for our society and our time, we must first ask, "What are our society's most deeply held and cherished shared beliefs and convictions?" These are not immediately obvious, given our society's pluralistic nature, but if there are any shared beliefs and convictions that are "sacred" to a majority of twentieth-century self-conscious humans (that is, if there are any self-conscious myths), perhaps they are these:[4]

1. A belief in the individual's right to pursue self-satisfaction, self-fulfillment, and self-gratification.

---

[4]Discounting the fear of annihilation, a negative factor that can hardly be expected to stimulate human creativity to any great extent.

2. Confidence in the potential of modern science to create for us an ever-improving quality of life, coupled with a fascination with the technology that is the result of modern science.

The kind of art that most clearly corresponds to the first belief is what we disparagingly call *kitsch* (art that makes us feel good about feeling). The art most properly aligned with the second belief centers on, in the words of Calvin Johansson, "media, presentation and image."[5] These are hardly the kinds of art envisioned or promoted by most educators and arts advocacy groups. It is evident, in fact, that they do not need to be promoted at all, since they are so omnipresent in our society. Is this conception of art in a self-conscious society accurate? If so, it raises profound questions about value and meaning, indeed about the very nature of modern culture and society (questions that are beyond the scope of this book).

Do the fine arts have any profound significance in modern society? Is there a meaningful role for artists of genius and total commitment? Is great art incompatible with modern, egalitarian society? Of course, it is too early to answer this question definitively, since modern society is, relatively speaking, still in its infancy. But a certain tension between the two is unmistakable. The pursuit of the fine arts has always been by nature labor-intensive and has often required expensive materials. Artists of genius and commitment have not typically proved to be skillful at or eager to raise funds to support their calling. Therefore the fine arts have in the past flourished only with generous patronage, either by the community or state[6] or by wealthy individuals with a developed taste for the arts. As for the present situation, U.S. government support for the fine arts, through the agency of the National Endowment for the Arts, is minimal compared with other developed countries, and yet intelligent, sensitive people (including many artists) have continually raised a hue and cry against it.

Yes, the NEA is a drop in the budget bucket, but it never will write a great book, compose a timeless symphony, or paint in sublime hues. Only the single man or woman, animated by what Jack Kerouac called "the unspeakable vision of the individual," can create. The government arts bureaucracy is, even at its most benign, superfluous. As publisher Eric Baizer said, "No great poet has ever been produced by a Washington backroom deal."...

Rock'n'roll receives not a penny of NEA money, yet it thrives; not only the formulaic rock heard on the radio, but vital, roots rock played in small clubs, in every nook and cranny in America. The punks of the late 1970s had a slogan-DIY, or "Do It Yourself." They did not ask the cultural establishment for a handout, or even a place to play. They founded their own clubs, bought secondhand guitars, paid the bands out of the gate proceeds, recorded in cheap studios, and disseminated tapes through and wrote themselves up in hand-stapled little magazines... They made music that will last and they did it by themselves. (Kauffman, "Art and Politics Don't Mix," pp. 20 & 21)

---

[5]In a letter to the author, October 23, 1991.
[6]State support, of course, presumes either a high degree of cultural solidarity or dictatorial control by a totalitarian regime.

Chapter 16 has already mentioned the dearth of private patronage of the arts in the United States. The following anecdote may help elucidate that phenomenon further. Recently, an elderly woman with whom I am acquainted made an appointment with me to discuss plans for music at her eventual funeral. She wanted to remove as many burdens as possible from her family. (This thoughtful concern confirmed my previous impression of her as an intelligent, reflective human being.) She told me that she loved the music (especially the piano music) of a particular famous composer, and she wanted to know if it would be possible to incorporate this music in some way into her funeral. I suggested the composer's works for organ as an alternative, and then continued by saying that if she really loved the piano works, she might consider arranging for a simple funeral and then providing funds for a concert of the composer's piano music. (That, it seemed to me, would be a thoughtful, appropriate parting gift to one's friends). She immediately reacted negatively to the suggestion, and her objection had nothing to do with the expense, but with the fear that folk would consider her ostentatious. Is it perhaps seen as too prideful, too pretentious, too self-serving for an upright, sober, common citizen in a democratic society to provide funds for such a lavish, extravagant undertaking?

The question of modern support for endeavors in the fine arts, however, pales before a far more profound question: what can the term *fine arts* mean in a pluralistic, egalitarian society that cannot reach a consensus in matters of artistic value (indeed, that sometimes rejects the very notion of making artistic value judgments as racist or elitist). Inherent in the term *fine arts* is the notion of discrimination; in the past, the *fine arts* were those artistic endeavors commonly recognized as exhibiting a greater degree of skill, as reflecting reality more subtly, profoundly, and insightfully (and consequently as requiring a higher degree of discernment, refinement and taste to appreciate).[7] What can the term mean in a society that moves ever further from agreement on what is real, and on what reflects reality more skillfully, profoundly and insightfully? In a society in which a very vocal element is outraged at the mere suggestion that the traditional fine arts are in any way superior to more popular artistic expression, or the artistic expression of minority groups? Is the attack on the notion of the fine arts the work of a few extremists that will eventually backfire on them? Or is it a long-overdue, just reaction against a repressive, racist (specifically, pro-Western-European), high-brow, elite minority that has for centuries ruthlessly imposed its taste on an oppressed majority? Is it just another twentieth-century fad, or is it a sign of a major shift, establishing that the fine arts never were significant except for the few who could appreciate them, and that the idea has passed into history with the coming of a truly egalitarian society?

The fine arts as we know them are the products of aristocratic Western European culture (and cult). What significant role can the fine arts assume in today's egalitarian, post-industrial Western culture, as the aristocratic European culture passes from a living force into a distant memory?

---

[7]Thus the nobility and other wealthy persons were willing to patronize the fine arts, either for altruistic reasons or because they expected to increase their prestige by being associated with "the best."

Do the arts have any profound significance for the church in the modern world? Christians, after all, are part of modern society; churches are not divorced from the world, nor should they be. If the great mass of humanity (the church's constituency) no longer finds artistic activity to be profoundly significant for human well-being, should the church continue to promote the arts sporadically and half-heartedly (as most churches have done in modern times)? Or should the church abandon the pretense that participating in the arts promotes both human wholeness and a deeper bond between humans and God? Should the church, for example, continue to practice a half-hearted congregational song,[8] or should the church gradually phase it out, allowing it to deteriorate in favor of a more nonparticipatory, entertainment-oriented musical practice?

A decision to renew commitment to the arts probably would also present the church with the challenge of revitalizing its understanding of cult and myth (no small feat!). A demythologized, amnesiac Christianity may appeal to a certain segment of self-conscious humanity, but can it sustain artistic vigor?[9] The cry of the psalmist, "How shall we sing the Lord's song in a foreign land?" (Psalm 137:4) takes on a certain poignant urgency in the modern world.

There is a great deal at stake in determining appropriate responses to these questions. Mantle Hood observes:

I have discovered that the arts are a kind of camera obscura of society. Like that optical wonder, they reduce the whole of its identity--sanctions and values, sacred and secular beliefs and customs--to a faithful reflection in miniature, in living colors. (Hood, *The Ethnomusicologist*, p. xviii)

If this observation reflects a past state of affairs, one that no longer has any validity in the modern world, then the church should abandon the promotion of artistic activity as soon as it is practical, since the arts are essentially a waste of the church's time and effort. If Hood is right, on the other hand, then the church ignores the arts at the peril of losing its soul.

Do the fine arts have any profound significance for the church in the modern world? Judging from the present state of affairs, the church in the modern world (through its indifference) has already given a negative answer to this question. There are, of course, great artists of our time who have created their art around religious, even specifically Christian themes. And there are a few churches that continue to patronize the arts to a limited degree.[10] (Church patronage of the fine arts in certain areas of Europe was strong after World War

---

[8] Whatever vigor sophisticated, partially self-conscious people can bring to their communal song normally pales in comparison to the intensity that world-conscious peoples generate in communal singing.

[9] I am speaking here not about appreciating Christian art treasures of the past, but of sustaining a present-day vital, creative artistic activity.

[10] I do not include among these the large number of affluent churches whose facilities exhibit second-rate, derivative (largely mass-produced) arts based on styles of the past.

II,[11] but since the eighteenth century it has always been sporadic, and in recent years it has declined.[12] It was never a vital, widespread movement in the United States.) As we have noted above, there has been renewed activity in church music in the twentieth century--but what in this swell of creativity is of primary *musical* interest? What, for example, would the compilers of a musical anthology find sufficiently interesting and meritorious to warrant its inclusion with earlier pieces of church music by, say, Josquin or Bach?

Do modern Christians consider the notion of the fine arts relevant enough to Christian faith and wholeness to resist being indifferent to it, or should they follow the lead of the surrounding self-conscious culture and cultivate the arts largely for their value as entertainment? Would it be beneficial for the church to try to muster enough solidarity to fashion a theological foundation that could provide guidelines for artists of genius and total commitment as they create works of fine art for the church? Such a foundation would have to be comprehensive and convincing to Christians in the modern world; it could not simply be a restatement of ideas that have energized past endeavors in the fine arts. It would, of course, have to relinquish any claim to universal validity or any hope of universal acceptance, since the Christian worldview (if one can still speak of such a thing), or even a religious worldview, is now only one worldview among many. Is it reasonable to hope that fine arts thus informed could become vigorous, vital, and creative within their own sphere, that they could provide a revitalized practice of the fine arts in the service of the church?

Of what significance (if any) to the church in the modern world are the great Christian artistic accomplishments of the past? The nineteenth-century revivals of historic liturgies, together with the rebirth of church music treasures of the past (see Chap. 15, pp. 188-9) were predicated in part on the presumption that the heritage of Christian creativity from past ages is a treasure of inestimable worth, that the lessons that heritage teaches are the surest foundation for facing the present and growing into the future. By the middle of the twentieth century the force of those revivals was spent, and since then the church's interest in its historic liturgies[13] and its artistic heritage has waned. The church in the modern world does not deny the significance of the past, but it does largely ignore it.

Why does it ignore it? Because the church no longer establishes society's ideals and attitudes. Indeed, it does not even influence them to any appreciable extent; it only reacts to them as they are presented from exterior, secular sources. Continuity with tradition, with the past, then, is rejected not by the church so much as by the whole of an ever more self-conscious society. The church has

---

[11]Consider, for example, the large number of churches in and around Cologne, Germany, built after the war by first-rate architects and exhibiting superb examples of modern art.

[12]Julius Cardinal Döpfner, the late archbishop of Munich-Freising, is reported to have accepted the plans for an unimaginative, utilitarian church building, observing wryly that if the building were ever abandoned it could always be used as a supermarket.

[13]In particular, those of the Middle Ages and the Reformation, that gave birth to the great Christian artistic accomplishments of the past.

had little success in stemming or channeling the tide of self-consciousness, not only in the society at large, but even among members of the church itself. To the extent that this is so, it is to be expected that the potential value of artistic creations of earlier world-conscious ages will be overlooked, dismissed.

One is compelled to suspect that the nineteenth-century revivals, despite all the energy they imparted to church music, were naïve in thinking they could simply resurrect the elements of earlier cultures that appealed to them (i.e., liturgical practices, art of earlier ages) while dismissing other less savory aspects (witch-burning, say, or superstitions arising out of ignorance). Can works of art, when they are removed from the world-conscious cultural fabric that generated them, continue to communicate to increasingly self-conscious people the force of their former meaning? When modern audiences (indeed, modern *Christian* audiences) listen to concerts of early sacred choral music or to recitals of early organ music, are they listening primarily out of piety or devotion? (How many of them are even aware of the works' cultic significance?) Or are they there for the most part because they expect to enjoy the music? Is it possible that the ideas of music as a means of communication with God and as a force for the ennoblement of the human spirit are becoming passé for some or (eventually) for all people? Or is there some way that the meaning of great Christian art of the past can be reinterpreted so that it has a renewed religious significance, not just to a few aesthetes, but to a broad spectrum of modern believers?

The question posed above, then, is indeed a vexing one. Just how distasteful and unfathomable it is may be judged from the fact that, in our time, questions concerning the religious significance of music and the arts in general, though sensed by some, seem to be of relatively little interest, even to people who are religious. On the one hand, the music of the Christian past seems to have very little relevance to the lives of the majority (even the majority of Christians). On the other hand, if Christians try to ignore or escape their heritage, it may well rise up to haunt them. When all is said and done, perhaps the greatest challenge facing the church today is to come to terms with the heritage of its past, and in particular its past as represented and embodied in the arts.

If the great Christian artistic accomplishments of the past are of any significance to the church in the modern world, should these artistic expressions be integrated into today's liturgies? How can this be done meaningfully? Can abstruse art contribute significantly to egalitarian worship? How?

It should be obvious to all who have read this book that the issues and questions raised here are neither inconsequential nor peripheral; rather, they penetrate to and affect the most intimate recesses of human well-being. In the present age, it seems that the more profound the question, the more inscrutable and elusive the answer. Some will be disappointed that I have refrained from offering at least some suggestions or provisional answers. But others (such as Gabe Huck,[14] for example, or Calvin Johansson,[15] or Paul Westermeyer,[16] or

---

[14]Gabe Huck. *How Can I Keep from Singing* ([Chicago:] Liturgy Training Publications [c.1989]).

212 Wiser than Despair

Paul Wohlgemuth[17]) have already charted viable and responsible courses to address immediate needs and shortcomings. The key to a deeper understanding of how much these issues really matter for all humans lies in formulating the right questions to ask about them, and I shall be satisfied for the present if I have contributed in some small measure to that goal.

While I offer no immediate answers, I am convinced that faith and grace will in due time provide more adequate and enduring answers to those who are willing to confront and probe and listen. In attempting to focus attention on the essence of the questions, therefore, I confess that I have often played the devil's advocate. If I have at times been brutal, my candor grows out of the deeply held conviction that those who are named Christian ignore at their peril the realities of a situation that has brought turmoil and insecurity not only to church music and musicians, but to the whole of the Christian Church (and, if the truth be known, to all of modern society). Only by facing these realities, by probing them and putting them into perspective, will it be possible to understand all the ramifications of the present situation and to try to chart a course toward more fruitful days.

Anyone who is a true believer cannot ultimately be a pessimist; that would deny the very ground of our hope. But given the magnitude of the dis-ease in an increasingly self-conscious society and the extent of human dislocation that the questions above reveal, it seems that the most realistic expectations for the foreseeable future must involve a degree of cynicism and pessimism. Things are likely to get worse (perhaps much worse) before they get better, and the arts (including, nay, *especially* church music) will faithfully reflect that deterioration. For this gloomy assessment I offer two reasons: (1) the prosaic modern age seems fated to judge human well-being largely in terms of material comfort and prosperity, and (2) in a society increasingly bereft of world-consciousness, human material and physical comfort seems eternally cursed to obscure human spiritual poverty. It is not reasonable to expect change (conversion) until the magnitude of human unfaithfulness and need becomes apparent. The present age conspires in countless ways to veil it. What is left for believers, then, is to live their lives hoping for, praying for, believing in, working toward health and blessing, authentic human fulfillment--longing for it, receiving it joyfully when it comes. For the present, believers have no alternative: they must continue to pursue and cultivate what is good while trying not to be distracted and disheartened by what is unworthy, and they must be extraordinarily astute in trying to determine the difference.

As part of the unending quest to name God in the all the varieties of human language, the twentieth-century hymn-writer Brian Wren has fashioned a hymn, "Bring Many Names," in which he has attempted to name the breadth and depth of God's personhood. To those who understand what is at stake in these matters, the words of the fourth stanza of that hymn take on a peculiar urgency:

---

[15]Calvin Johansson. *Music and Ministry: A Biblical Counterpoint* (Peabody, Mass: Hendrickson Publishers, Inc. [1984]).

[16]Paul Westermeyer. *The Church Musician* (San Francisco: Harper & Row [1988]).

[17]Paul W. Wohlgemuth. *Rethinking Church Music* (Carol Stream, Ill.: Hope Publishing Co. [c.1973, 1981]).

> Old, aching God, grey with endless care,
> calmly piercing evil's new disguises,
> glad of good surprises, wiser than despair:
> Hail and hosanna, old, aching God!
> (Wren, *Bring Many Names*, No. 9)

Christianity stands in relation to the modern, self-conscious world as the art music it has generated stands in relation to modern music in general. (Indeed, the same forces that threaten the one likewise menace the other.) For both of them--Christianity and its art music--represent what is old. There are those who maintain that the values they defend and promote are ageless, ever new. Yet in relation to the modern world they are old: embodiments of ancient, timeless, deep-rooted, deeply human values in a world enthralled by what is novel, hasty, shallow, and dehumanizing. In this context the image of the "old, aching" God is haunting, unforgettable. It provides an imperative for those whose allegiances are with the old: be "glad of good surprises"--not distracted by what is shabby and mean in the quest for what is excellent, rejoicing in every good and honest thing that survives and thrives against formidable odds. And: be "wiser than despair"--understanding what it means to be in the world but not of it, confident that when the time is ripe humankind will be renewed (as it has so often been in the past), and will be given new energy, new direction, new possibilities.

There is no way to hurry time to its ripeness. In the meanwhile, those who are faithful will know, as creatures made free and responsible, to seek patience, courage, and wisdom to make right choices for the present. The choice of ideas and attitudes to which they develop an allegiance will inevitably form and inform their ideals. That choice will make all the difference in how they make their music.

Appendix 1: The Organ

> "...Almighty God alone can never be given sufficient thanks for having granted to man in His mercy and great goodness such gifts as have enabled him to achieve such a perfect, one might almost say the most perfect, creation and instrument of music as is the organ...in its arrangement and construction; and to play upon it with hands and with feet in such a manner that God in Heaven may be praised, His worship adorned, and man moved and inspired to Christian devotion. (Michael Praetorius, *Syntagma musicum II: De Organographia* (1619), pp. 117-8; translated by W. L. Sumner)

> "...the monster never breathes... (Igor Stravinsky, *Dialogues and a Diary* (1961), p. 46)

The special place of honor accorded the pipe organ in Christian worship presents a curious paradox. On the one hand, the Christian church through most of its history has had an abiding antipathy toward instruments; on the other hand, the organ (together with bells) has, at least since the late Middle Ages, become so identified with the church that it embodies the very essence of "churchliness." How could this have happened?

The early church's rejection of instruments in worship and its mistrust of instrumental music of any kind is well established. In particular, the Roman *hydraulis* or water organ, a predecessor of the medieval church organ, was linked with pagan rites and games and with the theater; the early Church Fathers had no more use for it than for any other pagan instrument. St. Jerome (fourth century) spoke out sharply against the organ, warning that Christian virgins should be deaf to its music.[1] The Eastern Orthodox churches have never accepted instruments into their liturgies. In the West, the use of instruments in worship did not become commonplace until the Renaissance, and Roman Catholic

---

[1] Epistle CVII, 8: "Let her be deaf to *organa*; let her not know why the tibia, lyre and cithara are made" (McKinnon, *Music in Early Christian Literature* 324). Quasten (*Music and Worship in Pagan and Christian Antiquity*, p. 125; p. 112, n. 128) interprets *organa* as "organs"; McKinnon, on the other hand, asserts that the correct translation is the more generic "musical instruments." In any event, the organ as it was known in antiquity is surely included within the meaning of the term.

ecclesiastical authorities remained in some ways averse to them until well into the twentieth century.

Yet, in spite of its general hostility toward instruments, the Western church accepted the organ into its worship at a relatively early date (perhaps at some point during the tenth century), far in advance of any other instrument except bells. Why? The normal explanation for this paradox begins with the gift of an organ from the Byzantine Emperor Constantine Copronymus to Pepin, King of the Franks, in 757. The gift excited great curiosity (many contemporary chronicles mention it), not only because all knowledge of the organ seems to have perished in the West, but also because of the organ's imperial connotations. The organ played a central role in ceremonial occasions at the Byzantine court; indeed, it had become the unmistakable symbol of imperial majesty. This helps to explain the delight with which the instrument was received in the West. Pepin's organ was later destroyed, but in 826 there arrived at the court of Louis the Pious (Pepin's grandson) a Venetian priest, Georgius, who was trained in the art of organbuilding, and who at Louis's behest constructed an organ to replace the earlier instrument. A contemporary poem indicates just how significant the organ was to the self-esteem of the Frankish monarchs:

> Thus, Louis, do you bring your conquests to Almighty God
> And spread your aegis over noble kingdoms.
> The realms your forebears could not gain by force of arms
> Beg you of their own accord to seize them today.
> What neither mighty Rome nor Frankish power could crush,
> All this is yours, O Father, in Christ's name.
> Even the organ, never yet seen in France,
> Which was the overweening pride of Greece
> And which, in Constantinople, was the sole reason
> For them to feel superior to Thee--even that is now
> In the palace of Aix [the Frankish capital].
> This may well be a warning to them, that they
> Must submit to the Frankish yoke,
> Now that their chief claim to glory is no more.
> France, applaud him, and do homage to Louis,
> Whose valour affords you so many benefits.
> (from: E. Faral, *Ermold le Noir*; trans. in Perrot, *The Organ*, p. 213)

Scholars have generally assumed that the respect (indeed, the adulation) accorded a distinguished Eastern court instrument by the more primitive Western court and church led to its rapid appreciation and eventual admission into the liturgy of the Western church. There may be some truth in this assumption--church and state were indeed much intertwined throughout the Middle Ages. But it does not suffice to explain why the Western church should so summarily dismiss its centuries-old prejudice against all instruments and so wholeheartedly embrace an instrument with hitherto unmistakably secular connotations (to the extent that the most recognized early medieval experts in organbuilding were in fact monks, e.g., Gerbert of Aurillac, later Pope Silvester II, r. 999-1003, and Constantius of Fleury). Nor does it explain why early medieval accounts of organs place them in churches but do not link them with liturgical functions. These curious inconsistencies are perhaps best explained by understanding the organ of that time as an embodiment of cosmic harmony and as a means of manifesting and teaching basic neo-Platonic doctrines associated with the *quadrivium* and the medieval cosmic worldview.

The evidence from primary sources is scanty and inconclusive (as is much source material from the early Middle Ages), but in it there is a slender thread of support for conjecturing that the organ might have served as a symbol of cosmic harmony. The evidence begins with a statement by the early Christian writer Tertullian (third century), a proto-puritan who would, it seems, be least likely to approve a pagan instrument such as the organ.

> Look at that very wonderful piece of organic mechanism by Archimedes--I mean his hydraulic organ, with its many limbs, parts, bands, passages for the notes, outlets for their sounds, combinations for their harmony, and the array of its pipes; but yet the whole of these details constitutes only one instrument. In like manner the wind, which breathes throughout this organ, at the impulse of the hydraulic engine, is not divided into separate portions from the fact of its dispersion through the instrument to make it play: it is whole and entire in its substance, although divided in its operation... [Tertullian continues by saying that, precisely like the wind blown in the pipes throughout the organ, the soul displays its energies in various ways by means of the senses, being not indeed divided, but rather distributed in natural order.] (Tertullian, *De Anima* 14; trans. in Skeris, Χρομα Θεου, p. 43, and McKinnon, *Music in Early Christian Literature* 83)

In this statement, Tertullian praises the organ because its complex mechanism, made up of many diverse parts, results in one unified instrument.[2] It is reasonable to detect behind his words not only an assumed Christian monism, but also the Greek (neo-Platonic) presupposition of a harmonically ordered cosmos.

Some early medieval writers merely hint at this interpretation of the organ (rather as if they take it for granted). Thus St. Aldhelm (c.639-709), English poet, scholar, and teacher, wrote:

> If a man longs to sate his soul with ardent music,
> And spurns the solace of a thin cantilena,
> Let him listen to the mighty organs with their thousand breaths,
> And lull his hearing with the air-filled bellows,
> However much the rest [of it] dazzles with its golden casings
> Who can truly fathom the mysteries of such things,
> Or unravel the secrets of the all-knowing God?
> (Aldhelm, *De virginitate* ; trans. in Perrot, *The Organ*, p. 224)

And in 873 Pope John VIII charged Anno, bishop of Freising in Bavaria, "to send us, for the purpose of teaching the science of music, an excellent organ together with an organist capable of playing upon it and drawing the maximum amount of music from it" (*Monumenta Germania Historica*, Epist. Merov. et Karol. Aevi. V, anno 873, p. 287; trans. in Perrot, p. 222). Baldric, bishop of

---

[2]Michael Praetorius, some 1,400 years later, hints at the same sentiment in the quotation that begins this chapter. It is possible that one reason for the medieval fascination with the organ was the fact that it continued to represent one of the most complex technological achievements until the coming of the scientific age.

218 Appendix 1

Dol, however, is much less ambiguous in his estimation of the organ in a letter to the people of Fécamp, written sometime between 1114 and 1130:

> For myself, I take no great pleasure in the sound of the organ (ego siquidem in modulationibus organicis non multum delector); but it encourages me to reflect that, just as divers pipes, of differing weight and size, sound together in a single melody as a result of the air in them, so men should think the same thoughts, and inspired by the Holy Spirit, unite in a single purpose... All this I have learned from the organs installed in this church. Are we not the organs of the Holy Spirit? And let any man who banishes them from the church likewise banish all vocal sound, and let him pray, with Moses, through motionless lips... For ourselves, we speak categorically--because organs are a good thing, if we regard them as mysteries and derive from them a spiritual harmony; it is this harmony that the Moderator of all things has instilled in us, by putting together elements entirely discordant in themselves and binding them together by a harmonious rhythm... As we listen to the organs, let us be drawn together by a deeper harmony, and be cemented together by a two-fold charity. (*Patrologiae latinae* clxvi, pp. 1177-8; trans. in Perrot, *The Organ*, pp. 220-1)

The early appearance of organs in churches, then, may well not have been so much for practical music-making as for symbolic and didactic ends: symbolic in that the instrument was the material embodiment of cosmic harmony, and didactic in that it provided a visible, tangible "sermon" on that harmony. Together with the complex astronomical clocks that are still extant in some of the medieval cathedrals, organs may have witnessed to the divine basis for the *quadrivium* and the cosmic worldview that underlay it. Just as the clock represented divine order evident in the heavens, the organ represented it in music. (The other disciplines of the *quadrivium*, mathematics and geometry, were represented by the very architecture of the cathedral church itself.)[3]

Organs in the earlier Middle Ages normally seem to have consisted of only a single rank of pipes. At some point during the later Middle Ages, however, the organ underwent a new development in which each key began to control a number of pipes sounding intervals of fifths and octaves above a fundamental pitch. Thus the instrument became, in effect, a single large mixture (a *Blockwerk*, to use the proper German term). It may well be that the perception of the overtone series by an organ theoretician or builder caused this development. Given the medieval preference for theory over practical observation, however, it seems likely that such an advance was at least partially grounded in a desire to make the organ embody even more perfectly the Pythagorean "proof" of cosmic harmony.

If the medieval organ had possessed a sensuous, affective tonal quality, however, no amount of praise for its perfect structure would have won it the church's approval. (Bishop Baldric, quoted above, makes it clear that he prizes the organ not for its sound, but for its symbolism.) The very quality of the sound produced by the medieval organ had an affinity to the Christian ideal of cosmic harmony and to the objective, non-affective music which that ideal produced. The sound had practically no expressive qualities and only the slightest capacity for nuance (if indeed it had any at all), little variety in tone, very limited rhythmic capabilities, and no potential for crescendo and

---

[3] See Simson, *The Gothic Cathedral*, Introduction, p. 43.

diminuendo. It was remote in its playing mechanism, remote from its listeners (often in a balcony or "swallows-nest" high up on the church wall), and in a remote, mystic and awe-inspiring acoustical environment. Its most unique musical characteristic, the ability to hold a tone at a static dynamic level, theoretically endlessly, was distinctly superhuman. If one assumes, as the Middle Ages did, that variation and fluctuation belong to the human sphere, while awe, remoteness, and constancy are characteristic of the divine, the mysterious, the holy, then the qualities enumerated above would seem to render the organ a peculiarly hieratic musical instrument.

Whether or not the organ gained entry into the church because it was the embodiment of cosmic harmony, it seems fairly certain that it was not brought in at first to aid in the conduct of the liturgy. Again the sources are few and inconclusive, but the gradual incorporation of organ music into liturgical celebrations seems to parallel the rise to prominence of polyphony[4] (a development that may also have gained impetus from neo-Platonic musical speculation; see Chap. 8, pp. 113-4; 117-20). In that the organ's mechanical advances succeeded in keeping pace with the demands placed on it by musical developments, the organ became capable of performing intellectual, contrapuntal music as that music evolved within the church. Thus with the support of both speculation and practice, the organ gained a firm foothold in the church. By the thirteenth century, most major churches in Europe, especially large abbeys and cathedrals, possessed an organ, and by the fifteenth century many of them had two: a large one for solo performance and a smaller one to accompany or support choral singing.

By the same conservative process that granted approval to other previously foreign elements after long-established use, the Roman Catholic Church hierarchy gradually sanctioned the organ's official use in the church's liturgy. This process is best traced through papal and conciliar decrees that include statements on the organ. The only instrument that the decrees of the Council of Trent mention is the organ; its playing had to be free from any element that might be considered "lascivious or impure." Other sixteenth-century ecclesiastical ordinances (e.g., St. Charles Borromeo, Council of Milan in 1565; *Ceremoniale Episcoporum*, 1600) also mention no instrument other than the organ. By the eighteenth century, the use of the organ in churches was well-nigh universal, yet Pope Benedict XIV was less than enthusiastic about it, as were his successors up through the early twentieth century.[5] Only during the course of the twentieth century have Roman Catholic decrees gradually adopted a more friendly stance toward the organ (though still with reservations).

The organ experienced its golden age during the Renaissance. Its mechanism was by that time much refined and improved, and sixteenth-century writings attest to the high level of proficiency attained in organ performance. This art is unfortunately lost to us, since it was largely improvised; the extant compositions from this period represent only a minute fraction of its glory. There was enormous activity in organ building during this period, as not only prominent

---

[4]See Williams, *A New History of the Organ*, pp. 47ff.
[5]See Hayburn, *Papal Legislation*, pp. 96, 141, 331, 353, as well as Abbot, ed., *The Documents of Vatican II*, "The Constitution on the Sacred Liturgy," §.120, p. 173.

churches but also ordinary parish churches acquired organs. The use of the organ in worship was already well enough established by the time of the Reformation that its use continued undisturbed among Lutherans and Anglicans, even though Luther and other reformers were in fact less than enthusiastic about it:

> Luther rarely mentioned organ playing, but occasionally he did express an opinion against it, reckoning it among the externals of the Roman service; on the other hand, he was also musician enough in this area to appreciate and praise the art of a Protestant organist like Wolff Heintz... Most Lutheran church regulations, at least in the Reformation period, paid no attention to the organ; a few left it as "adiaphorous" (neither forbidden or approved) as long as "psalms and sacred songs" rather than "love songs" were played upon it, and as long as the organ playing did not, through its length or autocracy, encroach upon the principal parts of the service. (Blume, *Protestant Church Music*, p. 107)

The growth of *alternatim praxis* (chants divided into versets for choir and organ in alternation--also applied to the Lutheran chorale) continued to ensure an important role for the organ in worship. By this means, the organ was raised to a prominence equal to the pastor or priest, congregation, and choir, since it could "sing" by itself an entire segment of chant or stanza of a chorale, leaving the people to meditate on the text (which they usually knew by heart) while the organ performed the music. The organ's role in *alternatim praxis* reveals how well it was integrated into the prevailing world-conscious conception of worship, as one more means to fulfill the cultic requirement of self-effacing praise.

The Baroque era began to witness a decline in enthusiasm for the organ in southern Europe. Its mechanical development was arrested, less and less music was written for it (also, what was written was increasingly not of the highest quality), and there were fewer well-known organists. Calvinism stifled the organ in Switzerland, and Puritanism inflicted mortal wounds on it in Great Britain:

> [Ordinance of 1644] for the speedy demolishing of all organs, images and all matters of superstitious monuments in all Cathedrals, and Collegiate or Parish churches and Chapels, throughout the Kingdom of England and the Dominion of Wales, the better to accomplish the blessed reformation so happily begun and to remove offences and things illegal in the worship of God. (Ordinance of Lords and Commons, 1644; quoted in Sumner, *The Organ*, p. 135)

> The use of organs in the public worship of God is contrary to the law of the land, and to the law and constitution of our Established Church [of Scotland].
> (Proceedings of the Presbytery of Glasgow, 1807; quoted in Crofton & Fraser, *Dictionary of Musical Quotations*, p. 107:15)

In the early seventeenth century, however, Protestant north Germany found a new purpose for the organ: to accompany congregational singing. Thus the organ continued to be assured a secure place in the church, not only for philosophical or theological reasons, but for practical ones as well. The instrument reached another mechanical and artistic highpoint in middle and northern Germany during the seventeenth and early eighteenth centuries, announced by Michael Praetorius's enthusiastic affirmation quoted at the beginning of this chapter.[6] It is surely more than coincidence that the authors who furthered ideas about world harmony during this period are the same ones that show the greatest interest in the organ: Praetorius, Kircher, Werckmeister. Indeed, it seems that in general the organ has flourished wherever the Christian neo-Platonic worldview has been cultivated; the seventeenth-century English poets who eulogize the neo-Platonic concept of world harmony also praise the instrument:

> Ring out, ye crystal spheres,
> Once bless our human ears,
> (If ye have power to touch our senses so)
> And let your silver chime
> Move in melodious time;
> And let the Bass of Heav'ns deep Organ blow,
> And with your ninefold harmony
> Make up full consort to th' Angelick symphony.
> (John Milton, *Hymn on the Morning of Christ's Nativity*, 1645)

> But oh! what art can teach,
> What human voice can reach
> The sacred organ's praise?
> Notes inspiring holy love,
> Notes that wing their heav'nly ways
> To mend the choirs above.
> (John Dryden, *A Song for St. Cecilia's Day*, 1687)

> When the full organ joins the tuneful choir,
> Th'immortal Pow'rs incline their ear.
> (Alexander Pope, *Ode for Musick, on St. Cecilia's Day*, c.1708)

J. S. Bach's organ music represents the final glorious flourish, both for the concept of cosmic harmony in music and for the organ as a vitally important factor in the music world; even during Bach's lifetime it was being relegated to the fringe, where it has remained. By Bach's time, however, the interplay of sacred and secular ideas made paradox the order of the day: it is a measure of Bach's profound synthesizing genius that he made the organ "dance"--and a less likely instrument for dancing can hardly be imagined!

The pressures of Pietism and of the radically new Enlightenment ideas about music (e.g., music exists primarily to express and reflect human emotion, or to provide entertainment and relaxation) had an enormous impact on the status of the organ and its music. As self-consciousness transformed earlier cultic attitudes toward worship, the instrument was required to conform to the new requirement that music should edify the congregation. Its music then, instead of being understood as yet another voice in self-forgetting praise, was expected to speak to and to move the hearts of listeners. The latter half of the eighteenth century witnessed a rapid decline and trivialization of the organ and its music, a trend that prevailed through the first half of the nineteenth century. The

---

[6]The splendid organs (housed in equally splendid cases) that grace many seventeenth- and eighteenth-century churches (especially in Germany and the Netherlands) are as much expressions of civic pride as of religious devotion.

instrument could not compete with the new intimate affective gestures, rapid shifts of mood and emotional range of pre-classical and classical symphonies and secular keyboard music (e.g., the works of the Mannheim School, or of C.P.E. Bach, or of Haydn). Compared with them, "the organ quite naturally was thought of as a clumsy, screeching, dynamically monotonous instrumental monster"[7] (Arnfried Edler, "The Organist in Lutheran Germany," in Salmen, *Social Status*, p. 89).

If it were to be asked what instrument is capable of affording the GREATEST EFFECTS? I should answer, the Organ... It is, however, very remote from perfection, as it wants expression, and a more perfect intonation. (Charles Burney, *A General History of Music*, 1776: "Definitions")

...[organ playing] in France was generally irreverent, although once in a while a significant talent came to my attention within this irreverence. Not rarely is a gay pastorale heard during a church service which turns into a thunderstorm before closing with a sort of operatic grand finale in free style. Given that this is untenable from the German religious point of view, it must be admitted that such things are often done quite talentedly. A requiem mass for Lafitte in the church of Saint-Roch gave me the opportunity to hear one M. Lefébure-Wély play in a solemn, appropriate manner, whereas he worked up a tremendous gay mood during the mass on Sunday. In response to my astonishment over this I was told that the clergy as well as the congregation expect light-hearted music. (Adolph Hesse, "On organs, their appointment and treatment in Austria, Italy, France and England [observations on a trip made in 1844]; in *Neue Zeitschrift für Musik*, 1853, p. 53; trans. by Rollin Smith in "Saint-Saens and the Organ," pp. 190-1)

In spite of this decline, the organ continued to solidify its position as *the* musical instrument of the church. By the nineteenth century, its sound had come to be regarded as the epitome of churchliness; even those church bodies whose puritan heritage had hitherto rejected the organ now began to embrace it. Yet significant composers of the period between 1750 and 1850 wrote little or nothing of note for the organ, and no organist of this period was accorded the degree of international recognition granted to the premier violinists, pianists and singers of the time. (This last observation continues to hold true up to the present day.)

The mid-nineteenth century marked the beginning of attempts to rescue the organ from neglect and trivialization (e.g., the outstanding work of Mendelssohn in Germany, S. S. Wesley in England, Cavaillé-Coll, Hesse, Lemmens and Franck in France). These attempts were essentially within the framework of the church; the corresponding groundswell to restore the organ to a position of prominence in the world of secular music never attained the same degree of intensity. The revival of the organ within the church was bound up almost entirely with thrusts toward church renewal after the first disastrous encounter

---

[7] In a letter to his father dated October 18, 1777, Mozart writes, "When I told Herr Stein I would like to play the organ..., he was very surprised and asked why a man like me, such a great clavier player, wanted to play an instrument which has no sweetness, no expression, no piano and no forte, but which goes along always sounding the same..."

with Enlightenment ideas, a renewal that was largely fueled by romantic sentiments, especially those of historicism and aestheticism. Neither of these movements had a firm theological basis, however, and so the organ's continued existence in the church came to rest on its practical usefulness as a means of supporting large-group singing, as well as on the by-now unshakeable conviction among the majority of Christian worshipers that the organ is the church's instrument.[8]

Nineteenth-century attempts to make the organ conform to the new taste (and the new "enlightened" worldview), for example, enclosed divisions with swell shades and devices for rapid change of registration, were rather clumsy (especially when compared with the flexible expressivity of the orchestra or piano) and only partially successful. Thus there arose in the early twentieth century a counter-movement (the *Orgelbewegung*, or Organ Reform Movement) that did away with the questionable "improvements" and once again promoted the building of organs that were in greater conformity with older musical ideals--and, inevitably, with the old worldview. The revival of older organbuilding techniques and concepts has only exacerbated the antipathy toward the organ from those increasingly prevalent forces within the twentieth-century church that promote the ideal of a popular, intimate, human-scaled church and worship. The notion that the organ is the proper instrument of the church is still strong in many quarters, but it has its increasingly influential detractors. The rise of alternative styles of worship that de-emphasize or exclude the organ (while at the same time featuring the use of other instruments) underlines the gradual dethronement of the organ as the privileged instrument of the church.

The demise of the antique medieval worldview has relegated the organ to the fringe of the post-Enlightenment musical scene, since to the degree that the modern instrument participates in the characteristics of the medieval organ, it evokes and espouses by the very character of its sound the medieval worldview. Many twentieth-century composers harbor an antipathy toward the organ; not the benign neglect characteristic of the Enlightenment and Romantic eras, but an active dislike of the instrument. Stravinsky expressed this attitude bluntly and without apology: he disliked the organ because of its " *legato sostenuto* and its blur of octaves, as well as the fact that the monster never breathes."[9] There could hardly be a more succinct expression of the change in attitude toward the organ, a change that corresponds perfectly to the rejection of the old worldview and the shift to a new one.

The nineteenth-century revival of the organ (especially in France and England) led to its introduction into that most eminent of Enlightenment musical institutions, the concert hall, as well as to the practice of giving organ concerts in churches.

From the end of the 18th century on, the organ was used as a solo instrument in public concerts. As in the field of organ building, Abbé Vogler was a pioneer here. During the course of the 19th century there was a steady increase in the number of

---

[8]The latter notion has at times created problems for the organ, as well as discomfort for organists, especially those who do not wish to be associated with the church.

[9]Igor Stravinsky and Robert Craft, *Dialogues and a Diary*, p. 46.

virtuosi on the organ, both touring artists as well as those who concertized on their regular organs. There was also a corresponding growth in the literature for the instrument, despite the vehement protests of ecclesiastic authorities who viewed such use of the church as sacrilege. (Arnfried Edler, "The Organist in Lutheran Germany," in Salmen, *Social Status*, p. 91)

Organ concerts had, of course, existed long before this time, especially at organ dedications (e.g., Schütz, Scheidt, and Praetorius all participated in the dedication of the organ at Braunschweig in 1615), but also as civic events, such as Sweelinck's concerts[10] at the Oudekerk in Amsterdam. These public concerts were normally paraliturgical, however, and seem to have been conceived largely as *Andachtskonzerte* (devotional concerts), in which the organ was viewed as another "voice" to praise God--an extension of the idea underlying *alternatim praxis*. Not until the nineteenth century did the idea of a paid, secular organ concert become common (prefigured in the eighteenth century by Handel's performances of his own organ concertos as *intermezzi* at presentations of his oratorios). The alliance between the organ and the concert hall, however, remains an uneasy one. Concert-hall ettiquette--overt gestures and generally affective behavior on the part of the organist, applause and adulation from the listeners--is somehow ill at ease with an instrument that forces the player, with his or her back to the audience, to play literature that is often emotionally neutral, and whose structure and intellectual content by right demand that as much or more attention be paid to them as to the performer.

---

[10]These events seem to be something of an anomaly: entirely secular expressions of civic pride in the community's ability to create a splendid instrument and to furnish and support a person of talent and skill to play it.

Appendix 2: Performance Practice

The way in which music is performed might seem to be beyond the purview of a book concerned with ideas about music. But in fact, the ideas that people hold about music do have an influence on how they make music and how they like to hear music made. This book has traced the course of a major shift in ideas as the modern age replaced the age of Christian dominance. It should come as no surprise, then, that the changing ideas about music that flanked the Enlightenment radically transformed performance practices in sacred as well as secular music, and that many modern practices are ill-suited to the performance of earlier church music--and, for that matter, of early secular music, as well. The exploration of ideas on church music that we have been pursuing cannot and will not *prove* anything about performance practices, but it may prove useful in thinking about them.

In accord with its more objective conception, the early music that has been preserved for us is characterized by a more objective approach to performance as well as to composition. Evidence also indicates that early music made its point in performance with a much more limited supply of means, in conformity with the conceptual limitations imposed on it. This is not to say that musicians then were less capable or less ingenious or less human than today. Rather, they adhered to a different ideal of beauty, a more objective ideal that tried to express not primarily feeling or sensual pleasure, but order, balance, and wholeness. Such an ideal rendered many of the devices and practices superfluous that are considered to be indispensable features of modern performance practice (especially those that promote a heightened expression of human emotion).

As we have seen, there was a uniform Christian attitude of disdain for the element of sensual pleasure in music that prevailed to some degree at least until the Renaissance. The few earlier Christian sources that seem to recognize pleasure in music usually turn out on closer inspection to be saying something else. For example, one early Christian author who seems to speak of sensual pleasure in music in something more than disparaging terms is Hucbald of St. Amand (c.840-c.930).

The flute and lyre players and other secular musicians and singers exercise the utmost care to evoke pleasure by their artistic productions, melodies, and compositions. And we, who have the honor to utter the words of divine majesty, pronounce them without any art and with negligence. We should, perhaps, seek the beauty of art for the saintly things, the beauty which is abused by the histrions and musicians for their vanities. (Hucbald, *Commemoratio brevis de tonis et psalmis modulandis* in: Gerbert I, p. 213; trans. in Lang, *Music in Western Civilization*, p. 87)

A careful reading will reveal that Hucbald was imputing pleasure only to secular music (which he then condemns as vanity). Ultimately he is only advocating a more careful, correct model of performance, not a more sensual or emotive one. The same emphasis on correctness is perceptible in a statement from (pseudo-) Odo of Cluny's *Enchiridion musices* (tenth century; see Chap. 8, p. 117).

Nowhere is this contrasting conception of beauty more evident than in relation to the ideal tonal quality for singers (and by inference for instruments as well) as it is expressed in early sources right up to the seventeenth century.[1] There is well-nigh complete agreement in them that a good voice is marked by sweetness, clarity and moderation; it is subdued and soothing, and is accompanied by a modest, grave deportment on the part of the singer. None of them mentions expressing emotion, or suggests that the singers should try to move their audiences. This is the case not only for church music, but for secular music as well, although there is some indication that sacred music should be composed (and by inference sung) in a slower, less lively fashion.

When he wishes to write a motet... the composer must see to it that the voices sing with continual gravity and majesty...
The manner, or style, to be observed in composing a mass agrees with that of the motet as regards the slow movement which the parts should maintain. (Pietro Cerone, *El melopeo y maestro*, 1613, Book XII, 12 & 13; trans. in Strunk, *Source Readings*, pp. 263 & 265)

All of this is not to say that performances of early music were completely devoid of any expressive quality; it may well have been there to some degree, but it can

---

[1] Isidore of Seville, *Etymologiae*, Book III, Chapter XX (seventh century; trans. in Cattin, *Music of the Middle Ages*, p. 171) writes that "a perfect voice is high, sweet and clear." "Sweet" he describes as "thin and compressed, clear and acute." In his *Concordia regularis* (c.975), Ethelwold, bishop of Winchester, in describing the performance of the Easter play *Quem quaeritis*, calls for "a dulcet voice of medium pitch" (trans. in Smoldon, "The Easter Sepulchre Music Drama," p. 5). Pope John XXII, in his Bull *Docta sanctorum* (1324) decrees that "we...must sing, with modesty and gravity, melodies of a calm and peaceful character..." (trans. in Hayburn, *Papal Legislation*, p. 20). In his *Istitutioni harmoniche* (1558), Gioseffo Zarlino writes, "A singer should...not force the voice into a raucous, bestial tone. He should strive to moderate his tone and blend it with the others singers' so that no voice is heard above the others... The singer should know too that in church and in public chapels he should sing with full voice, moderated of course as I have just said, while in private chambers he should use a subdued and sweet voice and avoid clamor... Singers...should refrain from bodily movements and gestures that will incite the audience to laughter as some do who move...as if they were dancing (Zarlino, *The Art of Counterpoint*, pp. 110-11).

only have arisen from whatever instinctive "musicality" (in the modern sense of the term) the musicians might have possessed, and not from any cultivated intention. This holds true especially with regard to the performance of church music, both monophonic and polyphonic, and in general for all complex polyphonic music.

It is only reasonable to expect that changes in performance practice should coincide with changes in ideas about music. When changing ideals decreed that an important part of music's function was to express emotion (specifically, in the sixteenth century, the emotion of the text), then performance practices had to begin to cooperate in achieving that goal.

> In the Holy Year of 1575, or shortly thereafter, a style of singing appeared which was very different from that preceding. ...every composer took care to advance in the [accompanying new] style of composition, particularly Giaches [de] Wert [1535-1596] in Mantua and Luzzasco [Luzzaschi, d.1607] in Ferrara. They were the superintendents of all music for those Dukes, who took the greatest delight in the art, especially in having many noble ladies and gentlemen learn to sing and play superbly... The ladies of Mantua and Ferrara were highly competent, and vied with each other not only in regard to the timbre and training of their voices but also in the design of exquisite passages of embellishment delivered at opportune points, but not in excess. Furthermore, they moderated or increased their voices, loud or soft, heavy or light, according to the demands of the piece they were singing; now slow, breaking off with sometimes a gentle sigh, now singing long passages legato or detached, now *gruppi*, now leaps, now with long trills, now with short, and again with sweet running passages sung softly, to which sometimes one heard an echo answer unexpectedly. They accompanied the music and the sentiment with appropriate facial expressions, glances, and gestures, with no awkward movements of the mouth or hand or body that might not express the feeling of the song. They made the words clear in such a way that one could hear even the last syllable of every word, which was never interrupted or suppressed by passages and other embellishment. They used many other particular devices that will be known to persons more experienced than I. (Vicenzo Giustiniani, *Discorso sopra la musica*, c.1628; trans. in MacClintock, *Hercole Bottrigari...and Vicenzo Giustiniani*, pp. 69-70)

The Foreword to Giulio Caccini's *Le nuove musiche* of 1602[2] bears witness that by 1600 it was considered desirable for singers in Italy to be adept at performing in an emotionally expressive style of singing. The transformation of performance ideals, however, was gradual and irregular, just as was the transformation of the musical ideals behind them. In the early eighteenth century, for example, the Frenchman Le Cerf de La Viéville expressed a perference for an accurate, but also an expressive and powerful voice.[3]

The emotionally expressive manner of performance initiated among solo singers seems to have spread rather rapidly to include instrumental performance as well. By the mid-eighteenth century, the German flautist J. J. Quantz, confident in his ability to play expressively, can still look back and remember a time when this ability was not common among musicians in Germany.

---

[2]Translated in John Playford's *Introduction to the Skill of Music* (1693), quoted (with corrections) in Strunk, *Source Readings*; see in particular pp. 378 and 381.
[3]See *Comparaison de la Musique italienne et de la musique française* (1705), trans. in Strunk, *Source Readings*; see in particular pp. 501-2.

78. Now, if we were to make a thorough examination of the music of the Germans of more than a century ago, we should find that, even that far back, they had reached a very high point, not only in correct harmonic composition, but also in the playing of many instruments. Of good taste, however, and of beautiful melody we should find little trace, save for a few old chorales; on the contrary, we should find their taste and melody alike... rather plain, dry, thin, and simple.

79. In composition they were, as indicated, harmonious and many-voiced, but not melodious or charming.

Their writing was more artful than intelligible or pleasing, more for the eye than for the ear...

To arouse and still the passions was something unknown to them.

(J.J. Quantz, *Versuch einer Anweisung die Flöte traversière zu spielen*, 1752; trans. in Strunk, *Source Readings*, p. 595)

Of course, neither Quantz's assertion ("To arouse and still the passions was something unknown to them") nor any other like it can be taken at face value. Surely there were German musicians in the seventeenth century whose singing and playing were to some degree emotionally expressive. What such dicta *do* reveal is an awareness in every generation since the advent of the humanist outlook (until the twentieth century) that performance practices of the past were in general less advanced with regard to affective expression.

From the time that the medieval conception of music deteriorated sufficiently to allow the subjective element to become a paramount concern in musical performance, musicians have had to struggle to balance correctness, dignity, and self-restraint in performance with dramatic expressiveness and emotional intensity; the element of "taste" became an important ingredient in musical performance. When performance practice began to move decisively in the direction of subjectivity and emotional immediacy, then the performance of works composed in comformity with older ideals inevitably suffered. This was already evident in the early nineteenth century in statements by musicians who continued to prize the older music and who remembered the former ways of performing it. Here, for example, are some remarks on the proper performance of Bach's *Chromatic Fantasy* by F. W. Griepenkerl (whose connection with the Bach performance tradition lies in his keyboard training under J. N. Forkel, Bach's first biographer).

Touch [on stringed keyboard instruments] can only be compared with enunciation. There is more to beautiful musical declamation than mere clarity, neatness, security and facility with complete command of all the technical aspects of performance. Most compositions by J. S. Bach are genuine, eternal works of art, and thus must of necessity be treated objectively. Any sort of sentimentality and affectation, anything fashionable, subjective and individual, is therefore banished from their performance. Anyone who tried to impose on them his own personal feelings, or the emotional and expressive style of the present or any other particular era, without possessing the receptiveness and training to allow his spirit to be guided solely by the work of art itself--that person would thereby unavoidably distort and spoil them. Purely objective artistic performance, however, is the most difficult thing of all, and is understood and achieved only by a few, because it requires not merely talent and broad artistic awareness, but also a broad liberal education. The lack of this is what so often engenders unhealthy pretension instead of modest insight and and innocent joy--in total self-forgetfulness--in the beautiful work of art. (Griepenkerl, in Bach, *Chromatische Fantasie* [1819])

There is, of course, no way to establish conclusively how the ideals held by musicians in times past might have affected their performance styles. It might be enlightening, however, to hypothesize what performance characteristics composers and musicians might have appreciated if they understood their music more as an expression of sounding cosmic order rather than as an expression of feeling:

1. They might prefer to perform music of great intellectual substance, music in which expressiveness is to a great extent already composed into the music (an inherent part of the pieces's structure), to which the performer is not compelled to add or bring a high degree of his own emotional expressiveness--music that in some way strives to embody perfection in its own composition.
2. They might prefer a more refined, controlled, objective approach to performance.
3. They might be concerned to reproduce the compositions they played with a high degree of accuracy, so as to ensure their perfect, precise translation from paper into sound.
4. They might be concerned with accuracy of tuning and pitch, as manifestations of mathematical perfection.
5. The instruments on which they felt most at home might be ones that lent themselves most naturally to objective performance and to the restrained, controlled expression of emotion (e.g., the organ).

What performance practices might they find foreign or excessive?

1. Any element or gesture that might be considered today as affective or seductive, especially kaleidoscopic change in color or volume.
2. Extremes of volume, either loud or soft.
3. Any flamboyance in performance.
4. Those intimate performance gestures and techniques that suggest intense emotional involvement--indeed, any music that depends for its effect on such gestures and techniques.

Here a word of caution is in order: in such matters as these there are no absolutes, only inclinations and degrees. Nor is it practical to expect consistency in them, anymore than in the twentieth century when serial composers, otherwise excruciatingly exact in matters of pitch, nevertheless can tolerate the use of vibrato and tremolo in the performance of their compositions.

In reading comments on performance practices from early primary sources, it is important to consider not simply what is said, but also what is *not* said. Not until Josquin des Prez is anything said about expressing emotion in composition; in fact, all elements of early liturgical music and many as well in secular pieces (e.g., haphazard word placement) seem to contradict this notion. Not until the latter half of the sixteenth century is emphasis laid on expressing emotion in performance. The growth of the sensuous element in musical performance is the counterpart to humanistic developments in other arts, for example, perspective in painting or anatomical correctness in sculpture. It is unreasonable to expect that emotional expressivity was practiced in music before it became evident in other arts.

In conclusion: what can we hope to gain from an understanding of earlier ideas and attitudes about music that will help us to determine appropriate performance practices? First, such an understanding can help us put the music of any period into proper perspective. The lute songs of John Dowland, for example, are undeniably expressive of human emotion--but Dowland was hardly working with the same attitudes toward music that generated emotionally expresive works two or three centuries later. The lute songs belong to an entirely different ideological milieu, and their performance ought to reflect that difference. Second, in preparing a work for performance, it might be fruitful to try to decide what the composer was intending to express: was he motivated by the desire to represent order or emotion, and in each case to what degree? One's performance cannot help but reflect how one answers these questions.

Purely objective artistic performance, however, is the most difficult thing of all, and is understood and achieved only by a few, because it requires not merely talent and broad artistic awareness, but also a broad liberal education. The lack of this is what so often engenders unhealthy pretension instead of modest insight and and innocent joy--in total self-forgetfulness--in the beautiful work of art. (Griepenkerl, in Bach, *Chromatische Fantasie* [1819])

Bibliography

BOOKS

Abbott, Walter M., ed. *The Documents of Vatican II*. New York: Guild Press [1966].
Abert, Hermann. *Die Musikanschauung des Mittelalters*. Halle: Max Niemeyer, 1905.
Adlung, Jacob. *Musica mechanica organœdi*. Berlin: Friedrich Wilhelm Birnstiel, 1768.
Anderson, Warren D. *Ethos and Education in Greek Music*. Cambridge, Mass.: Harvard University Press, 1966.
Aristotle. *Aristotle on His Predecessors*, extracts from the *Metaphysics*. Trans. A. E. Taylor with an introduction by Herman Shapiro, ed. Eugene Freeman. LaSalle, Ill.: Open Court, 1969.
Aristotle. *De mundo*. Trans. E.S. Foster. Oxford: Clarendon Press, 1914.
Augustine of Hippo. *Confessions*. Trans. R. S. Pine-Coffin. Hammondsworth: Penguin Classics, 1961.
Augustine of Hippo. *De musica*. In J.-P. Migne, ed., *Patrologiae Latinae*. Paris, 1845, Vol. XXXII, Col. 1081-1194.
Augustine of Hippo. *On Music (De musica)*, introduction & translation by Robert C. Taliaferro. In *The Fathers of the Church: A New Translation*. Vol. 4: *Writings of Saint Augustine*. Vol. 2. New York: CIMA Publishing Co., 1947 (reprint ed., Washington, D.C.: Catholic University of America Press, 1984), pp. 169-379.
Austen, Jane. *Pride and Prejudice*. New York: Charles Scribner's Sons [1813; c.1918].
Bacon, Francis. *The Works of Francis Bacon*. London: H. Bryer, 1803.
Babb, Warren, Trans. *Hucbald, Guido and John on Music; Three Medieval Treatises*. New Haven, Conn.: Yale University Press, 1978.
Barker, Andrew, ed. *Greek Musical Writings*. Cambridge: Cambridge University Press, 1984.
Beerbohm, Max. *Zuleika Dobson*. New York: Modern Library [Random House] [1911].
Benser, Caroline Cepin, and David Francis Urrows. *Randall Thompson: A Bio-Bibliography*. New York: Greenwood Press [1991].
Bieler, Ludwig. *Ireland, Harbinger of the Middle Ages*. London: Oxford University Press, 1966.
Billings, William. *The Continental Harmony*. Boston: Thomas & Andrews, 1794.

Bibliography

Bloch, Ernst. *Essays on the Philosophy of Music.* Trans. Peter Palmer. Cambridge: Cambridge University Press [1985].

Blume, Friedrich. *Protestant Church Music: A History.* New York: W. W. Norton & Company [1974].

Boethius, Anicius Manlius Severinus. *De institutione musica.* Trans. into English, with introduction and notes, by Calvin M. Bower, as *Fundamentals of Music* (ed. Claude V. Palisca). New Haven, Conn.: Yale University Press [c.1989].

Bouleau, Charles. *The Painter's Secret Geometry: A Study of Composition in Art.* London: Thames & Hudson, 1963 (trans. from the French, published in the same year).

Braunfels, Wolfgang. *Monasteries of Western Europe: The Architecture of the Orders.* Princeton, N.J.: Princeton University Press [1972].

Budd, Malcolm. *Music and Emotions: The Philosophical Theories.* London & Boston: Routledge & Kegan Paul [1985].

Bukofzer, Manfred F. *Studies in Medieval and Renaissance Music.* New York: W. W. Norton [1950].

Burney, Charles. *A General History of Music*, Vol. I. London: 1776 (ed. Frank Mercer. New York: Harcourt & Brace [1935]).

Campbell, Joseph (with Bill Moyers). *The Power of Myth.* New York: Doubleday [c.1988].

Carpenter, Nan Cooke. *Music in the Medieval and Renaissance Universities.* Norman: University of Oklahoma Press, 1958.

Cassiodorus Senator. *An Introduction to Divine and Human Readings [Institutiones, Books I & II].* Trans. Leslie Webber Jones. New York: Columbia University Press, 1946.

Cattin, Giulio. *Music of the Middle Ages I.* Trans. Steven Botterill. Cambridge: Cambridge University Press [1984].

Chagnon, Napolean A. *Yanomamö: The Fierce People.* New York: Holt, Rinehart & Winston [c.1968],

Coates, Kevin. *Geometry, Proportion and the Art of Lutherie.* London: Oxford University Press, 1985.

Coclico, Adrian Petit. *Compendium musices* [1552]. Trans. Albert Seay. Colorado Springs: Colorado College Music Press, 1973.

Craig, Gordon A. *The Germans.* New York: Meridian (Penguin Books USA), c.1982/1991.

Crofton, Ian, and Donald Fraser. *A Dictionary of Musical Quotations.* New York: Schirmer Books [1985].

David, Hans T., and Arthur Mendel. *The Bach Reader.* Revised edition. New York: W. W. Norton [1966].

Davison, Archibald T. *Church Music.* Cambridge, Mass.: Harvard University Press, 1952.

Debussy, Claude. *Debussy Letters.* Trans. Roger Nichols. Cambridge, Mass.: Harvard University Press, 1987.

Debussy, Claude, Ferruccio Busoni and Charles Ives. *Three Classics in the Aesthetic of Music.* New York: Dover Publications [1962].

Deiss, Lucien. *Springtime of the Liturgy*, Trans. Matthew J. O'Connell. Collegeville, Minn.: Liturgical Press ([1967] c.1979).

Dictionary: The Compact Edition of the Oxford English Dictionary. [New York:] Oxford University Press, 1971.

Donne, John. *Sermons.* Ed. Potter & Simpson. Berkeley: University of California Press, 1955.

Dronkë, Peter. *Poetic Individuality in the Middle Ages.* London: Oxford University Press, 1970.

Bibliography 233

Elders, Willem. *Composers of the Low Countries.* Trans. Graham Dixon. Oxford: Clarendon Press, 1991.
Elders, Willem. *Studien zur Symbolik in der Musik der alten Niederländer.* Bilthoven: A. B. Creyghton, 1968.
Eliade, Mircea. *Myths, Rites, Symbols: A Mircea Eliade Reader.* Ed. Wendell C. Beane and William G. Doty. New York: Harper & Row [c.1975].
Eliot, T. S. *Notes towards the Definition of Culture.* London: Faber & Faber Ltd. [1948].
Eliot, T. S. *They Asked for a Paper: Papers and Addresses.* London: Geoffrey Bles, 1962.
Engel, Gabriel. *Gustav Mahler: Song-symphonist.* New York: David Lewis [n.d.].
Fellerer, Karl Gustav. *The History of Catholic Church Music.* Trans. Francis A. Brunner. Baltimore: Helicon Press, 1961.
Forbes, Elliot, ed. *Thayer's Life of Beethoven.* Rev. ed.. Princeton, N.J.: Princeton University Press, 1967.
Galle, Philip. *Encomium musices.* Antwerp: c.1590. (facs. Cambridge: Heffer [c.1943])
Gallo, F. Alberto. *Music of the Middle Ages II.* Trans. Karen Eales. Cambridge: Cambridge University Press [1985].
Gardner, Howard. *Frames of Mind: The Theory of Multiple Intelligences.* New York: Basic Books [1983].
Garside, Charles, Jr. *Zwingli and the Arts.* New Haven, Conn., and London: Yale University Press, 1966.
Geiringer, Karl. *Symbolism in the Music of Bach.* Washington, D.C.: The Library of Congress, 1956.
Gelineau, Joseph, S.J. *Voices and Instruments in Christian Worship.* Trans. Clifford Howell, S.J.. London: Burns & Oates [1964].
Geminiani, Francesco. *The Art of Playing on the Violin.* London: J. Johnson, 1751.
Georgiades, Thrasybulos. *Music and Language: The Rise of Western Music as Exemplified in Settings of the Mass.* Trans. Marie Louise Göllner. Cambridge: Cambridge University Press [1982].
Gerbert, Martin. *Scriptores ecclesiastici de musica sacra potissimum.* St. Blasien, 1784 [Hildesheim: Georg Olms, 1963].
Giustiniani, Vicenzo. *Discorso sopra la musica,* Trans. Carol MacClintock. Musicological Studies and Documents, IX. Rome: American Institute of Musicology, 1962.
Guthrie, W.K.C.. *A History of Greek Philosophy,* Vol. I. Cambridge: At the University Press, 1962.
Hamilton, E., and H. Cairns. *The Collected Dialogues of Plato.* New York: Pantheon Books, 1961.
Haweis, H. R. *Music and Morals.* New York: Harper & Brothers, 1904.
Hawkins, John. *A General History of the Science and Practice of Music.* London: Payne & Son, 1776 (2nd ed. reprinted by New York: Dover Publications, 1963).
Hayburn, Robert F. *Papal Legislation on Sacred Music, 95 A.D. to 1977 A.D..* Collegeville, Minn.: Liturgical Press [1979].
Haydn, Joseph. *Gesammelte Briefe und Aufzeichnungen.* Kassel: Bärenreiter, 1965.
Heine, Heinrich. *Selected Works.* Trans. & ed. by Helen M. Mustard. New York: Random House (c.1973).
Henze, Hans Werner. *Essays.* Mainz: B. Schott's Söhne [1964].
Henze, Marianne. *Studien zu den Messenkompositionen Johann Ockeghems .* Berlin: Merseburger Verlag, 1968.
Hindemith, Paul. *The Craft of Musical Composition.* Book I. Trans. Arthur Mendel. New York: Schott Music Corp., 1937, 1945.

234 Bibliography

Hollander, John. *The Untuning of the Sky: Ideas of Music in English Poetry, 1500-1700*. Princeton, N.J.: Princeton University Press, 1961.
Holy Bible: *The Jerusalem Bible*. Garden City, N.Y.: Doubleday & Co. [1966].
Hood, Mantle. *The Ethnomusicologist*. New York: McGraw-Hill [1971; 1982].
Hopper, Vincent Foster. *Medieval Number Symbolism: Its Sources, Meaning, and Influence on Thought and Expression*. New York: Columbia University Press, 1938.
Horace (Quintus Horatius Flaccus). *Ars Poetica*. Trans. as C.H. Sisson, *The Poetic Art: a translation of Horace's Ars Poetica*. [Cheadle, Cheshire]: Carcanet Press [1975].
Huck, Gabe. *How Can I Keep from Singing*. [Chicago:] Liturgy Training Publications [c.1989].
Hughes, David G. *A History of European Music*. New York: McGraw-Hill [1974].
Hughes, Dom Anselm, ed. *New Oxford History of Music II: Early Medieval Music up to 1300*. London: Oxford University Press [1954, 1955)
Hughes, Dom Anselm, and Gerald Abraham, eds. *New Oxford History of Music, Vol. III: Ars Nova and the Renaissance 1300-1540:* VI. "English Church Music of the Fifteenth Century," by Manfred Bukofzer. Oxford: Oxford University Press [1960].
Hutchings, Arthur. *Church Music in the Nineteenth Century*. New York: Oxford University Press, 1967.
The Hymnal of the Protestant Episcopal Church 1940. New York: Church Pension Fund [1940].
Irwin, Joyce L. *Neither Voice nor Heart Alone: German Lutheran Theology of Music in the Age of the Baroque*. New York: Peter Lang [1993].
Johansson, Calvin M. *Music and Ministry: A Biblical Counterpoint*. Peabody, Mass.: Hendrickson Publishers [1984].
Kant, Immanuel. *The Critique of Judgment* (1790). Trans. James Creed Meredith. In *Great Books of the Western World*. Chicago: Encyclopædia Brittanica [1952], Vol. 42.
Kepler, Johannes. *The Harmonies of the World*, Trans.Charles Glenn Wallis, in: *Great Books of the Western World*. Chicago: Encyclopædia Brittanica, Inc. [1952], vol. 16.
Klibansky, Raymond. *The Continuity of the Platonic Tradition during the Middle Ages*. Millwood, N.Y.: Kraus International Publications, 1982.
Knight, W.F. Jackson. *St. Augustine's De Musica: A Synopsis*. Westport, Conn.: Hyperion Press [1979] (Reprint of 1949 edition, published by The Orthological Institute, London).
Koenker, Ernest Benjamin. *The Liturgical Renaissance in the Roman Catholic Church*. St. Louis: Concordia Publishing House [1954, 1966].
Krenek, Ernst. *Horizons Circled*. Berkeley: University of California Press, 1974.
La Croix, Richard R., ed. *Augustine on Music: An Interdisciplinary Collection of Essays*. Lewiston/Queenston: Edwin Mellen Press [c.1988].
Lang, Paul Henry. *Music in Western Civilization*. New York: W. W. Norton [1941].
Leaver, Robin A. *J. S. Bach and Scripture: Glosses from the Calov Bible Commentary*. St. Louis: Concordia Publishing House [c.1985].
Leibniz, Gottfried Wilhelm. Letter #154, IV (Hanoverae, 17 April 1712). In: *Epistolae ad diversos, theologici, iuridici, medici, philosophici*. Ed. Christian. Kortholtus. Lipsiae: Breitkopfii, 1734-42, p. 239.
Lippman, Edward A., ed. *Musical Aesthetics: a Historical Reader*. New York: Pendragon Press, c.1968.
Long, Kenneth R. *The Music of the English Church*. London: Hodder & Stoughton [c.1971].
Luther, Martin. *D. Martin Luthers Werke; kritische Gesamtausgabe*. Weimar: Hermann Böhlaus Nachfolger, 1883ff..

Luther, Martin. *Luther's Works*. Vol. 53: *Liturgy and Hymns*. Philadelphia: Fortress Press [c.1965].
MacClintock, Carol (Trans.). *Hercole Bottrigari: Il Desiderio* and *Vicenzo Giustiniani: Discorso sopra la musica*, Musicological Studies and Documents, IX. Rome: American Institute of Musicology, 1962.
McKinnon, James. *Music in Early Christian Literature*. Cambridge: Cambridge University Press, [c.1987].
Macrobius. *Commentary on the Dream of Scipio*. Trans. W. H. Stahl. New York: Columbia University Press, 1952.
Maguire, Eunice Dauterman, Henry P. Maguire, and Maggie J. Duncan-Flowers. *Art and Holy Powers in the Early Christian House*. Urbana: University of Illinois Press, 1989.
Mahler, Alma. *Gustav Mahler: Memories and Letters*. Trans. Basil Creighton. New York: Viking Press, 1946.
Mattheson, Johann. *Der volkommene Kapellmeister*. Hamburg: Christian Herold, 1739.
Merriam, Alan P. *African Music in Perspective*. New York: Garland Press, 1982.
The Methodist Hymnal. Cincinnati: Jennings & Graham [c.1905].
Meyer-Baer, Kathi. *Music of the Spheres and the Dance of Death; Studies in Musical Iconology*. Princeton, N.J.: Princeton University Press, 1970.
Morgenstern, Sam, ed. *Composers on Music: An Anthology of Composer's Writings from Palestrina to Copland*. New York: Pantheon Books [c.1956].
Mowinckel, Sigmund. *The Psalms in Israel's Worship*. Trans. D. R. Ap-Thomas. New York: Abingdon Press, 1967 [original German publication: 1951].
Neumann, Werner, and Hans-Joachim Schulze, eds. *Bach-Dokumente, Vol. II: Fremdschriftliche und gedruckte Dokumente*. Kassel: Bärenreiter, 1969.
Niedt, F. E. *Musicalischer Handleitung, Anderer Teil*. Ed. by J. Mattheson. Hamburg: Benjamin Schillers Witwe & J.C. Kistner, 1721.
Ortega y Gasset, José. *Dehumanization of Art*. Trans. Helene Weyl. Gloucester, Mass.: Peter Smith, 1951.
Otto, Rudolf. *The Idea of the Holy*. Trans. John W. Harvey. New York: Oxford University Press, 1958.
Palisca, Claude V. *Humanism in Italian Renaissance Musical Thought*. New Haven, Conn.: Yale University Press [1985].
Palmer, Tony. *All You Need is Love*. [n.p.] Weidenfeld & Nicolson & Chappell [c.1976].
Panofsky, Erwin. *Abbot Suger on the Abbey Church of St. Denis and its Art Treasures*. Princeton, N.J.: Princeton University Press, 1946/1979.
Perrot, Jean. *The Organ from Its Invention in the Hellenistic Period to the End of the Thirteenth Century*. Trans. Norma Deane. London: Oxford University Press, 1971.
Petzoldt, Martin. *Johann Sebastian Bach: Ehre sei dir gesungen: Bilder und Texte zu Bachs Leben als Christ und seinem Wirken für die Kirche*. Göttingen: Vandenhoeck & Ruprecht, c.1988.
Pirotta, Nino. *Music and Culture in Italy from the Middle Ages to the Baroque: A Collection of essays*. Cambridge, Mass.: Harvard University Press, 1984.
Plato of Athens. *The Laws of Plato*. Trans. Thomas L. Pangle. New York: Basic Books [1980].
Plato of Athens. *The Republic*. Trans. Paul Shorey. London: W. Heinemann, 1930.
Plato of Athens. *Timaeus and Critias*. Trans. Desmond Lee. New York: Penguin Books [1965, 1971].
Portnoy, Julius. *Music in the Life of Man*. New York: Holt, Rinehart & Winston [1963].

Bibliography

Portnoy, Julius. *The Philosopher and Music: A Historical Outline.* New York: Humanities Press, 1954.
Praetorius, Michael. *Syntagma Musicum, Vol. II: De Organographia.* Wolfenbüttel: Elias Holwein, 1619.
Quantz, Johann Joachim. *On Playing the Flute (Versuch einer Anweisung die Flöte traversiere zu spielen,* 1752). Trans. Edward R. Reilly. London: Faber & Faber, 1966.
Quasten, Johannes. *Music and Worship in Pagan and Christian Antiquity.* Trans. Boniface Ramsey. Washington, D.C.: National Association of Pastoral Musicians [1983].
Quintilian (Marcus Fabius Quintilianus). *Institutio Oratoria.* Trans. H. E. Butler. London: William Heinemann, 1921.
Reese, Gustave. *Music in the Middle Ages.* New York: W. W. Norton [c.1940].
Reese, Gustave. *Music in the Renaissance.* New York: W. W. Norton [c.1954, 1959].
Richards, Jeffrey. *Consul of God: The Life and Times of Gregory the Great.* London: Routledge & Kegan Paul [c. 1980].
Routley, Erik. *The Church and Music.* London: Gerald Duckworth [1967].
Routley, Erik. *Twentieth Century Church Music.* New York: Oxford University Press [c. 1964].
Rowell, Louis. *Thinking About Music: An Introduction to the Philosophy of Music.* Amherst: University of Massachusetts Press [c.1983].
Sachs, Curt. *The Rise of Music in the Ancient World East and West.* New York: W. W. Norton [1943].
Sachs, Curt. *The Wellsprings of Music.* [New York]: Da Capo [reprint of The Hague: Martinus Nijhoff, 1962].
Salmen, Walter, ed. *The Social Status of the Professional Musician from the Middle Ages to the 19th Century.* New York: Pendragon Press [1983].
Santayana, George. *The Life of Reason.* IV: Reason in Art. New York: Charles Scribner's Sons, 1937.
Schaff, Philip. *Nicene and Post-Nicene Fathers*, XII. New York: Christian Literature Company, 1886.
Schalk, Carl F. *Luther on Music: Paradigms of Praise.* St. Louis: Concordia Publishing House [c.1988].
Schedel, Hartmann. *Liber chronicarum.* Nuremberg: Anthonius Koberger, 1493.
Schelling, F.W.J. von. *The Philosophy of Art.* Trans. A. Johnson. London: John Chapman, 1845.
Schoenberg, Arnold. *Arnold Schoenberg Letters.* Ed. Erwin Stein. New York: St. Martin's Press [1965].
Schopenhauer, Arthur. *The World as Will and Idea.* London: Routledge & Kegan Paul [1883]
Schweitzer, Albert. *J. S. Bach.* London: Breitkopf & Hartel, 1911.
Seay, Albert. *Music in the Medieval World.* 2nd Ed. Englewood Cliffs, N.J.: Prentice-Hall [c.1975].
Seeger, Anthony. *Why Suyá Sing.* Cambridge: Cambridge University Press [c.1987].
Sendrey, Alfred. *Music in Ancient Israel.* New York: Philosophical Library [1969].
Shands, Alfred. *The Liturgical Movement and the Local Church.* [London:] SCM Press, Ltd. [c.1965].
Shaw, [George] Bernard. *Music in London, 1890-94; Criticisms Contributed Week by Week to the World* , Vol. II. New York: Vienna House, 1973 (c.1931).
Simson, Otto von. *The Gothic Cathedral.* New York: Harper & Row [1962].
Skeris, Robert A.. χρομα θεου. Musicae Sacrae Melethmata, Vol. I. Altötting: Coppenrath, 1976.
Slonimsky, Nicolas, ed. *Music Since 1900.* 4th ed. New York: Charles Scribner's Sons, 1971.

Bibliography 237

Snyder, Kerala J. *Dieterich Buxtehude, Organist in Lübeck.* New York: Schirmer Books [c.1987].
Sparks, Edgar H. *Cantus Firmus in Mass and Motet, 1420-1520.* Berkeley & Los Angeles: University of California Press, 1963.
Spitzer, Leo. *Classical and Christian Ideas of World Harmony.* Baltimore: Johns Hopkins University Press, 1963.
Stanford, Charles Villiers, and Cecil Forsyth. *A History of Music.* New York: Macmillan, 1917.
Stephenson, Bruce. *The Music of the Heavens: Kepler's Harmonic Astronomy.* Princeton, N.J.: Princeton University Press [1994].
Stevenson, Robert. *Spanish Cathedral Music in the Golden Age.* Berkeley: University of California Press, 1961.
Stiller, Günther. *Johann Sebastian Bach and Liturgical Life in Leipzig.* Trans. Herbert J.A. Bouman et al. St. Louis: Concordia Publishing House [1970/1984].
Stravinsky, Igor, and Robert Craft. *Dialogues and a Diary.* London: Faber & Faber [1961].
Strunk, Oliver. *Source Readings in Music History.* New York: W. W. Norton [1950].
Studdert-Kennedy, Geoffrey Anketel. *The Best of G. A. Studdert-Kennedy.* New York: Harper & Brothers [1929].
Sumner, William Leslie. *The Organ, Its Evolution, Principles of Construction and Use.* London: Macdonald [1962].
Talley, Thomas J. *The Origins of the Liturgical Year.* New York: Pueblo [1986].
Thomson, Virgil. *A Virgil Thomson Reader.* New York: Houghton Mifflin, 1981.
Tillyard, E.M.W. *The Elizabethan World Picture.* London: Chatto & Windus, 1943.
Tolkien, J.R.R. *The Silmarillion.* New York: Ballantine Books [1977].
Tomlinson, Gary. *Music in Renaissance Magic.* Chicago: University of Chicago Press, 1993.
Toulmin, Stephen. *Cosmopolis: The Hidden Agenda of Modernity.* New York: Free Press (Macmillan) [1990].
Tredennick, Hugh. *The Last Days of Socrates.* New York: Penguin Books, 1967.
Tuchman, Barbara W. *A Distant Mirror: The Calamitous 14th Century.* New York: Ballantine Books [1978].
Von Rad, Gerhard. *Old Testament Theology.* New York: Harper & Row [1962].
Waite, William G. *The Rhythm of Twelfth-Century Polyphony.* New Haven, Conn.: Yale University Press, 1954.
Weiss, Piero, and Richard Taruskin. *Music in the Western World: A History in Documents.* New York: Schirmer Books, [1984].
Werkmeister, Andreas. *Musicalische Paradoxal-Discourse.* Quedlinburg: Calvisius, 1707 (facsimile, Hildesheim: Olms, 1970).
Westermeyer, Paul. *The Church Musician.* San Francisco: Harper & Row [1988].
Whitcomb, Ian. *After the Ball.* New York: Simon & Schuster [1972].
Wiener, Philip P., ed.-in-chief. *Dictionary of the History of Ideas.* New York: Charles Scribner's Sons [1973]
Williams, Peter. *A New History of the Organ.* Bloomington: Indiana University Press, 1980.
Winter, Arthur, and Ruth Winter. *Build Your Brain Power: The Latest Techniques to Preserve, Restore and Improve Your Brain's Potential.* New York: St. Martin's Press, 1986.
Winthrop, Robert H. *Dictionary of Concepts in Cultural Anthropology.* New York: Greenwood Press [c.1991].
Wittkower, Rudolf. *Architectural Principles in the Age of Humanism.* New York: Columbia University Press [1962, 1965].
Wohlgemuth, Paul W. *Rethinking Church Music.* Carol Stream, Ill.: Hope Publishing Co. [1973, 1981].

Zarlino, Gioseffo. *Istitutioni harmoniche.* Venice: 1558 (Part Three trans. as *The Art of Counterpoint*, trans. by Guy A. Marco and Claude V. Palisca. New Haven, Conn.: Yale University Press, 1968).

ARTICLES

Abert, Hermann. "Geistlich und Weltlich in der Musik." *Gesammelte Schriften und Vorträge,* herausgegeben von Friedrich Blume. Tutzing: Hans Schneider, 1968 [1929].
Anderson, Warren. "Plato." *New Groves Dictionary of Music and Musicians.* Ed. Stanley Sadie. London: Macmillan, 1980, Vol. XIV, pp. 853-7.
Ashbee, Andrew. "Robert Fludd." *New Groves Dictionary of Music and Musicians.* Ed. Stanley Sadie. London: Macmillan, 1980, Vol. VI, p. 663.
Babbitt, Milton, "Who Cares If You Listen." *High Fidelity* 8, No. 2 (February 1958): 38-40, 126-7.
Barber, Benjamin R. "Jihad Vs. McWorld," *Atlantic Monthly* 269, No. 3 (March 1992): 53-63.
Bell N Yung. "China: IV. Theory." *New Groves Dictionary of Music and Musicians.* Ed. Stanley Sadie. London: Macmillan, 1980, Vol. IV, pp. 260-2.
Bent, Ian D. "Léonin." *New Groves Dictionary of Music and Musicians.* Ed. Stanley Sadie. London: MacMillan, 1980, Vol. X, pp. 676-7.
Bent, Ian D. "Pérotin." *New Groves Dictionary of Music and Musicians.* Ed. Stanley Sadie. London: Macmillan, 1980, Vol. XIV, pp. 540-3.
Bent, Margaret. "John Dunstable" *New Groves Dictionary of Music and Musicians.* Ed. Stanley Sadie. London: Macmillan, 1980, Vol. V, p. 720.
Bower, Calvin M.. "Natural and Artificial Music: The Origins and Development of an Aesthetic Concept." *Musica Disciplina* 25 (1971): 17-33.
Buelow, George J. "Athanasius Kircher." *New Groves Dictionary of Music and Musicians.* Ed. Stanley Sadie. London: Macmillan, 1980, Vol. X, pp. 73-4.
Bukofzer, Manfred F. "Speculative Thinking in Medieval Music." *Speculum* 17, No. 2 (April 1942): 165-80.
Buszin, Walter E. "Luther on Music." *The Musical Quarterly* 32, No. 1 (January 1946): 80-97.
Cohen, Albert. "Marin Mersenne." *New Groves Dictionary of Music and Musicians.* Ed. Stanley Sadie. London: Macmillan, 1980, Vol. XII, pp. 188-90.
Dahlhaus, Carl. "Harmony." *New Groves Dictionary of Music and Musicians.* Ed. Stanley Sadie. London: macMillan, 1980, Vol. VIII, pp. 175-88.
Dalglish, William. "The Origin of the Hocket." *Journal of the American Musicological Society* 31 (1978): 3-20.
Dent, Edward J. "The Social Aspects of Music." *Oxford History of Music I.* Oxford: Oxford University Press, 1901.
Evans-Pritchard, Edward E. "Religion and the Anthropologists." In *Essays in Social Anthropology.* New York: Free Press of Glencoe [c.1962], pp. 29-45.
Fallows, David. "Specific Information on the Ensembles for Composed Polyphony, 1400-1474." In *Studies in the Performance of Late Mediaeval Music,* ed. Stanley Boorman. Cambridge: Cambridge University Press [c.1983], pp. 109-59.
Ficker, Rudolf. "Formprobleme der mittelälterlichen Musik." *Zeitschrift für Musikwissenschaft* 7 (1924-1925): 195-213.
Ficker, Rudolf. "Polyphonic Music of the Gothic Period." *Musical Quarterly* 15, No. 4 (October 1929): 483-505.
Finney, Gretchen Ludke. "Harmony or Rapture in Music." *Dictionary of the History of Ideas.* New York: Charles Scribner's Sons [1973], pp. 388-95.

Bibliography 239

Gatens, William J. "What does the Avant-garde Controversy Mean?" *The American Organist* 18, No. 12 (December 1984): 84-5.
Haar, James. "Marsilio Ficino." *New Groves Dictionary of Music and Musicians*. Ed. Stanley Sadie. London: Macmillan, 1980, Vol. VI, pp. 526-7.
Haar, James. "Music of the Spheres." *New Groves Dictionary of Music and Musicians*. Ed. Stanley Sadie. London: Macmillan, 1980, Vol. XII, pp. 835-6.
Handschin, Jacques. "Die Musikanschauung des Johannes Scotus (Erigena)." *Deutsche Vierteljahrsschrift für Literaturwissenschaft und Geistesgeschichte* 5 (1927): 316-41.
Hannick, Christian. "Christian Church, Music of the Early." *New Groves Dictionary of Music and Musicians*. Ed. Stanley Sadie. London: Macmillan, 1980, Vol. IV, pp. 363-71.
Hansen, Edward A. "President's Address to the AGO National Meeting." *The American Organist* 20, No. 9 (September 1986): 62-3.
Higgins, Paula. "In Hydraulis Revisited: New Light on the Career of Antoine Busnois." *Journal of the American Musicological Society* 39 (Spring 1986): 36-86.
Jansen, Martin. "Bachs Zahlensymbolik, an seinen Passionen untersucht." *Bach Jahrbuch*, 34. Jahrgang (1937): 96-117.
Kauffman, Bill. "Art and Politics Don't Mix." *USA Today* 120, No. 2554 (July 1991): 17-21.
Lowinsky, Edward. "The Goddess Fortuna in Music." *Musical Quarterly* 29 (1943): 45-77.
Lowinsky, Edward E. "Ockeghem's Canon for Thirty-six Voices: An Essay in Musical Iconography." *Essays in Musicology in honor of Dragan Plamenac on his 70th Birthday*. Eds. Gustave Reese and Robert J. Snow. Pittsburgh: University of Pittsburgh Press [c.1969], pp. 155-80.
Marty, Martin E. "Don't Sing." *Christian Century*, December 4, 1991, p. 1151.
Miller, Clement A. "Franchinus Gaffurius." *New Groves Dictionary of Music and Musicians*. Ed. Stanley Sadie. London: Macmillan, 1980, Vol. VII, pp. 77-9.
Mirandola, Giovanni Pico della. "*Oratio de dignitate hominis*" (1486). Trans. as "The Dignity of Man." In *Latin Writings of the Italian Humanists*, ed. F. A. Gragg, trans. M.M.M. New York: Charles Scribner's Sons, 1927.
Nabers, Ned, and Susan Ford Wiltshire. "The Athena Temple at Paestum and Pythagorean Theory." *Greek, Roman and Byzantine Studies* 21, No. 3 (Autumn 1980): 207-15.
Palisca, Claude. "Gioseffo Zarlino." *New Groves Dictionary of Music and Musicians*. Ed. Stanley Sadie. London: Macmillan, 1980, Vol. XX, pp. 646-9.
Pestell, Richard. "Medieval Art and the Performance of Medieval Music." *Early Music* 15, No. 1 (February 1987): 57-68.
Portnoy, Julius. "Similarities of Musical Concepts in Ancient and Medieval Philosophy." *Journal of Aesthetics and Art Criticism* 7 (1948/49): 235-243.
Ratzinger, Joseph (Cardinal). "Liturgy and Church Music." *Sacred Music* 112, No. 4 (Winter 1985): 13-22.
Ratzinger, Joseph (Cardinal). "Theological Problems of Church Music." *Sacred Music* 113, No. 1 (Spring 1986): 8-16.
Rifkin, Joshua. "Bach's "Choruses"--Less Than They Seem?" *High Fidelity* 32, No. 9 (September 1982): 42-44.
Rosenthal, Helene. "Hildegard von Bingen: Twelfth-Century Innovator." *Musick* 7, No. 1 (Summer, July 1985). Vancouver: Vancouver Society for Early Music, pp. 25-32.
Rulan Chao Pian. "China: I. General." *New Groves Dictionary of Music and Musicians*. Ed. Stanley Sadie. London: Macmillan, 1980, Vol. IV, pp. 245-50.
Sachs, Curt. "Primitive and Medieval Music: A Parallel." *Journal of the American Musicological Society* 13 (1960): 43-9.

Bibliography

Sanders, Ernest, H. "The Early Motets of Philippe de Vitry." *Journal of the American Musicological Society* 28 (Spring 1975): 24-45.
Schrade, Leo. "Music in the Philosophy of Boethius." *Musical Quarterly* 33 (1947): 188-200.
Serwer, Howard. "Martin Gerbert." *New Groves Dictionary of Music and Musicians*. Ed. Stanley Sadie. London: Macmillan, 1980, Vol. VII, pp. 249-50.
Sessions, Roger, "Music in Crisis: Some Notes on Recent Musical History." *Modern Music* X (1932-1933): 63-78.
Sherr, Richard. "*Illibata Dei Virgo Nutrix* and Josquin's Roman Style." *Journal of the American Musicological Society* 41, No. 3 (Fall 1988): 434-64.
Smith, Rollin. "Saint-Saens and the Organ." *The American Organist,* Vol. 20, No. 4 (April 1986): 184-94.
Smith, Timothy. "J.S. Bach the Symbolist." *Journal of Church Music* 27, No. 7 (September 1985): 8-13, 46.
Smoldon, W. L. "The Easter Sepulchre Music Drama." *Music and Letters* 27 (1946): 1-17.
Söhngen, Oskar. "Music and Theology: A Systematic Approach." In Joyce Irwin, ed., *Sacred Sound: Music in Religious Thought and Practice*. Chico, Calif.: Scholars Press [c. 1983].
Sparshott, F. E.. "Æsthetics of Music." *New Groves Dictionary of Music and Musicians*. Ed. Stanley Sadie. London: Macmillan, 1980, Vol. I, pp. 120-34.
Staff Notes: "Religious Denominations Asked: Will You Worship with Music in the Year 2000?" *Journal of Church Music* (April 1988): 42.
Taruskin, Richard. "Antoine Busnoys and the *L'Homme armé* Tradition." *Journal of the American Musicological Society* 39, No. 2 (Summer 1986): 255-93.
Todd, R. Larry. "Retrograde, Inversion, Retrograde-Inversion, and the Related Techniques in the Masses of Jacobus Obrecht." *Musical Quarterly* 64, No. 1 (January 1978): 50-78.
Tolnay, Charles de. "The Music of the Universe." *Journal of the Walters Art Gallery* VI, pp. 82-104.
Van Dijk, S.P.J., "Papal Schola *versus* Charlemagne." *Organicae voces: Festschrift Joseph Smits van Waesberghe*. Amsterdam: Instituut voor Middeleeuwse Muziekwetenschap, 1963.
Wagner, Edward. "The Holiness of Beauty: Healey Willan as Church Musician." *The Diapason* 72, No. 2 (February 1981): 1, 3-4, 8.
Warren, Charles W. "Brunelleschi's Dome and Dufay's Motet." *Musical Quarterly* 59 (1973): 92-105.
White, James F. "Church Choir: Friend or Foe?" *The Christian Century*, March 23, 1960, pp. 355-6.
Wright, Craig. "Dufay's *Nuper rosarum flores*, King Solomon's Temple, and the Veneration of the Virgin." *Journal of the American Musicological Society* 47, No. 3 (Fall 1994): 395-441.
Wright, Craig. "Leoninus, Poet and Musician." *Journal of the American Musicological Society* 39, No. 1 (Spring 1986): 1-35.
Wurm, Karl. "Christus Kosmokrator: Ein hermeneutischer Versuch zu D. Buxtehudes Passacaglia in d BuxWV 161 und zu J.S. Bachs Präludium und Fuge C-dur BWV 547." *Musik und Kirche*, Jg. 54:6 (November/December 1984). Kassel: Bärenreiter. pp. 263-71.

UNPUBLISHED DISSERTATIONS

Ellefsen, Roy Martin. Music and Humanism in the Early Renaissance: Their Relationship and its Roots in the Rhetorical and Philosophical Tradition. Ph.D. diss., Florida State University, 1981.
Funkhouser, Sarah. Heinrich Issac and Number Symbolism: An Exegesis of Commemorative Motets dedicated to Lorenzo de' Medici and Maximilian I. D.M.A. diss., University of Missouri-Kansas City, 1981.
McKinnon, James William. The Church Fathers and Musical Instruments. Ph.D. diss., Columbia University, 1965.
Willheim, Imanuel. Johann Adolph Scheibe: German Musical Thought in Transition. Ph.D. diss., University of Illinois, 1956.

MUSIC

Bach, Johann Sebastian. *Chromatische Fantasie* für das Pianoforte. Ed. by Conrad Friedrich Griepenkerl. Leipzig: C. F. Peters, [1819].
Bernstein, Leonard. *Mass*. [New York:] Jalni Publications (Boosey & Hawkes) [c. 1971].
Byrd, William. *Psalmes, Songs, and Sonnets*. London: Thomas Snodham, 1611.
Carter, Sydney. *Songs of Sydney Carter*, Book 2. Norfolk: Galliard (New York: Galaxy), 1969.
Dufay, Guillaume. *Opera omnia*. Ed. Heinrich Besseler, vol. II. Rome: American Institute of Musicology, 1966.
Hildegard of Bingen, Abbess. *Sequences and Hymns*. Ed. Christopher Page. [n.p.: Antico Church Music, 1982].
Josquin Des Prez. *Missa Pange Lingua*. New York: Kalmus [n.d.].
Miffleton, Jack. "Give Thanks and Remember." In *From Earthenware Jars*. Cincinnati: World Library Publications, c.1975.
Obrecht, Jacobus. *Opera omnia*: Missae VI. Sub tuum presidium. Ed. M. van Crevel. Amsterdam: Vereniging voor Nederlandse Muziekgeschiedenis [c.1960].
Ockeghem, Johannes. *Collected Works*. Ed. by D. Plamenac. Vol. II: Masses and Mass Sections IX-XVI. New York: published for the American Musicological Society, 1947.
Palestrina, Giovanni Pierluigi da. *Pope Marcellus Mass*. Ed. by Lewis Lockwood. New York: W. W. Norton, 1975.
Resinarius, Balthasar. *Responsoriorum numero octoginta* [Georg Rhau, 1543]. Kassel: Bärenreiter [1955].
Wren, Brian. *Bring Many Names*. Carol Stream, Ill.: Hope Publishing Co., c.1989.

Index

Aaron, 7
Absurd, cult of the, 196
Acclaim, popular, 176-177
Adam of Fulda, 76, 91
Adlung, Jacob, 174n.7
Aequalitas, 75
Aestheticism, 188, 189, 223
Aesthetics of Music, 74, 192
Alcuin of York, 81
Aldhelm, Saint, 217
Alexander the Great, 36
Allegory, 63
Alternatim praxis, 220, 224
American Guild of Organists, 204, 205
Amnesia, cultural, 169, 208
Amos (Prophet), 11
Amusement, 54
Anaesthetic, 71
Anarchy, 45
Anno (Bishop of Freising), 217
Anthony, Saint, 58
"Anti-hero," 196, 198
Antiphonal singing, 51
Applause, 224
Aristocratic, 43, 88, 103, 109, 193, 208
Aristotle, 30, 32, 35, 38, 46, 47, 61, 143, 144
Ark of the Covenant, 7
"Art for art's sake," 8, 109
Art music, 149-151, 169, 170, 172, 199, 200

Art vs. nature, 206
Art, suspicion of, 12
Artes liberales, 105
Artifice, 91, 126, 149, 180
Artificial, 149-151, 158, 177
Artisan, 154
Artusi, Giovanni, 115
Asaph (Priest), 22
Asceticism, 12, 50, 57-60, 67, 74, 79
Atonement, substitutionary, 11
Augmentation, 124, 125-126, 149
Augustine of Hippo, Saint, 33n.6, 47, 56, 58-59, 71, 73, 74-76, 78, 84, 100, 104, 110, 137, 138
Aulos, 39n.18, 42n.24, 45n.29, 47
Austen, Jane, 173

Baal, priests of, 20
Babbitt, Milton, 176
Babylonian Captivity, 12, 18, 19, 22
Bach, C.P.E., 174, 222
Bach, J. S., 13, 24n.9, 84, 111, 126, 131-133, 145, 149, 156, 158, 170, 180, 185, 210, 221, 228, 229, 230
Background music, 178, 202
Baker, Dame Janet, 172
Balance, 75
Baldric (Bishop of Dol), 217-218
Bali, 9, 161, 169, 201n.19, 205
Bardi, Giovanni de', 145
Basil, Saint, 51

244 Index

Bäumker, Wilhelm, 203
Beerbohm, Max, 202
Beethoven, Ludwig van, 150, 174, 176, 184-186, 188n.14
Bells, 215
Bembo, Cardinal Pietro, 153
Benedict XIV (Pope), 219
Benefices, choral, 145
Berg, Alban, 197
Berlioz, Hector, 197
Bernstein, Leonard, 168n.15
Bible, 78
Biblical criticism, 169
Biedermeyer, 187
Blessing, 1, 6
Blockwerk, 218
Blume, Friedrich, 203
Bobbio, 82
Boethius, 60, 73, 74 , 76-78, 82-84, 93, 94, 99, 102n.20, 107, 109
Book of Kells, 81n.16
Bourgeois culture, 187
Bowing, 6
Boy singers, 58
Brazil, 9, 14
Britten, Benjamin, 192
Bruckner, Anton, 189
Brunelleschi, Filippo, 128
Bultmann, Rudolf, 169
Burgundian School, 124
Burney, Charles, 183, 222, 173n.6, 175, 180
Busnois, Antoine, 129
Busoni, Ferruccio, 175
Buxtehude, Dietrich, 131, 145
Byrd, William, 158
Byzantine, 87, 23, 216

Caccini, Giulio, 227
Calov Bible, 24n.9, 132
Calvin, John, 136, 166n.9
Calvinism, 220
Campbell, Joseph, 13n.29
Canon, 124, 125, 149
Canticles, 25
Cantor, 77, 108, 109, 154
Carmina burana, 144
Carolingian Renaissance, 81, 82
Carter, Sydney, 197
Cassiodorus, 60, 75, 78, 79
Castiglione, Baldassare, 68n.63
Catherine of Siena, Saint, 94
Cavaillé-Coll, A., 222
Celestin, Saint (Pope), 51

Celtic religions, 88
Censorship, 42-46, 71, 136
Ceremony, 2, 6-8, 11, 23, 57, 167, 168
Chalcidius, 94
Chansons de geste, 118
Chant, 8, 72, 79, 114, 115, 117, 120, 188
Chaplin, Charlie, 196
Charles Borromeo, Saint, 219
Chaucer, Geoffrey, 144
China, 29
Chinese, 15
Choir schools, 58 (see also *Maîtrise*)
Chorale, Lutheran, 180, 181
Church Fathers, 54, 59, 68, 78, 109, 118, 136, 215
Church Growth Movement, 204n.2
Cicero, 35, 94, 100
Cistercian, 57, 90
Cithara, 94
Clement of Alexandria, 61
Clement XIV (Pope), 179
Clementine Recognitions, 109
Clownishness, 40, 154, 173
Columba (Columbcille), Saint, 81
Columbanus, Saint, 81, 82
Commonwealth, English, 137, 145
Composer, 108-109
Composition, 113
Confirmation, 7
Congregational singing, 136, 138, 199, 203, 204, 209, 220, 223
Conservatism, 40, 68, 88, 114-116, 131, 135, 146, 176, 193, 219
Constantine Copronymus, Emperor, 216
Consumerism, 194, 202
Contrition, 57, 71
Conversion, 11
Copland, Aaron, 196
Coptic Church, 56
Corybants, 38
Cosmic Harmony, 30, 32, 47, 64-65, 77, 83, 93-102, 105, 106, 116, 117, 119n.17, 123, 126, 127, 136, 137, 147, 217, 218, 219, 221, 228 (see also: Harmony)
Council of Trent, 140, 141, 153n.1, 219
Counter-reformation, 140, 146
Covenant, 5, 10, 17, 49, 166
Craftsmanship, 91
Cross, 57

Index 245

Crusades, 123
Cult, 4, 5-12, 18, 21-23, 49-52, 54, 57, 65n.51, 73, 165-169, 180, 188, 190, 198, 208, 209, 211, 220, 221
Culture, definition of, 162n.2, 206
Curriculum, classical, 84
Curse, 1

Damon (Philosopher), 36
Dance, 19, 145, 146, 221
Danhauser, Josef, 187
Dante, 94
David (King), 19, 21, 22, 24n.9
Davison, Archibald, 202n.21
De-sacralization, 143, 144
Deborah (Prophetess), 19
Debussy, Claude, 176
Delius, Frederick, 173n.5
Democracy, 43
Democratic ideal, 199
Demythologization, 169, 208
Didache, 51
Diminution, 124, 125-126, 149
Diocletian, 87
Dionysius the Areopagite, 82, 89n.2
Distler, Hugo, 192, 203
Docta sanctorum, 115
Donaueschingen, 201
Donne, John, 101
Dowland, John, 229
Döpfner, Julius, Cardinal, 210n.12
Dream of Scipio, 94, 100
Dryden, 99
Dufay, Guillaume, 109, 128, 158
Dumas, Alexandre, 188n.14
Dunstable, John, 109, 170, 175
Dura Europos, 50

Early music, 188-189
Ecclesiological Movement, 145, 146, 188
Ecstasy, 18-20, 22, 26, 51, 56, 116
Edification, 180, 221
Egalitarianism, 199-202, 207, 208, 211
Egypt, 29, 42n.25, 61
Egyptians, 15
Eli (Priest), 20
Eliade, Mircea, 4n.2, 6n.10, 13n.28, n.29, 52n.16, 68n.63
Elijah (Prophet), 12, 20
Eliot, T.S., 162n.2, 206
Elisha (Prophet), 20
Elitism, 208

Emotions, 71, 104, 105, 117, 118, 144, 151, 155, 157, 172, 177, 180, 183, 186-187, 189, 190, 192, 221, 222, 224, 225-230
Empfindsamer Stil, 174
England, 81
Entertainment, 173, 183, 194, 198, 206, 209, 210, 221
Entertainment Evangelism, 203n.2
"Enthusiasm" (fanaticism), 179
Epcot Center, 205-206
Erasmus, Desiderius, 120, 122, 166n.9
Eschatology, 25
Ethelwold, Bishop of Winchester, 226n.1
Ethics, 30, 36-46, 65, 166, 183
Ethiopia, 56
Ethos, 4
Ethos, Doctrine of, 36, 66, 93, 99-105, 132, 138, 144, 147, 178
Eucharist, 7, 22, 23, 50
Evangelical churches, 189, 190
Ex opere operato, 7, 12
Exorcism, 7

Fellerer, Karl Gustav, 203
Ferdinand I, Emperor of Spain, 141
Fibonacci numbers, 124, 130
Ficino, Marsilio, 97, 102
Figural music, 181
"Fine arts," meaning of, 208
Florentine Camerata, 145
Fludd, Robert, 97
Folk music, demise of, 194
Forkel, J.N., 228
Formula missae, 139
Franck, César, 222
Franco-flemish composers, 141, 84, 124, 126, 155 (see also Netherlanders)
Franks, 81, 216
Fratres operarii, 81
Fürstenberg, Prince Egon, 201

Gabrieli, Giovanni, 157
Gaffurius, Franchinus, 97, 102
Galant, 68n.63, 99n.14, 103
Galle, Philipp, 159
Gardner, Howard, 201n.20
Gelineau, Joseph (S. J.), 4n.4, 8n.15, 9, 115n.5, 203
Genesis, Book of, 15
Geneva Psalter, 136

246 Index

Genius, musical, 154, 157, 178, 186
Georgius (priest, organbuilder), 216
Gerbert of Aurillac (Pope Silvester II), 216
Gerbert, Martin, 115
Gideon, 21
Gill de Zamora, 94
Giustiniani, Vicenzo, 227
Glarean, 156
Glosses, 114
Glossolalia, 26, 51n.15
Gluck, C.W. von, 174n.7
Gnosticism, 36, 60, 67
Golden Section, 124, 130
Goliards, 144
Gothic architecture, 118
Gothic revival, 187n.13, 188
Gozbert (Abbot), 116
Graun, K. H., 180
Great Awakening, 180
"Great music," demise of, 192
Greatness in music, 150
Gregory the Great (Pope), 78-80, 94
Griepenkerl, F.C., 228-229, 230
Gymnastics, 39

Haito (Abbot), 116
Handel, G.F., 180, 224
Hannah, 20
Harmonia, 30, 33, 36, 37, 39, 46
Harmoniai, 38n.16, 40n.20, 41n.22, 47
"Harmony of the Spheres," 35-36
Harmony, 30, 32, 34, 36, 47, 65, 66, 75, 77, 93-102, 106, 116, 117, 119n.17, 123, 127, 136, 137, 139n.12, 146, 147, 184, 185, 190, 217, 218 (see also: Cosmic Harmony)
Harp, 21
Haydn, F.J., 84, 158, 175, 179, 181, 184, 222
Heine, Heinrich, 187
Henze, Hans Werner, 194
Hesse, Adolph, 222
Heunisch, Caspar, 132
"High-church," 190
Historicism, 188, 189, 223
Holy Spirit, 4, 7, 79, 80, 110, 111, 218
Homophony, 141, 177, 227
Honorius of Autun, 94, 108n.33
Hood, Mantle, 9n.21, 161-162, 201n.19, 209
Horace, 53, 55

Houphouet-Boigny, Felix, 168n.14
Howells, Herbert, 203
Hucbald of St. Amand, 225-226
Huck, Gabe, 211
Hugo, Victor, 188n.14
Humanism, 11, 93, 97, 115, 127, 124, 135n.1, 146, 153-158, 163-166, 185, 228, 229
Humanitarianism, 179, 186
Hume, David, 178
Hydraulis, 215, 217

Iconoclastic, 50
Ideals, 14
Imitation, 124, 149
Immanence, 164, 166
Improvisation, 9, 51, 117, 219
Indians, 15
Individuality, 175-176
Indonesia, 161
Industrial Revolution, 168
Industry, music, 177, 190, 194
Innovation, 40, 46
Instruments, 19, 20, 39, 47, 55-56, 63, 67, 157-159, 172-173, 181, 215-216, 223
Intuition, 29, 32
Inversion, 124, 126 149
Iona, 81
Irish monks, 57, 79-83
Isaac, Heinrich, 130
Isidore of Seville, 75, 94, 226n.1
Islam, 143
Isorhythm, 124, 125
Israel, 5, 6, 9, 10, 12, 17-23n.9, 72
Ives, Charles, 196
Ivory Coast, 167-168n.14

Jacob of Liège, 114, 120
Jacobus de Kerle, 141
Jansen, Martin, 133
Java, 161
Jazz, 193
Jericho, fall of, 21
Jesuits, 141, 179
Jesus, 4, 7, 10-12, 22, 24, 50, 52, 57, 89, 93, 127, 166, 196n.12, 199
Job (Prophet), 12
Johannes Scotus Erigena, 82-84, 89n.2, 94, 99
Johansson, Calvin, 206, 207, 211
John Chrysostom, Saint, 27
John of Luxembourg (King of Bohemia), 109

Index   247

John the Deacon, 79
John VIII (Pope), 217
John XII (Pope), 226n.1
John XXII (Pope), 115
Josquin des Prez, 120, 121, 130, 149, 156, 157, 210, 229
Jubilus, 117
Julian, John, 203

Kant, Immanuel, 172, 179
Kepler, Johannes, 36, 97, 98, 99
Kerouac, Jack, 207
Keyboard instruments, 177
King, 6
Kinnor, 21
Kirchenagenden, 146, 188
Kircher, Athanasius, 98, 99, 115, 141, 221
Kithara, 39n.18, 42n.24, 46n.24
Kitsch, 207
Kneeling, 6
Krenek, Ernst, 191n.1, 193

Last Judgment, 89
Lefébure-Wély, L.-J.-A., 222
Leibniz, Gottfried Wilhelm, 107, 132
Leipzig, *Thomasschule*, 84
Lemmens, Jacques, 222
Leonardo da Vinci, 101
Leonin, 108, 118, 119
Levites, 19, 22
Lewis, C.S., 17n.17
Liber chronicarum, 95
Liberace, 200
Liszt, Franz, 184, 185, 187, 188n.14
Literacy, music, 201-202
Liturgical Movement, 198-199
Liturgical Year, 73
Liturgy, 22, 49-52, 54, 56, 57, 63, 70, 79, 89-90, 114, 115, 117, 145, 148, 157, 158, 179, 180, 181, 188, 189n.20, 198, 199, 210, 211, 216, 219, 229
Lord's Supper, 23, 24, 50
Louis the Pious (King), 216
Luther, Martin, 24, 138-140, 166n.9, 201
Lutheran, 131, 179
Luxeuil, 82
Luzzaschi, Luzzasco, 227
Lyre, 21

Machaut, Guillaume de, 109, 144
Macrobius, 35, 94, 100

Madrigal, Italian, 155
Magic, 18, 20, 89
Magisterium, 89
Mahler, Gustav, 192
Maîtrise, 84, 99, 145, 180-181
Manetti, Giannozzo, 157
Manger, 57
Mannheim crescendo, 172
Mannheim School, 222
Marchetto of Padua, 108
Marie d'Agoult, Countess, 188n.14
Martianus Capella, 82
Mary, Blessed Virgin, 89
Mass Ordinary, 91
Mathematics, 30, 32-35, 46, 75, 76, 118, 123, 124, 127-130, 172
Mattheson, Johann, 99n.14, 131
Mechanization, 194
Media, mass, 194
Melanchthon, 166n.9
Memory, systemic, 170
Mendelssohn, Felix, 222
Mersenne, Marin, 98
Messiah, 7
Microphone, 194
Milton, John, 98
Minor orders, 145
Miriam (Prophetess), 19
Misogyny, 58
Missa Luba, 193
Missa Pange Lingua, 120
Mizler, Lorenz, 132
Modes, church, 83, 102, 103, 119
Module, 75
Moengal (Marcellus), 82
Monasticism, 57, 74, 78-82, 84, 87, 136, 137, 179
Monism, 217
Monochord, 31
Monody, 151
Montaigne, Michel de, 97n.11
Monteverdi, Claudio, 115, 155, 157
Morals, 65
More, Sir Thomas, 166n.9
Morley, Thomas, 174
Moses, 5
Motivicity, 124
Mousike, 36, 37n.12, 39
Mowinckel, Sigmund, 4-5, 21
Mozart, W.A., 158, 181, 184, 186, 222n.7
Muris, Jean de, 85, 110, 127
Music and poetry, 9, 144

248 Index

Music of the spheres, 93-97, 100, 143
Music, good and bad, 66-67, 76
Music, value of, 8
Musica artificialis, 83
Musica enchiriadis, 105, 119n.17
Musica humana, 76, 77, 93
Musica instrumentalis, 76, 77, 93, 100, 106
Musica mundana, 76, 77, 93, 99, 107, 119n.17
Musica naturalis, 82
Musica reservata, 109
Musicality, 91, 227
Musicology, 146
Musicus, 77, 82, 107-109, 154, 180, 196
Muzak, 202
Mystery, 165, 167, 179, 198n.16
Mysticism, 186, 187, 219
Myth, 2, 4, 12-15, 34, 35, 52, 65n.51, 73, 165, 169, 206, 209
Mythology, 62, 64, 131

National Endowment for the Arts, 162, 207
National Endowment for the Humanities, 162
Nationalism, 193
Neo-Platonism, 35, 60, 74, 77, 83, 91, 94, 98, 99, 109, 110, 115n.5, 116, 127, 139, 141, 143, 144, 191, 217, 219, 221
Neo-Pythagoreanism, 74, 77, 110, 127, 141
Netherlanders, 126 (see also Franco-flemish composers)
New Testament, 10, 12, 20, 23-27, 36, 51, 64, 68, 109, 111, 135, 136
Nibelungenlied, 118
Nichomachus (Philosopher), 32, 110
Niedt, F.E., 132, 174n.7
Nihilism, 196, 198
Nobility, 88
Noble, 38, 53, 68, 103, 104, 156, 183-186 194, 196, 199, 211
"Non-heroic ideal," 196
Norse raiders, 81
North, F. Mason, 195
Notation, music, 117
Notker Balbulus, 82
Notre Dame Cathedral, Paris, 108, 118, 119
Novelty, 40, 46, 69

Number symbolism, 93, 109-111, 126-133
Number, 29, 30, 32-35, 47, 75, 77, 105, 106, 109-111, 116, 123, 124, 127, 128, 177
Numeri, 75
Numerology, 47, 109-111
Numerositas, 75
Numerosity, 118
Numinous, 3n.2, 8

Obrecht, Jacob, 129
Ockeghem, Johannes, 128
Office, 22
Old Testament, 2, 9-12, 17-24, 36, 54, 57, 61, 62, 68, 110, 111, 128, 138,
Opera, 145, 146, 149, 157, 181
Optimism, 194, 196, 200
Organ concertos, 224
Organ Reform Movement, 223
Organ, 136, 137, 181, 215-224
Organum, 118, 127, 151
Orgelbewegung, 223
Originality, 175, 177, 198
Ornament, 5, 7-8, 50, 57, 131, 166, 167-168
Orpheus legend, 30
Orthodox, Eastern, 164, 215
Oxford Movement, 145, 146, 188
Oxyrhynchus hymn, 51

Paganini, N., 185, 187n.14
Pageants, beauty, 167
Paideia, 37, 39, 40n.20, 84
Palestrina, Giovanni da, 146, 188
Papal decrees, 144, 181, 219
Paraphrase, 124
Parody, 124
Parousia, 49
Participation, popular, 198
Patrick, Saint, 81
Patriotism, 6
Patronage, music, 201, 208
Paul (Apostle), 13n.30, 24-27n.10
Penderecki, Krzysztof, 197
Pentecost, 4
Pepin (King), 216
Performance practice, 225-230
Periodic melodic structure, 177
Perotin, 118, 119
Pessimism, 194, 198, 212
Petrarch, Francesco, 144
Philo, 109

Philolaus (Philosopher), 30
Pietism, 163-164, 189, 221
Pius VII (Pope), 179
Plato (of Athens), 15, 30, 33-47, 61, 63, 71, 75, 94, 95, 102n.20, 107, 115, 136, 143, 154
Pleasure, 40, 46, 54, 69, 70, 71, 117, 136, 137, 141, 143, 154, 225-226
Plotinus, 99
Pluralism, cultural, 191, 192n.3, 206
Plutarch, 109
Polyphony, 84, 105, 108, 109(n.37), 113-115, 117-127, 138, 141, 149, 150, 154, 177, 178, 185, 188, 219, 227, 186
Popular music, debased, 200
Popular opinion, 88
Prayer, 7
Preces speciales, 141
Presley, Elvis, 192
Pride, sin of, 76
Printing, music, 157
Prophecy, 18-20, 22, 26
Prophet, 57
Prophetess, 19
Prosody, rules of, 74
Prætorius, Michael, 24n.9, 97, 99, 107, 215, 220, 221, 224
Puritanical, 76
Puritanism, 57, 136-137, 220
Pythagoras, 30-33, 61, 100, 104n.26
Pythagorean, 64, 93, 105, 110, 111, 114(n.7), 118-120, 123, 128-130, 218
Pythagoreans, 30, 32, 35, 40, 47, 75, 76, 77

Quadrivium, 47, 62, 84, 85, 105n.28, 217, 218
Quality, 6
Quantz, J.J., 174n.7, 176n.10, 227-228
Quietism, 188

Racism, 208
Rameau, J.-P., 178
Ramshorn, 20
Rational religion, 165
Rationalization, 29
Ratpert, 82
Ravel, Maurice, 150
Reformation, 7, 135-140, 220
Regino of Prüm, 82
Reichardt, J.F., 186n.8

Reichenau, 82, 116
Remigius of Auxerre, 82
Repentance, 11
Resinarius, Balthasar, 120
Responsorial singing, 51
Retrograde, 124, 126
Retrograde inversion, 124, 126
Revelation, 29, 32, 34
Revival, 189
Revivalism, 180
Revolution, French, 179
Rhau, Georg, 120
Rhythm, 47
Rhythmic modes, 127
Riddles, 124, 125
Ritual, 2, 5-8, 11, 22, 166, 167, 168
Roaring Twenties, 186
Rock and roll, 207, 198
Rococo, 103, 173, 186
Root proportionals, 124
Rore, Cipriano de, 155
Rossini, Gioacchino, 187n.14
Routley, Eric, 203
Rule of St. Benedict, 82
Russolo, Luigi, 174

Sachs, Curt, 8n.15, 9n.17, n.18, 18n.1, 29
Sacrament, 5, 7, 166, 167, 168
Sacramental principle, 7
Sacraments, 7
Sacred/secular dichotomy, 4, 8
Sacred/secular tension, 146, 189
Sacrifice, 10
Sacrifice, animal, 6
Sacrifice, bloody, 63
Sadoleto, Jacopo, 166n.9
St. Denis (Abbey), 91
St. Gall, 82, 116
St. Peter's Basilica, Rome, 141
St. Stephen's Cathedral, Vienna, 84
Saints, 7n.12, 89
Salvation history, 52, 68, 169
Samuel (Prophet), 18, 19
Sand, George (Aurore Dudevant), 188n.14
Santa Maria del Fiore (Cathedral, Florence), 158
Saul (King), 18, 19, 21
Schedel, Hartmann, 95
Scheibe, Johann Adolph, 158
Scheidt, Samuel, 224
Schleiermacher, Friedrich, 164n.4
Schola cantorum, 58, 79

250 Index

Schola, 91
Scholia enchiriadis, 105, 106, 113. 114
Scholiae, 114
School of Notre Dame, 118
Schools, cathedral, 84, 180-181 (see also *Maîtrise*)
Schools, monastic, 84, 99
Schönberg, Arnold, 193, 197, 201
Schumann, Robert, 185
Schütz, Heinrich, 155, 157, 224
Science, 29
Scotti, 82
Scottish monks, 79-83
Scribes, 81
Scriptorium, 78, 81
Scripture, canon of, 68
Seconda prattica, 155
Self-abasement, 6
Self-conscious, 2, 3, 6n.9, 13, 135, 146, 151, 153, 161-170, 172, 194, 199, 202, 205, 206, 209-213, 221
Seminaries, 204
Sentimentality, 166, 187, 189
Separation of church and state, 6
Sequentia cum prosa, 117
Sessions, Roger, 191n.1
Shakespeare, William, 100, 102
Shaw, George Bernard, 185
Shepherd of Hermes, 109
Shofar, 20
Silvester II (Pope), 216
Simson, Otto von, 75, 118
Sinai, Mount, 5
Sinatra, Frank, 172
Singing, community, 194, 205
Sistine Chapel, 157
Smend, Julius, 188
Sobriety, 186
Social status of musician, 179
Socrates, 2, 36
Solesmes, St. Pierre de, 146, 188
Solidarity, 5, 131, 166, 169
Solomon, 21, 24n.9
Song, spiritual, 180
Sowerby, Leo, 203
Söhngen, Oskar, 33, 138
Speculation, 60-61, 82, 84, 85, 93, 95, 98, 106, 110, 113-119, 123, 124, 127, 130, 131, 139, 141, 143-146, 149-151, 155, 157, 178 187, 219
"Spiritual sacrifice," 62-63

Spirituality, 165
Sports events, 167
Stanley, Thomas, 97n.11
Stile antico, 146
Strauss, Richard, 197
Stravinsky, Igor, 215, 223
Studdert-Kennedy, G.A., 196
Subjective, 172
Suger, Abbot, 91
Supernatural, 89
Superstition, 79, 89, 165, 166
Suspicion of Music, 23, 47, 57, 64, 137, 138
Suya, 9
"Swallows-nest," 219
Sweelinck, J.P., 224
Symmetry, 75
Symphony, 162
Synagogue, 22, 49, 52, 63
Syria, 50
Systemic memory, 170

Talmud, 22
Taste, good, 173, 177, 228
Tax support of music, 201
Te Deum, 164n.5
Telemann, Georg, 180
Temple, Jerusalem, 11, 19, 21-24, 56, 63
Ten Commandments, 5
Tertullian, 51, 53, 217
Text painting, 157
Thematic development, 149
Theodosius, 87
Third World, 164n.7, 193
Thomism, 35
Thompson, Randall, 197
Thomson, Virgil, 191n.1
Timaeus, 15, 33, 34, 94
Tinctoris, Johannes, 127, 143, 175-176
Tithe, 6n.7
Tolkien, J.R.R., 15, 35, 169, 196
Tonal quality, ideal, 226
Toulmin, Stephen, 163, 164
Transcendence, 89, 164, 166, 167
Transubstantiation, 7n.11, 35
Tremolo, 229
Tribe, 1, 6, 8, 9, 11, 14, 17, 18, 20
Trinity, Holy, 110
Trivium, 84, 105n.28
Tropes, 114, 117
Troubadours, 118, 144
Trouvères, 118, 144

Truchsess, Otto Cardinal, 141
Tuotilo, 82

Universities, 84-85

Variety, 40, 46, 69, 174, 194
Vatican II, 165, 198
Venezuela, 14
Vesica piscis, 124
Vibrato, 229
Victoria, Queen of England, 186
Victorian, 187, 189, 190
Virtuosity, 40, 46, 54, 133, 172, 224
Vitry, Philippe de, 108
Vivarium, 78
Vogler, Abbé, 223

Wackenroder, W.H., 184, 186n.7, n.10
Wagner, Richard, 174, 177, 187
Water organ, 215
Watts, Isaac, 102n.17
Weimar Republic, 186
Werckmeister, Andreas, 99, 101, 132, 221
Wert, Giaches de, 227
Wesley, S.S., 222
Westermeyer, Paul, 211
Willan, Healey, 188n.15
Wittkower, Rudolf, 123
Wohlgemuth, Paul, 212
Women excluded from singing, 58
Word painting, 157
World, 2n.1
World-conscious, 2-14, 49, 56, 88, 131, 144, 151, 161, 163, 166, 167, 169, 170, 199, 202, 205, 206, 211, 212, 220
Worship, 5, 49-51, 56, 57, 58, 63, 89, 131, 157, 166, 167-169, 180, 188, 193, 198, 204, 215, 216, 220, 221, 223
Wren, Brian, 212

Yahweh, 5, 10, 17-22, 166, 167n.12
Yamoussoukro, 167n.14
Yanomanö, 14

Zahn, Johannes, 203
Zarlino, Gioseffo, 97, 102, 120, 226n.1
Zurich, 136
Zwingli, Ulrich, 57, 136, 153

About the Author

QUENTIN FAULKNER is Steinhart Distinguished Professor of Music at the University of Nebraska, Lincoln. He teaches organ and has developed a unique series of courses in church music. Dr. Faulkner's articles on various aspects of church music have appeared in *The American Organist*, *The Diapason*, *The Christian Ministry*, and *Liturgy*.

www.ingramcontent.com/pod-product-compliance
Lightning Source LLC
Chambersburg PA
CBHW071704160426
43195CB00012B/1570